Devotional Islam in British India

Devotional Islam and Politics in British India

Ahmad Riza Khan Barelwi and His Movement, 1870 – 1920

DELHI
OXFORD UNIVERSITY PRESS
CALCUTTA CHENNAI MUMBAI

Oxford University Press, Great Clarendon Street, Oxford OX2 6DP

Oxford New York
Athens Auckland Bangkok Calcutta
Cape Town Chennai Dar es Salaam Delhi
Florence Hong Kong Istanbul Karachi
Kuala Lumpur Madrid Melbourne Mexico City
Mumbai Nairobi Paris Singapore
Taipei Tokyo Toronto
and associates in
Berlin Ibadan

Second impression 1999
Oxford India Paperbacks 1999

ISBN 0 19 564862 5

Typeset by Print Line, New Delhi 110048
Printed in India at Wadhwa International, New Delhi 110 020
and published by Manzar Khan, Oxford University Press
YMCA Library Building, Jai Singh Road, New Delhi 110 001

To the memory of
my beloved father

Bimalendu Kumar Sanyal

Acknowledgements

It is with the greatest pleasure that I acknowledge the help of the many institutions and individuals who have enabled me to reach the end of the long road that this book represents. I would like to thank the American Institute of Indian Studies for a junior fellowship in 1986–7, which enabled me to travel to India and spend almost a year there on fieldwork and the analysis of key texts. This research was also assisted by a grant from the International Doctoral Research Fellowship Program for South Asia of the Social Science Research Council and the American Council of Learned Societies with funds provided by the Ford Foundation and the National Endowment for the Humanities, for three months' research in Pakistan during 1986–7. Finally, a Charlotte W. Newcombe Doctoral Dissertation Fellowship in 1989–90 permitted me to devote myself fulltime to writing in my final year of research.

Of the individuals who have helped me, I am heavily indebted to my many teachers. To Tony Milner, whose MA student I was at Canterbury, UK, I owe my interest in history. It was he who first raised interpretive questions about Southeast Asian history, and encouraged me to do research. His expression of confidence in me contributed importantly to my decision several years later to pursue an interest in history.

Since coming to Columbia, I have been greatly influenced in my thinking by Bill Roff. I owe to him in particular my sensitivity to internal forms of discourse within the Islamic world, and my awareness of the importance of understanding these on their own terms, within their own historically determined cultural systems of meaning. Working on the dissertation under his supervision has been a rewarding experience, given his keen interest in the research. Always at hand to guide, raise questions, and ensure that the work moved forward, he nevertheless gave me the opportunity to set my own pace and agenda. In more recent years, he has commented on portions of the revised manuscript from Scotland, where he now lives in retirement.

I have had the benefit throughout the period of research, also, of suggestions and criticism to drafts of the dissertation by Barbara Metcalf. It was she who first suggested the topic, then helped me get started. David Lelyveld has offered useful criticism and taken an unflagging interest in the work's progress. I am grateful to Frances Pritchett for having taught me Urdu and for correcting my poetry transliterations. Khalid Mas'ud, of the Islamic Research Institute, Islamabad, periodically suggested new ways of thinking about the material, at long distance. Christian Troll gave me the benefit of his knowledge of Muslim theology when commenting on several chapters. Greg Kozlowski gave encouragement and moral support.

In the course of revision, Muzaffar Alam has helped me with the sections on Rohilkhand history and the intricacies of eighteenth- and nineteenth-century land tenure systems. I am grateful to Yohanan Friedmann for his careful reading of the dissertation, and particularly for correcting my translations and transliterations of Arabic words and titles.

I owe a great deal to Sandy Freitag, who has been unstintingly generous with time and in offering suggestions as to new ways of conceptualizing the study. She has tried to get me to stand back, to disengage from the details and think about the 'big picture' of what I was describing.

To those who offered hospitality and access to source materials I owe the deepest gratitude. As Pakistanis, and particularly as emigrants (*muhajirs*) from India after the Partition of 1947, I can only imagine how difficult it must have been for them to take in an unknown Indian Hindu woman into their homes. Professor Muhammad Mas'ud Ahmed, currently retired in Karachi, was my host for several weeks at Thatta (Sind) in 1986, where he was then Principal of the Government Degree College. His wife accompanied me to Karachi more than once, staying with me and looking after me at their apartment there while the family managed without her at Thatta.

Furthermore, it was through Professor Mas'ud Ahmed that I made contact in Karachi, Lahore, and Delhi with others whose assistance proved crucial to my work. My special thanks go to Maulana Yasin Akhtar Misbahi of Delhi, Vice-President of the All-India Muslim Personal Law Conference and Director, Almajmaul Islami, to whom I was introduced by Professor Mas'ud Ahmed (the two men had never met, but knew of each other by reputation). For four months Maulana Yasin Akhtar was my *ustad*, reading Ahmad Riza's fatawa with me and helping me understand the difficult and often technical vocabulary and style of argument. It was largely due to work done in Delhi with Misbahi Sahib, as I called him, that after returning to New York I was able to follow other texts by myself.

I would also like to thank the many persons who generously permitted me to photocopy journals and pamphlets in their possession, several of which are unavailable in national libraries. Mr. Khalid S. Hasan, Senior Executive Vice-President of the National Bank of Pakistan at Karachi, gave me access to his personal collection of Jinnah's correspondence with Maulana Burhan ul-Haqq Jabalpuri in the 1940s. Khwaja Razi Haidar of Karachi shared with me his *Tuhfa-e-Hanafiyya* collection as well as other Nadwa-related material. Maulana Muhammad Athar Na'imi of Karachi permitted me to copy issues of *Al-Sawad al-A'zam*. Professor Muhammad Mas'ud Ahmed allowed me to copy unpublished documents such as Ahmad Riza Khan's letters. Mr Mustafa 'Ali Razwi, advocate in Bareilly, whose personal collection of Ahmad Riza's fatawa was the richest source of its kind in the subcontinent (surpassing by far the major national libraries), put me greatly in his debt by permitting me to make photocopies of whatever I wished. Maulana Muhammad Zuhur ud-Din Khan of Lahore gave me newspaper cuttings and books no longer in print. Maulana Rizwan ud-Din Na'imi of Muradabad permitted me to photocopy issues of *Al-Sawad al-A'zam*. Syed Jamaluddin, lecturer of history at Jam'iyya Milliyya Islamiyya, shared with me a precious family history of the Barkatiyya Sayyids of Marahra and copies of the journal *Ahl-e Sunnat ki Awaz* published by 'ulama' of this family. In addition, the staff of Jam'iyya Na'imiyya, Muradabad, and of Manzar al-Islam, Bareilly, gave me valuable original source material.

In June 1987, the librarian of Raza Library, Rampur, helped me generously as well. Thanks in large part to his personal interest in my research, and the practical assistance of Mr. Ashutosh Gaur of Modi Xerox Company, Rampur, I was able to photocopy sections of the *Dabdaba-e Sikandari* newspaper from the Raza Library's vast holdings. Mr Gaur arranged for the temporary installation of a photocopying machine in the library, as rules did not permit any library materials to leave the building, and personally supervised the photocopying under trying circumstances resulting from frequent electricity breakdowns in a searing June heat.

Other useful source materials were obtained from the Islamic Research Institute Library at Islamabad, the Khuda Bakhsh Library at Patna, the National Archives at Delhi, and the Nehru Memorial Library at Delhi. I am most grateful to the staff of each of these institutions for assistance rendered.

Finally, I owe a great deal to the affection and unfailing moral support offered by friends and family. In Pakistan, Dushka Saiyid and Anwar Kamal provided periodic breaks from work, and the opportunity occasionally to be a tourist in Lahore. Anwar's skilful management also averted the dreadful prospect that I would have to leave behind the materials so painfully collected, for a Pakistani law forbade Indians from transporting books published in Pakistan back to India.

To my parents, I give grateful thanks for loving support and encouragement of my work. It was they who made my education at Columbia possible in the first few years. I dedicate this work to my father, who, sadly, is not there to see it completed. Together with my mother, he had welcomed my interest in Muslim society and culture, and rendered tremendous practical help and advice, as well as moral support, in the course of fieldwork. My husband, Gautam Bose, has been indispensable to my ability to see this book through to completion. His willingness to act as sounding board on diverse matters, and his talent for finding humour where I have failed to see it, are the least of the many things he has done for me these last several years. For this, and much besides, I thank him.

I end with the warmest thanks to all those at Oxford University Press, Delhi, who have shepherded this book through to print, thereby enabling me—as Adil Tyabji, formerly an editor at the Press, so memorably put it—to become a 'convoluted author'. Thanks to friends and onetime colleagues at OUP, Delhi, I have thoroughly enjoyed the experience of publishing this, my first, book.

U. S.

Contents

Note on Transliteration

The transliteration system followed here is based on John T. Platts, *A Dictionary of Urdu, Classical Hindi, and English*. I differ from his usage, however, in the following respects: the letter *che*, as in *chilla*, is transliterated as 'ch' rather than 'c', and *ghain*, as in *tabligh*, is transliterated as 'gh' rather than 'g'. I use '-e' to indicate the *izafat*, and 'al-' for the Arabic definite article. The transliteration of South Asian personal names, however, follows Urdu pronunciation: thus Zafar ud-Din rather than Zafar al-Din (but 'Abd al-Qadir Jilani, rather than 'Abd ul-Qadir Jilani, because the latter is not South Asian).

Likewise, in spelling usage I have been guided by Urdu pronunciation where this differs from the classical Arabic, as in *hadis*, *azan*, and *qazi*. Departing from standard practice with regard to words like 'Haramayn', I substitute an 'i' for the 'y': thus, Haramain rather than Haramayn, shaikh rather than shaykh, and Haidarabad rather than Hyderabad. Also, the word 'sunna', when used in a compound, is transliterated 'sunnat'.

An apostrophe is used to signify the *hamza*. With the exception of '*ain*, diacritical marks above and below the letters are indicated only in the glossary.

Introduction

The Ahl-e Sunnat and Identity Formation, Late Nineteenth Century

Given the increasing prevalence of religious nationalism—Sikh, Buddhist, Hindu, and Muslim—in late twentieth-century South Asia, it is not surprising that historians are asking questions about the relationship between 'religion' and 'politics' and making connections between the current scene and its history (or histories) in colonial and pre-colonial India. Such issues are also in the forefront for students of inter-religious conflict or communalism in the subcontinent over the past century or so. While such interest is not new, scholars now seem to be paying more attention to the 'religion' in the 'politics' of religious nationalism than they did earlier. More specifically, some historians are taking religious practice seriously, and attending to the discourse and debate that accompanies that practice, seeing in these exchanges important clues that could help us see and understand underlying processes of social change.

The present study, of a religious movement led by a group of Sunni Muslim scholars of Islamic law (*'ulama'*) in late nineteenth and early twentieth century north India, may appear rather exclusively centred on 'religion' and not at all on 'politics'. While it is true that the 'ulama' of the Ahl-e Sunnat wa Jama'at movement maintained a largely apolitical stance towards British rule in India, and were not directly concerned with 'politics', there are several indications that their movement did have political implications.

In the formative period of this movement, a period that coincides with the leadership of Maulana Ahmad Riza Khan (b. 1856) from the 1880s until his death in 1921, the debates in which the Ahl-e Sunnat 'ulama' engaged with other north Indian 'ulama' do not deal specifically with politics. They deal instead with issues such as the qualities of the Prophet Muhammad, the permissibility or otherwise of the intercession of dead 'saints' (*pirs*), or the correct manner of calling believers to the mosque for the Friday congregational prayer. In laying out the arguments of the Ahl-e Sunnat 'ulama' on these and other matters in the chapters that follow, I hope to show, however, that the debates themselves were intricately related to the larger socio-political context of north India at the time. The religious discourse of the Ahl-e Sunnat was at the core of a process of identity formation which had wider ramifications, for relations with competing Muslim and non-Muslim groups as well as the colonial state.

In this context, the connections Freitag makes between local community activities, the British Indian state, and the process of identity formation which fed into a wider political process in the late nineteenth and early twentieth centuries, are most helpful.[1] She points out that in late nineteenth century British India, religious and cultural activity carried out by Indians in public spaces (such as festival processions, Muharram mourning rituals, voluntary organizations, and the like) 'became an alternative world to that structured by the imperial regime, providing legitimacy and recognition to a range of actors and values denied place in the imperial order'.[2] Freitag argues that in this alternative world, people made conscious choices about self-definition that enabled them to create a new-found sense of 'community':

> Key to understanding the underlying connections between organizations, ideology, and popular participation is the process by which participants constructed the respective 'communities' for which they acted. In this process certain shared values and behaviors were self-consciously chosen for emphasis: participants simultaneously defined their own community and created an 'Other' encompassing those outside the boundaries they drew. The articulation

[1] Sandria B. Freitag, *Collective Action and Community: Public Arenas and the Emergence of Communalism in North India* (Berkeley: University of California Press, 1989).

[2] Ibid., p. 6.

of these constructions, in turn, calls to our attention the universe in which community came to be expressed.[3]

Thus what people said and did in the 'public arena' (Freitag's term, following Habermas's 'public sphere'), in the colonial state was intrinsic to the process of community formation. Based on shared religious or cultural concerns, in the early decades of the twentieth century, some of these local communities mobilized around issues like cow-protection or the defence of mosques to come together on a larger national stage.

As Freitag indicates, and as my study of the Ahl-e Sunnat amply bears out, the process of community formation was inherently conflictual. In the period studied here, the 'Others' against whom the Ahl-e Sunnat defined themselves were primarily fellow Sunni Muslims. They were for the most part 'ulama' who belonged to important contemporary Sunni Muslim movements, such as the Deobandi.[4] The Ahl-e Sunnat also wrote against, and debated with, the Tablighi Jama'at,[5] the Ahl-e Hadis, the Panjab-centered Ahmadiyya movement,[6] and the Nadwat al-'Ulama'. Each of these movements, defining itself in terms of Islamic 'reform' (which term I examine below), was in competition with the others for hegemonic influence over the Indian Muslim population as a whole. The seriousness of the debate between them was motivated by a sense that only one of them could be right, only one of the many alternatives offered would survive the test of time and provide the tools with which to build an alternative world to that dominated by the state.

However, the very process of competition, divisive as it was at one level, was also instrumental in creating common discursive ground between the competitors, in this case a shared language of Islamic reform.[7] Or, to put this somewhat differently—and borrowing Roff's

[3] Ibid., p. 13.

[4] On the Deobandi movement, see Barbara D. Metcalf, *Islamic Revival in British India: Deoband, 1860–1900* (Princeton: Princeton University Press, 1982).

[5] M. Anwarul Haq, *The Faith Movement of Mawlana Muhammad Ilyas* (London: George Allen & Unwin, 1972).

[6] Yohanan Friedmann, *Prophecy Continuous: Aspects of Ahmadi Religious Thought and its Medieval Background* (Berkeley: University of California Press, 1989).

[7] A point also made by Metcalf in *Islamic Revival*, p. 358.

memorable phrase—the 'ulama' were arguing in part about 'how to argue', thereby making discourse about change possible.[8] Those with whom the Ahl-e Sunnat shared less common cultural space were thus also more remote 'Others'. After the immediate array of 'ulama' movements mentioned above, the Ahl-e Sunnat 'ulama' defined themselves as distinct from Shi'i Muslims. Then, at considerable remove, they did so in opposition to 'Hindus' (a term which came into currency as a working category only during British rule, as Freitag reminds us) and the colonial state.

The creation of cultural space and alternative worlds removed from state concerns was accomplished by the institutionalization of religious belief and practice in a number of novel ways. Several of these institutions were based on use of the printed word. Historians have frequently noted the importance of print technology in furthering community formation in the late nineteenth century. In *Imagined Communities*, Benedict Anderson argues that 'print capitalism' contributed powerfully to the growth of nationalism in colonized countries.[9]

My research confirms the crucial role the written and printed word played in the crystallization of the Ahl-e Sunnat movement in the late nineteenth and early twentieth centuries. Ahmad Riza's writings, chiefly *fatawa* (legal jurisprudential rulings), said to number about a thousand, were made available to followers in a variety of formats: sometimes hand-written, they were also published in newspapers, pamphlets (*risalas*), and as book-length treatises. They constituted a good proportion of the literature published by the printing houses of the Ahl-e Sunnat in Bareilly and elsewhere in north India. Through the dissemination of these writings, other Muslims in far-flung parts of British India were able to read Ahmad Riza's judgments on a variety of issues. Those who agreed with him were able to signal their support by participating in a range of

[8] William R. Roff, 'Whence Cometh the Law? Dog Saliva in Kelantan, 1937', in Katherine P. Ewing (ed.), *Shari'at and Ambiguity in South Asian Islam* (Delhi: Oxford University Press, 1988), pp. 25–42.

[9] Benedict Anderson, *Imagined Communities: Reflections on the Origin and Spread of Nationalism* (London: Verso, 1983).

collective activities. Thus the movement was gradually transformed from a local one to one with a following in many parts of India.

In the late nineteenth and early twentieth centuries, a whole range of institutional structures furthered the ongoing process of community formation among the Ahl-e Sunnat. These included seminaries (*madrasas*), periodic journals, and oral debates with 'ulama' of competing movements. Voluntary organizations followed, focusing on specific causes such as aid for Ottoman Turkish Muslims in the early decades of the twentieth century. Like Ahmad Riza's published writings, these activities were instrumental in creating a sense of community between members, and in enlarging the audience addressed. From an exclusive and relatively small circle of religious scholars, this audience fanned out to include a larger educated lay Muslim public.[10]

Controversy and contestation among the 'ulama', in verbal form and in print, was particularly strong when it came to Ahl-e Sunnat ritual practices. These included the observance of the death anniversaries (*'urs*) of dead sufi preceptors (pirs) venerated by the members of the movement. In particular, veneration of the Prophet Muhammad and occasions such as his birth anniversary (*milad*), were definitive to the self-image of the movement.

The intercessionary ritual practices of the Ahl-e Sunnat movement appeared to its opponents to invalidate its claims to being 'reformist', rendering it 'backward', and 'ignorant'. This continues to be the image of the Ahl-e Sunnat movement among adversarial groups in the subcontinent today. To the Ahl-e Sunnat themselves, however, following the Prophet's path (*sunna*) with the help of saintly intermediaries, provided a template for behaviour in the modern world. Shrine-centred devotion, carried out in a spirit of reform, was a conscious choice. In its self-consciousness the movement was based on a sense of individual responsibility, not on attachment to ancient custom (*rawaj*, Ar. *'adat*) as its detractors alleged.

[10] On 'lay' leaders of Hindu and Muslim reform movements in the late colonial period, see Barbara D. Metcalf, 'Imagining Community: Polemical Debates in Colonial India', in Kenneth W. Jones (ed.), *Religious Controversy in British India: Dialogues in South Asian Languages* (Albany: State University of New York Press, 1992), pp. 232–4.

Van der Veer suggests in *Religious Nationalism* that 'if we want to take religious discourse and practice as relevant to the project of religious nationalism, we have to attempt to understand religious identities as historically produced in religious institutions that are in a constant process of transformation'.[11] This study of the Ahl-e Sunnat 'ulama' at the height of the colonial period until the second decade of the twentieth century and the political transformations of the post-World War I period (when segments of the Ahl-e Sunnat leadership began to more towards some form of nationalism) examines how, through shifting emphases during these forty-odd years, they created an Indian Muslim identity that denied a dichotomy between shrine and mosque. Indeed, the integration of mosque- and shrine-based worship belies the general assumption that mosque-based activities are divisive and shrine-based ones inclusive. On the contrary, it is clear that the sufi institutions of the movement were as instrumental in the process of drawing exclusive boundaries as were other mosque-centred activities.

The historical context of British Indian colonialism was crucial to the emergence of the Ahl-e Sunnat movement, as were events in the wider Muslim world which shaped this and other Sunni Muslim movements in the subcontinent. The annual pilgrimage to Mecca (*hajj*), sometimes followed by extended periods of study in centres of learning such as the al-Azhar in Cairo, was of course the most important avenue for the exchange of ideas between Muslims from different parts of the world.[12] Ahmad Riza Khan performed the hajj twice, at a twenty-year interval, and both occasions were important for his stature as the leading *'alim* of the Ahl-e Sunnat movement. Moreover, he corresponded with several 'ulama' in Mecca and Medina over the years, sometimes to ask their opinion on controversial issues at home, but sometimes also to offer an opinion of his own. The 'ulama' of other contemporary movements

[11] Peter van der Veer, *Religious Nationalism: Hindus and Muslims in India* (Berkeley: University of California Press, 1994), p. 30.

[12] The classic study for the nineteenth century is by C. Snouck Hurgronje, *Mekka in the Latter Part of the 19th Century: Daily Life, Customs and Learning—the Moslims of the East-Indian-Archipelago,* tr. J. H. Monahan (London: Luzac and Co., 1931), Reprint (Leiden: E. J. Brill, 1970).

in British India likewise had sustained contacts with the Haramain. Such contacts were a powerful source of validation in contestations amongst the Indian 'ulama'.

The north Indian 'ulama' were consequently aware of intellectual currents in other parts of the Muslim world, and, to varying degrees, were influenced by them. In the eighteenth and nineteenth centuries, participation in study circles at Mecca may have acquainted some Indian 'ulama' with the reformist ideas of the Arabian Muwahhidun movement, widely known as 'Wahhabi'. However, the exact nature of the interchange of ideas between the Arabian movement and nineteenth century Indian ones characterized as 'Wahhabi' remains unclear.

The Khilafat movement of the early twentieth century, in which a number of the 'ulama' played leading roles, was notable in this regard. In the late nineteenth century, Sayyid Jamal al-Din al-Afghani (1838–97), the Iranian scholar and activist, had travelled around the Muslim world (visiting India in the 1850s and 1860s) exhorting Muslims of all nationalities to unite under the spiritual leadership of the Turkish sultan in order to free themselves of Western colonial rule.[13] The enduring hatred of the British which al-Afghani imbibed during his Indian stay led him to attack Sir Sayyid Ahmad Khan (1817–98) as a tool of British imperialism.[14] In the Khilafat movement of 1919–22, members of the 'ulama', influenced by al-Afghani's pan-Islamic message, entered into an alliance with the Indian National Congress. While M. K. Gandhi, representing the Congress leadership, supported the 'ulama' in their demand for British recognition of the Turkish sultan as Caliph, the 'ulama' in turn lent their support to the Indian nationalist struggle against British rule. These decisions were made after extensive debate in meetings held by the Jam'iyyat al-'Ulama'-e Hind, the political party formed by several north Indian 'ulama' in 1919. Ahmad Riza Khan, then a well-known public figure in 'ulama' circles as leader of the

[13] Nikki R. Keddie, *Sayyid Jamal ad-Din 'al-Afghani': A Political Biography* (Berkeley: University of California Press, 1972).

[14] Nikki R. Keddie, *An Islamic Response to Imperialism: Political and Religious Writings of Sayyid Jamal ad-Din 'al-Afghani'* (Berkeley: University of California Press, 1983). On Sir Sayyid Ahmad Khan, see the discussion in Chapter I.

Ahl-e Sunnat movement, refused however to support the Khilafat movement or the pan-Islamic idea, for reasons that I explore in Chapter IX.

Many in South Asia are more familiar with the term Barelwi than 'Ahl-e Sunnat wa Jama 'at'. Barelwis are to be found today in Pakistan and India, as well as Britain. The term Barelwi is, however, rejected by those who identify themselves with the movement, and has therefore not been used here. It may be useful to clarify at the outset what is at issue in this particular disagreement over nomenclature.[15]

Ahmad Riza's followers were called Barelwi simply because he was a resident of the town of Bareilly, in Rohilkhand (the western portion of present-day Uttar Pradesh).[16] It is common practice for Muslims in South Asia (as elsewhere) to identify themselves by place-name, or by profession, association with a sufi order (e.g., Qadiri, Chishti, or other), or family lineage (such as Qureshi or 'Usmani), so as to distinguish between individuals with the same personal name.[17] As Ahmad Riza was the central figure around which the movement sharing his views took shape, the name Barelwi has come to stand not simply for him but for the movement itself.

I deliberately use the words 'central figure' rather than 'founder' to describe Ahmad Riza's relationship to the movement, because followers consider the term founder misplaced. It is their belief that Ahmad Riza was reviving the prophetic sunna (path, way) as embodied in the Qur'an and the literature of the traditions, *hadis*. Because Muslims had become forgetful (*ghafil*) of the Prophet's message and had fallen away from it, Ahmad Riza had assumed the task of 'reminding' them and bringing them back to the ideal way.

[15] Thus van der Veer, *Religious Nationalism*, p. 43: '. . . names are very significant parts of one's social identity.'

[16] Bareilly, in Rohilkhand, is not to be confused with Rae Bareilly, in Awadh. Ahmad Riza and the Barelwi movement have no relationship to Sayyid Ahmad Barelwi (d. 1831), from Rae Bareilly, who led the jihad movement of the 1820s.

[17] Such names are called *nisbat* or *nisba*. See Mohammed Haroon, *Cataloguing of Indian Muslim Names* (Lahore: Islamic Book Centre, 1986), for a useful introduction to Indian Muslim names and the technical terms for different kinds of names.

The Ahl-e Sunnat looked upon him as a *mujaddid* or renewer, a term with specific meaning in Islamic tradition.[18] It being their collective purpose to return to the prophetic way—certainly not to found a new group—they called themselves the 'Ahl-e Sunnat wa Jama'at, or 'people of the [Prophet's] way, and the majority community'. Simply stated, they regarded themselves as 'Sunnis', part of the world-wide Sunni community.

I use the term 'Ahl-e Sunnat wa Jama 'at' (or Ahl-e Sunnat, for short) as a means of grasping the self-perception of those being described. It allows one to recognize the centrality of the figure of the Prophet Muhammad to the movement, and to understand the internal logic of the positions that were taken by Ahmad Riza on various issues as a consequence of his Prophet-centred vision. In other words, it enables one to see the movement in its own terms rather than those imposed on it from the outside. On the negative side, however, because the term 'Sunni' has a very wide application (standing in opposition to the other major Muslim category of Shi'i), such usage has the disadvantage of possible confusion about its denotation. Followers of the movement use the term in reference to themselves and to those they consider faithful to the prophetic sunna—that is to say, those whose vision of Islam coincides with their own. I have used the word Sunni within quotes whenever it signifies the particular meaning it had to the movement. This necessary precaution will, I hope, dispel any impression that I share the self-image of the movement.

As indicated above, the Ahl-e Sunnat movement was one of several British Indian movements led by 'ulama' in the nineteenth century. Scholars have characterized some of these as 'fundamentalist' or 'orthodox', or, speaking of those that seem to have roots in 'popular religion', as 'syncretist', 'traditional', or (in Bengal) *sabiqi*. Such characterizations are inevitably imprecise, as they mean different things to different people. Moreover, they are often value-laden, and as in the case of the Barelwi versus 'Ahl-e Sunnat wa Jamma 'at'

[18] I discuss the concept of tajdid and the Ahl-e Sunnat claim in Chapters VI and VII.

discussion, involve imposing categories that are foreign to the people being discussed.[19]

Most recently, Kenneth Jones has spoken of movements led by the 'ulama' (and certain Hindu movements, led by Hindu religious figures as well) as 'transitional'. He defines this term as follows:

> Transitional movements had their origins in the pre-colonial world and arose from indigenous forms of socio-religious dissent, with little or no influence from the colonial milieu, either because it was not yet established or because it had failed to affect the individuals involved in a particular movement. The clearest determinant of a transitional movement was an absence of anglicized individuals among its leaders and a lack of concern with adjusting its concepts and programmes to the colonial world.[20]

It is plain that for Jones the point of reference is British colonialism. The movements that come under this rubric are viewed as transitional between a pre-colonial past and—where the movements concerned survived the colonial era—a post-colonial present. While necessarily shaped by the reality of British political rule, Jones sees these as definably different from movements that sought to 'acculturate' to that reality, to use his term for movements whose members sought to take advantage of the changed situation and opportunities created by colonial rule.

While this conceptualization may be useful as a means of thinking about movements originating in a variety of religious traditions (Jones examines several Hindu and Sikh movements in addition to Muslim ones), for our purposes it seems best to describe the 'ulama'-led movements of the nineteenth century with reference to their own terms of discourse. Because the self-proclaimed goal of the Ahl-e Sunnat and several other 'ulama'-led movements of this period was *tajdid* (renewal), the most appropriate way to describe

[19] For a critical essay on the interpretive implications of imposing categories on the data, in the Southeast Asian context, see William R. Roff, 'Islam Obscured? Some Reflections on Studies of Islam and Society in Southeast Asia', *Archipel* 29 (1985), 7–34. Also see Roff, 'Islamic Movements: One or Many?' in William R. Roff (ed.), *Islam and the Political Economy of Meaning: Comparative Studies of Muslim Discourse* (Berkeley: California University Press, 1987), pp. 31–52, for a related discussion of the analytical difficulties associated with the term 'Wahhabi'.

[20] Kenneth W. Jones, *Socio-Religious Reform Movements in British India*, The New Cambridge History of India, III: 1 (Cambridge: Cambridge University Press, 1989), p. 3.

them would seem to be as renewal movements. The term 'reform' (*islah* in Arabic and Urdu) is also used in the literature, though usually in the context of a desire to improve 'worldly' conditions of some sort, such as education or living standards, rather than to effect religious change. In this book I have used the word 'reform' as synonymous with 'renewal', as it is close in meaning to the intent of the word tajdid. Reform in our context should not be understood, however, to mean either 'reformation' in the Christian sense of restructuring of ecclesiastical authority or 'reformulation' of the Islamic message. Rather, it implies restatement of that immutable message with the purpose of recreating in an existing society or community of Muslims the moral climate thought to have existed at the time of the Prophet. As will become evident in the course of this study, the Ahl-e Sunnat conception of tajdid and of the role of the Prophet as Allah's messenger differed considerably from that of other 'ulama'-led movements of the period.

The question remains, who were the Ahl-e Sunnat wa Jama'at? And how did they relate to the British colonial framework, and to the other renewal movements of the nineteenth century?

To the extent that the Ahl-e Sunnat have been subject to scholarly investigation thus far, a certain amount of confusion exists about who they were and the social background they came from. They are generally said to have been influential in the rural areas (unlike the Deobandis, who are thought to have been urban-based). Hamza Alavi, for instance, writes:

> Historically, Deobandis have tended to be mainly urban and from middle and upper strata of society whereas Barelvi influence has been mainly in rural areas, with a populist appeal . . . . Traditionally Barelvi influence has been weaker in the UP (with the exception perhaps of the peasantry of South-Western UP) than in the Punjab and to some degree in Sind. On the other hand the main base of Deobandis was in the UP especially among urban Muslims . . . .[21]

It seems clear that Alavi is talking of rural sufi pirs rather than the 'ulama' who called themselves the 'Ahl-e Sunnat wa Jama 'at' in the

[21] Hamza Alavi, 'Pakistan and Islam: Ethnicity and Ideology', in F. Halliday and H. Alavi (eds.), *State and Ideology in the Middle East and Pakistan* (New York: Monthly Review Press, 1988), p. 86.

late nineteenth century. While 'ulama' such as Ahmad Riza were sympathetically inclined towards ritual worship centred around the tomb-shrine complexes (*khanqahs* and *dargahs*) of sufi pirs, it is not the case—as is suggested by Alavi's account—that all sufi pirs necessarily regarded themselves as, or were regarded by Ahl-e Sunnat 'ulama' as, members of the Ahl-e Sunnat movement. Only some self-consciously 'reformist' pirs of the late nineteenth and early twentieth century period were actively involved in the Ahl-e Sunnat movement as leaders. Failure to make these internal distinctions creates the impression that all rural shrines were Barelwi in orientation and that the movement was therefore made up of a large, undifferentiated mass of Muslim peasants. In this view anyone not a Deobandi or a Nadwi or an Ahl-e Hadis (or a member of some other distinct movement) appears (by default) to be a Barelwi. This is not far from the Ahl-e Sunnat claim that as 'Sunnis', they represent all South Asian (and other Sunni) Muslims, other than a small number of 'deviant' groups such as the Deobandi, Nadwi, and others, but it would be misleading nonetheless.

In order to delimit our group, then, I shall use the criterion of self-conscious identification with the Ahl-e Sunnat. It will not be assumed that every visitor to a shrine in our period was a member of the Ahl-e Sunnat movement simply because the Ahl-e Sunnat looked upon shrine-associated rituals favourably. We have no way of knowing whether at that time the term Ahl-e Sunnat (or even Barelwi) had any meaning for people of the rank and file, nor whether, in the event that people had heard of the name, they thought of themselves in those terms.[22]

Consequently, I confine myself to the leadership of the movement centred around Ahmad Riza. Family histories and biographical dictionaries (*tazkiras*) of the 'ulama' indicate that the core Ahl-e Sunnat leadership in the late nineteenth century consisted of 'ulama' and pirs from well-to-do, frequently landowning families, living in

[22] Knowledge of affiliations of this sort is probably easier to gauge for the post-colonial period, given the emergence of political parties among the 'ulama'. I doubt we can talk of 'Barelwi' or Ahl-e Sunnat influence at all precisely for our period, other than from our knowledge of the schools, journals, or organizations established where the term 'Ahl-e Sunnat' was specifically invoked. I have attempted to do this in Chapter III.

small agricultural towns (*qasbas*),[23] or, as in Ahmad Riza's case, in larger urban centres. In one way or another, they all had a close intellectual relationship with Ahmad Riza.

The central source-material for this study has been the fatawa of Ahmad Riza Khan. I do not claim to have made a complete study of all the fatawa he wrote: their volume (said by some to number a thousand) precludes this, as does the fact that they are not all published. Nevertheless, on the basis of those that are known to have been important to an understanding of his thought, as well as several less well-known ones, it has been possible to establish a pattern of thought and belief that is for the most part consistent.

Ahmad Riza also wrote a *diwan* or collection of poems, on themes such as his love for the Prophet. Known as *na'ts*, these poems give us a glimpse of Ahmad Riza's 'softer, gentler' side as 'lover of the Prophet'. Verses from these poems have been quoted in Chapters II and III, which deal with the sufi aspects of the Ahl-e Sunnat movement.

I have not attempted to study Ahmad Riza's translation into Urdu of the Qur'an. Though this would undoubtedly have added to our understanding of his thought, I do not think it would have materially altered the picture that emerges from his fatawa.

Among the other sources that have been important are the full-length biographies and biographical dictionaries (tazkiras) of Ahl-e Sunnat 'ulama'. The main biography of Ahmad Riza is *Hayat-e A'la Hazrat* by his disciple Zafar ud-Din Bihari, a didactic, not historical, work that tells us a great deal about the Ahl-e Sunnat ideal of personal conduct, which Ahmad Riza naturally exemplified to his followers. Yet it speaks only tangentially about his personal experience, the sequence of historical events or the larger social and political context. Such details have to be put together (to the extent

[23] For a discussion of the qasba and its eighteenth-century history in north India, see C. A. Bayly, 'The Small Town and Islamic Gentry in North India: The Case of Kara', in Kenneth Ballhatchet and John Harrison (eds.), *The City in South Asia: Pre-Modern and Modern* (London: School of Oriental and African Studies, University of London, 1980), pp. 20–48; and C. A. Bayly, *Rulers, Townsmen and Bazaars: North Indian Society in the Age of British Expansion, 1770–1870* (Cambridge: Cambridge University Press, 1988), paperback edition, Chapter 9.

possible) by consulting other tazkiras, cross-referencing between them, and, most importantly, by consulting newspapers and journals published by Ahl-e Sunnat 'ulama' in the late nineteenth and early twentieth centuries.

Of these, the *Dabdaba-e Sikandari* published from Rampur has been the most valuable. To a large extent, I have been able to date events and learn of calendrical rituals such as 'urs and milad meetings in different north Indian towns and cities by reading the columns of this weekly. Where available, secondary sources in English have helped to provide a picture of the internal organization of schools, papers and journals in comparable settings.

I should add perhaps that there is a vast secondary literature on the Ahl-e Sunnat movement which has only very occasionally been consulted in the course of this study. The movement is currently in the midst of an intellectual revival in Pakistan, and some of Ahmad Riza's fatawa are being published for the first time. While this has been enormously helpful to me in the attempt to locate original sources, I have ignored present-day judgments on Ahmad Riza's achievements and chosen to form my own by reading his fatawa directly. This course was dictated partly by the practical difficulties of reading all that has been written about him in recent years. In part, of course, it is also in good Muslim and Western scholarly tradition to go back to the source.

Finally, fieldwork in Pakistan for three months (October-December 1986) and in India for almost a year (during most of 1987) has contributed importantly to my understanding of the movement. Interviews with contemporary Ahl-e Sunnat 'ulama', scholars and others listed in the bibliography, as well as extended discussion with some of them, enabled me to approach the texts with an empathy that would otherwise have been lacking.

Chapter I

Politics and Religion, Eighteenth and Nineteenth Centuries

Bareilly, the city which has given the Barelwi or Ahl-e Sunnat wa Jama'at movement its name, lies in Rohilkhand, in the western portion of what came to be known, under British rule, as the North-Western Provinces and Oudh (map 1).[1] In the seventeenth century rival Rajput chiefs had encouraged the immigration of Pathan or Rohilla Afghans, skilled mercenaries, into their territories as a means of shoring up their power against one another. In the eighteenth century two potentially powerful Afghan chieftaincies grew to prominence in the region: the Rohillas centred on Bareilly, and the Bangash centred on Mau-Farrukhabad farther south.

The Rohillas of Rohilkhand

When Mughal power began to decline with the death of Aurangzeb in 1707, the Rohillas came into their own under the strong and able leadership of 'Ali Muhammad Khan (d. 1748) and his successor, Hafiz Rahmat Khan (d. 1774). Between about 1720 and 1740 'Ali Muhammad Khan, a soldier in the Mughal army, was able to carve out an independent kingdom centred on the town of Aonla (then

[1] During Mughal times Rohilkhand had been a Rajput-dominated province known as Katehr. For this period of Rohilkhand (and more particularly Bareilly) history, see, e.g., Esha B. Joshi, *Gazetteer of India, Uttar Pradesh: Bareilly District* (Lucknow: Government of Uttar Pradesh, 1968), pp. 50–4.

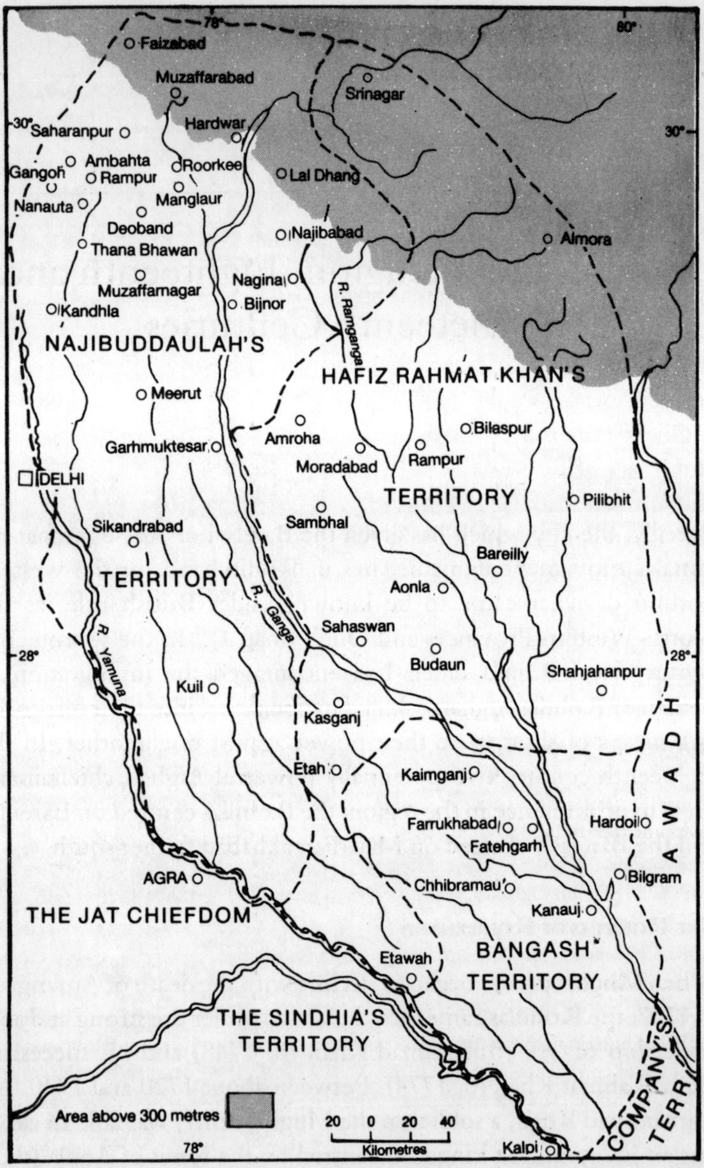

Map 1: Rohilkhand in 1768
(Adapted from Iqbal Husain, *The Ruhela Chieftaincies*, Delhi, Oxford University Press, 1994, p. 109. By permission of the author.)

part of *sarkar* Muradabad, an administrative division of Delhi province) at the Mughals' expense, and came to control much of Rampur, Sambhal, Muradabad, Amroha, Shahjahanpur, Pilibhit, and other districts in the region.[2] Many of these towns and districts had formerly been under Rajput control.

This region, known after the Rohillas as Rohilkhand, was bounded on the north by the foot-hills of the Himalaya (the *terai*) and by the Ganga in the south. It was characterized by rich alluvial soil. Indeed, early eighteenth-century European reports included northern Rohilkhand among those regions deemed 'the most fertile' in the subcontinent.[3] It could therefore easily accommodate Afghan troopers joining an up-and-coming Rohilla chief.

Given that the Rohillas were a threat to the authority of the Mughals, conflict was inevitable.[4] At first the Mughal Emperor, Muhammad Shah (r. 1719–48) had been pleased with 'Ali Muhammad Khan's military successes. In 1737, in recognition of services rendered, he granted the latter 'a *mansab* of 5,000/5,000'.[5] However, by about 1740 'Ali Muhammad Khan's growing power[6] began to worry the Mughal court. He was forced to spend the last years of his life fending off repeated attacks on his territory by Safdar Jang (d. 1754), then Nawab of Awadh and grandmaster of artillery (*mir-e atish*) in the imperial army.[7]

[2] Amar Singh Baghel, *Gazetteer of India, Uttar Pradesh: Rampur District* (Lucknow: Government of India, 1974), pp. 37–8.

[3] See Muzaffar Alam, *The Crisis of Empire in Mughal North India: Awadh and the Punjab, 1707–1748* (Delhi: Oxford University Press, 1986), pp. 252–3, 254.

[4] For a detailed treatment of eighteenth-century Rohilla history, see Iqbal Husain, *The Ruhela Chieftaincies: The Rise and Fall of Ruhela Power in India in the Eighteenth Century* (Delhi: Oxford University Press, 1994).

[5] Iqbal Husain, *The Ruhela Chieftaincies*, p. 46. A *mansab* is a military rank reflecting the number of horsemen the holder of the title was supposed to bring to the battlefield. As Iqbal Husain comments, with this mansab 'Ali Muhammad Khan 'obtained the status of a Mughal noble', and was entitled to use kettle-drums (*naubat*), a royal privilege. Ibid., p. 47.

[6] Joshi, *Gazetteer of India, Uttar Pradesh: Bareilly*, p. 56, estimates that 'Ali Muhammad Khan had a private army of between 30,000 and 40,000 men, though Iqbal Husain appears to think this an exaggeration.

[7] As Iqbal Husain explains, Safdar Jang's anti-Afghan sentiments (and actions) were rooted in the politics of Turani-Irani factionalism in the imperial capital. The Rohillas

In 1745 Safdar Jang led a Mughal force against 'Ali Muhammad Khan, forcing him to surrender. After being deprived of his recent conquests, he was given a revenue assignment (*jagir*) in Sirhind (Panjab) to prevent him from regrouping his forces in Rohilkhand. Furthermore, his eldest sons 'Abdullah Khan and Faizullah Khan were kept under royal custody in Delhi, as a guarantee for his good behaviour.[8]

Despite these setbacks, 'Ali Muhammad Khan was able to recoup his losses when in 1748 confusion overtook Mughal ranks in the wake of Ahmad Shah Abdali's invasion of Delhi and the death of Emperor Muhammad Shah that year. While Mughal forces were pre-occupied with Ahmad Shah's invasion, he swiftly returned to Rohilkhand and repossessed himself of his former territories with the help of Afghan troops happy to desert to him once again.

'Ali Muhammad Khan's unexpected death in September 1748, however, resulted in political confusion in Rohilkhand. With his two eldest sons still in captivity (now in Kabul), and the next in line a minor, control over Rohilla affairs fell to Hafiz Rahmat Khan (d. 1774), whom 'Ali Muhammad Khan had appointed regent prior to his death.[9]

The Nawabs of Farrukhabad

Meanwhile, south of Bareilly and across the Ganga in the Doab, another Pathan tribe, the Bangash, was establishing its political control centred on the town of Mau. Led by Muhammad Khan (1665–1743), the Bangash Afghans enlisted as soldiers in Farrukhsiyar's army during the latter's bid for the throne in 1713. When

were, by and large, supported by the Turani faction, while Safdar Jang was part of the Irani group. Iqbal Husain, *The Ruhela Chieftaincies*, pp. 53, 61.

[8] Baghel, *Gazetteer of India, Uttar Pradesh: Rampur*, pp. 40–1.

[9] Hafiz Rahmat Khan and 'Ali Muhammad Khan had a complex relationship themselves, as 'Ali Muhammad Khan's adoptive father, Daud Khan, had been responsible for the murder of Hafiz Rahmat Khan's father, Shah Alam Khan. A blood feud between them was avoided when they agreed to set aside old animosities in the 1730s, and Rahmat Khan accepted 'Ali Muhammad Khan's leadership of the Rohillas. 'Ali Muhammad Khan's ancestry was his weak spot, since he had been a Hindu prior to his adoption by Daud Khan. Ibid., pp. 37, 39.

Farrukhsiyar became emperor, Muhammad Khan assumed the title of Nawab, receiving among other things eight subdistricts (*parganas*) in Bundelkhand for the upkeep of his troops.[10] In 1714, seeking to build up a power base in and around Mau, he founded the fortified towns of Kaimganj and Muhammadabad, and also began the construction of Farrukhabad, which he named after Farrukhsiyar.[11]

As with 'Ali Muhammad Khan, Muhammad Khan's fortunes initially rose during the reign of Emperor Muhammad Shah, Farrukhsiyar's successor, but then fell. In favour with the Emperor at least until 1720, he was appointed governor (*subahdar*) of the province of Allahabad.[12] Thereafter, the Mughal court appears to have tried to curb his growing influence. Ordered to proceed to Gwalior to lead a campaign against the Marathas, his jagirs were resumed in the late 1720s. In 1729, when the Marathas besieged his fort at Farrukhabad, no help was forthcoming from Delhi. Moreover, Allahabad, a lucrative province, was taken away from him, and the troubled one of Malwa (subject to repeated Maratha incursions) allotted him instead.[13]

Despite these setbacks, by the time of his death in 1743, Muhammad Khan's authority extended over a considerable area:

> Nawab Muhammad held the western half of the Cawnpur district . . . the whole of the Farrukhabad district; all of the Mainpuri district except perhaps one parganah; the whole of the Eta district . . . nearly one half of the Budaon district across the Ganges; and one parganah of the Shahjahanpur district . . . . The local tradition states that parganah Marahra in the Eta district was obtained in farm . . . in 1738.[14]

[10] Farrukhsiyar rewarded Muhammad Khan with a ceremonial robe, and more importantly with the 'rank of Commander of four thousand. From that day [in January 1713] he was styled Nawab'. Irvine, 'The Bangash Nawabs of Farrukhabad', *Journal of the Asiatic Society of Bengal*, IV (1878), 274.

[11] Ibid., 275–80.

[12] Ibid., 282–3. Earlier honours had included the following: In 1719, the Emperor raised Muhammad Khan's rank to 6,000 as reward for having backed him against his rivals; in 1720, he raised it to 7,000, also bestowing on him the title of 'Ghazanfar Jang' ('The Lion of War'), and some more parganas.

[13] Ibid., 287–308.

[14] Ibid., 348.

Muhammad Khan was succeeded by his eldest son Qa'im Khan (d. 1748). Well liked by Emperor Muhammad Shah, he was confirmed in his possession of Muhammad Khan's territories, and obtained from the Emperor the title of 'Farzand Bahadur'.

Thus far the two regional Pathan powers—'Ali Muhammad Khan's Rohillas in the Muradabad-Bareilly region, and Muhammad Khan's Bangash Pathans around Farrukhabad—had expanded at the expense of the Mughal centre without coming into conflict with each other. But when 'Ali Muhammad Khan died in 1748, Safdar Jang attempted to divide them by appointing Qa'im Khan *faujdar* (military and administrative officer) of Muradabad. The latter accordingly led his forces against Rohilkhand.[15] In the battle that ensued, he was killed by Hafiz Rahmat Khan's forces. Farrukhabad and many other Bangash territories now fell to Hafiz Rahmat Khan.

These events were to eliminate the Afghans of Rohilkhand as a regional power on par with Bengal or Awadh. Hitherto, strong military leadership coupled with an ethic of loyalty amongst Afghans had enabled them to unite in the face of outside threat. So strong was their sense of loyalty that the Afghans even had Ahmad Shah Abdali's support against Mughal or Maratha attack. By the end of the eighteenth century, however, they were a spent force both in terms of military strength and economic resources. Moreover, the political landscape was changing. New threats had emerged.

Awadh's Domination Over Rohilkhand

Rohilla expansionism was decisively checked in the second half of the eighteenth century by a combination of forces: the westward expansion of Awadh as an autonomous province under Safdar Jang[16] and his son Shuja ud-Daula (d. 1775); Maratha incursions in the region, whether as an independent power or in alliance with the

[15] Muzaffar Alam, *Crisis of Empire*, p. 269. Also see Iqbal Husain, *The Ruhela Chieftaincies*, pp. 62–4.

[16] As Muzaffar Alam points out, Safdar Jang 'regarded the possibility of a powerful chief on the borders of Awadh as a threat to [his] ambition'. (*Crisis of Empire*, pp. 269–70.) Consequently he saw the Bangash nawabs and the Rohilla chiefs as a potential threat.

Nawab of Awadh and Mughal forces; and, after 1774, the British presence.

Safdar Jang's response to Qa'im Khan's death and the defeat of the Bangash forces by Hafiz Rahmat Khan was to attempt to annex Farrukhabad to Awadh. Initially the attempt was repulsed by Qa'im Khan's successor, Ahmad Khan Bangash (d. 1771). Indeed, the Bangash retaliated by occupying 'the important Awadh town of Bilgram' and sacking the town in 1750.[17] Later that year, they occupied Malihabad, on the outskirts of Lucknow,[18] and then entered Lucknow itself. Their occupation of Lucknow, however, was of short duration. According to Cole, 'the haughtiness of the new conquerors and the harshness of their exactions provoked sanguinary riots between the Afghans and the Shaykhzadahs [Sunni landholders in Lucknow]'.[19] More importantly, the local 'Sunni middle landholders based in small [Awadh] towns chose the Shi'i Safdar Jang over the Sunni Bangash tribesmen because his rule offered more continuity of political culture and revenue structure than did that of the coarse new conquerors'.[20] By 1752, Safdar Jang, with assistance from Maratha and Jat forces, had succeeded in defeating the Bangash and putting the Rohillas on the defensive as well. But Ahmad Shah Abdali's invasion of north India that year prevented him from decisively beating the Rohillas.

During the 1750s the Rohillas were also being attacked on their southern and western flanks by successive waves of Marathas. Their only source of hope and support at this stage lay with Ahmad Shah Abdali (now styled 'Durrani'), who, as a fellow Afghan, wanted to see their power restored and that of the Marathas crushed. Thus both the regional Rohilla powers (Ahmad Khan Bangash and Hafiz Rahmat Khan) supported Ahmad Shah in the Battle of Panipat of 1761. Despite their victory at this important battle, however, the

[17] J. R. I. Cole, *Roots of North Indian Shi'ism in Iran and Iraq: Religion and State in Awadh, 1722–1859* (Delhi: Oxford University Press, 1989), p. 46.

[18] Abdul Halim Sharar, *Lucknow: The Last Phase of an Oriental Culture*, tr. and ed. E. S. Harcourt and Fakhir Hussain (Delhi: Oxford University Press, 1989), p. 43, mentions Malihabad.

[19] Cole, *Roots of North Indian Shi'ism*, p. 46.

[20] Ibid., p. 47.

tide of events was not reversed, this time because of the growth of East India Company power in north India, clearly indicated by the British victory over Shuja ud-Daula at the Battle of Baksar in 1764. That, in turn, was to lead to Awadh's increasing load of debt to the British, and, ten years later, to Awadh's annexation of Rohilkhand with British help.

Rampur State, The Last Rohilla Outpost

Ironically, while the eighteenth-and-nineteenth century regional courts of Muradabad–Bareilly–Aonla, Farrukhabad, and even Lucknow (not to speak of Delhi, the Mughal capital) came gradually under direct British rule between 1774 and the Revolt of 1857, Rampur survived as an autonomous princely state down to 1949 following Indian independence. In large part, the political astuteness of successive nawabs of Rampur seems to have kept the state from being swallowed up by the British; perhaps its small size and lack of strategic importance for the British also offers an explanation.

Rampur state was created in 1774. After the British and the Nawab of Awadh defeated the Rohillas that year and usurped their territory, Warren Hastings concluded a treaty with Faizullah Khan (d. 1794) granting him Rampur, a small estate (*c.* 900 square miles) wedged between Muradabad and Bareilly districts, in return for a promise to render military assistance to the Nawab of Awadh.[21] This Faizullah Khan, the first Nawab of Rampur, was none other than 'Ali Muhammad Khan's son, who had been taken to Qandahar and Kabul by Ahmad Shah Abdali in 1748. Abdali had sent him back in 1751 to Aonla to help the Rohillas fight the Marathas and the Nawab of Awadh.[22] Given his aristocratic origins, leadership qualities and fighting skills, he became over the next two decades an important

[21] On these events, see Sir John Strachey, *Hastings and the Rohilla War* (Oxford: Clarendon Press, 1892), Indian reprint (Delhi: Prabha Publications, 1985), p. 275; Baghel, *Gazetteer of India, Uttar Pradesh: Rampur District*, pp. 52–3.

[22] Ibid., p. 44. The terms of the Treaty of Laldhang (1774) requiring Faizullah Khan to furnish military troops to the Nawab of Awadh were revised in 1783. Under the terms of the new treaty, Faizullah Khan absolved himself of any such future obligations by paying fifteen lakhs of rupees to the Nawab of Awadh. Ibid., pp. 54–6.

Rohilla leader in Hafiz Rahmat Khan's circle. When the latter was killed in 1774, Faizullah Khan became 'the acknowledged chief of the Rohillas, . . . daily joined by men who had nothing to lose by striking one more blow for their lands'.[23] Deeming further warfare against the combined forces of the East India Company and Awadh to be futile, however, Faizullah Khan consented a few months later to the terms of the treaty mentioned above.

With the end of Rohilla military might, Faizullah Khan devoted the remaining years of his life to administering his little state and attracting men of artistic and literary talent to his court. There is some evidence that the Raza Library was founded by Faizullah Khan.[24] Furthermore, the late eighteenth century poet Qa'im (d. 1793–4), a pupil of Sauda, was patronized by the Rampur court.[25] Sauda himself (1713–80), a poet of Shi'i persuasion, was patronized by Nawab Ahmad Khan Bangash for seventeen years until his departure for the Awadh court in 1771–2.[26]

The nawabs of Rampur and Farrukhabad appear to have been strongly influenced by the Shi'i court of the then reigning Nawab of Awadh, Asaf ud-Daula (d. 1797).[27] Following Asaf ud-Daula's decision to move the capital of Awadh from Faizabad to Lucknow in 1775, Lucknow experienced a construction and population boom. Over the next quarter-century, Cole estimates, Lucknow's population grew from 200,000 to 300,000.[28] Given the Shi'i faith of the nobility and upper classes of the Awadh court, Lucknow also began at this time to acquire a reputation for Shi'i scholarship, religious practice, poetic talent, and grand architecture.[29]

In time, the nawabs of Farrukhabad and Rampur became Shi'i as well. Cole reports that the 'nawabs of Farrukhabad became Shi'is in

23 Ibid., p. 51.

24 Abid Raza Bedar, *Raza Library* (Rampur: Institute of Oriental Studies, 1966), p. 5. (Urdu text.)

25 Muhammad Sadiq, *A History of Urdu Literature*, 2nd ed. (Delhi: Oxford University Press, 1984), pp. 142–3.

26 Ibid., p. 108.

27 I owe this insight to Carla Petievich. Personal communication, 12 May 1993.

28 Cole, *Roots of North Indian Shi'ism*, p. 94.

29 Ibid., pp. 93–100 and passim. Also see Sharar, *Lucknow: The Last Phase*, pp. 44–9.

the late eighteenth century'.[30] Those of Rampur appear to have converted to Shi'ism somewhat later, for the writer of the 1911 *Gazetteer of the Rampur State* suggests that the first nawab to become a Shi'i was Muhammad Sa'id Khan (r. 1840–55), and that he did so under the influence of Nawabs Amjad 'Ali Shah (r. 1842–7) and Wajid 'Ali Shah (r. 1847–56) of Awadh.[31] Subsequently, all the succeeding nawabs of Rampur—except one, Kalb 'Ali Khan (r. 1865–87)—were Shi'i Muslims.

Rampur's patronage of religious learning and the arts blossomed in the mid-nineteenth century, during Muhammad Sa'id Khan's reign. He initiated efforts to expand the Arabic, Persian, and Urdu Manuscripts in his library :

> There were several calligraphers, gilders, decorators of wood slates, and bookbinders employed [at the library]. New books were copied. Gold work was done on precious books . . . . The Nawab invited . . . preeminent copyists and Arabic hand-writers [from Kashmir]. After them, their sons kept their skills alive. From Lucknow, the Nawab invited and employed Mir Auz 'Ali Khushnavisi [a calligrapher] . . . . The Madrasa 'Aliyya, that famous centre for Oriental sciences, also came into being at this time.[32]

Nawab Muhammad Sa'id Khan was also acquainted with some of the leading literary and religious figures of his day: among them were Mufti Sadr ud-Din Khan Azurda (d. 1863), a poet and scholar of Persian who held the judicial post of Sadr al-Sudur until the 1857 Revolt; Maulana Fazl-e Haqq Khairabadi (d. 1862), a leading scholar of his day who was held in great esteem by the Ahl-e Sunnat wa Jama'at; and Hakim Momin Khan Momin (d. 1851), who came from a well-known family of Yunani physicians in Delhi and was also a poet and scholar of repute.[33]

Muhammad Sa'id Khan's successor Yusuf 'Ali Khan had only been in power about a year when the British ousted Wajid 'Ali Shah as ruler of Awadh in 1856. The collapse of the Awadh court left a

[30] Cole, p. 103.

[31] Baghel, *Gazetteer of India, Uttar Pradesh: Rampur District*, p. 68. Baghel's source is the 1911 Rampur Gazetteer whose author appears (though this is not made entirely clear) to be Syid A. H. Khan. See Baghel, 'Preface'.

[32] Abid Raza Bedar, *Raza Library*, p. 6.

[33] Ibid., p. 5.

number of poets, writers and scholars without patronage, and many consequently chose to come to Rampur. Sharar names a number of them in his history of Lucknow: among them Sayyid Muzaffar 'Ali Khan Asir (d. 1881), a scholar from Firangi Mahal; Munshi Mufti Amir Ahmad Amir Minai (d. 1900), a writer of ghazal poetry; and Hakim Sayyid Zamin 'Ali Jalal (d. 1909), a Yunani doctor and scholar of Arabic and Persian.[34]

While the eclipse of the court of Awadh as patron had thus helped enlarge the circle of luminaries in Rampur, the Revolt of 1857, which led to the formal liquidation of the Mughal empire, had the same effect. Yusuf 'Ali Khan had chosen to be loyal to the British during their hour of peril; in fact he administered Muradabad district on behalf of the British during their absence in 1856-7.[35] Rampur was thus spared the widespread destruction of homes and displacement of families that the British visited upon the citizens of Delhi. Among those who found refuge in Rampur were, according to Sharar, Nawab Mirza Dagh Dehlavi (d. 1905), stepson of Bahadur Shah Zafar's heir-apparent, and a writer of ghazals, and the poet Mir Mahdi Majruh (d. 1902).[36]

The star of the court circle at Rampur was, however, Mirza Ghalib (d. 1869), teacher (*murshid*) of poetry to Nawab Yusuf 'Ali Khan who wrote under the pen name (*takhallus*) 'Nazim'.[37] In 1859, Yusuf 'Ali Khan began to send Ghalib a regular monthly grant for correcting his poetry and writing occasional panegyrics on important state occasions. Contrary to custom (and the preference of the Nawab), Ghalib was permitted to live in Delhi, making only occasional visits to the Rampur court. In letters to friends Ghalib sometimes referred to his relationship with the Nawab and visits to Rampur. In 1865, he wrote:

> About ten to twelve years ago the late Nawwab of Rampur Yusuf Ali Khan began sending me his verses to correct; and every month he had a draft for a hundred rupees sent me. Judge of his tact and courtesy by the fact that he never

[34] Sharar, *Lucknow: The Last Phase*, pp. 256–7, notes 278, 283, 288.

[35] E. I. Brodkin, 'The Struggle for Succession: Rebels and Loyalists in the Indian Mutiny of 1857', *Modern Asian Studies*, 6:3 (1972), 277–90.

[36] Sharar, *Lucknow: The Last Phase*, p. 256, notes 284 and 287.

[37] Abid Raza Bedar, *Raza Library*, p. 6.

demanded receipts for the money . . . . Besides this monthly allowance he would send me other sums from time to time—sometimes two hundred, sometimes two hundred and fifty. During the time of the troubles [the Mutiny of 1857] my income from the Fort [i.e., the Mughal court] ceased and my pension from the British was stopped. This good man continued to send my monthly allowance and occasional extra gifts from time to time; and that is how I and my dependants managed to survive. The present Nawwab [Kalb 'Ali Khan]—may God preserve and prosper him for ever and ever—continues to send the draft for my monthly allowance as of old. Let us see whether he continues the practice of the occasional gifts or not.[38]

Although Ghalib did not fare as well under Kalb 'Ali as he had under his father, for reasons set out by Daud Rahbar,[39] he must have been too important an asset to the Rampur court for Kalb 'Ali to disown entirely: as Rahbar adds, for all the differences between them, Kalb 'Ali Khan continued the monthly payments and helped defray other costs such as the wedding expenses of one of Ghalib's sons. After the poet's death he settled some of his outstanding debts.[40]

Ghalib's association with the Rampur court illustrates, in fact, the increasingly important role of the Muslim princely states in fostering and preserving an Indo-Persian culture at a time when most of India was under British rule. In patronizing Ghalib, Kalb 'Ali's larger purpose must have been to make Rampur an important (if small) regional court where Persianate cultural traditions associated with learning, the arts, and Urdu letters, might flourish. To this end, he also built up the resources of the Raza Library, and in 1886

[38] Ralph Russell and Khurshidul Islam, tr. and eds., *Ghalib 1797–1869, vol. 1: Life and Letters* (Cambridge: Harvard University Press, 1969), pp. 319–20. As the editors clarify, the grant from Yusuf 'Ali Khan began in July 1859, not in 1853 or 1854, as Ghalib here suggests.

[39] Daud Rahbar, tr., *Urdu Letters of Mirza Asadullah Khan Ghalib* (Albany: State University of New York Press, 1987), p. xxxviii: 'the two men had never been, nor were ever to be, terribly comfortable with each other. Ghalib's grandfatherly attitude towards the Prince was taken as condescension, and the former's steadfast refusal to take up residence in Rampur was not unreasonably taken as a slight. In addition, Kalb-i 'Ali was a staunch Sunni while Ghalib, though raised in a Sunni family, leaned towards the Shi'ite faith. The Prince took an exceedingly dim view of drinking and gambling, two activities in which Ghalib was known to indulge. To make matters worse, the two also clashed over their divergent views of literature and Persian usage'.

[40] Ibid.

inaugurated the construction of a new library building.[41] In addition such patronage provided a favourable environment for the 'ulama' and institutions of religious education such as the Madrasa 'Aliyya.

In the late nineteenth and early twentieth centuries, the Rampur court attracted some figures who were later to be important in the Indian nationalist movement. Pre-eminent among them was Hakim Ajmal Khan (1863–1927), who was in charge of the Raza Library for seven years, from 1896 to 1903, and under whose direction the collection of books on medicine (*tibb*) 'grew to become one of the most priceless' in the country.[42] A protégé of Nawab Hamid 'Ali Khan (r. 1889–1930), he continued to visit Rampur after 1903, whenever summoned by the Nawab for medical or other reasons. When he died in 1927, Hamid 'Ali Khan declared that even though Ajmal Khan had been a Sunni while he, Hamid 'Ali, was a Shi'i, he knew 'that if [he] were anyone's disciple in this world, [he] would have been Ajmal Khan's.'[43]

Rohilkhand Under the East India Company, 1801–57

While Rampur retained its nominal independence, the rest of Rohilkhand came under Awadh in 1774, and then under the East India Company in 1801. The economic prosperity of Rohilkhand became a thing of the past, the result of heavy revenue demands from Nawab Asaf ud-Daula in Lucknow (who was himself under pressure to pay the British in keeping with treaty obligations entered into by his father Shuja ud-Daula). Brodkin writes, 'Rohilkhand . . . staggered into the British Raj in 1801, an exhausted and impoverished state ravaged both by war and by twenty-seven years of malign rule from Lucknow'.[44]

Rohilkhand's impoverishment grew worse under the East India

[41] Abid Raza Bedar, *Raza Library*, p. 7.

[42] Ibid., p. 9.

[43] Barbara D. Metcalf, 'Hakim Ajmal Khan: *Rais* of Delhi and Muslim 'Leader",' in R. E. Frykenberg (ed.), *Delhi Through the Ages: Essays in Urban History, Culture and Society* (Delhi: Oxford University Press, 1986), pp. 306–7.

[44] E. J. Brodkin, 'British India and the Abuses of Power: Rohilkhand Under Early Company Rule', *Indian Economic and Social History Review*, X:2 (June 1973), 130.

Company, Brodkin argues, because of the absence of a landholding class and an unrealistically high revenue demand: 'The Pathans had effectively destroyed the old proprietary body [the Rajput élite that had governed the area before Pathan rule] and the Lucknow administration had hardly taken measures to reinstate it'.[45] Settling for the revenue with registrars or record-keepers (*qanungos*) and local headmen or *muqaddams* by means of auction, successive British collectors fixed the revenue demand at a high and continually increasing rate. The new 'proprietors' were promised that their title would be made permanent after a ten-year period; but before the end of this period, their inability to meet the revenue demand resulted instead in their indebtedness to the British administration and eventual dispossession.

At the end of thirty years of British rule, in Brennan's view the ryots or peasants seemed no better off than before.[46] Despite rack-renting by those who engaged for the revenue, the availability of uncultivated land provided possibilities of escape while the force of custom also kept a lid on the extent to which the ryots might be oppressed. Brennan argues that there were two significant changes at the end of this period: an increase in the acreage under agriculture (and the growth of an important new cash-crop in the 1820s, sugarcane), and the creation of a new landlord class of government officials, muqaddams, revenue-farmers, and bankers and merchants. The last group (bankers and merchants), which was drawn largely from Hindu bania castes, made up close to ten percent of the landlord class. It had come to own property through money-lending and control over cash resources.[47]

Such changes in the countryside were accompanied by changes in the social composition of the major towns of Rohilkhand. During Rohilla rule, Bareilly had been dominated by the Rohilla élite. Essentially a military élite, its members also occupied important positions in government, administration, and landownership.

[45] Ibid., p. 138. Iqbal Husain, however, disputes the view that the Afghans destroyed the old zamindari class. See *The Ruhela Chieftaincies*, pp. 197–9.

[46] L. Brennan, 'Social Change in Rohilkhand 1801–33', *Indian Economic and Social History Review*, VII:4 (December 1970), p. 465.

[47] Ibid., pp. 458–60.

Additionally, the Rohillas had fostered religious education and preserved an Indo-Persian cultural style. With the onset of British rule their material base in landownership and military service disappeared. This urban 'gentry', as Bayly calls them, consequently suffered a decline in fortune and influence, while certain Hindu castes (Brahmins, Rajputs and Banias) profited at their expense. It is illustrative of the social conflict generated by this process that Bareilly, the largest and most important town in Rohilkhand, experienced two major riots in the first half of the nineteenth century, in 1816 and 1837.[48] Bayly believes that the 'local decline of the Rohilla gentry was the real cause' of the 1816 riot.[49]

Driven by the need to increase revenues, the British had decided to impose a house tax in Bareilly. However, both Hindu and Muslim community leaders—the *muhalladars* or leaders of the city's neighbourhoods or *muhallas*—were united in their opposition to the new tax. As Bayly notes, their opposition was rooted in part in their notions of propriety and status: 'There was a profound objection to any system which not only released police spies into the neighbourhood communities, but which also invited people of dubious origin to assess others' status and honour as represented in exchanges with the rulers'.[50] So great was public clamour against the tax that 'business [came to] a standstill, the shops were shut, and crowds assembled at the cutcherry to petition against the impost'.[51]

Leading the revolt was Mufti Muhammad Ewaz, a descendant of Hafiz Rahmat Khan, who apparently perceived the tax as a new kind of *jizya*, one which the Christian British were imposing on the Muslims in a total reversal of its legitimate use.[52] 'For him India was no longer a land of Islam, but *dar ul-harb*, a land of war in which

[48] My account of these events is based on two sources: Sandria Freitag, *Collective Action and Community*, chapter 3; and, on the 1816 riot, also C. A. Bayly, *Rulers, Townsmen and Bazaars: North Indian Society in the Age of British Expansion, 1770–1870* (Cambridge: Cambridge University Press, 1988), pp. 323–8.

[49] Bayly, p. 323.

[50] Ibid., p. 328

[51] Freitag, p. 105, quoting from the *Bareilly District Gazetteer* of 1911.

[52] Bayly, p. 325.

jihad (holy war) was possible'.[53] The crowd's perception that the Mufti's life was in danger led the call to war to be sounded:

> It was when the crowds began to think that the *mufti* was in danger of arrest that the real explosion of mob anger began. A very large crowd retired to the Shahdana mosque and the green flag of holy war was unfurled. The British moved troops and cannon to surround the rebels.[54]

The rebellion was notable both for the cooperation between élite Muslims and lower-class Muslims—artisans, day labourers, dyers, weavers, and others—and for that between Hindu and Muslim élites. Freitag notes that British rule in Rohilkhand had imperilled the economic fortunes not only of Pathans, but also those of Khatris and Kayasthas, who had shared in the Indo-Persian culture of the Pathans. Indeed, both these 'old élites' were in retreat before the rising new class of Hindu merchants who were profiting from the revenue-farming and money-lending opportunities being created by the British.[55] As Freitag shows, the old élites responded to their economic dislocation by groping for new cultural forms that would at once recognize ascribed status and make space for a new style of devotionalism which placed the individual at the centre.

By 1837 community leadership had moved more decisively into the hands of the new class, though the old élite families still enjoyed some influence. In the twenty-one-year interval between the two riots, the expansion of sugar cane cultivation in the countryside had further boosted the wealth and standing of the new élite. These changes in social structure found expression in 1837, when the dates of the Hindu festival of Ramnaumi (commemorating the god Rama's birth) and the Shi'i Muslim mourning rituals of Muharram (commemorating Imam Husain's martyrdom at Karbala) coincided. When British administrators 'permitted full-scale observances of the *Ramnaumi*'

[53] Ibid.

[54] Ibid. In footnote 63 on p. 325, Bayly incorrectly identifies Sayyid Ahmad Barelwi (d. 1831) as a resident of Bareilly rather than Rae Bareilly, in Awadh. This leads him to the further conclusion that 'Key members of the Rohilkhand *ulema* were thus closely related to the more militant strain of north Indian Islam'. In fact, the 'Barelwi' 'ulama' of Rohilkhand were *opposed* to Sayyid Ahmad Barelwi's movement, as I show in the course of this book.

[55] Freitag, pp. 106–7.

members of the old élite tried to defuse Muslim discontent by disarming the Muharram crowd and leading it in the direction of the Karbala, or field set aside for Muharram rituals.[56] The Muslim leaders then worked out a compromise with the Hindu leadership, agreeing 'to refrain from killing cattle in the bazaar on Hindu festival days in return for keeping the days of Muharram free of Hindu processions'.[57] As Freitag notes, the agreement reflected the growing influence of the Hindu mercantile élite, inasmuch as they were able to persuade the Muslims to recognize their ceremonial rights in the first place. And while the search for a compromise, led by the old Hindu and Muslim élites, showed that the latter were still influential in Bareilly city politics, the compromise was fragile.[58] By the 1870s, when Hindus and Muslims clashed again over similar issues, the Hindu mercantile élite refused to be bound by previous agreements.

I shall end this brief survey of major landmarks in eighteenth and early nineteenth century Rohilkhand history with a few comments about the 1857 Revolt in the region. According to Brodkin the disappearance of British authority in Rohilkhand in the first phase of the revolt led to a struggle for control by Rohilkhand's old rivals, the Rajputs and Pathans. Because the Pathans won, the British later generalized that 'Muslims' were 'rebels' while 'Hindus' were 'loyal'. Brodkin argues that these labels are misleading, because the picture was in fact much more complex. The British assumption of 'Muslim' guilt in fact led some Pathan leaders into rebellion by late 1857 against their will.[59] In Rohilkhand the districts of Bareilly, Badayun,

[56] Ibid., pp. 107–8.

[57] Ibid., p. 108.

[58] The Hindu leader of the compromise, Chaudhari Basant Rai, was murdered a few years later by a Muslim carpet maker, 'and when *Ramnaumi* and Muharram again overlapped in the early 1850s, his son had great difficulty extending the agreement of 1837'. Ibid., p. 108.

[59] Brodkin's paper, 'The Struggle for Succession', illustrates this basic argument with reference to Mahmud Khan, Nawab of Najibabad (in northern Rohilkhand). The fact that Mahmud Khan came from a family that had looked to the nawabs of Rampur for leadership is important, Brodkin argues. Rampur's Nawab Yusuf 'Ali remained loyal to the British throughout 1857–8. See E. I. Brodkin, 'The Struggle for Succession: Rebels and Loyalists in the Indian Mutiny of 1857', *Modern Asian Studies*, 6:3 (1972), 278–86.

and Shahjahanpur were controlled during the summer of 1857 by anti-British forces led by Khan Bahadur Khan, a grandson of Hafiz Rahmat Khan. Nawab Yusuf 'Ali Khan of Rampur, as noted earlier, remained loyal to the British, even administering Muradabad on their behalf until the British re-established control in 1858. The Nawab of Farrukhabad, Tafazzul Husain Khan, though labelled a rebel by the British (and deported to Aden for his alleged role in the rebellion), had by his own account reluctantly co-operated with the anti-British forces for fear of his life in October 1857.[60]

Religious Debates and Renewal Movements

If the political situation in north India had been highly fluid in these two centuries, the religious climate among the 'ulama' was hardly any less so. As early as 1803, shortly after the British assumption of control over the city of Delhi, debate started among the north Indian 'ulama' as to the *shar'i* (Islamic jurisprudential) status of India under British rule: was it still (as it had been under Mughal domination) *dar al-islam* (a land of peace) or had it become dar al-harb (a land of war), Shah 'Abd ul-'Aziz Dehlawi (d. 1824), son of the famous eighteenth-century 'alim, Shah Wali Ullah (d. 1762), was asked.[61] Shah 'Abd ul-'Aziz's answer, though equivocal, is thought to have inspired the jihad movement led by Sayyid Ahmad Barelwi (d. 1831) in the North-West Frontier Province and Panjab in the late 1820s.[62]

In Bengal, in 1821 another 'alim, Haji Shari'at Ullah (d. 1840), inspired by long residence in the Haramain, launched a reform movement among Bengali Muslim weavers and peasants known as the Fara'izi movement.[63] The movement took its name from

[60] Ibid., 277.

[61] The debate on the religious status of British India is addressed more fully in Chapter VII below.

[62] On this movement, see Harlan Otto Pearson, 'Islamic Reform and Revival in Nineteenth Century India: The Tariqa-i Muhammadiyah', Ph.D. dissertation, Department of History, Duke University, 1979.

[63] On the Fara'izis, see Mu'in ud-Din Ahmad Khan, *History of the Fara'izi Movement in Bengal (1818–1906)*, (Karachi: Pakistan Historical Society, 1965).

Shari'at Ullah's insistence that the people fulfill their fundamental duties (*fara'iz*, sing. *farz*) as Muslims—the daily prayer and other so-called 'pillars' of Islam—and discard practices seen by him as reprehensible innovations (*bid'a*). Under Shari'at Ullah's leadership, the Fara'izis were also markedly anti-British. While not jihadists, they refused to recognize the legitimacy of British rule. In view of the absence of duly functioning *qazis* (judges) and *amirs* (commanders), they forbade the observance of the Friday congregational prayer (*namaz-e jum'a* or *jum'a ki namaz*) and 'Id (festival) prayers.[64] Haji Shari'at Ullah's son, popularly known as Dudhu Miyan (d. 1862), subsequently constructed a political framework based on a complex hierarchy of *khalifas* (deputies) reporting ultimately to himself. Refusal to pay land taxes brought the Fara'izis into increasing conflict with the (largely Hindu) landowners and with the British Indian government as well.[65]

Yet another Muslim reaction to the ongoing intensification of British control was migration (*hijra*) to the Hijaz. Abu'l Kalam Azad's (1888–1958) great-grandfather Munawwar ud-Din was one of those who chose this option in the early nineteenth century.[66] Not until the end of that century did the family return, led by Azad's father Khair ud-Din (1831–1908). Maulana Muhammad Ishaq (1778–1846), Shah 'Abd ul-'Aziz's successor at the Madrasa Rahimiyya in Delhi, also migrated in 1841, along with his younger brother Ya'qub.[67]

Several others left in the aftermath of the 1857 Revolt. Because the British believed at the time that Muslim participation in the Revolt had been decisive, they were particularly harsh toward

[64] The absence of qazis was the result of the progressivc anglicization of the law, both in terms of content and administration, starting in the late eighteenth century. See Uma Yaduvansh, 'The Decline of the Role of the *Qadis* in India, 1793–1876', *Studies in Islam*, 6 (1969), 155–71.

[65] This brief summary of the Farai'zi movement is based on Roff, 'Islamic Movements: One or Many?', pp. 40–1.

[66] On Azad, see Ian Henderson Douglas, *Abul Kalam Azad: An Intellectual and Religious Biography*, eds. Gail Minault and Christian W. Troll (Delhi: Oxford University Press, 1988), pp. 32–3. Munawwar ud-Din probably left India in the early 1830s.

[67] Metcalf, *Islamic Revival*, p. 71

Muslims in its aftermath. Haji Imdad Ullah (1817–99) was one of several 'ulama' to migrate from India at this time.[68]

As for the 'ulama' who stayed, many retreated from large cities such as Delhi to the relative security of the qasbas dotting the north Indian landscape:

> The 'ulama now tended, by and large, to leave their beloved but desolate Delhi behind in favor of the qasbahs in which many of them had their roots. The places they chose, such as Deoband, Saharanpur, Kandhlah, Gangoh, and Bareilly, were less touched by the British presence and were, increasingly, the centers for preserving Muslim culture and religious life.[69]

Although Muslims suffered disproportionately from the after-effects of the 1857 Revolt, the transformation in the conditions under which social and economic life was conducted after this date affected a wide range of Indians of diverse religious and professional affiliations. With the absorption of several princely states into British India by the mid-nineteenth century, large numbers of soldiers who had served in the private armies of various princes came to be unemployed. Like Rampur, other princely states had also been a source of patronage to the 'service gentry', a category which included poets, musicians, medical practitioners (*tabib*), and the 'ulama'.[70] The loss, or substantial reduction at any rate, of state patronage naturally caused the livelihoods of many literary, artistic and religious families to suffer.[71] Inversely, merchants (*banias*) in newly-emerging towns along British-built railway routes prospered.

The late nineteenth-century Muslim renewal movements of north India, of which the Ahl-e Sunnat was one, emerged in this

[68] Ibid., pp. 76, 79–80. Haji Imdad Ullah was pir to Maulanas Muhammad Qasim Nanautawi (1833–77), and Rashid Ahmad Gangohi (1829–1905), two of the founders of the Dar al-'Ulum at Deoband.

[69] Ibid., p. 85.

[70] On state patronage of medical practitioners, see Metcalf, 'Hakim Ajmal Khan,' in Frykenberg (ed.), *Delhi Through the Ages*, pp. 301, 305. On court patronage of musicians, both Hindu and Muslim, see Daniel M. Neuman, *The Life of Music in North India: The Organization of an Artistic Tradition* (Detroit: Wayne State University Press, 1980), pp. 170–1.

[71] See Bayly, *Rulers, Townsmen and Bazaars*, pp. 354–9, for a vivid and multi-dimensional picture of the causes for the decline of the qasbas under colonial rule.

context of a post-1857 British-dominated India. A new cultural system was taking shape, dominated by Hindu merchant patronage in an urban milieu. The non-viability of the military option, given the supremacy of British power, and new developments in communications technology, were also determining factors. The rapid building of railroads facilitated travel and advances in printing methods opened up new possibilities for the 'ulama' in the fields of education and publication. Not surprisingly, therefore, the late nineteenth century renewal movements concentrated their efforts on education and publication in an attempt to provide personal guidance to individual Muslims, rather than on state-related action. As the Ahl-e Sunnat movement indicates, the new technologies could be used both to preserve older cultural forms that emphasized ascribed, hierarchical statuses and roles, and to promote newer, more egalitarian ones focused on individual action and responsibility. Each of the major Muslim renewal movements made its own distinctive choices from those available.

The Renewal Movements

To understand the religious perspectives and distinctive features of the renewal movements that arose in north India after 1857, it is necessary to go back to the eighteenth century. For, numerous and diverse as these movements were, many saw themselves in one way or another as heirs and followers of the teachings of the famous eighteenth-century theologian of Delhi, Shah Wali Ullah.[72] The eclecticism and originality of his thought are indicated by the range of those who have claimed to be his intellectual followers. Among the 'ulama'-led renewal movements, the Deobandis and the Ahl-e

[72] The most recent work to appear on Shah Wali Ullah's thought is J. M. S. Baljon, *Religion and Thought of Shah Wali Allah Dihlawi 1703–1762* (Leiden: E. J. Brill, 1986). Briefly, Baljon's research indicates the importance of certain currents in Shah Wali Ullah's thought which had not thus far been appreciated by earlier scholarship on him. Shah Wali Ullah's leaning toward Ibn al-'Arabi (d. 1240) against Shaikh Ahmad Sirhindi (d. 1624) on the *wahdat al-wajud* vs. *wahdat al-shuhud* debate, for instance, does not seem to have previously been recognized: see pp. 60–3. Shah Wali Ullah apparently incorporated elements of the teachings of theologians as different from one another as Ibn al-'Arabi, Shaikh Ahmad Sirhindi and Ibn Taimiyya (d. 1328).

Hadis advanced a particularly strong claim. At the other end of the spectrum, modernist intellectuals such as Sir Sayyid Ahmad Khan (1817–98), founder of the Muhammadan Anglo-Oriental College at Aligarh in 1875,[73] Maulana Abu'l Kalam Azad, and Sir Muhammad Iqbal (1876–1938) acknowledged their debt to him.

What men like Sir Sayyid and Azad imbibed from Shah Wali Ullah's thought has naturally been very different from that which the 'ulama' have incorporated. The former interpreted Shah Wali's rejection of *taqlid* (legal conformism, following one of the main Sunni law schools) in favour of *ijtihad* (the exercise of individual reasoning or deduction) and *talfiq* (jurisprudential eclectism),[74] for instance, in the light of their own modernist inclinations.[75] The 'ulama', for the most part, took from Shah Wali Ullah different aspects of his legacy, such as a renewed emphasis on hadis scholarship. The Deobandis, who were in sufi terms primarily Chishtis but shared Shah Wali Ullah's affiliation to the Naqshbandi order, also saw him and his successors as a 'source of spiritual blessing'.[76] Finally, the 'ulama' followed Shah Wali Ullah's lead in their efforts to provide moral guidance to the Muslim community, although the context of political subjection to the non-Muslim British was far from what Shah Wali Ullah had hoped and striven for.[77]

The Tariqa-e Muhammadiyya, the early nineteenth-century movement led by Sayyid Ahmad Barelwi, was closely linked to Shah Wali Ullah's successors at Delhi. Sayyid Ahmad himself became a disciple of Shah 'Abd ul-'Aziz in 1806; later, Muhammad Isma'il (1781–1831) and 'Abd ul-Hayy (d. 1828), two of Shah Wali Ullah's descendants, became Sayyid Ahmad's disciples and close associates.

[73] On Sir Sayyid, see David Lelyveld, *Aligarh's First Generation: Muslim Solidarity in British India* (Princeton: Princeton University Press, 1978), and Christian W. Troll, *Sayyid Ahmad Khan: A Reinterpretation of Muslim Theology* (Delhi: Vikas, 1978).

[74] See Baljon, pp. 166–8.

[75] On Sir Sayyid's rejection of *taqlid*, see, e.g., Troll, pp. 128, 131, 275; on Azad and taqlid, see Doughlas, pp. 52, 75–6

[76] Metcalf, *Islamic Revival*, p. 160; also pp. 28, 37, 43.

[77] On Shah Wali Ullah's hopes for a stable Muslim political order in India and attempts to bring this about, see, e.g., ibid., p. 35.

Aziz Ahmad describes the Tariqa-e Muhammadiyya in glowing terms as

> the practical culmination of the religio-political thought of Shah Wali-Ullah . . . [a] movement of religious purification and political revolution . . . . [The movement marked] the progress of Shah Wali-Ullah's programme from theory to practice, from life contemplative to life active, from instruction of the elite to the emancipation of the masses, and from individual salvation to social organization.[78]

The programme of 'religious purification' was spelt out in detail in Muhammad Isma'il's *Taqwiyat al-Iman* (Strengthening the Faith), written in Urdu in the 1820s. It dealt with the centrality of the concept of *tauhid* (Allah's transcendental unity), and denounced popular devotional ritual at shrines and other beliefs or practices regarded as *shirk* (polytheistic). As the name 'Tariqa-e Muhammadiyya' indicates, its leaders took as their model the Prophet Muhammad. The term *'tariqa'* (sufi way or path) did not mean, however, that this was a new sufi order; rather, the leaders preached faithfulness to the prophetic sunna. The activist aspect of the movement, namely the jihad against the Sikh kingdom of Ranjit Singh, was also modelled on the Prophet's hijra to Medina.[79]

The Deobandi renewal movement, centred on the Dar al-'Ulum in Deoband, Saharanpur district, was dominated in its early years by Maulanas Muhammad Qasim Nanautawi (1833–77) and Rashid Ahmad Gangohi (1829–1905). The two men were united by a friendship that went back to the 1840s when they had both been private pupils at Delhi College. Subsequently, both became disciples of Haji Imdad Ullah Makki (1817–99) in the Chishti order (and secondarily in the Qadiri, Naqshbandi, and other orders).[80] Their common commitment to the reform of customary ritual practice, and to an emphasis on hadis scholarship in the Shah Wali Ullahi tradition, further cemented the relationship.[81] In 1867, following

[78] Aziz Ahmad, *Studies in Islamic Culture in the Indian Environment* (Oxford: Clarendon Press, 1964), p. 210.

[79] This summary is based on Pearson, pp. 46–8; Metcalf, pp. 56–62.

[80] Metcalf, p. 158.

[81] Ibid., pp. 76–9, 100–1.

the Revolt and the subsequent desolation of Delhi, both joined in founding the Dar al-'Ulum at Deoband.

As muftis (jurisconsults), the Deobandi 'ulama' attached great importance to the writing of fatawa as a means of providing moral guidance and instruction at the personal level. According to Metcalf, the fatawa reflected the Deobandis' concern for religious reform in the following important ways:

> The fatawa in general reflected three underlying principles: to revive lapsed practices such as undertaking the hajj and permitting widows to remarry; second, to avoid fixed holidays like the maulud [birth anniversary] of the Prophet, the *'urs* [death anniversary] of the saints, . . . and the elaborate celebration of 'Id [a Shi'i practice]; and, third, to prevent optional practices being made obligatory—for example, the reading of certain passages in supererogatory prayers or the distribution of sweets upon the completion of the reading of the Qur'an. On this foundation the reformers built, point by point, to convey to their followers the conviction that they conformed to the *sunnat.*[82]

As had Shah Wali Ullah, the Deobandi 'ulama' also integrated sufism into their lives. In their role as sufi guides and masters, they sought 'to influence people to conform to the sunnat',[83] and emphasized aspects of sufi belief and practice that reinforced the reformist message they sent out.

The Deobandis' insistence that the prophetic sunna be the measure of approved belief and action indicates that, as for the Tariqa-e Muhammadiyya of the early nineteenth century, so for them the Prophet was the ultimate model and exemplar of human conduct. He was also the object of spiritual devotion, approached through the experience of discipleship to a personal pir. The Prophet intervened directly in the lives of the Deobandi 'ulama', appearing to them in dreams, giving guidance, and sanctioning their educational work at the school.[84] As Metcalf says, the ' 'ulama' modeled themselves on the Prophet, and ordinary people modeled themselves on them'.[85]

The centrality of the prophetic model was expressed rather

[82] Ibid., p. 151.

[83] Ibid., p. 172.

[84] See, e.g., ibid., pp. 92, 175.

[85] Ibid., p. 350.

differently by the followers of the renewal movement of the Ahl-e Hadis. Initially calling themselves 'Muhammadi' to emphasize the importance they attached to the Prophet's example, they later used the name Ahl-e Hadis in response to criticism that they were exalting their relationship with the Prophet over that with Allah.[86] They believed that Muslims should act in accordance with the injunctions of the Qur'an and the prophetic sunna recorded in hadis, bypassing the opinions of the four Sunni law schools as embodied in *fiqh* (jurisprudential) scholarship. It was better to study the sources directly in light of the application of *qiyas* (analogy) and *ijma'* (consensus), as the founders of the law schools had themselves once done, they argued, than to depend on commentaries, glosses, and the like.

This approach to the religious tradition, as Metcalf notes, could hardly have been advocated for the uneducated. The Ahl-e Hadis leadership consisted overwhelmingly of the well-to-do and the well-connected, people who had the necessary learning to interpret the texts unaided.[87]

The Ahl-e Hadis preference for direct access to the sources of religious authority was also transparent in their disapproval of sufism, believed to be 'a danger to true religion'.[88] In this respect, as in their rejection of taqlid (i.e., of the authority of the Sunni law schools), they differed dramatically from the Deobandis who, like the majority of Indian Sunni Muslims, were followers of the Hanafi school. Yet the two groups to some extent had common intellectual roots in their affiliation to the Delhi reformists of the Shah Wali Ullahi family, in their disapproval of ritual practices such as 'urs and other shrine-related practices, and in their desire to promote social reforms such as widow remarriage.[89] These issues were the focus of

86 Ibid., p. 272. No scholarly monograph has yet been published on the Ahl-e Hadis movement. The following brief account is based on Metcalf, *Islamic Revival*, pp. 268–96.

87 In the front ranks of the leadership were Nawab Siddiq Hasan Khan (1832–90), who married into the Bhopal ruling family, Sayyid Nazir Husain Dehlawi (d. 1902), and Sayyid Mahdi 'Ali Khan, also known as Nawab Muhsin ul-Mulk, who was Sayyid Ahmad Khan's successor as administrative director at the Anglo-Muhammadan Oriental College at Aligarh. Metcalf, pp. 268–70.

88 Ibid., p. 274.

89 Ibid., pp. 273–4, 276–7.

'ulama' debate in the latter half of the nineteenth century, and provided the framework around which the 'ulama' created their new institutional structures.

Despite the common intellectual roots shared by the Deobandis and the Ahl-e Hadis, there was more to distinguish the Ahl-e Hadis from the Deobandis and other nineteenth-century 'ulama' than there was to bring them together. In addition to the heated debates engendered in 'ulama' circles by the Ahl-e Hadis's uncompromising positions on taqlid and sufism, the latter also incurred British displeasure by giving the appearance of political disloyalty.[90] This was further exacerbated by the Ahl-e Hadis's friendly relations with certain Arab Muslims, which aroused British fears that the movement might be sympathetic to the contemporary followers of the reform movement of Muhammad ibn 'Abd al-Wahhab of Arabia.[91] In the 1860s the British arrested Sayyid Nazir Husain, one of the Ahl-e Hadis leaders, for suspected involvement in the jihad movement on the north-west frontier.[92] Later, however, having proved his innocence, Nazir Husain received a title from the British.[93]

In the 1870s and 1880s the Ahl-e Sunnat movement emerged under Ahmad Riza's leadership in opposition to the movements described here. Like the others, the Ahl-e Sunnat too centred their vision of Islam on the Prophet, saw themselves as 'reformist', and traced their intellectual heritage to the Shah Wali Ullahi tradition.[94]

[90] The truth of these allegations is not known. According to a newspaper article dated 1881, Nawab Siddiq Hasan Khan of Bhopal had sent Bhopal state funds to aid the Mahdi of the Sudan, and had asked the Turks to help his state militarily. However Siddiq Hasan himself went to some lengths to point out the many ways in which he had been loyal to the British. See Metcalf, pp. 279–80.

[91] Ibid., pp. 277–8; Pearson, 'Islamic Reform', p. 162.

[92] This was the same jihad movement which had started in the 1830s under Sayyid Ahmad Barelwi's leadership. Kept alive by a small leadership based in Patna, Bihar, it was finally suppressed by the British in the 1860s and '70s. The movement provoked considerable debate in British circles, stimulated by the publication of one book in particular, namely W. W. Hunter's work, *The Indian Musalmans: Are They Bound in Conscience to Rebel Against the Queen?* published in 1871. On this, and the so-called 'Wahhabi Trials' of 1869–71, see Pearson, pp. 215–26.

[93] Metcalf, p. 281.

[94] Though not entirely: they did not accept Shah Wali Ullah's claim to be the mujaddid of the twelfth Hijri century, and disagreed with him on his position on ijtihad and talfiq.

Nevertheless, differing interpretatively from the Tariqa-e Muhammadiyya, the Deobandis, the Ahl-e Hadis and other 'ulama' groups about the significance to Muslims of the Prophet Muhammad, but also on other matters, the Ahl-e Sunnat came by the 1880s to speak with a voice distinctly their own.

Because the Ahl-e Sunnat 'ulama' were actively engaged in a network of relationships with certain sufi families in the United Provinces and elsewhere, we must turn finally to intellectual developments in north Indian sufi circles in the period of Ahl-e Sunnat influence. As later chapters will show, Ahmad Riza had close ties with the Barkatiyya Sayyids of Marahra, Etah district, and with the 'Usmani pirs of Badayun. Both considered themselves reformist. Reformist sufism, thus, constituted the third element (along with British colonial rule and the rise of reformist movements among the 'ulama') which shaped the direction taken by the Ahl-e Sunnat movement in the late nineteenth century.

Reformist Currents in Sufism

At the height of British rule in late nineteenth-century India, the Barkatiyya pirs of Marahra and the 'Usmani pirs of Badayun took pride in the belief that their ancestors (*buzurg*) had at all times accorded precedence to the shari'a over *tasawwuf* (sufi belief and practice). They considered the latter to be a necessary complement to the shari'a, enriching it but not superseding it in any way. This attitude, which accorded well with the Ahl-e Sunnat emphasis on following the sunna, was what defined a sufi as 'reformist'.[95] The Ahl-e Sunnat contrasted it with the 'excesses' of 'false' sufis who

However, they regarded Shah Wali Ullah's eldest son, Shah 'Abd ul-'Aziz, as the mujaddid of the thirteenth Hijri century. Their attitude to the next generation of scholars in the family, represented by the leaders of the Tariqa-e Muhammadiyya, was different again, for they rejected the Tariqa's legitimacy entirely. For the Ahl-e Sunnat and the mujaddid issue, see Chapter VII of this study; for the Ahl-e Sunnat on the Tariqa-e Muhammadiyya, see Chapter VIII.

95 The term reformist is widely used in the scholarly treatment of sufism, though it is not a translation of any single word in Arabic or Urdu by which the sufis may have described themselves. The word 'orthodox' is also frequently used in the scholarly literature to describe sufis who put the shari'a above tasawwuf.

thought they had attained such spiritual heights that they need not fulfill the daily ritual prayers and other prescribed duties. In his daily conversations with followers, Ahmad Riza frequently condemned such sufis, saying they were inspired by Satan.[96]

While Ahl-e Sunnat 'ulama' were affiliated with all the major sufi orders (tariqas) current in British India, as were 'ulama' in other movements, most emphasized their ties to the Qadiri order over the Chishti and Naqshbandi.[97] Nevertheless, their respect for the other orders was evident. For one thing, some of Ahmad Riza's followers belonged to the Chishti and Naqshbandi orders. Furthermore, the Ahl-e Sunnat regarded Shah 'Abd ul-'Aziz Dehlawi, whose affiliation was primarily Naqshbandi, as the mujaddid of the thirteenth Hijri century.

In each of these three orders—Qadiri, Naqshbandi, and Chishti—certain key figures were thought to have been particularly associated with the attempt to subordinate sufi 'excesses' to shar'i sobriety. Of them Shaikh 'Abd ul-Haqq Muhaddis Dehlawi (1551–1642) and Shaikh Ahmad Sirhindi (1564–1624) lived during some part of the reign of Emperor Akbar (d. 1605). Scholars have generally assumed that the hostile attitude of these two shaikhs toward Akbar's religious policy, including their objection to the occupation of important positions of state by Hindus and Shi'is,[98] was representative of the views of many Sunni Muslims in Akbar's day.

For Ahmad Riza, Shaikh 'Abd ul-Haqq Muhaddis Dehlawi, of the Qadiri order, was the more important of the two men. In part, this was related to Shaikh 'Abd ul-Haqq's valuable contributions to

96 See, e.g., Ahmad Riza Khan, *Malfuzat-e A'la Hazrat* (Gujarat, Pakistan: Fazl-e Nur Academy, n.d.), vol. 3, pp. 22–3.

97 The Suhrawardi order, though usually included as one of the four major Indian tariqas, is mentioned relatively infrequently in the lists of different orders into which individual 'ulama' were initiated.

98 Hostility to the Emperor is particularly associated with Shaikh Ahmad Sirhindi. See, e.g., S. A. A. Rizvi, *Muslim Revivalist Movements in Northern India in the Sixteenth and Seventeenth Centuries* (Agra: Agra University, 1965), pp. 210–24, and passim. Yohanan Friedmann, however, cautions against the tendency in modern scholarship to make more of this than is justified. See Yohanan Friedmann, *Shaykh Ahmad Sirhindi: An Outline of His Thought and a Study of His Image in the Eyes of Posterity* (Montreal and London: McGill-Queen's University Press, 1971), pp. 106–11.

hadis scholarship (acknowledged by Sunni Muslims of all schools, not just the Ahl-e Sunnat). Ahmad Riza cited him frequently in his fatawa. Additionally, Shaikh 'Abd ul-Haqq contributed to Qadiri intellectual discourse through his writings on sufi themes. According to S. A. A. Rizvi,

> [his] writings on sufism are generally an attempt to reconcile the Shari'a with the Tariqa; nevertheless they also assert the superiority of Shaikh 'Abdu'l-Qadir Jilani and the *Wahdat al-Wujud.* His celebrated *Akhbaru'l- akhyar,* relating to Indian sufis . . . emphasizes the belief that Shaikh 'Abdu'l-Qadir was superior to all his predecessors and that his precedence over all future generations of saints of God was also guaranteed. To Shaikh 'Abdu'l-Haqq, the Ghausul-A'zam's claim, 'My foot is on the neck of every saint of God' was a well-considered statement.[99]

Ahmad Riza shared in these views completely. He too revered Shaikh 'Abd al-Qadir Jilani (d. 1166), the founder of the Qadiri order in 'Abbasid Baghdad, over and above all other saints. He also affirmed his belief in the sufi doctrine of wahdat al-wujud (ontological or existential monism) against that of *wahdat al-shuhud* (phenomenological monism) which came to be associated with the Qadiri order after Shaikh 'Abd al-Qadir Jilani's death.[100] In part because he believed that discussion of this doctrine should be confined to the learned (the *khawass*, as against the *'awamm*, ordinary people), and in part perhaps because he was not particularly interested in the debate, the occasional references to this issue in Ahmad Riza's writings are (to my knowledge) rather brief.[101]

[99] S. A. A. Rizvi, *A History of Sufism in India*, vol. 2 (Delhi: Munshiram Manoharlal Publishers, 1983), p. 90.

[100] This important but complex philosophical debate among sufis has been frequently dealt with in the scholarly literature. The wahdat al-wujud position is associated with Ibn al-'Arabi (1165–1240), and takes a pantheistic view of creation. This is the Qadiri position as well, though it is opposed by the Naqshbandis. For details, see, e.g., Burhan Ahmad Faruqi, *The Mujaddid's Conception of Tawhid* (Lahore: Sh. Muhammad Ashraf, 1940).

[101] See, e.g., Ahmad Riza Khan, *Al-'Ataya li-Nabawiyya fi'l Fatawa al-Rizwiyya*, vol. 6 (Mubarakpur, Azamgarh: Sunni Dar al-Isha'at, 1981), p. 132; *Malfuzat*, vol. 1, p. 48. In the *Malfuzat* reference, Ahmad Riza specifically told someone who asked him to explain the doctrine of wahdat al-wujud that if he went into the details his explanation would not be understood by the questioner.

Ahmad Riza—and the Ahl-e Sunnat generally—were also drawn to Shaikh 'Abd ul-Haqq's approach to the Prophet. In *Madarij al-Nubuwwa,* a Persian 'biography of Prophet Muhammad in five . . . parts,' Shaikh 'Abd ul-Haqq defended the belief that Muhammad had performed miracles.[102] He also wrote in praise of *Faqr al-Muhammadi,* a book by the Arab sufi al-Wasiti (d. c. 932), on love of the Prophet and the excellence of the '*Muhammadiyya Tariqa*'. Al-Wasiti exhorted sufis to regard the Prophet as their 'Shaikh and Imam', and to strive to attain mystical union with him.[103] In outward behaviour, they were enjoined to be chaste, emotionally restrained, and faithful to the shari'a.

Shaikh Ahmad Sirhindi, a Naqshbandi sufi and contemporary of Shaikh 'Abd ul-Haqq, was widely accepted by the nineteenth-century 'ulama' as the renewer of the eleventh Hijri century, and perhaps even as 'Renewer of the Second Millenium' (*mujaddid-e alf-e sani*), whose task was of particular significance because it happened to inaugurate a millenium.[104] Ahmad Riza respectfully refers to him on one occasion as 'Hazrat Shaikh Mujaddid', and mentions with approval his work *Mabda' o Ma'ad.*[105] I am not aware of any discussion of Shaikh Ahmad Sirhindi's thought in Ahmad Riza's vast corpus of writings. Yet Ahmad Riza's evident familiarity with Sirhindi's works makes it unlikely that he would not have known about Sirhindi's 'unorthodox' views on Muhammad's prophethood, and of Shaikh 'Abd ul-Haqq's strong objections to

102 Rizvi, *Muslim Revivalist Movements*, p. 171; and *A History of Sufism in India*, p. 89.

103 Rizvi, *A History of Sufism in India,* p. 94.

104 Shah Wali Ullah accepted Shaikh Ahmad Sirhindi's claim to the title of renewer of the eleventh Hijri century, but makes no mention of the larger claim. See Friedmann, *Shaykh Ahmad Sirhindi*, pp. 103–4; Deobandis and Ahl-e Hadis looked upon him as a reformer, and presumably acknowledged him as renewer of the eleventh Hijri century, though Metcalf does not mention this specifically. Metcalf, pp. 183, 277, 353.

105 The context for this reference to Shaikh Ahmad Sirhindi was an argument about the second *azan* (call to prayer) on Fridays. Ahmad Riza supported his position against some Naqshbandi Mujaddidis on this issue by attempting to prove that their position was in opposition not only to him, Ahmad Riza, but also to Sirhindi, founder of their own line of Naqshbandi sufis. *Dabdaba-e Sikandari* (Rampur), 50:16 (March 16, 1914), 5 (Question 18). Sirhindi's work *Mabda' o Ma'ad* was apparently very popular in the seventeenth century. See Friedmann, *Shaykh Ahmad Sirhindi*, pp. 5–6.

these.[106] The controversy over Sirhindi grew even greater during Aurangzeb's reign. In 1682, some Indian 'ulama' asked certain others in the Haramain for their opinion, and the Sharif of Mecca wrote that 'the 'ulama' of Hejaz thought Shaykh Ahmad Sirhindi was a *kafir* (infidel)'.[107] In 1679 Aurangzeb issued a decree forbidding the teaching of those 'false ideas' contained in Sirhindi's *Maktubat* which 'are apparently opposed to the views of *ahl al-sunnah wa-al-jama'ah*'.[108]

Debate about Sirhindi appears to have ceased in the eighteenth century. Perhaps Shah Wali Ullah's acceptance of Sirhindi as renewer of the eleventh Hijri century (though not the Renewer of the Second Millenium) set the tone for later 'ulama', who do not appear to have interested themselves in the controversy. Metcalf writes that the Naqshbandi order, increasingly influential in eighteenth-century north India due to the contributions of mystics and poets like Mirza Mazhar Jan-i Janan (1700–80) and Mir Dard (1721–85), both of Delhi, 'was to shape the views of many 'ulama' toward sobriety in spiritual experience and rigorous adherence to the religious Law'.[109] In this their position resembled Shaikh 'Abd ul-Haqq Muhaddis Dehlawi's insistence that tasawwuf be guided by shari'a.

The same trend is also associated with the Chishti order, though along somewhat different lines than the Qadiri and Naqshbandi

[106] Friedmann, pp. 88–9, discusses 'Abd ul-Haqq's objections to aspects of Sirhindi's thought. For a clear and detailed exposition of Sirhindi's ideas themselves, Friedmann's book should be consulted, particularly Chapter 2.

[107] S. A. A. Rizvi, *Shah Wali-Allah and His Times: A Study of Eighteenth Century Islam, Politics and Society in India* (Canberra: Ma'rifat Publishing House, 1980), p. 324. John Voll thinks that one of the Medinese 'ulama' who opposed Sirhindi's ideas at this time may have been an ancestor of a nineteenth-century Medinese 'alim who in 1905 attested a fatwa by Ahmad Riza Khan in which certain Deobandi 'ulama', and Mirza Ghulam Ahmad, founder of the Ahmadiyya movement, were condemned as kafir. The family connection is suggested by similarity between the names Muhammad bin 'Abd al-Rasul al-Barzanji Shafi'i (one of the Medinese 'ulama' to consider Sirhindi a kafir) and Shaikh Sharif Ahmad Barzanji, Shafi'i mufti of Medina in 1905 (John Voll, personal communication, February 24, 1990).

[108] Friedmann, p. 94. Note that Sirhindi is here being described as being in opposition to the 'Ahl al-sunnah wa-al-jama'ah'. Ahmad Riza presumably did not share the opinion.

[109] Metcalf, p. 28.

orders. The Chishti has probably been, since its inception in the thirteenth century, the most popular of all the orders in India, both in court circles and among the population.[110] Founded by Mu'in ud-Din Chishti of Ajmer (d. 1235), the order quickly spread to Sind, the Panjab, and the Deccan through a network of disciples tracing their spiritual genealogy to Mu'in ud-Din.[111] In time it branched into two distinct *silsilas* (chains of spiritual authority), the Chishti Nizami and the Chishti Sabiri.

Subsequently, in the Panjab, Chishti influence apparently suffered a decline until the eighteenth century. A renewed emphasis on obedience to the shari'a then formed part of the Chishti attempt at spiritual regeneration.[112] Prior to this, however, during the years of Mughal decline, the order revived in Delhi under the leadership of Shah Kalimullah (1650–1729).[113]

At the initiative of Shah Fakhr ud-Din of Delhi, a khalifa (successor) of Shah Kalimullah, the Chishti resurgence spread to the Panjab, where the Muslims lived in subjection to the Sikhs. Working through the sufi mediational institutions of *khanqah* (hospice) and

[110] The most recent study of the order is P. M. Currie, *The Shrine and Cult of Mu'in al-din Chishti of Ajmer* (Delhi: Oxford University Press, 1989). Currie attempts to disentangle the Mu'in ud-Din of legend from the historical figure, and also gives a detailed picture of the current social and economic organization of the shrine. On this, also see Syed Liyaqat Hussain Moini, 'Rituals and Customary Practices at the Dargah of Ajmer', in Christian W. Troll (ed.), *Muslim Shrines in India* (Delhi: Oxford University Press, 1989).

[111] The early spread of the order has been studied by, among others, Simon Digby, 'The Sufi Shaikh as a Source of Authority in Mediaeval India', in Marc Gaborieau (ed.), *Islam and Society in South Asia* (Paris: Ecole des Hautes Etudes en Sciences Sociales, 1986). Digby has an illuminating discussion, on pp. 67–9, of the inherent contradictions between the 'professed aims and necessary practice in the pursuit of the role of a great Shaikh'. One of the greatest of these contradictions related to the order's ideal of poverty and independence from the state, as against its record of landownership, patronage by the state, and territorial jurisdiction.

[112] M. Zameeruddin Siddiqi, 'The Resurgence of the Chishti Silsilah in the Punjab during the Eighteenth Century', *Proceedings of the Indian History Congress, 1970* (New Delhi: Indian History Congress, 1971), 1, p. 409.

[113] According to Gilmartin, in the context of 'declining central power, he reorganized the Chishti order and emphasized the central importance of *tabligh*, or the active propagation of Islam, as its fundamental mission'. David Gilmartin, *Empire and Islam: Punjab and the Making of Pakistan* (Berkeley: University of California Press, 1988), p. 57.

dargah (tomb-shrines), rather than through madrasas as did the reformist 'ulama', leading Chishtis such as Khwaja Nur Muhammad Maharwi (1730–91) and Khwaja Suleman of Taunsa (1770-1850) extended the influence of the order in the western Panjab.

During British rule most Chishti pirs in the Panjab were drawn into association with the British government.[114] Reformist pirs such as Pir Mehr 'Ali Shah of Golra (1856–1937), a disciple of Khwaja Suleman, however, distanced themselves from such ties. As Pir Mehr 'Ali was directly associated with the Ahl-e Sunnat movement in the Panjab,[115] it is important to refer to Gilmartin on his career and intellectual orientation at some length:

> Like many Punjabis who sought an advanced religious education in British India, Mehr Ali Shah traveled to the United Provinces, where he studied hadis and *tafsir* (Qor'anic exegesis) with leading 'ulama' in the reformist tradition. Returning to Punjab with a concern for reform, he became the disciple of an important khalifa of Khwaja Suleman . . . ; under his influence Mehr Ali Shah transformed Golra into a major Chishti center . . . .
>
> He refused to be drawn into direct association with the British government. He maintained his deep reformist concern with the personal instruction of his disciples in the individual obligations of Islam, issuing numerous fatwas (rulings) on points of religious law and gaining a reputation for religious learning among a section of 'ulama'.[116]

As Gilmartin goes on to say, Mehr 'Ali illustrates two major aspects of the Chishti revival. One was a concern for obedience to the shar', the other a continued commitment to the mediational ties of the '*piri-muridi* bond, the shrine, and the urs'.[117]

In Gilmartin's view, sufi reformist pirs of the Panjab such as Mehr

[114] On the relationship between the Panjab pirs and the British government, see Gilmartin, *Empire and Islam*, pp. 39–72.

[115] He was at one time Muhaddis Surati's fellow student of hadis in a class taught by one Maulana Ahmad 'Ali Muhaddis Saharanpuri, and was associated with the Anjuman Nu'maniyya which administered the Dar al-'Ulum Nu'maniyya, an important Ahl-e Sunnat school in Lahore. Khwaja Razi Haidar, *Tazkira-e Muhaddis Surati* (Karachi: Surati Academy, n.d.), pp. 320–1.

[116] Gilmartin, *Empire and Islam*, pp. 58–9.

[117] Ibid., p. 59.

'Ali were helped by the emergence of the Ahl-e Sunnat movement in north India and Panjab. Ahl-e Sunnat 'ulama'

> championed a religious outlook in which religious mediation and custom had a continuing and central place . . . . The arguments of the Barelvi 'ulama' aimed at legitimizing the religious authority of all the sufi revival pirs, but according to the standards of religious education and debate developed by the reformers. To an important degree, the presence of these 'ulama' thus helped to justify the entire movement of rural sufi revival.[118]

While the Ahl-e Sunnat 'ulama' would probably not have defined their purpose as the desire to 'justify the entire movement of rural sufi revival' (they would have said they were reviving and following the sunna), Gilmartin's comments are useful in the connections he makes between the Ahl-e Sunnat, other nineteenth-century 'ulama', and the movement of sufi reform.

[118] Ibid., pp. 60–1.

Chapter II

A Sunni Muslim Scholar: Ahmad Riza Khan Barelwi

Colonialism set the framework for what could or could not be done in late nineteenth-century India: while appropriating political power the British nevertheless provided conditions favourable for the emergence of movements such as the Ahl-e Sunnat. The communications and transportation networks, so effectively utilized by the 'ulama' in order to organize and unite, were a British creation, put in place in order to further the needs of empire. The British also provided Western models of administration and organization that the 'ulama' adapted in innovative ways across the country. Most importantly, though, the British policy of support for pre-colonial élites enabled religious families who had acquired an economic base in landownership prior to British rule to survive, even to prosper. This was most evident in Panjab, where the rural pirs came to play a 'hinge' role, to use Gilmartin's term, mediating between the British at the top and ordinary villagers below.[1] As we shall presently see, religious families associated with the Ahl-e Sunnat movement in the United Provinces, such as the Barkatiyya pirs of Marahra and the 'Usmani 'ulama' of Badayun, suffered economically during the nineteenth century, though this was less the result of hostile British policy than of mismanagement. Some 'ulama'-led institutions benefitted from British patronage, as in the case of Badayun's

[1] See Gilmartin, *Empire and Islam*, pp. 56–62, and passim.

Madrasa Shams al-'Ulum, which also received material assistance from the independent nawabs of Haidarabad and Rampur. British rule also opened up new economic possibilities in government service, of which some 'ulama' availed themselves.

In addition, the 'ulama' accepted the British presence because of British non-interference in religious practice. The Ahmadis in the Panjab were notably pro-British, because that government, as Ghulam Ahmad saw it, 'allow[ed] everyone not only to profess and practice but also to preach and propagate his own religion'.[2] In the United Provinces both Deobandis and the Ahl-e Sunnat ruled for the same reason that late nineteenth-century British India was dar al-islam (a land of peace). Nevertheless, their acceptance of British rule was pragmatic rather than whole-hearted, and they distanced themselves from the sources of power.[3] For the most part, the Ahl-e Sunnat literature of the period takes the British presence for granted and ignores it.

Emerging in this political context, then, the Ahl-e Sunnat fashioned a movement centred on one 'alim in particular, Ahmad Riza Khan. The litany of titles with which his biographer, Zafar ud-Din Bihari, introduced Ahmad Riza in his 1938 *Hayat-e A'la Hazrat* illustrates the reverence in which his followers held him:

> [His] exalted presence, Imam of the Ahl-e Sunnat, Renewer of the present [fourteenth Hijri] century, Strengthener . . . (*mu'aiyid*) of the pure *millat*, Maulana Maulawi Haji, Reciter (*qari*) and Memorizer (*hafiz*) of the Qur'an, Shah Muhammad Ahmad Riza Khan Sahib Qadiri Barkati Barelwi, May his grave be hallowed . . . .[4]

Although the movement's self-perception denies the role of founder to Ahmad Riza, the sources make clear the centrality of his life and work in the formulation by the Ahl-e Sunnat of a particular interpretation of *din*—seen within the movement as a restatement of an original, pristine 'Islam' going back to Muhammad's day.

[2] Friedmann, *Prophecy Continuous*, p. 34.

[3] On the Deobandi attitude, see Metcalf, pp. 154–5; for that of the Ahl-e Sunnat, see Chapter IX below.

[4] Zafar ud-Din Bihari, *Hayat-e A'la Hazrat*, vol. 1 (Karachi: Maktaba Rizwiyya, 1938), Preface.

Ahmad Riza Khan: Childhood and Youth

Ahmad Riza Khan was of Baraich Pathan (or Rohilla) ancestry. Biographical sources are vague about when his ancestors first came to India. Perhaps it was in the seventeenth century that a branch of his family left its home in Qandahar for India, joining the Mughal imperial bureaucracy as soldiers and soldier-administrators.[5] A family ancestor eventually settled in Bareilly, where he was awarded a land grant for military service. Then followed a brief interlude during which Ahmad Riza's great-grandfather, Hafiz Kazim 'Ali Khan, served the Nawab of Awadh in Lucknow.[6] This may have occurred in the second half of the eighteenth century, when Mughal fortunes were in considerable decline and north Indian politics in a state of flux as a result of Maratha incursions and the growing British power.[7] As Rohilkhand had become subject to the suzerainty of Awadh in 1774, service under the nawabs must have seemed promising to a soldier. The Nawab is said to have granted Hafiz Kazim 'Ali two revenue-free (*mu'afi*) properties, which remained in the family's possession until 1954.[8]

But by the end of the eighteenth century Hafiz Kazim 'Ali probably returned to Bareilly, for Ahmad Riza's grandfather, Riza 'Ali Khan (1809–65/66), is said to have grown up in that town. Making a break with the family tradition of military service, he became well known as a *faqih* (jurisconsult) and sufi gnostic in the Qadiri order.[9] He was educated at Tonk, the only Muslim state in

[5] Ibid., p. 2 ; Hasnain Riza Khan, *Sirat-e A'la Hazrat* (Karachi: Maktaba Qasimiyya Barkatiyya, 1986), p. 40. The sources give no dates for these events beyond the fact that the move to India occurred during Mughal times. As it is implied that the Mughal empire was flourishing at the time, it seems plausible to suggest that the event may date to the sixteenth–seventeenth centuries.

[6] *Sirat-e A'la Hazrat*, p. 41. The move to Lucknow is not mentioned by Zafar ud-Din Bihari in his *Hayat-e A'la Hazrat.*

[7] On eighteenth-century politics in north India, see Richard B. Barnett, *North India Between Empires: Awadh, the Mughals, and the British, 1720–1801* (Berkeley: University of California Press, 1980).

[8] *Sirat-e A'la Hazrat*, p. 41.

[9] Zafar ud-Din Bihari refers, in this context, to numerous miracles performed by Riza 'Ali, as well as his fondness for a *majzub* or ascetic. See *Hayat-e A'la Hazrat*, pp. 4–5. Also see Metcalf, p. 298.

Rajputana, completing his study of the *dars-e nizami* syllabus at twenty-three.[10] After his time the warrior's profession became a thing of the past, as succeeding generations came to enjoy a reputation for Islamic scholarship and/or saintliness.

Historically speaking, this switch from the military to the scholarly life was a reflection in part of changing times, for (as the previous chapter indicated) one of the great changes brought about by British rule was the fact that large numbers of soldiers came to be unemployed in the mid-nineteenth century.[11] Fortunately for Riza 'Ali, the family's wealth was secure, for it owned several villages in Bareilly and Badayun, adjoining Bareilly to the south-west. The properties were looked after by Maulana Naqi 'Ali Khan (1831–80), Ahmad Riza's father, who was known both as a scholar and as a local notable (*ra'is*).[12]

In his biography of Ahmad Riza, Zafar ud-Din Bihari relates a story about Riza 'Ali following the British resumption of control over Bareilly after the 1857 Revolt:

> After the tumult of 1857, the British tightened the reins of power and committed atrocities toward the people, and everybody went about feeling scared. Important people left their houses and went back to their villages. But Maulana Riza 'Ali Khan continued to live in his house as before, and would go to the mosque five times a day to say his prayers in congregation. One day some Englishmen passed by the mosque, and decided to see if there was anyone inside so they could catch hold of them and beat them up. They went inside and looked around but didn't see anyone. Yet the Maulana was there at the time. Allah had made them blind, so that they would be unable to see him . . . . He came out of the mosque, they were still watching out for people, but no one saw him.[13]

[10] Maulawi Rahman 'Ali, *Tazkira-e 'Ulama'-e Hind*, tr. Muhammad Ayub Qadiri (Karachi: Pakistan Historical Society, 1961), p. 193. The course of studies is described as *'ulum-e darsiyya*. For the books included in the dars-e nizami course, see G. M. D. Sufi, *Al-Minhaj, Being the Evolution of Curriculum in the Muslim Educational Institutions of India* (Delhi: Idarah-i Adabiyat-i Delli, 1941), pp. 73–5.

[11] Metcalf writes, 'The greatest change [resulting from British rule] took place in military service, as successive princes were brought under British control and their armies, both formal and informal, were disbanded'. *Islamic Revival*, p. 49.

[12] *Sirat-e A'la Hazrat*, p. 36.

[13] *Hayat-e A'la Hazrat*, p. 5.

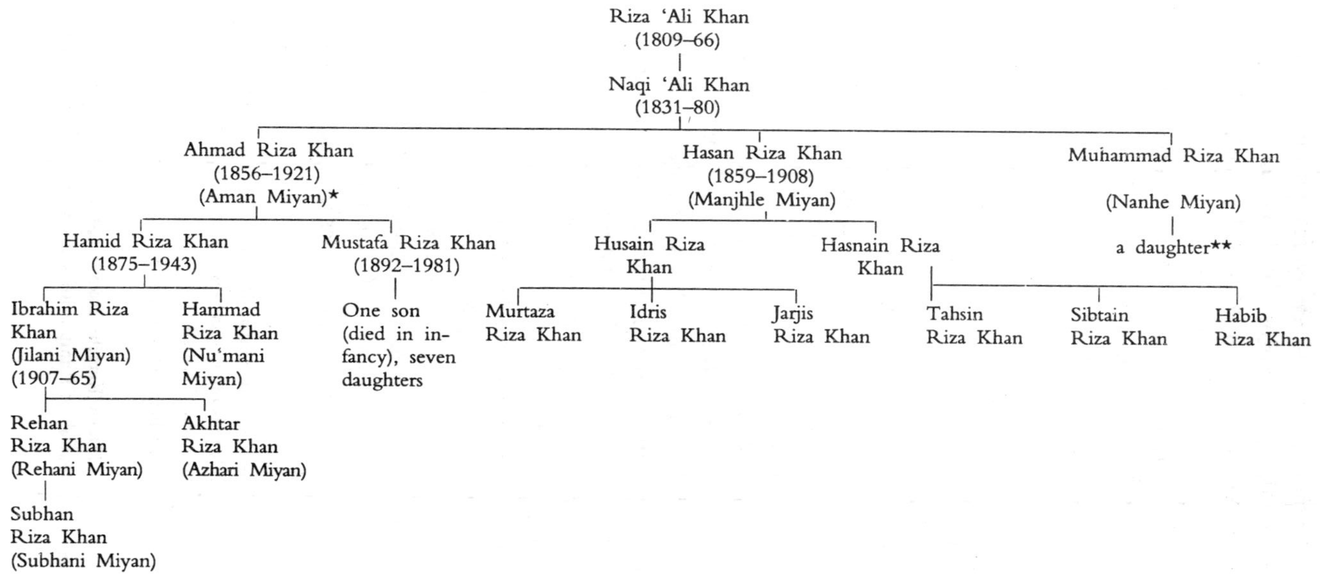

* Affectionate name used by elders or close family associates. All names in parentheses are of this category.

** Married to Mustafa Riza Khan, Ahmad Riza's younger son, whose uncle and father-in-law Muhammad Riza Khan regarded him as a son. Muhammad Riza resided in his house.

Dates are indicated where known.

Daughters were not regarded as bearers of spiritual or scholarly authority, and are therefore seldom mentioned. The marriage pattern was for the most part endogamous.

Figure 1 Family Tree of Ahmad Riza

Zafar ud-Din Bihari quotes the Qur'anic verse 'And We have put a bar in front of them and a bar behind them, and further, we have covered them up; so that they cannot see' (36:9, Yusuf 'Ali tr.) after narrating this miracle (*karamat*). It is one of the relatively few references to the relations between Ahmad Riza's family and the British in the biography. For Zafar ud-Din Bihari, as for others who revered Ahmad Riza, the telling of this story establishes both Riza 'Ali's piety and his distance from the British.

Indeed there is no evidence that Riza 'Ali was involved in the events of 1857 on either side. In later years Ahmad Riza's family (see figure 1), while never engaged in government service, appears to have had indirect but cordial relations with British officials. His father, a wealthy landowner, apparently suffered little loss of property after 1857.[14] Ahmad Riza's nephew Hasnain Riza (d. 1981), owner of the Hasani Press in Bareilly which published a number of Ahmad Riza's works (see Chapter III) was reportedly well regarded by the British. While he never worked in an official capacity, it is said that he used to collect fees (*chungi*) from the police tribunal for the British, act as arbitrator (*hakam*) in disputes between Muslims in the town, and exercise his personal influence with the administration on behalf of local citizens.[15] Ahmad Riza's father-in-law, Shaikh Fazl-e Husain, was a government officer in the Rampur Post Office, and attended the Nawab's court.[16]

By the time Ahmad Riza's education began in the 1860s, the family already had a well-established reputation for scholarship. Its inclination was toward rationalist studies (*ma'qulat*) and fiqh (jurisprudence), specialties also of the 'ulama' of Badayun and Khairabad (the latter lies east of Bareilly in Awadh). This was in contrast to the hadis (prophetic traditions) scholarship of the descendants of Shah

[14] Maulana Tahsin Riza Khan, a grandson of Ahmad Riza's brother Hasan Riza, said that two villages owned by the family in Rampur were lost to them after 1857, because of failure to find the title deeds. Interview, April 18, 1987.

[15] This was reported by Sibtain Riza Khan, son of Hasnain Riza. Interview, April 18, 1987.

[16] Hasnain Riza Khan, *Sirat-e A'la Hazrat* (Karachi: Bazm-e Qasimi Barkati, 1986), p. 152. As noted in Chapter I, the Nawab of Rampur himself was pro-British, though politically independent.

Wali Ullah.[17] In fact, by the second half of the nineteenth century, the 'ulama' of Badayun and Bareilly had distanced themselves considerably from the Delhi 'ulama'.

Ahmad Riza's first teacher was one Mirza Ghulam Qadir Beg, for whom Ahmad Riza is said to have retained a lifelong affection, sending him fatawa whenever he requested.[18] Ahmad Riza later studied the dars-e nizami under his father's direction. His father exerted an important intellectual influence on his thought in these formative years. From him he imbibed an attitude of opposition to Sayyid Ahmad Barelwi (d. 1831) and others of his Tariqa-e Muhammadiyya movement. Indeed, many of the major intellectual issues that later engaged Ahmad Riza are foreshadowed in Maulana Naqi 'Ali's own writings, which included works in opposition to the 'Nejdis' (the Muwahhidun in Arabia) in general and to Sayyid Ahmad Barelwi's *Taqwiyat al-Iman* in particular, defence of the practice of milad (birth anniversary of the Prophet) and *qiyam* (standing up at a designated moment during the milad), and works about the qualities of the Prophet Muhammad. Notably, he participated in a debate that had begun in the early nineteenth century in north India (and in which Sayyid Ahmad Barelwi had taken a prominent part) about Allah's omnipotence. In the 1870s some 'ulama' saw in the concept of Allah's omnipotence the implication that Allah could create another prophet equal to the Prophet Muhammad (an issue described as *imkan-e nazir*, the 'possibility of an equal') should He so wish. Naqi 'Ali opposed such a theoretical possibility, arguing that there never could be another person like the Prophet (a view described as *imtina'-e nazir* or *imtina'-e mumasalat-e rasul*, the impossibility of an exact equivalent to the Prophet). This debate was recorded by Maulana Hafiz Bakhsh (d. 1921) in his *Tanbih al-Juhhal bi-Ilham al-Basit*

[17] Metcalf, *Islamic Revival*, p. 298.

[18] *Hayat-e A'la Hazrat*, p. 32. Opponents of the Ahl-e Sunnat have alleged that the Mirza was a brother of Mirza Ghulam Ahmad, founder of the Ahmadi movement. See Ehsan Elahi Zaheer, *Bareilavis: History and Beliefs* (Lahore: Idara Tarjuman al-Sunnah, 1986), tr. Dr. Abdullah, p. 41. However, Mirza Qadir Beg was a resident of Bareilly who later moved to Calcutta. He had no connection with the Ahmadis.

al-Mut'al (Censure of the Ignorant People . . .) and published in 1875.[19]

We know little about Ahmad Riza's teachers other than his father and grandfather. He had a few other teachers as well, notably Maulana Abu'l Husain 'Nuri Miyan' Maraharwi. But unlike many others in his day, he had no madrasa education. This is surprising, given the presence of well-known centres of learning in the Rohilkhand area such as Rampur's Madrasa 'Aliyya and Badayun's Madrasa Qadiriyya, which shared his own inclination for ma'qulat. The biographical references to Ahmad Riza's scholarly abilities make the point that much of his knowledge was self-taught and was to be seen as a blessing from Allah.[20]

The biographies are replete with stories of Ahmad Riza's precociousness as a child: when learning the Arabic alphabet, he instinctively knew, Zafar ud-Din Bihari writes, the significance of *la* (composed of *lam* and *alif*), the word with which the Muslim attestation of the faith or *kalima* (also *shahada*, lit. 'witness') begins. Ahmad Riza's grandfather, in explaining the significance of the word to him, is said to have simultaneously communicated to him the secrets of gnostic knowledge.[21] Tales such as these indicated to Ahmad Riza's followers his lifelong and intuitive obedience to the shari'a as well as his eminence as a sufi pir.[22]

Ahmad Riza is also reported to have accomplished extraordinary intellectural feats. For instance, he had read the entire Qur'an by the time he was four, and at the age of six, addressed a large audience from the pulpit (*minbar*) of a mosque on the occasion of a milad.[23] Later, when learning the dars-e nizami from his father, he quickly

[19] These biographical details about Maulana Naqi 'Ali are based on Rahman 'Ali, *Tazkira-e 'Ulama'-e Hind*, pp. 530–2. Maulana Hafiz Bakhsh was associated with the scholarly circle of the 'ulama' of Badayun.

[20] *Hayat-e A'la Hazrat*, p. 35. As Zafar ud-Din writes, 'By [God's] grace, it was through his own efforts and his own intelligence that he [Ahmad Riza] mastered so many different fields of knowledge that his books cover as many as fifty different fields'.

[21] *Hayat-e A'la Hazrat*, pp. 31–2.

[22] On the sufis' interpretations of the kalima, see Annemarie Schimmel, 'The Sufis and the *Shahada*', in Richard G. Hovannisian and Speros Vryonis, Jr. (eds.), *Islam's Understanding of Itself* (Malibu: Undena Publications, 1983), pp. 103–25.

[23] *Hayat-e A'la Hazrat*, pp. 32–3.

demonstrated that he had outstripped the latter in knowledge, rewriting parts of a complicated text to answer a criticism noted on the margins by his father.[24] On another occasion, he solved in five minutes a complex mathematical puzzle brought to his attention by a mathematics professor at MAO College (later Aligarh Muslim University), with which the latter had been grappling for months.[25] These are but a few of the intellectual achievements credited to Ahmad Riza. The telling and retelling of such exemplary stories assured Ahl-e Sunnat followers of the special favours bestowed by Allah on their leader Ahmad Riza, and consequently, opposition from their critics notwithstanding, of the righteousness of their vision of din.

An important landmark in Ahmad Riza's early life was his assumption of responsibility from his father for writing fatawa in 1869, when he was about fourteen.[26] Fatwa-writing was to be his primary occupation for the rest of his life, the main medium through which he personally expressed his vision of din, engaged in controversy with other 'ulama', and defended his views with 'an armoury of erudition' based on quotation from Qur'an, hadis, and Hanafi authorities of fiqh.[27]

Writing in the scholarly solitude of his home in Bareilly, surrounded by books and a few devoted followers, was characteristic of Ahmad Riza's personal style and temperament. Modelling his life on the prophetic sunna as he interpreted it, he was attentive to the details of comportment, dress, and etiquette in daily life, and corrected those about him if they were not likewise attentive. Thus, when reading or writing he sat with his knees drawn up together, never stretching his legs out in the direction of the qibla in Mecca.

[24] This elicited the comment by Naqi 'Ali that Ahmad Riza was teaching him, rather than the other way around. Ibid., p. 137.

[25] Ibid., p. 151; *Sirat-e A'la Hazrat*, pp. 72–4; Burhan ul-Haqq Jabalpuri, *Ikram-e Imam Ahmad Riza* (Lahore: Markazi Majlis-e Riza, 1981), pp. 58–60. This incident is believed to have occurred some time between 1914 and 1917. Metcalf also refers to it in *Islamic Revival*, p. 299.

[26] *Hayat-e A'la Hazrat*, p. 11.

[27] The phrase within quotes is from Metcalf, p. 304. Chapters VI through VIII of this study examine Ahmad Riza's fatawa in some detail.

He always entered the mosque with his right foot first and left it with his left foot first.[28] Both teacher and patron to his followers, he was also personally generous, indeed lavish, in his periodic gifts to his students and disciples,[29] a characteristic one may attribute perhaps to his Pathan ancestry.[30] As Metcalf says, his style was 'aristocratic'.[31] This characteristic was also evident in his relations with fellow 'ulama'. As later chapters show, he seldom participated in large-scale organizational endeavours other than those associated with ritual observances or the annual graduation ceremonies at the Madrasa Manzar al-Islam founded by him in 1904.

If Ahmad Riza's scholarship and attentiveness to the details of personal conduct were among the sources of his moral authority, another important source was the approval of authoritative figures, gained in the course of journeys he undertook at various junctures in his life. Although the biographies, presenting him fully-formed from childhood (and therefore a 'born' leader), give us no sense of his growth of stature as a leader of the Ahl-e Sunnat movement, we do get some perspective on this by focusing on important journeys made by him in chronological order. Thus, his second hajj was very different, we find, from his first.

Important Journeys

Before going on hajj, Ahmad Riza went, in 1877, to Marahra, in order to receive discipleship (*bai'a*) from an elderly pir of the Barkatiyya Sayyid family resident there. Marahra is a qasba in Etah district, about 120 kilometres southwest of Bareilly. Ahmad Riza, about twenty-one years old at the time, was accompanied by his

[28] *Hayat-e A'la Hazrat*, pp. 27–8, 68, 177–9. See Francis Robinson, 'The 'Ulama of Farangi Mahall and Their *Adab*', in Barbara D. Metcalf (ed.), *Moral Conduct and Authority: The Place of Adab in South Asian Islam* (Berkeley: University of California Press, 1984), pp. 152–83, for an account of similar attention to the details of personal conduct among the 'ulama' of Firangi Mahal. As he says on p. 178, this was a source of moral authority.

[29] *Hayat-e A'la Hazrat*, pp. 50–4.

[30] Thus, Iqbal Husain writes: 'Hospitality was regarded as a necessary obligation, guests were held in great honour and all care was taken for their comfort. They [the Rohillas] were equally open-handed on ceremonial occasions . . .' *The Ruhela Chieftaincies*, p. 206.

[31] Metcalf, *Islamic Revival*, p. 306.

father, for both wanted to become *murids* (disciples) of Shah Al-e Rasul (d. 1878–79).[32] The sources tell us that this visit was preceded, for Ahmad Riza, by a period of painful spiritual longing during which his grandfather appeared to him in a dream and assured him that relief would soon be forthcoming.[33] This came to pass as prophesied when a revered friend and mentor of his father's, Maulana 'Abd ul-Qadir Badayuni (1837–1901), came to their house and advised father and son to seek bai'a from Shah Al-e Rasul of Marahra.[34]

According to the biographical accounts, when Ahmad Riza and his father arrived at Marahra they were welcomed with unusual honours. Shah Al-e Rasul accepted them both as his disciples right away, although a forty-day period of waiting (and training), called *chilla*, was customary. Ahmad Riza and his father received permission to accept disciples in all the sufi orders.[35] The sources suggest that Ahmad Riza and Shah Al-e Rasul shared an intuitive bond: while Ahmad Riza had experienced an internal longing, Shah Al-e Rasul had been waiting the last several days to see him. Now that he had done so, he said he could die in peace, knowing that when Allah asked him what he had brought Him from the world, he could offer Him Ahmad Riza in reply.[36]

That Ahmad Riza's biographers should seek to convey the

[32] Chapter IV deals with the Barkatiyya family of pirs to which Shah Al-e Rasul belonged. Also see Chapter V for the significance to Ahmad Riza of his tie of discipleship to Shah Al-e Rasul.

[33] *Sirat-e A'la Hazrat*, p. 55.

[34] 'Abd ul-Qadir Badayuni (1837–1901), son of Maulana Fazl-e Rasul Badayuni, studied under a number of well-known teachers. Among them were Maulana Fazl-e Haqq Khairabadi (d. 1861), who was imprisoned by the British in the Andaman Islands for anti-British activities during 1857. 'Abd ul-Qadir Badayuni was active against the 'Wahhabis', and in opposing the Nadwat al-'Ulama' in the 1880s. See Rahman 'Ali, *Tazkira-e 'Ulama'-e Hind*, pp. 311–13. Ahmad Riza was to involve himself forcefully in these concerns as well. For details, see Chapters VII and VIII below.

[35] Multiple affiliation into a number of sufi orders (tariqas) was the norm in the subcontinent in the nineteenth century. For discussion, see Metcalf, *Islamic Revival*, pp. 158–9, and passim. As she notes, usually one order was emphasized over others by different sufis. In the Ahl-e Sunnat's case, their primary affiliation was to the Qadiri order.

[36] *Sirat-e A'la Hazrat*, pp. 55–6.

impression that he was Shah Al-e Rasul's most valued disciple should not surprise us. Nevertheless, it must be remembered that he was accompanied by his father and by Maulana 'Abd ul-Qadir Badayuni, both revered elders, and that Shah Al-e Rasul had been approached at 'Abd ul-Qadir's behest. It had not been Ahmad Riza's personal decision to do so.[37]

Shortly after this journey, Ahmad Riza accompanied his father in 1878 on another important voyage, to the Haramain to perform hajj. At the time, the hajj from British India, in contrast to that originating in the Dutch East Indies for instance, was relatively unregulated by the government.[38] Recurrent outbreaks of cholera at Mecca during the pilgrimage season, however, had begun by the 1860s to cause colonial governments some alarm, particularly as cholera spread to Europe and America via the Hijaz and Egypt. It was in this context, as well as concern about the large number of indigent Indian pilgrims (*hajjis*) who failed to return after completion of the pilgrimage and unsanitary conditions on board ship, that the British Indian government began in the late nineteenth century to attempt some form of regulation.[39] Initially hesitant to do so, in succeeding years political considerations (the fear of subversion) reinforced the trend toward surveillance and control.[40]

Ahmad Riza's first hajj was thus conducted in circumstances quite different from those surrounding his second in 1905, about twenty-five years later.[41] In personal terms, and in those of the Ahl-e Sunnat

37 In Chapter V, I further explore the relationship between Shah Al-e Rasul and Ahmad Riza and suggest reasons for believing that the personal bond between them was not as close as the sources indicate, though the piri-muridi tie of discipleship with the Barkatiyya family was for Ahmad Riza a permanent one.

38 See William R. Roff, 'Sanitation and Security: The Imperial Powers and the Nineteenth Century Hajj', *Arabian Studies*, VI (1982), 146.

39 The 1878 hajj was accompanied, for the first time, by an Assistant Surgeon, one Abdur Razzack, charged with observing and reporting on the sanitary conditions surrounding the pilgrimage. Ibid., 147.

40 Government regulations a generation or so later were spelt out in considerable detail. See, e.g., *General Instructions for Pilgrims to the Hedjaz and a Manual for the Guidance of Officers and Others Concerned in the Red Sea Pilgrim Traffic* (Calcutta: Superintendent Government Printing, India, 1922).

41 A vivid account of this second pilgrimage is in Ahmad Riza Khan, *Malfuzat-e A'la*

movement as well, both pilgrimages had important but very different meaning. The first hajj was important because by performing it Ahmad Riza fulfilled one of the fundamental duties of a Muslim. Additionally, while in the Haramain he obtained certificates (*sanads*) in several fields of knowledge—hadis, fiqh, *usul-e fiqh* (principles of the law), and *tafsir* (Qur'anic exegesis)—from two well-known muftis (jurisconsults).[42] In Mecca, muftis, as expounders of the shari'a, were appointed by the Ottoman government. Sayyid Ahmad Dahlan (d. 1886), the then mufti of the Shafi'is, and one of the two who are said to have given Ahmad Riza a sanad on this occasion, was the Shaikh al-'Ulama' of Mecca. He issued fatawa in his capacity as mufti, and taught at the Haram mosque.[43] The other 'alim was one 'Abd al-Rahman Siraj, the mufti of the Hanafis; the holder of this position was consulted by the government whenever it wished to issue new rules or laws in Mecca.

Yet more honours were awarded Ahmad Riza. If the bestowal of sanads by the above-mentioned muftis had enhanced his stature as a scholar, the following incident seems to bear primarily on his spiritual role. It is said that Husain bin Saleh, the Shafi'i imam of the Maqam-e Ibrahim mosque near the Ka'ba noticed him one day during the evening (*maghrib*) prayer. Although they had not been introduced, the imam gazed at him intently, seized him by the hand, and took him home. There he held his forehead for a long time, saying at length that he saw Allah's light in it. He then gave him a new name, Zia ud-Din Ahmad, and a sanad in the six collections of hadis,[44] as well as one in the Qadiri order, signing it with his own hand. In this sanad there were only eleven names intervening between those of Husain bin Saleh and al-Bukhari.[45] Finally, Ahmad

---

Hazrat, vol. 2, pp. 2–4.

42 *Tazkira-e 'Ulama'-e Hind*, pp. 98–9.

43 C. Snouck Hurgronje, *Mekka in the Latter Part of the 19th Century*, pp. 173, 175, 187.

44 Known by the names of their compilers, these are: the *Sahih Bukhari* by al-Bukhari (d. 256/870); the *Sahih Muslim* by Muslim (d. 261/875); and the *Sunan* by Abu Da'ud (d. 275/888), al-Nasa'i (d. 303/915), al-Tirmidhi (d. 278/892), and Ibn Maja (d. 273/886). The first two are collectively known as the *Sahihain*, and are the most authoritative.

45 *Tazkira-e 'Ulama'-e Hind*, p. 99. The significance of this statement is rather confusing,

Riza received another sign of spiritual favour at Medina: a vision one night at the Hanif mosque that he had been absolved of all his sins.[46]

These and other spiritual honours bestowed on Ahmad Riza on his first hajj point us toward the *rite de passage* symbolism of hajj. At the end of his journey, Ahmad Riza returned to India imbued with the moral authority required to become the pre-eminent leader of the Ahl-e Sunnat movement. Having earlier been accepted as disciple by the Qadiri pir Shah Al-e Rasul, he had now also received the blessings of the 'ulama' of the Haramain. His new identity was symbolized by his new name.[47] In Ahl-e Sunnat terms, the significance of the first hajj was that as he was Allah's chosen instrument for the task of rebuking the 'ulama' of the subcontinent in this era of bid'a (reprehensible innovations), Allah had called him to the pure land of the Haramain before he embarked on his lifelong mission (as leader of the Ahl-e Sunnat) in India. The 'ulama' of the Haramain loved him, blessed him with the wealth of their knowledge in many fields, including gnosticism, and sent him back to India.[48]

Acknowledgement of Ahmad Riza's moral leadership of the Ahl-e Sunnat movement was publicly made in 1900, when he undertook another journey. This was to Patna, to attend a meeting of the Majlis-e Ahl-e Sunnat wa Jama'at, an anti-Nadwa organization

---

for if it was a sanad in the Qadiri order as mentioned (rather than in hadis), presumably it ought ultimately to be traceable to Shaikh 'Abd al-Qadir Jilani (d. 1166), the founder of the Qadiri order, rather than al-Bukhari, one of the major authoritative sources for hadis.

[46] *Tazkira-e 'Ulama'-e Hind*, p. 99. This last detail is significant in that it assured Ahmad Riza of an afterlife in heaven. The Ahl-e Sunnat (as do many other Muslims) believe that such assurance had been given to only a few Companions of the Prophet during their lifetimes.

[47] See Victor Turner, 'Pilgrimages as Social Processes', in his *Dramas, Fields, and Metaphors: Symbolic Action in Human Society* (Ithaca: Cornell University Press, 1974); William R. Roff, 'Pilgrimage and the History of Religions: Theoretical Approaches to the *Hajj*', in Richard D. Martin (ed.), *Approaches to Islam in Religious Studies* (Tucson: Arizona University Press, 1985). Arnold Van Gennep points out in *The Rites of Passage* (Chicago: University of Chicago Press, 1960), pp. 62–3, that the act of naming is an act of 'incorporation', that is, of acquisition of a new identity at the final stage of the rite of passage.

[48] Akhtar Shahjahanpuri, Introduction, in *Rasa'il-e Rizwiyya* (Lahore: Maktaba Hamidiyya, 1396/1976), p. 6.

of Ahl-e Sunnat 'ulama' founded by Qazi 'Abd ul-Wahid Azimabadi. It is reported that in the course of the week-long meetings Ahmad Riza was unanimously proclaimed the mujaddid (renewer) of the fourteenth Hijri century.[49] This proclamation was an important landmark not only in his career, but in the history of the Ahl-e Sunnat movement itself. An unambiguous statement of the Ahl-e Sunnat's self-perception as a—indeed the only—movement of renewal among contemporary Muslims, it was simultaneously a measure of self-confidence and a challenge to rival Muslim renewal movements (such as the Deobandi) which advanced similar claims. While rival 'ulama' groups did not accept the Ahl-e Sunnat claim, the mutual rivalry was itself indicative, as Metcalf points out, of common aspirations for Islamic 'reform'.[50]

Returning to the growth in Ahmad Riza's moral standing as reflected in his travels, we must attend to his second hajj in 1905. Unlike the first in which his position was that of a seeker and humble recipient of honours, the second was akin to a triumphal tour with important consequences back home. Ahmad Riza had already corresponded with many of the 'ulama' he met in the Haramain on this occasion. In the 1890s he had sought and received the confirmation of some Meccan 'ulama' of a controversial judgment made by him in certain fatawa condemning the Nadwat al-'Ulama'. But during this visit (judging by our Ahl-e Sunnat sources) the roles were to some extent reversed. He had again sought and received confirmations by several 'ulama' of a fatwa (this time an anti-Ahmadi and anti-Deobandi one). But more than this, many 'ulama' had sought

[49] Chapters VI and VII discuss the concept of the mujaddid and the circumstances in which Ahmad Riza was so proclaimed. Suffice it to say here that the proclamation by a group of 'ulama' of one of their number in a meeting, in a procedure resembling an election, was most unusual. The decision was generally made informally over an extended period of time (perhaps several years) when a consensus ('ijma') was felt to have been reached. I am grateful to Professor Yohanan Friedmann for pointing this out to me.

[50] Metcalf, *Islamic Revival*, p. 13. She also points to the important fact that many of the rival movements traced their intellectual heritage to Shah Wali Ullah. Ibid., pp. 276–7. As Chapter VII of this study indicates, the Ahl-e Sunnat also did so, though they looked to Shah 'Abd ul- 'Aziz, eldest son of Shah Wali Ullah, rather than to Wali Ullah himself.

sanads *from* him this time, bearing *his* signature.[51] These were in hadis and tafsir, among other things.

This is only the most dramatic of many events said to have occurred on this 1905 visit to the Haramain, in which Ahmad Riza is portrayed as teacher rather than pupil. For instance, when in the library of the Haram mosque in Mecca, he overheard some 'ulama' debating whether or not it was lawful to throw stones at the pillars of Satan in Mina before dusk. One Meccan 'alim had apparently said that it was lawful to do so. Ahmad Riza, asked his opinion, dissented with this judgment. A book was consulted, and Ahmad Riza's opinion was confirmed as the right one.[52] Ahmad Riza also relates in his *Malfuzat* that he received a warm and hospitable welcome from a number of 'ulama' in Mecca—in fact, there were few who did not personally visit him.[53] Another mark of respect was the fact that two 'ulama' asked him for a fatwa, posing a series of questions on the status of the paper note.[54] As one 'alim reportedly said of him, '[Although] he was a Hindi [an Indian], his light was shining in Mecca'.[55] The comment is significant in that it expresses succinctly the reversal of relations between centre (the Haramain) and periphery (the Indian subcontinent) implicit in many of the events which occurred during Ahmad Riza's second hajj.

The immediate result of his approximately three-month stay in

[51] Muhammad Mas'ud Ahmed, *Fazil Barelwi 'Ulama'-e Hijaz ki Nazar men* (Mubarakpur, Azamgarh: Al-Majma' al-Islami, 1981), pp. 70–2, lists the names of some of the 'ulama' to whom Ahmad Riza gave sanads. To many he reportedly promised that he would send them their sanads after he returned to Bareilly.

[52] *Malfuzat-e A'la Hazrat*, vol. 2, p. 8. The question related to part of the hajj rituals, in which the pilgrim 'stones three pillars [at Mina, a few miles outside Mecca] in memory of the way Abraham, Hagar and Ishmael rejected Satan's temptings to disobey God's command'. Francis Robinson, *Atlas of the Islamic World since 1500* (New York: Facts on File, 1982), p. 194.

[53] The one 'alim who was too proud to visit him, Ahmad Riza said, was the Hanafi mufti of Mecca, Shaikh 'Abd Allah bin Siddiq bin 'Abbas. When they met eventually, in the Haram library, it was in circumstances that put the mufti to shame. Before they had been introduced, Ahmad Riza had occasion to correct him on a small matter of etiquette relating to a book in the library. *Malfuzat*, vol. 2, pp. 18–19.

[54] The fatwa was entitled *Kafl al-Faqih al-Fahim fi Ahkam Qirtas al-Darahim*. Chapter VI below discusses some of the issues involved in this particular debate.

[55] *Malfuzat*, vol. 2, p. 17.

Mecca and Medina was that Ahmad Riza was able to establish close relations with a number of leading scholars in the Haramain, and secure their support in his anti-Deobandi efforts at home. The Deobandis of course responded with fatawa of their own, rebutting his. But whatever the merits of the arguments made, he was seen by Ahl-e Sunnat supporters as having scored a major victory against the Deobandi side. From their point of view, the events at the Haramain confirmed their belief that Ahmad Riza was a leader of 'Sunnis' world-wide, not merely in India.

There is one last journey I would like to refer to here, in which we see how Ahl-e Sunnat followers venerated him toward the end of his life. Unlike the hajj pilgrimages described above, Ahmad Riza's visit to Jabalpur (central India) in 1919 was a very personal one. It was undertaken to please a dear and devoted follower, Burhan ul-Haqq Jabalpuri (d. 1984), and to perform the latter's *dastar-bandi* (tying of the turban, a ceremony marking the end of a student's career).[56]

This was no simple visit, quietly undertaken. Ahmad Riza's stature within the movement by this time was far too elevated for such a possibility. Because his health was poor, elaborate arrangements were made all along the way to ensure his comfort. It was a long (perhaps two-day) journey by train, following an eastern route to Allahabad and then a southern one to Jabalpur, a distance of perhaps 800 kilometres. Arriving at the head of a large party of people, he was received like a royal visitor: great crowds greeted him not only at the Jabalpur station, but even at earlier halts at smaller stations. Thronging to touch and kiss his feet, they lined the streets all along the way.[57]

The royal metaphor, implicitly invoked by sufis in their own vocabulary, is an apt one for Ahmad Riza's relationship with the people who gathered about him daily during his month at Jabalpur. Like royalty, he bestowed lavish gifts on all around him. Zafar ud-Din Bihari comments on the amazement of those who witnessed

[56] The Epilogue at the end of this study contains some biographical information about Burhan ul-Haqq, with reference in particular to his stand on the Pakistan issue.

[57] For a description of this journey, see Burhan ul-Haqq Jabalpuri, *Ikram-e Imam Ahmad Riza*, pp. 83–98.

his generosity on this occasion. From a box he pulled out money, gold ornaments, clothes—something for every household servant, not just for the hosts, as well as for important merchants (*seths*) and their families.[58] The gifts were reciprocated in the form of *nazar* (gift to a sufi pir), as well as frequent feasts.

Most remarkable, however, is the unfortunately brief report of a series of public meetings in which large numbers of people did *tauba* (sought pardon) at Ahmad Riza's hands. A list of seventy-nine names is given in the *Malfuzat*, though perhaps even this is incomplete.[59] The sins confessed were not all colossal ones: shaving the beard and dyeing the hair black, both disapproved of by Ahmad Riza, for instance. Those whose omissions related to deeper spiritual ('hidden') matters, however, spoke to him in private.

This incident, which occurred about two years before Ahmad Riza's death in October 1921, shows the moral authority he enjoyed among those who called themselves the Ahl-e Sunnat wa Jama'at. In their eyes, his eminence was a gift from Allah, reflected in his depth of learning, piety, and personal rectitude. Above all, the certainty of his convictions, and his insistence that unlike those he accused of 'disrespect' to the Prophet (in ways that he set out in detail in his writings), his own views were 'correct', provided psychological reassurance in a time of great social change. To his followers, he was their saviour in a dark world.

Ahmad Riza, Pre-eminent Scholar and Exemplary Model

The picture presented by the Urdu-speaking biographers of Ahmad Riza is of a man who embodied in every act and thought the best in the scholarly tradition of Sunni Islam. Because he modelled his life and work on his vision of the Prophet, he in turn became a model for emulation and the centre for a movement of revival and reform. In so doing he attracted followers to Bareilly from other parts of the country and put Bareilly on the intellectual map for Sunni 'ulama' from as far away as Mecca and Medina.

58 *Hayat-e A'la Hazrat*, pp. 56–7.

59 *Malfuzat*, vol. 2, pp. 98–101.

Interestingly, the sense of timelessness that is evoked by the sources in their portrayal of Ahmad Riza as an eminent nineteenth-century Indian Muslim 'alim appears to echo a tradition of biographical writing in other parts of the Muslim world. Lucette Valensi describes the image of the ideal scholar embedded in a fifteenth-century biographical dictionary from the Maghreb:

> the learned man is one who has evinced since childhood a passion for learning and a capacity for understanding the sciences; one who is endowed with an infallible and powerful memory; one whose ability to endure [long hours of] study exceeds the norm; one who excels in not one but a great number of branches of learning; one who exhibits a subtle intelligence. He makes himself known particularly by the solving of an enigma: the paradigmatic anecdote that one looks for here is the presentation by the master of a problem that the other students are unable to solve, indeed that even the master is unable to solve, and that is impeccably resolved by the talented young man.[60]

The learned man must also, Valensi goes on to say, have mystic knowledge of God, and discharge an important function in his community. Most important, he must be both 'cosmopolitan', in touch with the sources of high religious tradition, and embedded in his society. This permits him to mediate, through his voluminous writings, between the universal and the local, for his corpus is the product as much of his local milieu as it is of a universalistic Islamic tradition.[61] Reading Valensi, I see a remarkable likeness with the image of Ahmad Riza conveyed by Zafar ud-Din Bihari and other biographers. In his life, his followers found a model for their own.

[60] Lucette Valensi: 'est bon lettré celui qui a manifesté dès son enfance son ardeur à apprendre et sa capacité à absorber la science; celui qui est doué d'une mémoire infaillible et inépuisable; celui dont l'endurance à l'étude excède la norme; celui qui excelle non pas dans une, mais dans un grand nombre de branches du savoir; celui qui fait montre d'une intelligence subtile. Celle-ci se revèle notamment, par la solution d'une enigme: l'anecdote paradigmatique que l'on attend ici est la presentation, par le maître, d'un problème insoluble par les autres élèves, voir par le maître lui-même, et sa resolution impeccable par le jeune talent'. 'Le jardin de l'Académie, ou comment se forme une école de pensée', pp. 15–16. Paper presented at Colloquium on Modes of Transmission of Religious Culture in Islam, Princeton University, and jointly sponsored by the Department of Near Eastern Studies, Princeton University, and Ecole des Hautes Etudes en Sciences Sociales, Paris, April 28–30, 1989.

[61] Ibid., pp. 17–20.

Chapter III

Institutional Bases of the Ahl-e Sunnat Movement, 1880s–1920s

Giving concrete shape to Ahmad Riza's vision of din—a vision set forth in his fatawa, commentaries, glosses, and malfuzat—were the 'ulama', students, and devoted followers who disseminated his thought by teaching, publishing, and debating with one another. Individually and in concert, they created institutions which carried the Ahl-e Sunnat message to a wider audience, and made it possible by the 1880s for followers to identify themselves as members of a 'movement', which they called the Ahl-e Sunnat wa Jama'at. These institutional structures were both 'ulama'-centred and pir-centred, both urban and rural. Indeed, the distinction between those who were primarily 'ulama' and those who were primarily pirs is sometimes hard to make, as the scholarly pirs of the Ahl-e Sunnat movement frequently appeared to be both. In this chapter I focus on scholarly institutions such as madrasas, journals, and voluntary associations. The next two chapters continue with an examination of important leaders and their institutional bases, paying close attention to rural shrine-centred activities.

The Class Composition of the Leadership

The core leadership of the Ahl-e Sunnat movement in the late nineteenth century consisted of 'ulama' and Qadiri pirs from Bareilly, Badayun, Rampur, Pilibhit, and Marahra in the Rohilkhand

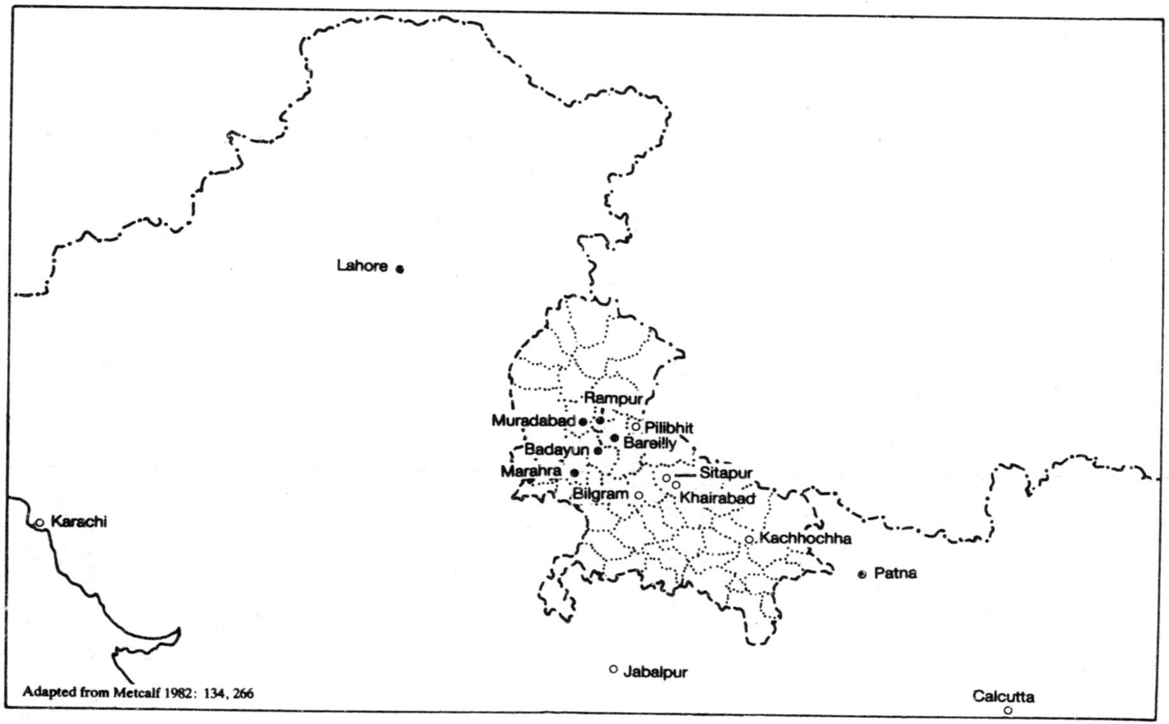

Map 2. Centres of Ahl-e Sunnat Influence in the Late Nineteenth Century. Black circles indicate areas of particular importance to the movement. (Adapted from Metcalf 1982: 134, 266)

region, and from Patna, Bihar (map 2). They were drawn from both urban and qasba (rural) centres, dependent variously on incomes from land, trade, teaching, the voluntary contributions of followers, or combinations thereof. In social terms they were part of the *ashraf*, or Muslim élite. Their status was based on ancestral lineage (whether Pathan, Sayyid, 'Usmani, or similar), religious learning, and wealth. Privileged social standing corresponded to the concepts of hierarchy central to the religious style they favoured. Like Ahmad Riza, they approved of and attended annual 'urs (death anniversary) celebrations around the country, and engaged in other mediational practices. So close knit were the scholarly and mediational aspects in Ahmad Riza's life and thought, in fact, that by the end of his life a khanqah (sufi hospice) known as the Khanqah-e 'Aliyya Rizwiyya had been established in Bareilly, where, among other things, the annual meeting of the Ahl-e Sunnat's Madrasa Manzar al-Islam took place.[1] The lifestyle fostered by Ahl-e Sunnat 'ulama' in the towns and that centred around rural khanqahs therefore shared a common tone, even if their emphases were different.

As noted previously, however, Ahl-e Sunnat 'ulama' and pirs stressed the need to follow the sunna and remain faithful to the shari'a. Consequently the pir families associated with the movement considered themselves to be 'reformist', identifying with a sufi movement that had been active in the countryside simultaneously with the urban renewal movements of 'ulama'. As Chapter IV will indicate, this concern for reform was evident among other things in religious ritual during annual 'urs pilgrimages, in which the attendance of women, and the holding of *sama'* musical sessions, for instance, were frowned upon.

Gilmartin notes that the sufi reformist pirs of the Panjab were less closely tied into the local patronage network than 'older' pirs, and were willing on occasion to join reformist 'ulama' 'in defense of Islamic symbols and, at times, in religious attacks on the colonial system'.[2] Two such pirs in the Panjab, with whom the Ahl-e Sunnat

[1] See report of the eighteenth such meeting of the Madrasa Manzar al-Islam in *Dabdaba-e Sikandari* (Rampur), 58:36 (May 8, 1922), 4–5.

[2] Gilmartin, *Empire and Islam*, pp. 58–60, 63–4. As Gilmartin goes on to say, however, co-operation between reformist pirs and reformist 'ulama' sometimes resulted in tension

movement worked closely in the course of the Khilafat movement and during the anti-*irtidad* (apostacy) campaign of the early 1920s to counter Arya Samaj conversions of Muslims to Hinduism (known as the Shuddhi movement), were Pir Jama'at 'Ali Shah, a Naqshbandi from Alipur Sayyedan, and Pir Mehr 'Ali Shah, a Qadiri from Golra Sharif. The political base of 'reforming' pirs such as these, Gilmartin indicates, consisted of a combination of rural and urban networks.[3] Thus the 'ulama' and pirs of the Ahl-e Sunnat movement were at once urban and rural, 'reformist' and mediationist.

As townsmen, some of the Ahl-e Sunnat competed for local administrative positions and played a part in the British power structure. Among subscribers to the *Tuhfa-e Hanafiyya*, an important Patna-based journal of the movement in the late nineteenth century, for instance, were qazis (judges of Islamic law), *wakils* (authorized public pleaders), *tahsildars* (revenue collectors), as well as municipal commissioners, barristers, doctors, and station masters.[4] Although the 'ulama' did not usually undertake government service, this was not unknown: Maulana Fazl-e Haqq Khairabadi (d. 1862), identified by the Ahl-e Sunnat as one of themselves, had served the East India Company as a *peshkar* (agent) early in the nineteenth century;[5] likewise, Maulana Fazl-e Rasul Badayuni (d. 1872) was at one time a legal expert (*mufti-e 'adalat*) and record-keeper (*sar-rishtadar*) in Badayun district.[6] Paradoxically, both 'ulama' also participated in the Revolt of 1857.[7]

between them.

[3] Ibid., p. 59. Although Jama'at 'Ali was a Qadiri, Gilmartin writes that 'he found his religious mission in one of the more active, reforming orders in Punjab—in this case, the Naqshbandi'.

[4] *Tuhfa-e Hanafiyya* (Matba'-e Ahl-e Sunnat wa Jama'at, 1315/1897–98), vol. 1, no. 9, p. 2.

[5] See A. S. Bazmee Ansari, 'Fadl-i Hakk', in *Encyclopaedia of Islam*, vol. 2 (*EI2*), pp. 735–6.

[6] Maulawi Rahman 'Ali, *Tazkira-e 'Ulama'-e Hind*, p. 381.

[7] Bazmee Ansari writes that Fazl-e Haqq Khairabadi played 'a leading part in the military uprising of 1857, was charged with high treason, arrested, tried and sentenced to transportation for life. He died in exile in the Andamans (*Kala Pani*), where he was interred, in 1862'. 'Fadl-i Hakk', in *EI2*, p. 735. Ahl-e Sunnat 'ulama' regard him with great respect, in part because of his participation in a debate with Muhammad Isma'il

In the agriculturally-based qasbas, great pir (and 'ulama') families such as the Barkatiyya Sayyids of Marahra, the 'Usmani pirs of Badayun, and the Ashrafiyya Ghausiya pirs of Kachhochha (Faizabad district, in the Awadh region), constituted the élite in their areas, being both landowners and purveyors of *baraka* (spiritual grace).[8] However, they probably never commanded the same influence in their localities as did the wealthy Panjab pirs described by Gilmartin as hinges in the political structure of that province. The Ahl-e Sunnat wa Jama'at's relationship to the British power and administrative structure, and the degree of their integration into networks dependent on British patronage, appear diverse enough to preclude any single characterization. Considering our limited knowledge of the family histories of some 'ulama' and the evidence of pertinent fatawa (to be examined below), it seems fair to say that while there was little active hostility toward the British during the nineteenth century, the Ahl-e Sunnat 'ulama' do not, on the other hand, appear to have been directly co-opted by the British Indian government in the United Provinces in a manner comparable to the Panjab religious élites.[9]

The new institutional structures the Ahl-e Sunnat created, the new madrasas, voluntary organizations, newspapers and publication houses, bore the imprint of British colonialism in India, in that they included features borrowed from British Indian organizations. They were thus by no means replicas of similar institutions in the past.

Madrasas

Ahmad Riza had founded a school in 1904, called the Madrasa Manzar al-Islam, though known more often as the Madrasa Ahl-e

---

in the 1820s on the doctrine of imkan-e nazir. On this issue, see Chapter VIII below. His autobiography, translated from Persian into Urdu under the title *Baghi-e Hindustan*, has been through several editions. It tells of the conditions of his capture and imprisonment, and is readily available in bookstores stocking Ahl-e Sunnat literature in Pakistan.

8 Chapter IV below examines the family history of the Barkatiyya Sayyids of Marahra.

9 It is probable that the pir families of the United Provinces did not enjoy either the vast landed wealth nor the corresponding political influence in their areas that their Panjab counterparts did, and that British policy in the U.P. was therefore different. On relations between the Panjab pirs and the British, see Gilmartin, *Empire and Islam*, p. 51.

Sunnat wa Jama'at. The Ahl-e Sunnat were in fact late starters in the educational field, for all the major late nineteenth-century Muslim movements in north India were organized around madrasas or colleges. Deoband had its Dar al-'Ulum, founded in the late 1860s, Sir Sayyid Ahmad Khan began his educational reforms at the Anglo-Muhammadan Oriental College in 1875, and the Nadwat al-'Ulama', founded in the 1890s, established their madrasa of this name at Lucknow in the early twentieth century.

The reason for the Ahl-e Sunnat's initial neglect of education was probably Ahmad Riza's relative lack of interest in teaching, as compared to fatwa-writing. As mentioned earlier, he spent much of his time writing fatawa in his own library at home. He presumably preferred erudite discourse to the routine and less challenging task of teaching at relatively elementary levels. Moreover, as he himself had never attended a madrasa, having learned all he knew either from books or from a few personal teachers, he may not have seen any pressing need for one.

At any rate, when Zafar ud-Din Bihari first came to Bareilly in 1904–5 desiring to become Ahmad Riza's student, the latter advised him to study at an existing madrasa, the Madrasa Dar al-Isha 'at, and help out in his spare time in the work of the Dar al-Ifta (office for the issuance of fatawa).[10] When the Madrasa Dar al-Isha'at turned out, some time later, to be under Deobandi influence, Zafar ud-Din Bihari took the initiative in establishing the Madrasa Manzar al-Islam, with help from Ahmad Riza's brother Hasan Riza (1859–1908), and elder son Hamid Riza (1875–1943). Ahmad Riza's consent to the creation of the madrasa was obtained by asking a Sayyid to recommend the idea to him.[11] A local ra'is donated space for the new school in his house.[12]

[10] The Ahl-e Sunnat Dar al-Ifta was not attached to a madrasa, as was usually the case, but operated out of Ahmad Riza's home. On Zafar ud-Din Bihari's early experiences regarding the Madrasa Dar al-Isha'at, see Muhammad Ahmad Qadiri, 'Malik al-'Ulama' Maulana Muhammad Zafar ud-Din Bihari aur Khidmat-e Hadis', *Ashrafiyya* (Mubarakpur, Azamgarh, April 1977), 29. In Chapter VI I discuss the work of the Dar al-Ifta and the manner in which fatwa-writing was taught.

[11] *Ashrafiyya* (July 1977), 15. For Ahmad Riza's respect for Sayyids, see Chapter V below.

[12] Ibid.

In subsequent years, it was Hamid Riza who was most closely associated with the madrasa in his capacity of *muhtamim*, or manager and chief administrator. In fact, the position became hereditary, being passed on from father to eldest son.[13] Ahmad Riza was the *sarparast*, rector or patron, helping the madrasa financially to some extent (no figures are indicated). Once a year, he addressed the gathering of 'ulama', pirs, and wealthy residents of the town at the madrasa's annual dastar-bandi ceremonies. Zafar ud-Din, the first student to graduate, also taught at the madrasa for some time.

Despite the fact that the term 'Dar al-'Ulum', a place of higher learning superior to a madrasa, is sometimes fondly used for the Madrasa Manzar al-Islam, the school was in fact not the great institution that some maintained.[14] A report by Na'im ud-Din Muradabadi, dated August 1920, is especially revealing:

> This [the Madrasa Manzar al-Islam] is a very special madrasa, for it is under the care of A'la Hazrat [Ahmad Riza]. Although it is not very old, it would not have been unreasonable to expect that at this time it could have been a great Dar al-'Ulum, and other madrasas in Hindustan would have considered it their centre. Although I have not visited this madrasa at length at any time, what I have seen superficially has led me to conclude that it has nothing in it which lives up to its worth. The room is small and space is short. The Muhtamim Sahib [Hamid Riza Khan] has found it fit to place his bed in the room. If instruction is given in a normal voice at one level [i.e., to students of one grade] the voice would surely reach the other level. Students have to sit with bent knees, and probably for this reason the muhtamim is obliged to send many away. In my estimation, there are approximately two hundred students. There are only nine or ten teachers.[15]

Na'im ud-Din went on to name the teachers, praising them for their learning. He noted, however, that the school needed a good

[13] It was later held by Hamid Riza's eldest son Ibrahim Riza 'Jilani Miyan' (1907–65), and after him by Rehan Riza, Jilani Miyan's eldest son. Ibid.

[14] For a contrasting picture to the description of the Madrasa Manzar al-Islam that follows, see Metcalf's account of the Dar al-'Ulum at Deoband, *Islamic Revival*, pp. 92–8, 100–11, and passim. The Madrasa Manzar al-Islam, it will be apparent, was much smaller and less well-endowed than the Dar al-'Ulum. Nonetheless, it shared with the latter several organizational features which were new to madrasas.

[15] Na'im ud-Din Muradabadi, 'Present Conditions [of Islamic Madrasas]', *Al-Sawad al-A'zam* (Muradabad), 1:9 (Zu'l Hijja 1338/August 1920), 27-8.

building, a better library, more teachers, and more space, both for classrooms and boarding facilities. He attributed the lack of money for these needs to Ahmad Riza's aversion to fund-raising:

> A'la Hazrat's greatness is such that he is unwilling to ask anyone for a contribution for any purpose. He has an aversion to anything to do with wealth. Alas. The Ahl-e Sunnat and the community (millat) sympathetic to it should . . . turn this madrasa into a central Dar al-'Ulum . . . instead of opening new schools here and there.[16]

Indeed, there are indications that local financial support for the madrasa was inadequate, particularly during World War I. A newspaper article appearing in Rampur's weekly *Dabdaba-e Sikandari* in 1916 was unusually blunt when it admitted that that year the school had suffered financial loss, and had received insufficient donations on account of the war.[17] Donations (*chanda*) were sought particularly at the annual dastar-bandi ceremonies which usually lasted three days. The size of individual contributions is unfortunately not recorded: only exceptionally large donations (Rs. 200 on two occasions)[18] find mention.

For the period for which I consulted newspaper reports (1908–17), the number of students graduating at any one time was usually between four and ten. Ahl-e Sunnat 'ulama', sufi shaikhs, and local *ru'asa* (pl. of ra'is) were invited to attend, to give sermons (*wa'z*), to read na'ts (poetry in praise of the Prophet) and to participate in the milad that sometimes followed at the end. Space permitting, local residents also came to listen and participate. The venue was a mosque near Ahmad Riza's house, known as Masjid Bibiji.[19]

Lists of the names of participants in some of the early dastar-bandi ceremonies tell us something of the school's range of influence during these years. In 1908, those attending included 'ulama' from Haidarabad, Pilibhit, Muradabad, Badayun, Allahabad, and

[16] Ibid., p. 30.

[17] *Dabdaba-e Sikandari* (Rampur), 53:8 (December 18, 1916), 5.

[18] Ibid., 44: 38 (October 26, 1908), 5; 58:36 (May 8, 1922), 4.

[19] The foregoing paragraph is based on the following entries in *Dabdaba-e Sikandari*: 44:38 (October 26, 1908), 3–5; 45:34 (September 20, 1909), 7; 47:34 (August 21, 1911), 9; 48:45 (October 28, 1912), 3; 50:46 (October 12, 1914), 3; 53:8 (December 18, 1916), 5; 53:49 (October 1, 1917), 5.

Rampur.[20] Many of the 'ulama' and sufis named were personally close to Ahmad Riza. Among them were Maulana Wasi Ahmad (1836–1916) of Pilibhit, known as 'Muhaddis Surati', who taught hadis at the Madrasa al-Hadis founded by him in Pilibhit; Didar 'Ali Alwari (1856–1935), founder of the Madrasa Hizb al-Ahnaf in Lahore in 1924; Irshad 'Ali Rampuri (1862–1910), nephew and son-in-law of Irshad Husain Rampuri (1832–93), a longtime associate of the family who was also close to Kalb 'Ali Khan, the late nineteenth century Nawab of Rampur (r. 1865–87);[21] 'Abd ul-Muqtadir Badayuni (1866–1915), from the family of 'Usmani 'ulama' and pirs who had close and longstanding ties to Ahmad Riza's family (though 'Abd ul-Muqtadir later opposed Ahmad Riza on some important issues); and Sayyid 'Muhammad Miyan' Kachhochhawi (1893–1963), the caretaker (*sajjada-nishin*) of a shrine in Kachhochha, district Faizabad. These pirs and 'ulama' were among the inner circle of the Ahl-e Sunnat leadership in the late nineteenth and early twentieth centuries.

Lacking detailed knowledge of the structure or finances of the madrasa, we can only guess that it suffered from neglect on the part of Ahmad Riza, which in turn led to the shortage of resources described by Na'im ud-Din Muradabadi. Following Ahmad Riza's death in 1921, its close association with Hamid Riza may also have been a source of weakness. Hamid Riza, whom Ahmad Riza had appointed his sajjada-nishin in 1915,[22] appears to have become immersed in sufi activities after his father's death; indeed, in 1922 the madrasa's annual dastar-bandi ceremonies were held in the Khanqah-e 'Aliyya Rizwiyya, as Ahmad Riza's home came to be known, and not in the Masjid Bibiji as before.[23] Several years later, in 1937, Mustafa Riza Khan (1892–1981), Hamid Riza's younger

[20] *Dabdaba-e Sikandari*, 44:38 (October 26, 1908), 3–5.

[21] Irshad Husain and other members of his family, unlike others mentioned in this paragraph, were followers of the Naqshbandi Mujaddidi order of sufis. Most Ahl-e Sunnat 'ulama' were primarily (though not solely) followers of the Qadiri order. It should also be noted that Kalb 'Ali, the Nawab of Rampur, was a Sunni, unlike other ruling nawabs in the family who were Shi'is.

[22] *Dabdaba-e Sikandari*, 51:51 (November 8, 1915), 3.

[23] Ibid., 58:36 (May 8, 1922), 4.

brother by seventeen years, founded another school, the Madrasa Mazhar al-Islam, attached to the Masjid Bibiji, which followed the same syllabus (the dars-e nizami) as Manzar al-Islam.[24]

Although the Ahl-e Sunnat failed to develop a Dar al-'Ulum at Bareilly comparable to either the Deobandi institution or to the one established by the Nadwat al-'Ulama' in Lucknow, a number of madrasas were started in different parts of north India in the late nineteenth and early twentieth centuries which identified themselves with the movement. Their size and longevity were inevitably uneven. As the preceding description of the Bareilly-based Manzar al-Islam shows, financial support from wealthy patrons and the setting up of an administrative framework independent of the founder were crucial to the long-term success of an institution.

One of the oldest of the Ahl-e Sunnat's madrasas was Rampur's Madrasa 'Aliyya. It was an eighteenth-century institution, funded by a *waqf* (endowment) based on income from two villages, which enjoyed state patronage under the nawabs.[25] In the politically disturbed conditions of the eighteenth century, it attracted scholars and students from the Panjab (including Delhi) and Lucknow. Maulanas Fazl-e Haqq Khairabadi (d. 1861) and 'Abd ul-Haqq Khairabadi (d. 1899), specialists in ma'qulat, were among its teachers and office-bearers.[26]

Organizationally, the Madrasa 'Aliyya (as originally conceived) was probably very different from madrasas set up by the Ahl-e Sunnat a century or so later.[27] In Badayun, Maulana 'Abd ul-

[24] Interview in Bareilly with Dr Mustafa Husain Nizami Niyazi, April 19, 1987. Dr Niyazi maintained that his father, Maulana Niyaz Ahmad, had founded the original madrasa in the Bibiji mosque which was later revived by Mustafa Riza under a new name. Ziaud-Din A. Desai, *Centres of Islamic Learning in India* (Delhi: Publications Division, Ministry of Information and Broadcasting, 1978), p. 41, gives 1937 as the year of its founding. Its student body is said to have been about 200 at the time of Desai's survey.

[25] Kalb 'Ali Khan Fa'iq Rampuri 'Madrasa 'Aliyya Rampur', in *'Ilm o Agahi* (Karachi: Government National College, 1974–75), pp. 29–32.

[26] Ibid., p. 32. Also see Desai, *Centres of Islamic Learning*, p. 35.

[27] Madrasas of the older style would have resembled that at Firangi Mahal described as follows by Metcalf: 'In . . . the famous Farangi Mahall in Lucknow, family members taught students in their own homes or in a corner of a mosque. There was no central

Qayyum (d. 1900) founded the Madrasa Shams al-'Ulum in 1899. His son, 'Abd ul-Majid (d. 1931), enabled it to grow and prosper by securing an annual grant from the Nizam of Haidarabad which continued until 1948, and other grants from the Nawab of Rampur and wealthy families in Bombay, Aligarh and elsewhere.[28] Individual donations from the people of Badayun were collected for a new building. Sir James Meston, Lieutenant-Governor of the United Provinces, and Mr. Ingram, Collector of Badayun, also contributed toward land and buildings for the school. Students were taught the dars-e nizami syllabus. Many then went on to pass exams at Panjab and Allahabad Universities, qualifying for the titles of Maulawi 'Alim and Munshi Fazil (Persian) which were held to be equivalent to the BA degree.[29] The madrasa had its own writing and publishing offices which published the works of different 'ulama'.

In Pilibhit in 1893 Maulana Wasi Ahmad Muhaddis Surati founded the Madrasa al-Hadis. This madrasa owed its reputation in hadis studies largely to the teaching of Muhaddis Surati himself. Many of Ahmad Riza's closest followers were Muhaddis Surati's students before they came to Bareilly and joined his circle.[30] Muhaddis Surati's position was rather special in the Ahl-e Sunnat movement on account of his close relations, established early in his career, with 'ulama' outside the movement, notably Nadwa leaders Lutf Ullah Aligarhi (d. 1916) and Muhammad 'Ali Mungeri.[31] These

library, no course required of each student, no series of examinations. A student would seek out a teacher and receive a certificate, a sanad, listing the books he had read, then move on to another teacher or return home'. Metcalf, *Islamic Revival*, p. 94.

[28] Muhammad Ayub Qadiri, 'Madrasa Shams al-'Ulum Badayun', in *'Ilm o Agahi*, pp. 94–5; Mahmud Ahmad Qadiri, *Tazkira-e 'Ulama'-e Ahl-e Sunnat* (Muzaffarpur, Bihar: Khanqah-e Qadiriyya Ashrafiyya, 1391/1971), pp. 146–9.

[29] *'Ilm o Agahi*, p. 96. The Panjab University exams which had to be passed to qualify for these titles were in grammar, literature, rhetoric, logic, the law of inheritance, prosody and moral philosophy. See G. M. D. Sufi, *Al-Minhaj*, pp. 115–19.

[30] Among them were Zafar ud-Din Bihari, Amjad 'Ali A'zami, and Sayyid Muhammad Kachhochhawi. See Khwaja Razi Haidar, *Tazkira-e Muhaddis Surati*, pp. 266, 269, 275–7.

[31] Muhaddis Surati was a disciple of Shah Fazl-e Rahman Ganj Muradabadi (1797–1895/96), the spiritual link between many of the Nadwa's early leaders. For details, see Chapter VII below.

early contacts also included men such as Didar 'Ali Alwari, Ashraf 'Ali Thanawi (of Deoband), and Pir Jama'at 'Ali Shah Alipuri.[32]

In Patna, Maulana Qazi 'Abd ul-Wahid Firdausi Azimabadi (d. 1908), the moving spirit behind the Ahl-e Sunnat's anti-Nadwa meetings and conferences in the 1890s, founded the Madrasa Hanafiyya in 1900. The school building[33] was a large house given in waqf by 'Abd ul-Wahid's father. A staff of six or seven teachers served a student body of about a hundred, many of them boarders.[34] Financed in part by voluntary contributions and in part from collections designated as *zakat* (mandatory alms-tax on accrued wealth), the school was apparently short of funds in its early years. However, Qazi 'Abd ul-Wahid was a splendid organizer and had access to well-to-do patrons, being himself a wealthy notable.[35] The school most likely prospered under his management. What became of it after his death in 1908, though, is not known.

Two other madrasas of importance must be mentioned: the Jam'iyya Na'imiyya in Muradabad founded by Na'im ud-Din Muradabadi in the early 1920s, and the Dar al-'Ulum Hizb al-Ahnaf started by Didar 'Ali Alwari in Lahore in 1924. The latter was particularly important in terms of providing leadership for the Ahl-e Sunnat movement in the Panjab.

The Jam'iyya Na'imiyya, apparently first known as the Madrasa Ahl-e Sunnat wa Jama'at, Muradabad, was administered in 1919–20 by an association (*anjuman*) headed by an influential local patron. After the death of the patron, the anjuman ceased to exist, and the

[32] Didar 'Ali and Pir Jama'at 'Ali Shah later played leading roles in the Ahl-e Sunnat movement. See Khwaja Razi Haidar, *Tazkira-e Muhaddis Surati*, p. 55, and below.

[33] This also served as the office of the *Tuhfa-e Hanafiyya* journal, discussed below, and the new printing press, Matba' Hanafiyya.

[34] *Rudad-e Majlis-e Imtihan-e Madrasa Hanafiyya 1320* (Patna: Matba' Hanafiyya, n.d.), pp. 2–3.

[35] Unfortunately I have been unable to learn anything of Qazi 'Abd ul-Wahid's life, as he is not included in the standard tazkiras. A recent book by an Ahl-e Sunnat follower states that Qazi 'Abd ul-Wahid spent over fifty thousand rupees in publishing and distributing anti-Nadwa materials in the late 1890s. Badr ud-Din Ahmad Gorakhpuri, *Sawanih-e A'la Hazrat*, 4th reprint (Ahmadnagar, Bihar: Madrasa Ahl-e Sunnat Gulshan Riza, 1986), p. 147. Whatever the truth of this estimate, his wealth was evidently considerable.

madrasa came to be associated solely with Na'im ud-Din. Its name changed to the Madrasa Na'imiyya. In time, it acquired local fame and grew larger, until in 1933–34 it became big enough to merit the title of Jam'iyya (a 'centre' of learning). It had a Dar al-Ifta and several teachers.[36] The school, located in the heart of the city of Muradabad amidst narrow lanes and bustling commerce, presently consists of a large handsome building surrounding a central courtyard. A mosque and Na'im ud-Din's mausoleum occupy a prominent position there.

Na'im ud-Din and many of his students were associated in various ways with the Dar al-'Ulum Hizb al-Ahnaf of Lahore, several of the Jam'iyya Na'imiyya's students going on to the Hizb al-Ahnaf as teachers.[37] Its founder, Sayyid Didar 'Ali Alwari (1856–1935), belonged to the Chishti Nizami order.[38] His teachers included eminent 'ulama' and sufi shaikhs such as Irshad Husain Rampuri and Shah Fazl-e Rahman Ganj Muradabadi. Ahmad Riza also gave him a sanad in fiqh, hadis, and other disciplines.[39] From 1912 to 1916 he was in Lahore as Shaikh al-Hadis at the Dar al-'Ulum Nu'maniyya (founded in 1887). After a period at Agra, he returned to Lahore in 1920, this time as khatib of the Wazir Khan mosque in that city. In 1924, he instituted the Markazi Anjuman Hizb al-Ahnaf (Central Association of the Hizb al-Ahnaf), to set policy and administer the Dar al-'Ulum Hizb al-Ahnaf, which began initially at the Wazir Khan mosque. Didar 'Ali was joined by several fellow 'ulama' in teaching the dars-e nizami syllabus. Although details of the subsequent

[36] Mu'in ud-Din Na'imi, 'Tazkira al-Ma'ruf Hayat-e Sadr al-Afazil', *Sawad-e A'zam* (Lahore: Na'imi Dawakhana, 1378/1959), pp. 20–1. See Epilogue for a biographical sketch of Na'im ud-Din Muradabadi.

[37] In 1948, when Na'im ud-Din visited Pakistan, he was the guest of 'ulama' associated with the Hizb al-Ahnaf. Ibid., p. 29. A list of his students, including those who taught at the Hizb al-Ahnaf, is given on pp. 20–1.

[38] Sayyid Mahmud Ahmad Rizwi, *Sayyidi Abu'l Barakat* (Lahore: Tabligh Department, Hizb al-Ahnaf, 1979), p. 117. The author is Didar 'Ali's grandson.

Didar 'Ali belonged to a family which had migrated from Mashhad, Iran, probably in the eighteenth century, and settled down in Awadh. After some time in Bilgram and Farrukhabad, the family moved to the Hindu princely state of Alwar in Rajputana. Ibid., p. 117.

[39] Ibid., pp. 121–4.

history of the school are not known, the Dar al-'Ulum later acquired buildings of its own, and began specialized departments in preaching (tabligh) and debate (*munazara*), for example, in addition to the regular classes. There was ample financial support for the school from influential Panjab pirs such as Pir Jama'at 'Ali Shah Alipuri,[40] with whom Didar 'Ali had a close relationship. As one writer says, 'hundreds of thousands of 'ulama' and teachers were born here, and today [1979] there is probably no town in Pakistan which does not have 'ulama' trained at the Hizb al-Ahnaf'.[41] Another Ahl-e Sunnat 'alim said of Didar 'Ali that had he not taught and preached in Lahore, the whole Panjab would today be full of 'Wahhabis'.[42]

This last remark draws attention to the competitive atmosphere in which the Hizb al-Ahnaf and other Ahl-e Sunnat madrasas were established and operated in the early twentieth century. A new emphasis on tabligh or preaching at this time is the most obvious indication of this. Tabligh was generally directed against fellow Muslims, but sometimes against Hindus as well, as during the anti-Shuddhi campaigns of 'ulama' of all persuasions in the United Provinces.[43] Even the addition of a Dar al-Ifta to madrasas of the time was competitive, for it was through the fatawa produced by the 'ulama' of different movements that they made known their stand on controversial issues and rebutted those of their rivals. Ahmad Riza, for instance, expressed his views for the most part in a daily stream of fatawa going out to people throughout British India, and beyond.

To sum up, the early twentieth century saw a proliferation of new madrasas of the Ahl-e Sunnat 'ulama' throughout north India. Unlike other renewal movements of the time, the Ahl-e Sunnat had

[40] Gilmartin writes of Pir Jama'at 'Ali that he donated 'hundreds of rupees to the madrasa Naumaniya and the anjuman Hizb al-Ahnaf'. Gilmartin, *Empire and Islam*, p. 61.

[41] Rizwi, *Sayyidi Abu'l Barakat*, p. 127.

[42] Quoted in Khwaja Razi Haidar, *Tazkira-e Muhaddis Surati*, p. 309.

[43] This was directed against the Arya Samaj, which in the 1920s began a movement for the reconversion of Hindus who had become Muslim back to Hinduism. For details, see G. R. Thursby, *Hindu-Muslim Relations in British India: A Study of Controversy, Conflict, and Communal Movements in Northern India 1923–1928* (Leiden: E. J. Brill, 1975).

no central institution to compare, for example, with the Dar al-'Ulum at Deoband. Rather, individual 'ulama' took the initiative in founding madrasas in their towns with help from wealthy patrons where possible. Often small and ephemeral, these madrasas were nevertheless instrumental in creating a network of personal links between 'ulama' and in producing new leaders. As did rival movements, the Ahl-e Sunnat madrasas too used novel organizational methods such as a fixed syllabus, annual examinations, the award of prizes to students with the best records, the publication of an annual report, and the institution of specialized departments for preaching, publication, and debate. The appeal to the local public for financial support was also an innovation, pioneered by the Dar al-'Ulum of Deoband.[44]

That debate and rivalry amongst the 'ulama' were central to the formation of Ahl-e Sunnat ideology, becomes particularly apparent from publications, oral debates, or voluntary associations (anjumans, *majlis*es) in support of particular causes. I turn now to a selective survey of some of these institutions.

Printing Presses and Publications

Although a number of Indian businessmen had owned their own printing presses as early as the 1820s and 1830s, the 1880s saw a dramatic increase in these, with a consequent spurt in Indian-language publishing. Till then, printing technology had been controlled, for the most part, by Christian missionaries and other Europeans who used it for the promulgation of Christian doctrine or to publish small editions of scholarly translations in English of Indian classical texts.[45] With the dramatic increase of Indian-owned presses in the 1880s, however, the north Indian 'ulama' (and Hindu religious leaders as well) began to make full use of printing to spread their ideas and reach out to wider audiences. As the 'ulama' wrote and published in Urdu, the language of the north Indian élite (both Hindu and Muslim in the mid-nineteenth century, though identified

[44] Metcalf, *Islamic Revival*, p. 94.

[45] Frances W. Pritchett, *Marvelous Encounters: Folk Romance in Urdu and Hindi* (Delhi: Manohar, 1985), pp. 20–5.

increasingly with Muslims alone by the end of that century), their writings contributed to the creation of a new corpus of Urdu literature.[46] In so far as religious debate was concerned, the printed word became *the* most important medium through which late nineteenth-century Muslims argued with one another. Because of the wide practice of reading aloud, a single copy of a book or pamphlet in the hands of a literate member of a community was sufficient to ensure that the ideas expressed therein became known to a widening circle of people.[47]

In Bareilly, the Ahl-e Sunnat had two major presses in the late nineteenth century, Hasani Press, owned by Ahmad Riza's nephew Hasnain Riza, and the Matba' Ahl-e Sunnat wa Jama'at managed (but probably not owned) by Amjad 'Ali A'zami (d. 1948), a close follower of Ahmad Riza. Between them they appear to have published all Ahmad Riza's important fatawa in the late nineteenth and early twentieth centuries. The earliest works date to the late 1870s. Books varied in length from as little as fifteen pages to several hundred, though fifty or sixty was probably closer to the average. The front cover, bordered on the corners and sides with a floral design, generally gave a brief résumé of the contents of the work at the top and recommended it for spiritual benefit. Then followed the title, chosen with great care: not only did the middle and the end usually rhyme, but it was also frequently a means of poking fun at an opponent.[48] In addition, the numerical values of the letters (in

[46] See Metcalf, *Islamic Revival,* pp. 199–210.

[47] See ibid., p. 201. On the orality of religious texts in the Hindu and Muslim contexts, see William A. Graham, *Beyond the Written Word: Oral Aspects of Scripture in the History of Religion* (Cambridge: Cambridge University Press, 1987), pp. 68–77, 88–92, and passim. Also see Dale F. Eickelman, 'The Art of Memory. Islamic Education and its Social Reproduction', *Comparative Studies in Society and History*, 20 (1978), 485–516, for a related discussion on the importance of memory and of oral repetition in the learning process in Muslim societies.

[48] For example, in 1314/1896 Hasan Riza (Ahmad Riza's brother) wrote an anti-Nadwa work entitled *Nadwe ka Tija—Rudad Som ka Natija* (The Nadwa's *Tija*—The Result of its Third Report). Here, not only do *tija* and *natija* in the title rhyme, but there is a play on the word *tija,* which is the third day after a person's death. Hasan Riza clearly implies that in light of the Nadwa's third report it is 'dead' as an institution. Most of Ahmad Riza's works had titles in this style, with or without the implied irony, and usually with heavy use of Arabic.

accordance with the *abjad* system whereby each letter of the alphabet is assigned a number) had to add up to the year of the writing of the book.

Print runs at the Hasani Press and Matba' Ahl-e Sunnat ranged from five hundred to a thousand copies. Occasionally a book ran to three editions: for example, Ahmad Riza's *Al-Kaukab al-Shahabiyya*, printed in 1894, in which he argued that although Shah Isma'il Dehlawi (d. 1831), leader of the Tariqa-e Muhammadiyya movement, was a 'Wahhabi' and a kafir, it was best to refrain from calling him a kafir.[49] The popularity of writings against the Deobandis (prominent among those styled 'Wahhabi' in the Ahl-e Sunnat literature) is indicated by the printing history of another fatwa by Ahmad Riza entitled *Ilhaq al-Wahhabiyyin 'ala Tauhin Qubur al-Muslimin* (The Wahhabis Join in Slandering Muslim Graves). Originally written in 1904, it went through a fourth printing, of a thousand copies, in 1928. The topic, the alleged disrespect of Deobandis toward graves, was obviously of interest to Ahl-e Sunnat followers; at a price of less than a rupee the reading public must have found the book affordable.[50]

In the late 1890s both presses published a large number of fatawa by Ahmad Riza against the Nadwat al-'Ulama'—it is estimated that he wrote about two hundred on this theme alone. In 1920 Hasnain Riza began a monthly journal called *Al-Riza*, containing articles by Ahmad Riza and other 'ulama' on a variety of topics. Some of Ahmad Riza's writings were serialized in the journal. It also contained na'ts, controversial articles in defence of milad and 'urs, as well as others decrying the shortage of madrasas. The annual cost of the journal was two rupees. Unfortunately we have no readership lists or other indication of the circulation of the journal.

Such information is available, however, for another Ahl-e Sunnat journal, the *Tuhfa-e Hanafiyya* (also called *Makhzan-e Tahqiq*). This

[49] The Ahl-e Sunnat position on the Tariqa-e Muhammadiyya movement, and on 'Wahhabis' generally, is the subject of Chapter VIII of this study.

[50] Ahmad Riza Khan, *Ilhaq al-Wahhabiyyin 'ala Tauhin Qubur al-Muslimin* (Bareilly: Hasani Press, 1928). In those cases where the price of a book or pamphlet is stated on the bottom left-hand corner of the title page it is generally in the range of one to ten annas. (Sixteen annas made up a rupee.)

was started in 1897–98 by Qazi 'Abd ul-Wahid Azimabadi of Patna (founder as noted earlier of the Madrasa Hanafiyya) in the context of the Ahl-e Sunnat's campaign against the Nadwat al-'Ulama'. A monthly consisting usually of forty-four pages, its stated purposes were to strengthen Islam and the *mazhab* (lit., school of law, here religious orientation within the Hanafi school) of the Ahl-e Sunnat, and to rebut their enemies. It contained articles on *'aqa'id* (tenets of Muslim belief), fiqh and hadis, stories from the lives of the prophets and the first caliphs, and of course those in rebuttal of rival 'ulama' groups, particularly the Nadwa. 'Abd ul-Wahid wrote most of the articles, though others contributed as well, among them well-known 'ulama' such as Maulana 'Abd ul-Qayyum Badayuni (founder of the Madrasa Shams al-'Ulum).[51]

Regular lists of buyers and donors published by the *Tuhfa-e Hanafiyya* reveal that the journal had a subscription list of about two hundred people in its early years, growing slowly but steadily to approximately two hundred and fifty. Both the geographic spread and the social composition of the subscribers are indicated in these lists. Geographically, the *Tuhfa* reached out to people in an impressive diversity of places throughout India. An early published list includes large cities such as Ahmadabad, Bombay, and Haidarabad, as well as district towns in the United Provinces (mainly the western districts of Bareilly, Badayun, Etah, and Bulandshahr), and of course Bihar (districts Muzaffarpur, Darbhanga, Munger, Patna, Shahabad, and Gaya in north Bihar).[52] Seventy-two names (out of 119) in this list are from Bihar; the U.P. comes next (23); then Bombay (12), Ahmadabad (5), and Haidarabad (3). In social terms, we find a heavy representation of the educated and well-to-do, not surprising for subscribers to a journal emanating from a section of the 'ulama'. Nevertheless, the number of those holding positions of authority in the British administration, or possessors of landed title, is noteworthy. Forty-two persons were identified as 'ra'is' or 'ra'is-e a'zam', persons of social standing in their towns; seven were legal

[51] The foregoing paragraph is based on a perusal of early volumes of the journal. See, e.g., *Tuhfa-e Hanafiyya* (Patna: Matba' Hanafiyya), 1:4–5 (Sha'ban and Ramazan 1315/Dec. 1897–Jan. 1898).

[52] Ibid., appendix at end of volume, after p. 44.

representatives of various descriptions (a barrister, a subjudge, a wakil or authorized public pleader, and four *mukhtars* or legal agents). There were also a station master, a doctor, two students in Western-style colleges in Patna, and a couple of tahsildars or revenue collectors. In addition, several munshis (writers, secretaries), qazis (judges), muhtamims of madrasas and imams of mosques were among the subscribers.[53]

It would probably be mistaken to assume on the basis of this and similar lists of subscribers and donors to the *Tuhfa* that all these people self-consciously identified themselves with the Ahl-e Sunnat movement. Keeping in mind the strong anti-Nadwa platform of the *Tuhfa*, some of its subscribers were, conceivably, interested in the journal as a validation of their own views. Nevertheless, we can identify a certain core group of 'ulama' and others whose involvement in Ahl-e Sunnat affairs was prolonged and multifaceted. These included the 'ulama' of Badayun, Bareilly, Pilibhit (listed as buyers in subsequent issues of the *Tuhfa*),[54] and Patna. The *Tuhfa* appears to have ceased publication soon after the death of 'Abd ul-Wahid in 1908.[55]

A publication of a different kind, and one that is an important source for the late nineteenth-and early twentieth-century history of the Ahl-e Sunnat movement, was a newspaper briefly mentioned above, the *Dabdaba-e Sikandari* (an untranslatable title, meaning something like 'Alexander's awesome majesty').[56] It began weekly publication around 1864 in Rampur.[57] Its editor and sub-editor in the early twentieth century, Maulanas Muhammad

[53] Ibid.

[54] *Tuhfa-e Hanafiyya*, 1:6 (Shawwal [?] 1315/1898), 2 (of appendix at end of journal).

[55] The last issue I was able to trace is 13 (Safar 1327/February 1910).

[56] The significance to be attached to this royal-sounding title is not clear. It suggests that the paper enjoyed the nawabs' patronage, though we have no information on this either way. Perhaps too much should not be read into the title: in Badayun, a British Indian district town (not a 'princely state' as Rampur was), a newspaper called *Zu'l-Qarnain* ('The Two-Horned', an epithet for Alexander the Great) was started some time in the nineteenth century.

[57] The year 1864 is indicated by a remark in one of the issues dated 1910, showing that the paper had been in continuous operation for forty-six years. *Dabdaba-e Sikandari*, 46:18 (May 16, 1910), 1.

Faruq Hasan[58] and Muhammad Fazl-e Hasan respectively, were followers of the Chishti Sabiri line of sufis, though also of the Qadiri order. They appear to have had a Dar al-Isha'at, or distribution centre, in a khanqah at Rampur, the Khanqah-e Sabiriyya.[59]

That the paper was pro-British is indicated by an editorial statement that by means of interesting news articles, the *Dabdaba-e Sikandari* had been 'creating unity (*ittihad*) between the people (*ra'ya*) and the government' ever since it began publication.[60] Its range of reporting was broad, covering events both primarily 'political' (such as the process of constitutional devolution of power to Indians in the early 1920s) and 'religious' (descriptions of periodic 'urs celebrations, for example), though of course much that was newsworthy fell between these two categories. On the political front, it covered news events in Rampur, in British India, in the Muslim world generally, and in Europe as well. In the early 1900s, for instance, it reported constitutional changes in the Ottoman empire and the building of the Hijaz Railway.[61] In the second decade of the new century it carried articles about the fate of Ottoman possessions in the Balkans, and efforts by Indian Muslim groups such as the Anjuman-e Khuddam-e Ka'ba (Society of the Servants of the Ka'ba) to protect the Hijaz from non-Muslim aggression.[62] In short, it kept its readers well-informed on local and world events, particularly those of concern to Muslims.

The editors' interest in issues relating to din was evident in numerous

[58] Described also as its owner (*malik*). See *Dabdaba-e Sikandari*, 52:13 (February 7, 1916), 3.

[59] *Dabdaba-e Sikandari*, 49:31 (July 14, 1913), 3. Unfortunately I have no further information on the connection between the khanqah and the *Dabdaba-e Sikandari* or its editors.

[60] *Dabdaba-e Sikandari*, 46:18 (May 16, 1910), 1. The nawabs of Rampur, as noted in Chapter I, were also pro-British, as were, indeed, most princely states during the late nineteenth and early twentieth centuries.

[61] See, e.g., *Dabdaba-e Sikandari*, 44:26 (August 1–3, 1908), 9–10, 12–13; 44:35 (October 5, 1908), 6; 45:22 (June 12, 1909), 3–5, on Sultan 'Abd al-Hamid.

[62] See, e.g., *Dabdaba-e Sikandari*, 49:36 (August 18, 1913), 12–13, on the Balkan wars; 50:44 (September 28, 1914), 3, for a fatwa by the Ahl-e Sunnat on the Anjuman-e Khuddam-e Ka'ba. The Anjuman was founded by Maulana 'Abd ul-Bari Firangi Mahali in 1913, but was opposed by Ahmad Riza on specific grounds. See Chapter IX below for details.

ways, ranging from periodic ʻurs announcements (Chishti, Qadiri, or other) to more substantive coverage of dispute and debate among the ʻulama'. During World War I, for instance, the paper gave wide coverage to a divisive debate among the Ahl-e Sunnat ʻulama' on a matter concerning the second *azan* (call to prayer).[63] Its respect for Ahmad Riza and other Ahl-e Sunnat ʻulama' was considerable. This was most dramatically reflected in November 1910 in the decision by Munshi Muhammad Fazl-e Hasan, the sub-editor, to start a column called *Chashma-e Dar al-Ifta-e Bareilly* (Fount of Bareilly's Dar al-Ifta) in which questions (*istifta*) from the public to the Ahl-e Sunnat ʻulama' at Bareilly were reproduced with their corresponding answers (fatawa).[64] The *Chashma* was generally accorded two full pages out of the paper's total of sixteen. From November 1910 to February 1912, two hundred questions had been answered in this section of the *Dabdaba-e Sikandari*. The answers were given for the most part by one ʻUbaid un-Nabi' Nawab Mirza ʻAli, not by Ahmad Riza.

The *Dabdaba-e Sikandari* regularly reported, in addition, Ahl-e Sunnat events, whether convocations at the Madrasa Manzar al-Islam at Bareilly, an ʻurs at Marahra, or a newly formed anjuman of the Ahl-e Sunnat elsewhere. Ahmad Riza himself sometimes contributed a naʻt to its columns. The paper also published annually before Ramazan a detailed chart worked out by Ahmad Riza and Zafar ud-Din Bihari, of the exact times of sunrise, sunset, and the daily evening prayers on each day of the fasting month, for people in different U.P. towns.[65]

Voluntary Associations

Given its sympathetic interest in Ahl-e Sunnat argument and debate, the *Dabdaba-e Sikandari* is a helpful guide to mapping the movement's range and diversity of organizational activity in fields

[63] See Chapter VI for details.

[64] See *Dabdaba-e Sikandari*, 46:43 (November 7, 1910), 3, for the first occurrence of this column.

[65] See, e.g., *Dabdaba-e Sikandari*, 44:35 (October 5, 1908), 14; 46:35 (September 12, 1910), 8.

other than education during the early twentieth century. One of these, common to reform and renewal movements across the religious spectrum in British India at this time, was the creation of voluntary associations or societies seeking to promote various group interests. All were organized along 'modern' lines, with presidents, secretaries, annual reports, and so on. As Jones says of the Arya Samaj in the Panjab,

> Sabhas, samajes, clubs, anjumans, and societies proliferated with amazing speed. These associations in turn established schools, colleges, libraries, reading rooms, orphanages, publication departments, and presses—a universe of social organization. Battles were fought, victories won, and defeats suffered according to the proper forms of parliamentary procedure.[66]

The proliferation of such societies among early twentieth-century Muslims is clear from the array of names appearing in the *Dabdaba-e Sikandari*. Thus, in 1906 Hakim Ajmal Khan of Delhi created the Tibbi Conference, and in 1910 followed up with the All-India Ayurvedic and Unani Tibbia Conference.[67] Around 1908 a group of Shi'is began an All-India Shi'a Conference;[68] in 1910 Muslims from Panjab, the U.P., and Bengal gathered at Badayun for their first Urdu Conference;[69] in 1913 Maulana 'Abd ul-Bari and associated 'ulama' started the Anjuman-e Khuddam-e Ka'ba noted above.

The Ahl-e Sunnat too had their anjumans and conferences. In 1909, a pir of the Barkatiyya family issued an invitation to 'sufi pirs (*masha'ikh*) of the Ahl-e Sunnat' to attend a two-day planning committee (*intizami committee*) meeting to be held during the

[66] Kenneth W. Jones, *Arya Dharm: Hindu Consciousness in 19th-Century Punjab* (Berkeley: University of California Press, 1976), pp. 318–19.

[67] For the background to these medical organizations and on the madrasa also founded by Hakim Ajmal Khan, see Metcalf, 'Hakim Ajmal Khan', in Frykenberg (ed.), *Delhi Through the Ages*: pp. 299–315. Reports of annual meetings and other events related to these organizations appeared in the *Dabdaba-e Sikandari*. See, e.g., 46:41 (October 24, 1910), 6; 46:42 (October 31, 1910), 6, dealing with a Tibbi Conference meeting; 54:19 (February 25, 1918), 6–7, reporting on an All-India Vedic and Tibbi Conference annual meeting at Bombay.

[68] *Dabdaba-e Sikandari*, 46:13 (April 11, 1910), 10.

[69] Ibid., 46:12 (April 4, 1910), 6.

forthcoming ʻurs for Muʻin ud-Din Chishti (popularly known as Khwaja Gharib Nawaz) at Ajmer.[70] As he pointed out, this ʻurs was always well-attended, and holding the meeting there would therefore result in the new organization of pirs quickly becoming well known. Its purpose was very broadly formulated as the need to instill a 'new spirituality' (*taza ruhaniyyat*) in Islam, which the writer described as currently 'oppressed' (*mazlum*).[71] The brief announcement in the *Dabdaba-e Sikandari* tells us that the annual ʻurs had acquired an important new function as a forum for sufis to meet for purposes entirely distinct from devotion to the pir whose death anniversary was being commemorated.[72]

In the second decade of the twentieth century, the *Dabdaba-e Sikandari* reported annual meetings of organizationally distinct associations called the 'Anjuman-e Ahl-e Sunnat' in Karachi,[73] Bareilly and Muradabad.[74] In each case the anjumans seem to have been related to the Ahl-e Sunnat madrasas in their respective towns. The report of the Bareilly anjuman tells us that the meetings consisted of

70 Ibid., 45:23 (June 28, 1909), 3–4. On the Ajmer shrine and ʻurs, see Currie, *The Shrine and Cult of Muʻin al-din Chishti of Ajmer*. Also see Syed Liyaqat Hussain Moini, 'Rituals and Customary Practices at the Dargah of Ajmer', in Troll (ed.), *Muslim Shrines in India*, pp. 60–75.

71 *Dabdaba-e Sikandari*, 45:23 (June 28, 1909), 3. The announcement was made by one Sayyid Irtiza Husain Qadiri Barkati, of Marahra and Sitapur.

72 This development is not too well documented, though we have some passing references to the ʻurs as an occasion for public statements or meetings on matters of current concern. Gilmartin, e.g., cites an instance when 'a radical ʻalim of strong reformist leanings . . . issue[d] a public challenge at the Sial ʻurs for a debate with the Pir of Golra, who opposed the radical phase of the Khilafat agitation' (*Empire and Islam*, p. 64). In Marahra, we see the ʻurs being an occasion for an association meeting in 1946, when Muhammad Miyan cretaed an organization called the 'Jama ʻat-e Ahl-e Sunnat', opposing the Pakistan idea. The Jamaʻat met during the annual ʻurs for Muhammad Miyan's father. See the Epilogue below for details.

73 The founder of this anjuman, and of the associated madrasa, was one Ghulam-e Rasul, an imam in the Jameʻ Masjid at Karachi. In a letter to the *Dabdaba-e Sikandari*, he referred to Ahmad Riza as the Mujaddid of the fourteenth century, thereby indicating that he considered himself a follower. A visit to the madrasa by a disciple of the Barkatiyya pirs in May-June 1912 signalled the approval of the leaders of the Ahl-e Sunnat. See *Dabdaba-e Sikandari*, 48:20 (May 6, 1912), 7–8; 48:24 (June 3, 1912), 7; 59:22 (May 12, 1913), 5–6.

74 Ibid., 49:31 (July 14, 1913), 6; 50:32 (July 6, 1914), 3; 52:32 (June 9, 1916), 4.

na'ts, sermons, and speeches, proceedings which also marked such occasions as 'urs and annual dastar-bandi ceremonies at the Manzar al-Islam.[75] In Muradabad, on the other hand, the anjuman meeting included a debate with some Arya Samajis, a field in which Na'im ud-Din's skills were highly regarded among the Ahl-e Sunnat.[76]

In 1916, the *Dabdaba-e Sikandari* announced the formation of a 'Halqa-e Ahl-e Sunnat' in Sikandra Rao, a town in Aligarh district about 40 kilometres southwest of Marahra.[77] The term *halqa* (circle) suggests a group of sufis engaged in *dhikr* (repetition of religious formulae).[78] However, this halqa, while expressly stating its respect for sufis and sufi institutions,[79] also sought to defend the Ahl-e Sunnat vision of din against its critics, both Muslim and Hindu. The *nazim-e a'la* (chief administrator) of the halqa was one Sayyid Muhammad Ghulam Qutub ud-Din, a preacher from Sahaswan, Badayun district.[80] Not surprisingly, therefore, the halqa displayed a particular interest in preaching: thirty-five preachers (*wa'ezin*) were said to have undertaken to do tabligh on the 'duties (*ahkam*) of Islam'.[81] Their preaching tours were reported periodically in the *Dabdaba* during 1917, but seem to have fallen off thereafter.

Much more ambitious in scope, and more far-reaching in influence

[75] Ibid., 49:31 (July 14, 1913), 6.

[76] See the biographical sketch of Na'im ud-Din in the Epilogue for more details.

[77] *Dabdaba-e Sikandari*, 53:2 (November 6, 1916), 3.

[78] See Annemarie Schimmel, *Mystical Dimensions of Islam* (Chapel Hill: University of North Carolina Press, 1975), p. 176.

[79] For instance, one of its purposes was 'to follow the tariqa (way) of the sufi masters'. Among its principles were the following: 'It is incumbent on every member [of the Halqa] that he be a follower of the tariqa of the sufis', and 'No one will have the right to criticize the old tariqa of the derwishes and the customs of the khanqah'. *Dabdaba-e Sikandari*, 53:2 (November 6, 1916), 6.

[80] He was commonly known by the unlikely name of 'Pardesiji Brahmachari', 'a Brahmin ascetic from foreign parts'. While not of Ahmad Riza's inner circle of followers, Ghulam Qutub ud-Din Brahmachari played a leadership role in various Ahl-e Sunnat activities. For instance, in 1920 he presided over the fourth annual meeting of the Madrasa Ahl-e Sunnat wa Jama'at, Muradabad (precursor, presumably, to the Jam'iyya Na'imiyya). *Al-Sawad al-A'zam* (Muradabad), 1:4 (Rajab 1338/April 1920), unnumbered page facing p. 32; in 1924, he was involved in the work of the Jama'at Riza-e Mustafa, on which see below.

[81] *Dabdaba-e Sikandari*, 53:2 (November 6, 1916), 6.

than any of the activities mentioned so far, were two organizations created in the early 1920s by 'ulama' at the centre of the Ahl-e Sunnat movement. In 1921 they created the 'Ansar al-Islam', or 'Helpers of Islam' (invoking, no doubt deliberately, the 'Ansar' of Muhammad's day, who helped him set up the first Muslim state in Medina), an organization dedicated to helping the Ottomans after their defeat in World War I.[82] In 1924, or perhaps earlier, the Jama'at-e Riza-e Mustafa (Society Pleasing to the Prophet Muhammad) was formed with the immediate purpose of reconverting to Islam large groups of people who had recently embraced Hinduism under the influence of the Arya Samaj.[83] Unlike all the preceding organizations, including the Ansar al-Islam, the Jama'at-e Riza-e Mustafa was quite long-lived, records of its meetings being available for as late as 1957.[84]

It would serve little purpose to describe the Jama'at-e Riza-e Mustafa in any detail here. Suffice it to say that in it we see, as in the other Ahl-e Sunnat endeavours, organized compartmentalization of different activities (preaching, publications, debate, finance, and so on), as well as competition with rival groups of 'ulama' for influence. This spirit of competition is evident in the following sentences in an annual report, for instance, where the role of the Tablighi Jama'at, affiliated to Deoband, is deprecated:

> It is entirely fitting to say that the boldness and courage of the Jama'at-e Riza-e Mustafa and its unhesitating entry into the field were an inspiration to many [branches of the] Tablighi Jama'at to enter the field as well. They did so when the Jama'at-e Riza-e Mustafa had cleared the field, and had prepared a course of action.[85]

[82] The collapse of the Ottoman empire after World War I and its impact on Indian Muslims of various persuasions is dealt with in some detail in Chapter IX of this study. The Ansar al-Islam is discussed in that context, in relation as well to other Indian Muslim organizations of relief such as the Anjuman-e Khuddam-e Ka'ba, mentioned earlier in this chapter.

[83] The date of the Jama'at-e Riza-e Mustafa's founding is in some doubt because a letter dated April/May 1920 by Ahmad Riza Khan suggests that he had blessed the new organization at that time; however, it does not appear to have been active until 1924 or thereabouts. The letter is reproduced in *Rudad-e Jama'at-e Riza-e Mustafa (1342/1924)*, 'Khutba', pp. 21–2. No publication details are indicated.

[84] The Jama'at may of course have continued to exist even beyond this date.

[85] *Rudad-e Jama'at-e Riza-e Mustafa*, p. 19.

Yet the Jama'at-e Riza-e Mustafa, for all its organization and efforts in the field, was in fact greatly overshadowed by the Tablighi Jama'at. The Jama'at-e Riza-e Mustafa's apparent need to set off its achievements against those of the Tablighi Jama'at would seem to confirm this.[86]

Oral Debates

Competition between rival Muslim movements was also expressed in oral debate or munazara, a phenomenon well documented in the scholarly literature.[87] As Metcalf has indicated, most oral debates in the mid-nineteenth century had taken place between Muslims and Christian missionaries (whose methods of preaching were a model for the tabligh efforts of later Muslims).[88] As early as the 1830s, however, the 'ulama' were debating one another. The debate between Shah Isma'il and Fazl-e Haqq Khairabadi (1797–1861) on the subject of imkan-e nazir ('the possibility of an equal'), that is to say, whether Allah had the power to create another prophet like Muhammad, was famous in 'ulama' circles.[89] It foreshadowed later debates along the same lines between the Ahl-e Sunnat and the Deobandis in the late nineteenth century and thereafter.

By the 1880s and 1890s the issues debated by the Ahl-e Sunnat

[86] On the Tablighi Jama'at's efforts in the anti-Shuddhi campaign, see Anwarul Haq, *The Faith Movement of Mawlana Muhammad Ilyas;* and S. Abul Hasan Ali Nadwi, *Life and Mission of Maulana Mohammad Ilyas*, tr. Mohammad Asif Kidwai (Lucknow: Academy of Islamic Research and Publications, 1979). The Shuddhi movement itself is described by Thursby, *Hindu-Muslim Relations in British India*, pp. 136–58, and passim.

[87] See Rafiuddin Ahmed, *The Bengal Muslims 1871–1906: A Quest for Identity* (Delhi: Oxford University Press, 1981), pp. 74–6, and passim, for discussion of the institution of *bahas* or debate among Bengal Muslims; Metcalf, *Islamic Revival*, pp. 215–34, has an illuminating discussion of debate in all its aspects, with reference to the north Indian 'ulama'; Friedmann, *Prophecy Continuous*, pp. 4–10, discusses Ahmadi debates with Christians, Arya Samajis, and Muslims in the Panjab.

[88] Metcalf, *Islamic Revival*, pp. 215–18.

[89] See Ibid., pp. 65–6, for an account of the two positions taken. The issues involved were Allah's transcendence and power on the one hand and the Prophet's uniqueness on the other. Ahmad Riza's father, Naqi 'Ali Khan, participated in debate on the same issue in the 1870s against an 'alim of the Ahl-e Hadis. See Rahman 'Ali, *Tazkira-e 'Ulama'-e Hind*, p. 531.

had become quite standard. Against the Deobandis, they frequently argued that the Prophet had knowledge of the unseen (*'ilm-e ghaib*), or 'proved' the *kufr* (unbelief) contained in one of several books by Deobandi 'ulama'.[90] With the Ahl-e Hadis, they argued on the absolute necessity of taqlid (following one of the four major Sunni law schools), and with the Nadwa, on the impermissibility of associating with 'bad' Muslims.[91] They also debated with the Arya Samaj on subjects such as the createdness of the Qur'an, Muhammad's personal excellence, or the 'falsity' of the Hindu doctrine of transmigration (*taṇasukh*).[92]

While Ahmad Riza never engaged in oral debates (preferring to do so in writing instead), some of his followers were known for their skill as debaters. Among them, notably, were Na'im ud-Din Muradabadi and Hashmat 'Ali (d. 1960). It was said that whenever a well-known opponent challenged the Ahl-e Sunnat to debate Ahmad Riza would send Na'im ud-Din a telegram, asking him to be the Ahl-e Sunnat representative (wakil) on the occasion.[93] His debating skills were said to be so good that even Swami Shraddhanand, leader of the Arya Samaj's Shuddhi movement, shied away from testing his skills against those of Na'im ud-Din:

> When Shraddhanand began his *fitna-e irtidad* (mischief of apostacy, i.e., the Shuddhi movement) . . . Hazrat [Na'im ud-Din] invited him to a debate. He accepted the invitation. Hazrat went to Delhi [to debate with Shraddhanand]. He ran from there and came to Bareilly. Hazrat went to Bareilly and challenged him to debate. He ran from there to Lucknow. When Hazrat went to Lucknow, he went to Patna. Hazrat followed him to Patna, but he went to Calcutta. Hazrat went there too, and caught him. He then clearly refused to debate.[94]

As for Hashmat 'Ali, known in Ahl-e Sunnat circles as an eminent

[90] See Chapter VIII below.

[91] On this, see Chapter VII.

[92] On debate with the Aryas, see, e.g., Ghulam Mu'in ud-Din Na'imi, 'Tazkira al-Ma'ruf Hayat-e Sadr al-Afazil', *Sawad-e A'zam*, 2 (Lahore: Na'imi Dawakhana, 1378/19–26 June 1959), 7–9; Zafar ud-Din Bihari, *Hayat-e A'la Hazrat*, pp. 218–19 (in which Ahmad Riza reportedly converted an Arya Samaji).

[93] 'Tazkira al-Ma'ruf Hayat-e Sadr al-Afazil', pp. 10–11.

[94] Ibid., p. 9.

munazir or debater, his biography gives the following account of his first debate:

> In 1919–20, [Ahmad Riza] sent this young man to debate with [a Deobandi 'alim], khalifa of [Maulana Ashraf 'Ali] Thanawi, at Haldwani Mandi, all by himself. He was only nineteen years old. He harassed his opponent (*naak chane chabwa diye*) [lit., 'made him chew gram with his nose'] and silenced his argument in favour of Thanawi's kufr-laden *Hifz al-Iman*. And on the question of 'ilm-e ghaib, [the opponent] was left astounded. This was his first debate . . . . After successfully defeating his opponent, he returned to [Ahmad Riza, who] was very pleased with his report, embraced him, and prayed for him. He gave him the name (*kunyat*) 'Abu'l Fath' ['the father of success'], as well as a turban and tunic (*angarkha*), and five rupees. He also said that henceforward [Hashmat 'Ali] would get five rupees every month. In this way he honoured him. And, by the grace of Allah, [Ahmad Riza's] favour was always with him, and he won a debate on every occasion.[95]

As Metcalf notes, there was no serious intellectual exchange on such occasions. As each competitor left the debate convinced that his side had 'won', that his view was morally 'right' and the rival opinion correspondingly 'wrong', all participants derived psychological satisfaction from the exchange[96]—the chief purpose of the debate, Metcalf suggests. The result was that a person's identification with his chosen group was intensified.

These debates, being social events often attended by large public audiences, were characterized by an element of competitive showmanship and theatre. Ahmed describes the atmosphere surrounding a late nineteenth-century bahas in a Bengali Muslim village as that of a 'fair . . . as if suddenly a city had sprung up in the middle of a jungle'.[97] Several factors lent drama to the event. These included the imposition of extravagant conditions on the loser (for instance, that he would embrace the views of his opponent if he lost[98]), and the occasional invocation by the competitors of the curse of God

[95] Muhammad Mahbub 'Ali Khan, *Buland Paya Hayat-e Hashmat 'Ali* (Kanpur: Arakin-e Bazm-e Qadiri Rizwi, 1380/1960–61), pp. 7–8.

[96] Metcalf, *Islamic Revival*, pp. 215–16, 219.

[97] Ahmed, *Bengal Muslims*, p. 79.

[98] Ahmad Riza said that it was *haram* (forbidden) for anyone to either impose or agree to such a condition. See *Malfuzat*, vol. 4, p. 19.

on the loser.[99] The length of the debate (three days, sometimes as much as fifteen[100]), the competitors' apparent licence to insult one another, and their insistence on having the last word (which frequently led one party or the other to ask for a second debate) point in fact to an element of 'social inversion' in some debates.[101] As Ahmed indicates in the context of the bahas in Bengal, debates sometimes ended in violence.[102]

While written and oral argumentation did not always have such dramatic consequences, there is no doubt that the combined effect of extensive publication, the creation of voluntary organizations, preaching tours in small towns and villages, sermons delivered at mosques and elsewhere, and the oral debates together created a self-consciousness about religion that was new in late nineteenth-century British India.

[99] Known as a *mubahala*, this was sometimes an element in Ahmadi debates with opponents. See Friedmann, *Prophecy Continuous*, pp. 6–7. The Ahl-e Sunnat are also known to have challenged a leader of the Nadwa on one occasion to a *mubahala*, a challenge that (according to Ahl-e Sunnat Sources) was not taken up. See Sayyid Ikhlas Husain Sahaswani Chishti Nizami, *Hadis-e Jankah Mufti Lutf Ullah* (Bareilly: Matba' Ahl-e Sunnat wa Jama'at, 1313/1895–96), pp. 13–14.

[100] See Friedmann, *Prophecy Continuous*, p. 7.

[101] I owe this concept to Katheryn Hansen, 'The Birth of Hindi Drama in Benaras, 1868–1885', in Sandria B. Freitag (ed.), *Culture and Power in Banaras: Community, Performance, and Environment, 1800–1980* (Berkeley: University of California Press, 1989), p. 73. Hansen's description of certain features of the Svang theatre seems to have much in common with the social setting in which munazaras (one imagines) must have taken place. These include 'the use of unbounded public space, . . . the open-ended time frame, . . . the competitive situation, . . . the absence of a controlling figure of authority, . . . the gathering together of spectators from all castes and classes'. Most if not all these characteristics seem to be shared by the munazara.

[102] Ahmed, *Bengal Muslims*, pp. 79–80.

Chapter IV

The Barkatiyya Sayyids of Marahra, Late Nineteenth Century

Ahmad Riza's discipleship to Shah Al-e Rasul (d. 1878), a Sayyid and pir of the Barkatiyya family based in the small town of Marahra near Aligarh, was of great significance to his life. In what way the sufi tie was important to the Ahl-e Sunnat in the larger context of 'being' Muslim, and what connection they saw between their claim to being the Ahl-e Sunnat or 'people of the [Prophet's] way' and sufi belief and practice, are some of the questions I try to address in this chapter and the next. Furthermore, in indicating wherein the Ahl-e Sunnat perceived the sources of the sufi master's authority to lie, I hope to say something about their perceptions of the nature of religious authority generally: how it is conferred, manifested, and passed on.

Here I turn to the Barkatiyya family. My account, based on a family history, indicates some of the ways in which the Barkatiyya pirs, regarding themselves as 'reformist', differed from—or believed themselves to be different from—other sufi pirs in the subcontinent in the late nineteenth century. By focusing specifically on the Barkatiyya pirs, I also hope to highlight the importance of the institution of the family in nineteenth-century British India as a source of authority.

THE BARKATIYYA SAYYIDS OF MARAHRA

The Barkatiyya family of Marahra traces its descent to certain Zaidi[1] Sayyids who were descended from the Prophet through his daughter Fatima and her husband 'Ali. In the course of time they settled in Iraq. In the eleventh century AD, a branch of the family went to Ghazni, joining the army of Sultan Mahmud of Ghazni (r. 998–1030) on one of the Sultan's incursions to India. However, it was in a later reign, that of Sultan Shams ud-Din Altamash (r. 1211–36), or Iltutmish, as he is often called, that a member of the family first acquired a land grant in Bilgram, a small rural town in western Awadh, as reward for a successful military campaign against a Hindu king.[2]

This ancestor of the Barkatiyya Sayyids was one of many Muslims to settle in the north Indian plains during the reign of the Delhi Sultans, and later that of the Mughals, as landowners. Encouraged by the Mughal policy of granting land in return for state service, the seventeenth and eighteenth centuries saw the Muslim gentry (ashraf) putting down roots in the countryside, and creating small agriculturally-based towns (qasbas) around them. During Aurangzeb's time, land grants were made heritable, thus further encouraging settlement on the land; under earlier Mughal rulers, they had been for the lifetime of the grantee only.[3]

Bayly describes the qasba town as 'a place with a distinct urban status which possessed a mosque, a public bath and a judicial officer (*kazi*). It was, however, an inward sense of cohesion which was

[1] The Zaidis (Ar., Zaydi) trace their origins to Zayd, son of Zayn al-'Abidin, the fourth Shi'i Imam (d. 712). Zayd claimed 'the Imamate on the basis that it belonged to any descendant of 'Ali and Fatima who is learned, pious and comes forward openly to claim the Imamate (i.e. raises a revolt)'. He raised a revolt in 740, but was killed at Kufa on the orders of the Caliph Hisham. His followers succeeded in establishing a state in north Iran between the ninth and eleventh centuries, and in converting the population to Zaidi Shi'ism. Zaidi Shi'is ruled Yemen from the tenth century down to modern times. See Moojan Momen, *An Introduction to Shi'i Islam: The History and Doctrines of Twelver Shi'ism* (Delhi: Oxford University Press, 1985), pp. 49–50.

[2] This family history is based, unless otherwise indicated, on Maulana Aulad-e Rasul 'Muhammad Miyan' Qadiri's *Khandan-e Barakat* (*c.* 1927).

[3] The foregoing is based on Bayly, *Rulers, Townsmen and Bazaars*, pp. 189–93, and Chapter 9.

important'.[4] As he points out, a 'sense of pride in home (*watan*) and urban tradition' was characteristic of the way the gentry felt about their qasba from the mid-eighteenth century. They stood at the centre of a literate, Perso-Islamic culture economically dependent on agriculture and landholdings. Frequently, Bayly adds, the presence of a Muslim saint's tomb, or hospice, further enhanced the sense of corporate unity and pride. All of these features appear to have been present in the case of the Barkatiyya Sayyids of Bilgram.

The name 'Barkatiyya' adopted by the family probably refers to Shah Barkat Ullah (1660–1729), who founded the hospice (khanqah) around which later generations of the family have lived and grown up. Although Shah Barkat Ullah was not the first in the family to move to Marahra (his paternal grandfather had made that move sometime in the seventeenth century),[5] he was in many senses the 'founder' of the Marahra branch of the family; their present settlement, known as 'Basti Pirzadagan', was founded by him. The reasons for Shah Barkat Ullah's grandfather's initial move from Bilgram are not clear; the sources mention his restless piety and search for spiritual truth. Whatever the reason, it was probably beneficial to later generations to be close to the centre of power at Delhi. Marahra, in Etah district, is located beyond Aligarh, about 170 kilometres due south-east of Delhi.

Shah Barkat Ullah is reputed to have been especially drawn to the Qadiri order of sufis, although he was also initiated into other orders, such as the Chishti, Suhrawardi, and Naqshbandi.[6] He was a learned man, with many books on mysticism and poetry to his credit, and enjoyed a reputation for piety which attracted a large number of disciples, many of them from the ruling classes (*umara*). His reputation also attracted the patronage of the Mughal rulers at Delhi, including Emperor Aurangzeb (r. 1658–1707); during the eighteenth century, revenue-free grants of whole villages were made

[4] Ibid., pp. 191–2.

[5] Shah 'Abd ul-Jalil, Shah Barkat Ullah's paternal grandfather, lived there during the last years of his life. He built a hospice, mosque, and a well, and lived there with his family until his death in 1647. *Khandan-e Barakat*, pp. 4–5.

[6] Ibid., pp. 8–9.

to the khanqah and dargah (shrine) by rulers attracted to the pirs of Marahra.[7]

Aurangzeb's death ushered in a period of weakness in the Mughal empire, encouraging a move toward greater regional autonomy in Rohilkhand as elsewhere. Patronage of the Barkatiyya family was assumed by the nawabs of Farrukhabad. In 1730, Nawab Muhammad Khan Bangash (d. 1743) ordered a tomb built for Shah Barkat Ullah and granted lands in mu'afi (or *madad-e ma'ash*) for its upkeep.[8] Some years later, Ahmad Khan Bangash (d. 1771), Muhammad Khan's second son who succeeded him as Nawab in 1750, made an annual grant of Rs. 450 available to Shah Barkat Ullah's grandson for the upkeep of the tomb. This sum was still being disbursed in the early twentieth century by the state government of the United Provinces.[9]

However, in the mid-eighteenth century, the Barkatiyya Sayyids' fortunes could not have been entirely secure. Along with the political vicissitudes of the times, in which now the Mughals and now the nawabs of Farrukhabad exercised control over the Marahra region,[10] there were also rural *zamindari* revolts and resentment of the Sayyids' privileged tax-free status. With the political system in flux, the local revenue system was unravelling as well: hitherto jagirdars (land grantees) had collected the revenue from the zamindars (local chieftains) and passed it on to the centre, but now, with the weakening of the Mughal empire, jagirdars had difficulty collecting

[7] Ibid., See, e.g., pp. 9, 15, 18.

[8] Ibid., p. 12. Irvine indicates more precisely that the tomb of Shah Barkat Ullah was built by Shuj'at Khan Ghilzai (probably an officer in the service of Muhammad Khan Bangash) in 1730. William Irvine, *The Bangash Nawabs of Farrukhabad—A Chronicle (1713–1857)*, Part II (1879), no. 2, 71 fn.

[9] *Khandan-e Barakat*, p. 16.

[10] In 1750, the town of Marahra was sacked by Safdar Jang's army in the course of a battle between Safdar Jang's forces (led by the Hindu Naval Rae, and then by Safdar Jang himself) and Ahmad Khan Bangash. Ahmad Khan returned to Farrukhabad victorious for the time being. A year later, however, the situation was reversed when Safdar Jang returned to the attack with Maratha help. Although the Rohillas put up a combined front, Ahmad Khan Bangash was defeated. Accepting an unfavourable treaty with the Mughal emperor, he managed to hold on to half his territories. Irvine, *The Bangash Nawabs of Farrukhabad*, 71–122.

the revenue. The zamindars also resented the fact that the lands granted in mu'afi to learned religious families such as the Barkatiyya Sayyids had been removed from their authority and revenue pool.[11]

However, the patronage of the nawabs of Farrukhabad appears to have allowed the Barkatiyya family to survive these troubles. The nawabs, for their part, needed the Sayyids to legitimize their rule. As Bayly says, 'A ruler needed to be legitimate in the eyes of the powerful Islamic élites of writers, jurists and service communities. He had to offer them patronage and also sustain the life of the community of the faithful'.[12] Likewise, Eaton describes the interdependence between political rulers and sufis in medieval India as follows:

> The court realized that hundreds, even thousands, of common folk—Hindu as well as Muslim—thronged to these dargahs . . . . by securing the loyalty of an elite group considered by the court to wield such influence among the lower population, the government hoped to deepen the roots of its own authority throughout the kingdom.[13]

Marahra's geographic location was also favourable, given its proximity to the Grand Trunk Road and to important trade routes and market towns such as Kasganj. Bayly notes that there were 'no less than eleven major markets in Farrukhabad and Etah Districts before 1750'.[14]

Notable Sufis in the Barkatiyya Family

In the course of the eighteenth and nineteenth centuries the family traditions of learning and sufi piety continued to be handed down from father to son, and the reputation of the family spread. After Shah Barkat Ullah's death, the Barkatiyya Sayyids divided into two *sarkars* ('houses' or 'branches'):[15] the descendants of Shah Barkat

[11] These comments are based on Muzaffar Alam, *Crisis of Empire*, Chapter III.

[12] Bayly, *Rulers, Townsmen and Bazaars*, p. 115.

[13] Richard M. Eaton, *Sufis of Bijapur 1300–1700: Social Roles of Sufis in Medieval India* (Princeton: Princeton University Press, 1978), p. 218.

[14] Bayly, *Rulers, Townsmen and Bazaars*, p. 119.

[15] Literally 'government' or 'master', the term has obvious connotations of worldly power and authority. For discussion of such terminology in the sufi context, see Simon

Ullah's elder son constituted the 'Sarkar Kalan', or 'Great House', while those of his younger son constituted the 'Sarkar Khurd' or 'Small House'. The Sarkar Khurd had its own khanqah and mosque and its own lands provided the revenue for their upkeep. The Sarkar Kalan, which was the better endowed of the two, also financed the running of its hospice, mosque and other buildings, through revenue derived from landed property. The branches maintained their separate identities in terms of marriage alliances, each tending to have its own networks, though marriage across the two sarkars was not ruled out.[16] The author of the *Khandan-e Barakat* ignores the Sarkar Khurd for the most part, or relegates it to relative unimportance.

In the Sarkar Kalan, on the other hand, the mid-eighteenth to mid-nineteenth centuries shone with illustrious personalities (see family tree below): notably, in the eighteenth century, the three brothers Shah Al-e Ahmad 'Achhe Miyan', Shah Al-e Barakat 'Suthre Miyan', and Shah Al-e Husain 'Sache Miyan'.[17] The first two distinguished themselves in very different ways: Achhe Miyan is said to have been so wise and popular that he had close to two lakh (200,000) disciples (murids)! In 1783, the Mughal king Shah 'Alam granted him several villages for the upkeep of the khanqah.[18] As to Suthre Miyan, he was a great builder, also a great sufi devotee and ascetic, and a poet. The youngest brother, Sache Miyan, was adopted by his mother's brother at the age of six, and grew up in Bihar, never again to return to Marahra. As his uncle was a nawab, he inherited the nawabi after the latter's death.

Digby, 'The Sufi Shaikh as a Source of Authority in Mediaeval India', in Marc Gaborieau (ed.), *Islam and Society in South Asia* (Paris: Ecole des Hautes Etudes en Sciences Sociales, 1986).

16 These comments are culled from the family history as a whole. See, e.g., ibid., pp. 10, 69–70, 82; on p. 82, the author, who belonged to the Sarkar Kalan, specifically distanced himself from certain trends of belief which he associated with the Sarkar Khurd.

17 *Miyan* is 'an address expressive of kindness, or respect', and its range of meanings includes 'Sir', 'good man', 'master', 'husband', 'lord and master'. John T. Platts, *A Dictionary of Urdu, Classical Hindi and English* (Oxford: Oxford University Press, 1982), p. 1103. It is frequently appended to a male child's nickname, which latter may be based (as is presumably the case here) on some trait of his personality. 'Achhe Miyan' may thus be rendered 'Good sir', 'Suthre Miyan' 'Handsome . . .', and 'Sache Miyan' 'Honest . . .'.

18 *Khandan-e Barakat*, pp. 18–19.

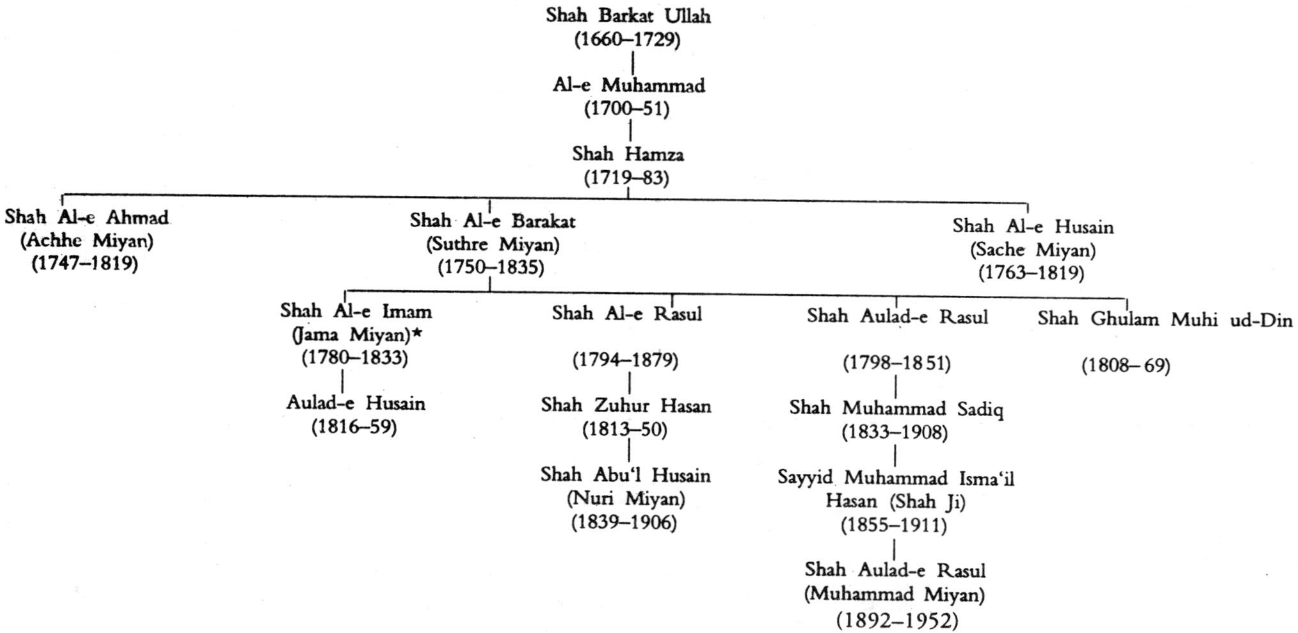

* Jama Miyan is described in the *Khandan-e Barakat* as a 'Tafzili Shi'i'.

Figure 2 Family Tree of the Barkatiyya Sayyids of Marahra

Several of Suthre Miyan's sons were also famous. Al-e Imam 'Jama Miyan', the eldest, was something of a *bête noire* in the Sarkar Kalan, for he was a Tafzili, whose beliefs verged on Shi'ism;[19] the author of the family history puts this down to his having lived in Lucknow and 'the East'. He was excluded from his father's inheritance, apparently because his father survived him. He died in Bihar and was buried there; his descendants appear also to be buried separately from the rest of the family, not at the main dargah in Marahra.[20]

Shah Al-e Rasul (1794–1879), Suthre Miyan's second son (and Ahmad Riza's pir), received his education from his father and his uncle, Achhe Miyan; he was taught, as well, by Shah 'Abd ul-'Aziz Dehlawi (son of the famous Shah Wali Ullah), and Maulana Nur ul- Haqq Firangi Mahali of Lucknow. Achhe Miyan gave him bai'a, and khilafat and *ijazat* (permission to enrol disciples in a silsila, or line of spiritual masters ending in one's own preceptor). His father also gave him khilafat. After his father's death, he and his two younger brothers jointly became Suthre Miyan's sajjada-nishins (successors as pir). All three brothers inherited equal portions from the khanqah, the dargah, the income of the two sarkars, and the landed properties (*ja'e-dad*). They were also joint caretakers (*mutawallis*) of these properties.[21]

Finally, in this list of eighteenth-and nineteenth-century luminaries in the Barkatiyya family must be mentioned Shah Abu'l Husain Ahmad 'Nuri Miyan' (1839–1906), a grandson of Shah Al-e Rasul. Orphaned as a young boy, he was brought up by his grandparents, and Shah Al-e Rasul was extremely fond of him. Nuri Miyan received bai'a and khilafat from his grandfather. In addition, he was taught by a vast array of teachers from within the family and outside; among the latter were Maulanas 'Abd ul-Qadir Badayuni

[19] *Tafzili*: a Sunni who assigns special importance to 'Ali. As noted in the Barkatiyya genealogical table, however, Jama Miyan is described as a Tafzili Shi'i in the *Khandan-e Barakat*. Apparently, being on the borderline of Sunni and Shi'i belief, the Tafzilis were regarded sometimes as Sunnis, at other times as Shi'is.

[20] Unlike the other sons, Jama Miyan was born of Suthre Miyan's first marriage; perhaps this also set him apart from them. His descendants are buried in a place called 'Bagh Pukhta', built by Jama Miyan. *Khandan-e Barakat*, pp. 25–9.

[21] Ibid., pp. 29–36.

and Fazl-e Rasul Badayuni, confidants and close associates of the family. Nuri Miyan wrote a large number of books on sufi-related themes (*wird, zikr, shaghl, 'amal*) as well as fiqh, and poetry. After Shah Al-e Rasul's death, he became his sajjada-nishin, jointly with Shah Al-e Rasul's son (brother of Nuri Miyan's deceased father; hence Nuri Miyan's uncle). He had many *khulafa'* (spiritual successors), and thousands of murids.[22]

The author of the *Khandan-e Barakat*, Aulad-e Rasul 'Muhammad Miyan' (1892–1952), was Nuri Miyan's (maternal) grandson. He was a learned scholar with a large number of books to his name, who regarded Ahmad Riza Khan with the greatest respect. Although he was quite young during Ahmad Riza's last years of life, he played a leadership role in the activities of the Ansar al-Islam, created in 1921 in order to find some means of helping the Ottomans in the aftermath of World War I.[23]

Religious Life at Basti Pirzadagan

The heart of the settlement of the Barkatiyya Sayyids was the dargah or cluster of tomb-shrines in which the ancestors were buried. Muhammad Miyan carefully documents the place of burial of each member of the family, including women, who were interred in a separate part of the dargah. Shah Barkat Ullah's tomb was the most important of them all. All Shah Barkat Ullah's male descendants of the Sarkar Kalan and Sarkar Khurd are buried close to his tomb-complex. A separate complex, that of Shah Al-e Muhammad, his son, is located close by, and around it, again, are the graves of several descendants.

The importance of these tomb-shrines to the family and to their followers may be understood in terms of the concept of baraka (or, more popularly, *barkat*). All sufi pirs, and particularly Sayyids, are held by believing Muslims, and indeed by some Hindus as well, to possess spiritual efficacy or grace caused by their closeness to God and the Prophet. Some believe that when a saint dies

22 Ibid., pp. 30–1.

23 On the Ansar al-Islam, see Chapter III above; also see the Epilogue below which includes a biographical account of Muhammad Miyan and discusses the reasons for his objections, in the 1940s, to the creation of Pakistan as a separate Muslim state.

his spirit is so powerful and so dominant over the body that the body itself does not die or decay but is merely hidden from the living. The baraka of the saint is not dissipated at the saint's death. It is both transmitted to his successors and remains at his tomb, which becomes a place of pilgrimage for later followers. The *pir* does not actually die in the ordinary sense of the term. He is 'hidden', and over time he continues to develop spiritually, so that his *baraka* increases, as does the importance of his shrine.[24]

The concept of baraka, thus, is central to the popular sufi practices associated with pilgrimage to shrines, and to the institutions of sajjada-nishini, overseeing the shrine of one's pir, as well as 'urs, the three- or four-day annual ceremony commemorating the death-anniversary of a pir. Religious life at Basti Pirzadagan was dominated by these concerns and the annual cycle of ritual observances.

The khanqah was where the family lived, amidst mosques, and other buildings built over the centuries by various ancestors; for instance, a Diwan Khana (Hall of Audience, in which important visitors would be received)[25] and a Haweli Sajjada-nishini (residence for sajjada-nishins) were built by Shah Haqqani in the eighteenth century, and subsequently rebuilt, while Suthre Miyan built numerous houses and rebuilt another haweli (the Haweli Mahal Sara'e). Thus one gets the picture of male descendants of the family living separately, each of them heir to his father's personal property and frequently to his sajjada-nishini. At the same time, together they constituted a core of closely related males living in proximity to one another, within Basti Pirzadagan. The Basti is located away from the main township of Marahra and enclosed by a boundary wall.

The strong sense of family unity that pervades Muhammad Miyan's history, the *Khandan-e Barakat*, is reflected in Basti Pirzadagan's obvious physical unity. As the Barkatiyya sufis were Sayyids with a genealogical memory that reached right back to the

24 Katherine Pratt Ewing, 'The *Pir* or Sufi Saint in Pakistani Islam', Ph.D. dissertation, University of Chicago, 1980, p. 29. This view is consonant with Ahl-e Sunnat views on the subject, as will be clear further.

25 Ewing, pp. 179–80, writes that among the Malangs near Lahore whom she studied, the Diwan Khana was used by the sajjada-nishin to receive other sajjada-nishins during an 'urs. The term is associated with a royal court. Adjoining the royal apartments in the Delhi Red Fort (built by Shah Jahan in the seventeenth century), for instance, was a Diwan-e 'Amm (public hall of audience) and a Diwan-e Khass (private hall of audience).

Prophet himself, marriages were carefully regulated, and almost invariably contracted either with other family members, or in the absence of a suitable mate, with Sayyids from other khandans. The occasional marriage to a non-Sayyid was strongly disapproved of, though the children of such unions seem to have been recognized as part of the family.[26] Family consciousness of Sayyid ancestry is most vividly reflected in the choice of personal names: 'Al-e Muhammad', 'Aulad-e Rasul', or 'Al-e Husain',[27] for sons, while daughters' names would invariably consist of some compound of the name 'Fatima', such as 'Khairiyat Fatima', or 'Ihtiram Fatima'. While such names were by no means limited to Sayyid families, their ubiquity in the Barkatiyya khandan is remarkable.

More importantly, however, family unity was expressed in the religious realm. The family owned, either collectively or individually, a large number of *tabarrukat* or sacred relics (literally, 'objects filled with baraka'). These were an important part of the inheritance that a father passed down to his sons. Tabarrukat contain baraka by virtue of their previous association with a saint; they are imbued with the spiritual qualities of the saint himself, 'as if [they were] an extension of his body or contained some of his essence'.[28] Consequently they are accorded great reverence. The Barkatiyya khandan was fortunate in having some especially prized relics. Chief among these were some hairs of the Prophet. One of them came into the family's possession during Shah Barkat Ullah's lifetime; it is kept in a pewter or silver needle-case, and viewed by pilgrims during 'urs ceremonies. Other valuable tabarrukat, also dating from Shah Barkat Ullah's time, are a robe belonging to 'Ali (*khirqa-e Murtazwi*), and hairs of Hasan and Husain.[29] Some of these relics claim fascinating histories,

[26] See, e.g., *Khandan-e Barakat*, pp. 40, 59, 65, 72, and 76. Maulana Tahsin Riza Khan, a great-grandson of Ahmad Riza, told me that a non-Sayyid family can give a girl in marriage to a Sayyid family, but cannot take one (i.e., marriage between a non-Sayyid male and a Sayyid female is not permissible). Interview, April 18, 1987, Bareilly. In anthropological terms, this would be said to be a case of hypergamy within an endogamous marriage system.

[27] In translation, 'Muhammad's family', 'son of the Prophet', and 'Husain's family'.

[28] Ewing, 'The *Pir* or Sufi Saint', p. 30.

[29] *Khandan-e Barakat*, pp. 10–11.

which are themselves statements of a hierarchy of spiritual authority: 'Ali's robe, thus, is said to have been worn after him by Shaikh 'Abd al-Qadir Jilani, founder of the Qadiri order. Thereafter it passed through the hands of a succession of famous sufi mystics: Sultan al-Hind (Mu'in ud-Din Chishti of Ajmer, d. 1236), the Qutb (Shaikh Bakhtiyar Kaki of Delhi, d. 1236), Baba Farid (Shaikh Farid ud-Din Ganj-e Shakar of Pakpattan, Panjab, d. 1265), Hazrat Mahbub Ilahi (Nizam ud-Din Auliya of Delhi, d. 1325), Chiragh-e Dehli (Shaikh Nasir ud-Din Chiragh of Delhi, d. 1356), and so on, ultimately reaching Shah Barkat Ullah.[30]

Shah Barkat Ullah acquired, and passed on to his descendants, a turban (dastar) which had originally belonged to 'Abd al-Qadir Jilani.[31] It is said to have come to Shah Barkat Ullah through Bu 'Ali Qalandar (Shaikh Sharf ud-Din of Karnal and Panipat, d. 1324). Shah Barkat Ullah believed it was 'Abd al-Qadir Jilani's gift to him for his devotion and love for the shaikh and the Qadiri order.[32] In succeeding generations, the number of tabarrukat in the family's possession grew quite large and in the eighteenth century Shah Hamza, a son of Shah Barkat Ullah, received another hair of the Prophet, and a pair of the Prophet's shoes.[33] These and other relics are viewed by pilgrims during the annual 'urs.

Apart from tabarrukat, the family also had certain special prayers (*du'a*) which were passed down from father to son, or sufi preceptor to disciple, and were part of the family's secret lore of mystic prayers and practices. Nuri Miyan, for instance, received special permission

[30] Ibid., p. 11. All the saints mentioned here were of the Chishti order, founded by Mu'in ud-Din Chishti, of Ajmer.

[31] Richard M. Eaton, 'Court of Man, Court of God: Local Perceptions of the Shrine of Baba Farid, Pakpattan, Punjab', *Contributions to Asian Studies*, 17 (1982), 57, describes the symbolism of the turban as follows: 'One symbol in particular, the turban, perhaps transcended all others in point of its repertoire and importance. Associated with traditional Sufi lore but also having ambiguous associations with the crown and thereby with royalty, the turban served as a vehicle both for religious legitimacy and for the distribution of [the pir's] grace'.

[32] *Khandan-e Barakat*, p. 11.

[33] For a rather negative view of such relics, and their veneration in India especially, see Ignaz Goldziher, *Muslim Studies*, vol. 2, tr. and ed. S. M. Stern (Chicago: Aldine, 1971), pp. 327–32.

(ijazat) from one of his teachers to recite (and to pass on to his disciples) the *Hirz-e Yamani*, a name given to certain verses from the Qur'an, 'written cabbalistically and sewn up in leather for carrying on the body for protection'.[34] There were several such special prayers which were closely guarded secrets within the family, considered so important that the dates on which a disciple acquired his teacher's permission to recite or use them, were recorded, and considered part of his progress on the sufi path.[35] Undoubtedly, these constituted part of the Barkatiyya sufis' baraka. The possession of such baraka, in turn, attracted disciples to the holy man. Thus Nuri Miyan, because of his reputation for piety and wisdom, had attracted 'several thousand' helpers (*khuddam*) to the dargah, and was responsible for their material and spiritual welfare.[36]

In terms of practice and tradition, there were certain shared institutions which also bound the family together. These included the institution of sajjada-nishini. The sajjada-nishin, or caretaker of a tomb-shrine, was appointed or designated by his pir to succeed him at his death. As his spiritual successor, he inherited his pir's baraka. Usually a son succeeded his father as his sajjada-nishin (thus creating a double link of spiritual as well as biological succession). In exceptional cases, a person chose to nominate a brother or nephew, or other relative, as in Shah Al-e Rasul's case, where he nominated his grandson jointly with his son. Muhammad Miyan's family history also records cases in which several brothers became their father's sajjada-nishins jointly; these are instances, undoubtedly, of uncommon family unity and amity, for the position was a highly coveted one, and is known to have frequently led to family discord.[37]

[34] Constance E. Padwick, *Muslim Devotions: A Study of Prayer-Manuals in Common Use* (London: S. P. C. K., 1961), p. 25. *Khandan-e Barakat*, p. 30.

[35] Thus, the dates on which Nuri Miyan was given permission by Shah Al-e Rasul to recite particular prayers are separately recorded (together with the names of the prayers) in a biography of Nuri Miyan. See Maulawi Ghulam Shabbir Qadiri Nuri Badayuni, *Tazkira-e Nuri* (La'ilpur, 1968), p. 59.

[36] Ibid., p. 60.

[37] There were frequent court cases in British India resulting from disputes over who the rightful successor was to a sajjada-nishini (also called *gaddi*, or 'seat', a term which emphasizes the aspect of 'rulership' in the role). See, e.g., Eaton, 'Court of Man, Court of God', for an example from the shrine of Baba Farid of Pakpattan.

The installation ceremony for a new sajjada-nishin at Marahra took place on the fortieth day of his pir's death, a day known as the *chehlum*. Family members and important guests, the élite of the town and neighbouring areas, and 'ulama' close to the family, would be invited. At the appointed time the new incumbent-to-be, and a small group of elders would together go to the dargah, taking with them some tabarrukat such as a khirqa, turban, or *tasbih* (rosary). They would halt at the recently deceased pir's grave, and lay the tabarrukat on it. Then they would pray to the elders of the silsila for union (*tawassul*) and guidance (*iste'anat*), and read the Fatiha. This done, the new sajjada-nishin would be bedecked with the tabarrukat, and they would leave the dargah.[38] This would be followed by speeches on the sanad (certificate of authority) of the sajjada-nishini in question, at the sajjada-nishin's house, and followers would offer gifts or *nazar*. It was also an occasion when believers sought bai'a from the new incumbent, and became his disciples. Muhammad Miyan laments the fact that in his day (the mid-1920s) people were sajjada-nishins in name only: they lacked the true devotion, piety and selfless service of their pirs and forefathers.

Debate and Disputation about Sufi Devotional Practice

As the Marahra pirs well knew, many of the practices in which they engaged were the subject of heated controversy in north India. Ever since the Dar al-'Ulum had been founded by Maulanas Muhammad Qasim Nanautawi (d. 1877), Rashid Ahmad Gangohi (d. 1905), and other 'ulama' at the town of Deoband in the North-Western Provinces in 1867, a renewal movement had been growing in British north India.[39] The Deobandi 'ulama' frowned upon customs such as 'urs, trying to discourage them on the grounds that asking a saint to intercede with God was tantamount to *shirk* or polytheism; moreover, the custom was economically wasteful and extravagant.

[38] This account is based on *Khandan-e Barakat*, pp. 84–5.

[39] The roots of this movement, however, went much further back in time than this, to Shah Wali Ullah. See Metcalf, *Islamic Revival*, Chapter III, for details about the Dar al-'Ulum, and Chapter VIII below for Ahl-e Sunnat perspectives on the Deoband movement.

Some of the Deobandi 'ulama', however, were themselves somewhat ambivalent about the issue. Moreover, Haji Imdad Ullah 'Muhajir' Makki (1817–99), a pir to whom many of them owed allegiance, had written a pamphlet (*risala*) in its favour.[40] Haji Imdad Ullah, who was the pir of Muhammad Qasim and Rashid Ahmad as also of some seven or eight hundred other 'ulama', many of them educated at the Deoband madrasa, in 1894 wrote a pamphlet entitled *Faisla-e Haft Mas'ala* (Decision on Seven Problems).[41]

In it he took a conciliatory line toward the seven issues he addressed, urging the 'ulama' and all Muslims generally not to allow questions such as 'urs,[42] which were ancillary to their faith, to divide them. Haji Imdad Ullah noted that after death the dead are tested on matters of belief by two angels who visit the grave, and enjoy the peace and happiness of union with the beloved, Allah, only upon passing the test. The origin of the word 'urs is a hadis about the two angels Munkar and Nakir (together known as 'Nakirain'), who approach the dead person in the grave and ask three questions: who is your Lord? What is your din? What do you say about this man (pointing to the Prophet)? If the person answers all three questions correctly—if he says, that is: My Lord is Allah, my din is Islam, and this is Muhammad, the Prophet of Allah—the angels tell him to 'sleep as the bride (*'urus*) sleeps'. The reward for true belief, thus, is peace after death and the joy of union with God, as of a new bride with her husband. In dying, it is as if one returns to one's beloved (husband), Allah. For the living, therefore, it is fitting (especially if the dead person had done them some tangible or intangible service during his lifetime) that they should pray for him and transfer the

[40] Metcalf, *Islamic Revival*, pp. 161–2, 181–2.

[41] This has since been republished, in 1986, by the Ahl-e Sunnat wa Jama'at in Pakistan, with extended glosses and comments. The original twelve-page pamphlet is now a thick 367-page book!

[42] The other issues were milad (celebration of the Prophet's birthday), *fatiha* (reading the Fatiha on certain fixed days after a person's death, seeking intercession for him or her with God), *nida-e ghair Allah* (calling upon one other than Allah for help), *jama'at-e sani* (the holding of a second *namaz* on Fridays), during zuhr, *imkan-e nazir* (can God create another being equal to the Prophet Muhammad?) and *imkan-e kizb* (can God lie?). The first five problems related to practice (*'amal*), the last to knowledge (*'ilm*).

merit (*sawab*) of their prayer to him,[43] so that he may answer the angels' questions correctly.[44]

Haji Imdad Ullah argued, furthermore, that the 'urs brings together a large number of pirs linked to different saintly lines (*salasil*, pl. of silsila), thus enabling those in search of a pir to find one and to become initiated to him in discipleship. The pirs too were able to meet each other. All this was a source of grace (baraka) to the participants. These were the advantages of honouring the dead on a specific day, rather than individually and randomly.[45]

The controversy about the permissibility of holding an 'urs was tied in with the question of sama', or singing, with or without instrumental accompaniment, which among sufis was a means of inducing spiritual ecstasy.[46] Haji Imdad Ullah quoted a hadis in which the Prophet said, 'Do not make my grave a place of rejoicing'. He interpreted this to mean that there should be no noisy dancing, or revelry, at the grave-site; but sama' itself was not prohibited as long as it is within the limits of the shari'a.[47] Haji Imdad Ullah's rather middle-of-the-road position on this issue was similar, it appears, to that of Nuri Miyan. While Nuri Miyan himself did not listen by choice to music, he did not prevent his guests from doing so, and, in fact, joined them at such gatherings (majalis). But he did this in very select (khass) company and under all the necessary conditions of sobriety.[48] The Marahra sufis, according to Maulawi

[43] *Isal-e sawab* is the concept that one can transfer the merit that one's good deeds call up, to someone else. This is done by specifically naming that person in private prayer, and asking God to 'transfer the merit' to the designated person. In this way an 'account' of good deeds may be built up even by a dead person, which may ultimately change his or her fate from Hell to Heaven on the Day of Judgment.

[44] Shah Imdad Ullah 'Muhajir' Makki, *Faisla-e Haft Mas'ala*, with commentary by Mufti Muhammad Khalil Khan Barkati (Lahore: Farid Book Stall, 1406/1986), p. 170.

[45] Ibid., p. 174. The context for this remark was the Deobandi objection to the practice of earmarking a specific day for the remembrance of the dead. See Metcalf, *Islamic Revival*, pp. 149, 151, 157, and passim.

[46] Sama' literally means 'to hear' in Arabic, and is thus related by extension to an important matter of faith, namely whether the dead can hear the living. On Ahmad Riza's views on this question, see below.

[47] *Faisla-e Haft Mas'ala*, pp. 184, 192, 194.

[48] *Tazkira-e Nuri*, pp. 102–3. Haji Imdad Ullah himself approved of 'urs, milad, and

Ghulam Shabbir Qadiri, Nuri Miyan's biographer, looked upon sama' and musical accompaniments to singing as aids in the sufi's path, helping him to reach a higher state (*hal*). Since Shah Al-e Rasul's time, however, sama' had been stopped at the 'urs at Marahra, and Nuri Miyan did not restore it.

The 'Urs-e Nuri

The largest and most important ceremony in the Barkatiyya khandan, which affirmed the family's corporate unity most forcefully, was the annual 'urs for one of the ancestors. Surprisingly, there is no account of this event in Muhammad Miyan's family history or in the *Tazkira-e Nuri*. Possibly Muhammad Miyan wished to glorify his line of the family tree against the claims of other branches, and therefore neglected some facts while emphasizing others.[49] At any rate, a picture of what took place at an 'urs at Marahra and how many people were involved can only be formed piecemeal, using varied sources and drawing on materials from other 'urs ceremonies.

Early twentieth-century accounts of one of the annual 'urs ceremonies at Marahra in the *Dabdaba-e Sikandari*[50] published in Rampur reveal that it was held in honour of Nuri Miyan, who had died in 1906. The 'urs lasted between four and six days.[51] As Nuri Miyan had had no male heirs, he had appointed his young first cousin, Sayyid 'Ali Husain, known as 'Iqbal Hasan' (1873–97), as

---

similar ritual observances being limited to the élite or khass. Metcalf, p. 151., writes, for instance, 'Haji Imdadu'llah actually joined in the elaborate celebration of the maulud [milad] in Mecca, although he approved of Rashid Ahmad's refusal to participate either at home or in the Hijaz . . . all felt they shared an understanding of the correct attitude to the practice, and tended to conform publicly to opposition to the custom'.

[49] Nuri Miyan was descended from Shah Al-e Rasul, while Muhammad Miyan was a descendant of Shah Aulad-e Rasul, Shah Al-e Rasul's younger brother.

[50] See Chapter III above for background on this newspaper. I consulted issues between the years 1909 and 1921 of the *Dabdaba*.

[51] 'Urs ceremonies for other Barkatiyya ancestors, particularly Shah Barkat Ullah, presumably also took place on their death anniversaries, though they were not reported in the *Dabdaba-e Sikandari*. Thus, Maulana Zafar ud-Din Bihari records various anecdotes in his *Hayat-e A'la Hazrat* which occurred when Ahmad Riza Khan had gone to Marahra to attend an 'urs for Shah Barkat Ullah. *Hayat-e A'la Hazrat*, pp. 39, 40, 131.

his sajjada-nishin. When the latter died he chose Iqbal Hasan's son, Hafiz Sayyid Aulad Husain, 'Safi Miyan' (1893–1910), for this position of honour. Unfortunately, Safi Miyan, who would have been a youth of thirteen at Nuri Miyan's death, also died young, at the age of seventeen or so.[52] In the circumstances, Nuri Miyan's 'urs was organized and managed by another first cousin, Sayyid Mahdi Hasan (b. 1870). He appears to have been an able organizer, and to have commanded great respect among the 'ulama'.

Each year Mahdi Hasan put a notification in the papers some weeks prior to the 'urs, extending a public invitation to all to attend, informing people of the location of Marahra on the railway route, and assuring them that their food and lodging needs would be looked after for the duration of the event. If they informed him in advance, he said, they would be met at the railway station. As to the 'urs itself, he emphasized that it was always conducted with full regard for, and within the limits of, the shari'a. Attendance at the 'urs-e Nuri would consequently be a source of merit (sawab).[53]

Although no detailed report exists of any single 'urs at Marahra, much less of the subjective experience of participating in one, the major events must have approximated those set out for the 'urs-e Nuri in the *Dabdaba-e Sikandari* in June 1912. In the course of five days, the first two were devoted to *khatma* of the Qur'an, or recital of the entire Qur'an in a single night,[54] recital of na't verses in praise of the Prophet, and sermons (*bayan* and wa'z) by well-known 'ulama'. The highlights of the third day, which was Nuri Miyan's actual death anniversary, were a *khirqa-poshi* ritual in which the sajjada-nishin (Mahdi Hasan, in this case) ceremonially wore 'Ali's robe (khirqa) and performed the Fatiha ceremony at Nuri Miyan's grave, and a *qul*, a ceremony apparently marking the exact time of

[52] *Khandan-e Barakat*, p. 31.

[53] See, e.g., *Dabdaba-e Sikandari*, 45:27 (July 26, 1909), 6–7; 48:24 (June 3, 1912), 7; 48:25 (June 10, 1912), 3.

[54] An achievement which brought merit to the reciters. See Fr. Buhl, 'Khatma', *EI2*, 1112–13. Ewing, 'The *Pir* or Sufi Saint', p. 142, describes a much more emotional khatma in honour of 'Abd al-Qadir Jilani 'who is regarded as the patron of all the sufi orders in South Asia', among the Malangs of Lahore. Unlike the 'urs-e Nuri, women were present at this khatma.

his death.[55] The fourth day included, apart from Qur'an reading, na'ts, and sermons—all a daily occurrence during this five-day period—a pilgrimage to the Prophet's holy relics, as also to those of Hasan, Husain, and Shaikh 'Abd al-Qadir Jilani. Finally, on the fifth and last day, there was a *ghusl*, or ceremonial washing of the tomb.[56]

It is noteworthy that the 'urs-e Nuri was characterized by the restrained piety of night-long Qur'an readings, and by sermons by the 'ulama', rather than by sama'. As Frederick M. Denny comments

> Reciting the Qur'an is akin to a sacramental act in that divine power and presence are brought near .... There is even a kind of 'divine Magic' to the Qur'an; [because its verses and formulae] come from God, . . . they are rather like a talisman which protects and guides man.[57]

It was this emphasis on Qur'an reading, together with the sermons of the 'ulama', that formed the basis for the claims of the Marahra pirs—as also of the pirs and 'ulama' of Badayun and Bareilly—that they followed the shari'a at all times. *Na't-khwani* (the recitation of poetry in praise of the Prophet), and *qasida-khwani* (recital of praise verse of religious figures generally) were also an integral part of these shari'a-inclined 'urs celebrations.[58]

We get some inkling of the popularity of the annual 'urs at Marahra, and the size of the crowds that were attracted to it, by incidental comments in the *Dabdaba-e Sikandari*: in 1921 it reported that that year the turnout had been much smaller than usual, on account of a recent death in the Barkatiyya family: Mahdi Hasan's

55 Unfortunately, I have no information on the nature of the *qul* ceremony. A recent article by Syed Liyaqat Hussain Moini describing 'urs-related rituals at Mu'in ud-Din's shrine at Ajmer indicates that qul was not a specific ritual but the totality of final-day ceremonial at the 'urs. See his 'Rituals and Customary Practices at the Dargah of Ajmer', in Troll (ed.), *Muslim Shrines in India*, pp. 73–5.

56 *Dabdaba-e Sikandari*, 48:25 (June 10, 1912), 3.

57 Frederick M. Denny, 'Islamic Ritual: Perspectives and Theories', p. 76, in Martin (ed.), *Approaches to Islam in Religious Studies*. See also William A. Graham, 'Qur'an as Spoken Word: An Islamic Contribution to the Understanding of Scripture', in the same volume, for a discussion of Qur'an recitation, or *qira'a*. A fuller discussion of the orality of scripture may be found in Graham, *Beyond the Written Word*.

58 It must be added, however, that qawwali and sama' were reported to have taken place one year, as a separate part of the 'urs. See *Dabdaba-e Sikandari*, 51:29 (June 7, 1915), 7.

only surviving child, a young girl, had died in childbirth along with her baby a week earlier at Lucknow, and her body had been brought to the dargah for burial. This had prompted Mahdi Hasan to put out notices announcing a postponement of the 'urs, a decision which had later been reversed. With time running short, the final decision not to postpone the 'urs had not reached the public, leading to confusion and the low turnout. The report says that that year there were only four or five thousand people, instead of the usual 20,000.[59]

The scale of the organization on the part of the sajjada-nishin and his helpers appears to have been impressive. At arrival, each guest was met at the railway station. The road from the station to the khanqah was especially lit for the occasion with gas lights. Police were deputed to keep law and order, and ensure that nothing went wrong. The khanqah was brilliantly lit with lights and mirrors.[60] Each person who attended the 'urs, regardless of social standing, was given a straw mat (*chattai*) to sleep on, earthenware water-containers (*ghara, lota*) for bathing or drinking, and food, drink, betel (*pan, challi*), and tobacco, twice a day—all delivered to the lodgings from the start of the 'urs until the very last day.[61]

As might have been expected, given the above and given, as well, that the Barkatiyya pirs were Sayyids of standing, the 'urs-e Nuri was attended by many people of distinction, apart from ordinary folk from the surrounding countryside. Amongst the nobility were, at least occasionally, a nawab or ra'is[62] and 'ulama' and sufi pirs from places as distant as Bombay, Calcutta, Bhopal, Gwalior, Ajmer, Pakpattan, and Bankipur, as also from districts in the North-Western Provinces themselves.[63] The core group, however, consisted of men whose principal allegiance was to the Qadiri order. Apart from the

[59] Ibid., 57:29 (December 1, 1921), 4.

[60] Ibid., 51:29 (June 7, 1915), 6.

[61] Ibid., 57:29 (April 4, 1921), 4. As may well be imagined, the costs of the 'urs must have been of a very high order. Unfortunately, I have no figures as to the expenses incurred for any single year, nor of the nazar (voluntary gifts of money or in kind) collected from the pilgrims.

[62] See, e.g., ibid., 50:29 (June 15, 1914), 18.

[63] Ibid., 51:29 (June 7, 1915), 6–7.

'ulama' of Marahra, these were from Bareilly, Badayun, Pilibhit, and Rampur, with a sprinkling from other towns in the North-Western Provinces (such as Kachhochha) and the Panjab. In several reports of the 'urs-e Nuri, Ahmad Riza Khan's presence and his delivery of a sermon are singled out for mention.

The lack of detailed information on the rituals involved, and more importantly, of first-hand participants' accounts, makes it difficult to amplify this discussion of the 'urs-e Nuri. Nevertheless, some tentative comments, based in particular on Victor Turner's essay 'Pilgrimages as Social Processes',[64] are in order even if his discussion is based largely on non-Islamic examples, and, when he does turn to the Islamic world, on hajj rituals alone.

The 'urs is a pilgrimage. The Arabic term *ziyara* (from the root *zara*), which means 'to pay a visit', is commonly used in the Urdu in the specific sense of visiting a saint's tomb. The Urdu word *mazar*, meaning tomb or shrine, is likewise derived from the same Arabic root. Whether one visits a tomb during an 'urs or at any other time of the year, such a visit is respectfully termed *ziyarat*.

Unlike the hajj, the 'urs at Marahra was (apparently) attended only by men.[65] Women were strongly discouraged from visiting graves, and various ill-effects were believed to occur to them if they did so.[66] When Ahmad Riza Khan was asked whether women could attend the 'urs at Ajmer, his reply was unequivocal: a woman would be cursed by Allah and by the person whose grave it was from the moment she resolved upon making such a visit, until she returned home. The only grave which women may visit, and indeed *must*

[64] Victor Turner, *Dramas, Fields, and Metaphors: Symbolic Action in Human Society* (Ithaca and London: Cornell University Press, 1974).

[65] While I have no way of verifying this, when attending Ahmad Riza's annual 'urs at Bareilly in October 1987 I found that women attended only tangentially as observers from enclosed quarters—I myself was unable to witness the ceremonies, and this was unrelated to being a non-Muslim. Women were not allowed to approach the tomb itself. (However, it is conceivable that these restrictions might be relaxed at other times.)

[66] See, for example, Mrs. Meer Hassan Ali, *Observations on the Mussulmauns of India: Descriptive of their Manners, Customs, Habits, and Religious Opinions. Made during a Twelve Years' Residence in Their Immediate Society* (London, 1832), reprinted by Idarah-i Adabiyat-i Delli, 1973, vol. 2, p. 321.

visit (such an act being sunna, and almost *wajib*) was the Prophet's grave at Medina, should they go on hajj.[67]

Beliefs about the dead are clearly central to what takes place at an 'urs. Ahmad Riza wrote at some length on the subject, citing hadis to support his arguments. When asked whether it was permissible to dig up an old graveyard of Sunnis and build residential houses on the land, Ahmad Riza responded in a fatwa in 1904–5 that this would be an act of disrespect toward the dead buried there, and was not permitted in the Hanafi school.[68] Citing proofs from hadis, *riwayats* from the *sahaba* (companions of the Prophet) and *tabe'in* (those who followed the Prophet's Companions), in addition to proofs from fiqh, he argued first that the bodies of the highest categories of beings (prophets, sufi saints, and martyrs) do not disintegrate after death.[69] Further, after death the spirits of the *auliya* become even more powerful than before. When someone reads the Fatiha at the grave of a *wali* ('a friend of Allah'), the spirit (*ruh*) of the latter recognizes him. Similarly, if someone acts disrespectfully toward his grave, he is troubled by it. Nuri Miyan related the following incident:

> Close to our home in Marahra, in a jungle, there is a graveyard of martyrs (*ganj-e shahidin*). Someone used to take his buffalo there. In one place the ground was soft. Suddenly, the foot of the buffalo went in. It was discovered that there was a grave at that spot. A voice came from the grave, 'O you! you have caused me great discomfort. The foot of your buffalo hit me on the chest'.[70]

As for ordinary Muslims, although their bodies decay over time, their spirits continue to inhabit their graves, and must be respected. The fatwa continues:

> Dear God! when the Prophet has told us not to sit on graves, or lean against them, or put our feet on them, and when the 'ulama' have warned us against walking on new paths in a graveyard, or sleeping near a grave, it is incumbent on us, when we go to pay our respects and do pilgrimage (ziyarat) at a grave,

[67] *Malfuzat*, vol. 2, p. 107.

[68] Ahmad Riza Khan, *Ihlak al-Wahhabiyyin 'ala Tauhin Qubur il-Muslimin* (Bareilly: Hasani Press, 1322/1904–5).

[69] On the bodies of prophets being preserved from decay after death, see the hadis reported in the *Sunan* of Abu Da'ud: Ahmad Hasan, *Sunan Abu Dawud: English Translation with Explanatory Notes* (Lahore: Sh. Muhammad Ashraf, 1988), vol. 1, p. 249.

[70] Ahmad Riza Khan, *Ihlak al-Wahhabiyyin*, p. 18.

to do so from a [respectful] distance . . . . We have been told that dead Muslims and live ones both derive honour from the same things.

In his *Malfuzat,* Ahmad Riza also said that the dead can hear better than the living, and can communicate with the living, just as the living, in turn, can intercede for the dead and be instrumental in changing their fate in the hereafter.[71]

This interactive relationship between the living and the dead helps us understand the concept of *isal-e sawab,* or transfer of merit, in which the prayers of the living act as a kind of intercessionary factor in changing the fate of the dead person. This was what Haji Imdad Ullah was referring to in his defence of the 'urs, when he said that the prayers of the living could help the dead man answer the questions of the two angels correctly, and thereby ensure his ultimate entry into heaven. Equally, however, ordinary folk approach a shrine in the hope that the dead man will intercede for them. The chain of intercession starts at the grave of the local pir, and goes right up to the Prophet, who is closest to Allah, and whose intercession on one's behalf will never be denied.[72]

To return now to the 'urs-e Nuri, we can imagine, following Victor Turner, that there was a sense in which 'communitas' was created in the course of the pilgrimage. As the sources indicate that women were not participants in the 'urs, we may be justified in supposing that for a week, perhaps more, a large number of men had left their homes and families, and their ordinary occupations, to attend the 'urs. Although there was no communal eating at the Marahra 'urs, each person being served at his own lodging-place, fellow-feeling was (we assume) created in the course of the all-night sessions of khatma, na't-khwani, and sermons. Starting at about 8 p.m., the prayers and other events continued until the early morning, and the day wound up after the *zuhr* (midday) prayer.

The sources convey a sense that the pilgrims approached the occasion with joyousness and eager anticipation, rather than a mood of penitence. There was splendour (*raunaq*) in the large crowds, the

[71] *Malfuzat,* vol. 2, pp. 73–4. Also see vol. 3, pp. 29–30.

[72] The question of intercession, and of the Prophet's intercession with Allah in particular, will be more fully discussed in the next chapter in the context of Ahmad Riza's life.

ornamentation of the shrine, and the decoration of the route leading to the dargah from the railway station. We could say, with Turner, that when setting out for Marahra the pilgrim began a long sacred journey, voluntarily undertaken, in order to arrive at

> a threshold, a place and moment 'in and out of time', [where he hoped] to have . . . direct experience of the sacred, invisible, or supernatural order, . . . and [where he] participate[d] in symbolic activities which he believe[d] [were] efficacious in changing his inner and, sometimes, hopefully, outer condition from sin to grace, or sickness to health.[73]

Relations with the Outside World

The Sayyids of the Barkatiyya khandan lived, as noted, just outside the qasba of Marahra. Their landholdings were acquired as madad-e ma'ash from Mughal rulers and the nawabs of Farrukhabad, in what was agriculturally the best pargana (subdistrict)[74] of Etah district. In theory, such grants could be resumed at the death of the grantee; in practice, the grants to the Barkatiyya family had tended to become permanent and hereditary. Irrigation had become available through a branch of the Ganges Canal by the 1870s and sugar and indigo were widely grown.[75] That the Barkatiyya khandan had been affluent by the standards of its time in the eighteenth and nineteenth centuries is therefore a reasonable assumption. In the early twentieth century, however, one senses that economic decline had set in, for Muhammad Miyan suggests that the family had lost much of its landed property in sales or mismanagement by the mutawallis.[76] Bayly's analysis of economic change in the qasbas during colonial rule also points to a decline in the fortunes of the agriculturally-dependent Muslim gentry.[77]

Nevertheless, the family continued to own considerable land, and

[73] Turner, 'Pilgrimages as Social Processes', p. 197.

[74] Several parganas made up an administrative district.

[75] Elizabeth Whitcombe, *Agrarian Conditions in Northern India: The United Provinces under British Rule, 1860–1900* (Berkeley: University of California Press, 1982), p. 72.

[76] See, e.g. *Khandan-e Barakat*, pp. 9, 15, 18.

[77] Bayly, *Rulers, Townsmen and Bazaars*, pp. 354–8.

to be fairly well-to-do.[78] As landowners, the Barkatiyya Sayyids would have had relations with tenants and agricultural labour, many of whom were probably Hindus. Indeed, according to one scholar, the town's *chamars* ('untouchables' whose traditional occupation was leather-tanning) were a source of cheap labour for the Sayyids of Marahra.[79] Despite the suggestion in this of economic exploitation and conflict, the fact that the Barkatiyya Sayyids were sufi pirs probably played a considerable role in ameliorating relations with their Hindu tenants and labour:

Though there always remained lines of social difference between the landholding Muslim gentry and their Hindu cultivators, and though compulsion played a considerable part in agrarian relations, gentry patronage and Hindu veneration of the shrines of Muslim holy men significantly diminished the scope for conflict and enhanced the solidarity of the qasbah as a society until well into the colonial period. Gentry families, both Hindu and Muslim, communed in Indo-Persian literary culture, while peasants and craftsmen participated in the same festivals and feast days.[80]

Apart from being landowners, the Barkatiyya Sayyids as pirs came into daily contact with a large number of people. Maulawi Ghulam Shabbir Qadiri describes a typical day in Nuri Miyan's daily life as follows:

When not reading the namaz, praying [*waza'if*] or meditating, [Nuri Miyan] would enquire into the affairs of [his] *khuddam* (helpers) and those who came to him with petitions [*sa'ilin*], reply to letters received, visit the sick, write amulets [*nuqush, ta'wiz*], take a break and get some rest, then spend some time with his books, reading or writing . . . . He also paid his respects to Shah Al-e Rasul, presenting himself at his *darbar*, learning of various affairs and receiving advice. [In addition,] he was responsible for the well-being of hundreds of thousands of khuddam. Every day a variety a problems presented themselves

78 It must be remembered that they also had an income (the size of which is unknown) from their sufi activities, for pilgrims, petitioners, and well-wishers always brought gifts in accordance with individual means.

79 S. Jamaluddin, 'Religiopolitical Ideas of a Twentieth Century Muslim Theologian—An Introduction', in *Marxist Miscellany*, 7 (March 1977), p. 17.

80 Bayly, *Rulers, Townsmen and Bazaars*, pp. 192–3. I recognize, of course, that Bayly is here talking of the eighteenth, and perhaps most of the nineteenth centuries, certainly not of the early twentieth century when Hindu–Muslim relations had deteriorated markedly.

before him, and he would deal with them. Never did he put off dealing with something till the next day on the plea that he was too busy, or fail to do something at its proper time. In everything he did, the spirit of the shari'a and the rules of tariqa reigned.[81]

As Ewing points out, 'pirs interact with their followers in a wide variety of ways'.[82] Most people came with everyday problems to be solved, problems such as illness, barrenness, marriage, and business, which required a minimum amount of the pir's time, and were dealt with by writing amulets, giving some advice, and admonishing the person to perform his or her prayers regularly. In addition to this 'outer circle' of followers, a pir might have a smaller number of serious disciples who constituted his 'inner circle', and in whose training he took a great interest. A large part of this training, Ewing says, had to do with the interpretation of dreams.[83]

The relationship between a pir and his murid has frequently been described in the literature. Its main feature is its authoritarianism, modelled on the father-son relationship, in which the pir's authority over his murid, though absolute, is mediated by affection and concern for the disciple.[84] As for the disciple, his pir is his model in everything he does. Ghulam Shabbir Qadiri describes how Nuri Miyan's life-style reflected Shah Al-e Rasul's:

[Nuri Miyan] loved and respected his shaikh; indeed he loved everyone who was associated with him, and all the members of his family. He followed his shaikh ['s commands]; he presented himself before him at his darbar; he sought his company; he was completely absorbed in him. His face had the same radiance [as his shaikh]; his personality had the same stamp (hal); he walked with the same gait; when he spoke, it was in the same tone. His clothes had the same appearance; he dealt with others in the same way. In his devotions and strivings, he followed the same path (*maslak*). The times set apart for rest in the afternoon and sleep at night were times when he went to his shaikh particularly, receiving from him guidance in every matter and warning of every danger.[85]

Among the 'ulama', the Marahra pirs had close relations with

[81] *Tazkira-e Nuri*, pp. 59–60.
[82] Ewing, 'The *Pir* or Sufi Saint', p. 108.
[83] Ibid., pp. 109–10.
[84] Ibid., pp. 87–8; Metcalf, *Islamic Revival*, p. 165.
[85] *Tazkira-e Nuri*, p. 91.

other families of the Qadiri silsila in particular. Their relations with the 'Usmani khandan of Badayun went back to the time when someone in the 'Usmani family became a disciple of Achhe Miyan's in the eighteenth century.[86] Both the Barkati and 'Usmani families had produced several generations of gifted, learned and eminent scholars or sufis, and the relationship between them had thus been one of mutual learning and respect. To cite a few examples, Shah Al-e Rasul had attended classes given by Shah 'Abd ul-Mujid Badayuni at the Madrasa Qadiriyya at Badayun, and Muhammad Miyan's paternal grandfather, Shah Muhammad Sadiq (1833–1908), had studied tibb (Yunani medicine) from the famous 'alim Shah Fazl-e Rasul Badayuni (1798–1873). Nuri Miyan used to consult Maulana 'Abd ul-Qadir Badayuni on matters of fiqh.[87]

One matter which concerned both Nuri Miyan and the 'ulama' of Badayun was the influence of Shi'i and Tafzili ideas in their midst. As noted, the Barkatiyya Sayyids had originally lived in Bilgram (Hardoi district of Awadh), and some branches of the family had been influenced by Shi'ism. Indeed, despite the long-term residence of the Barkatiyya Sayyids at Marahra, marriage networks with the eastern branch of the family remained quite active well into the early twentieth century, when Muhammad Miyan was writing. Daughters who married into 'eastern' families in Kawat (Arrah district, Bihar) or Bilgram generally adopted Shi'i or Tafzili beliefs and brought up their children to do likewise.[88] Two branches of the Sarkar Kalan at Marahra—descendants of Jama Miyan (1780–1833), Suthre Miyan's eldest son, and descendants of Muhammad Taqi Khan (1803–63), Sache Miyan's second son—were reputed to be Tafzilis or Shi'is, in addition to some members of the Sarkar Khurd, who had marriage ties to Jama Miyan's descendants.

The situation in Badayun was of concern to the 'Usmani 'ulama' for a different reason: the spread of Tafzili khanqahs in Badayun and Bareilly. These khanqahs attracted students and disciples, who published books defending their views and popularizing the

[86] Ibid., Introduction, pp. 4–5.

[87] Ibid., p. 72. Ahmad Riza Khan also respected Shah 'Abd ul-Qadir's opinion a great deal, and the two men co-operated closely on the anti-Nadwa issue.

[88] *Khandan-e Barakat*, pp. 25, 28–9, 81–3. *Tazkira-e Nuri*, pp. 24–5.

celebration of Muharram, complete with *ta'ziya* processions, rituals of mourning, and the recital of *marsiyas*.[89] Shah 'Abd ul-Qadir Badayuni, Ahmad Riza Khan, and Nuri Miyan all rebutted the Tafzilis vigorously in numerous books; indeed, their books constituted one side of a learned debate conducted in print rather than verbally, each book or pamphlet being a response or challenge to something the Tafzilis had written.[90] In the opinion of Muhammad Ayub Qadiri, who wrote the introduction to Nuri Miyan's biography, however, the influence of the Ahl-e Sunnat 'ulama' was consequently limited to the learned, and did not reach the public. People continued to flock to Badayun from distant towns in order to see the Muharram processions, which were famous.[91]

The Barkatiyya Pirs' Rise to Prominence

As Peter Brown points out in his essay 'Relics and Social Status in the Age of Gregory of Tours',[92] it needs 'a large measure of hard work on the part of the human community' to ensure that the tombs of saints receive the reverence that they are due. Not every tomb is revered, and many are forgotten. What, then, ensures that they enjoy social status? More specifically, how did a pir family from Bilgram come to establish such a large khanqah in Marahra?

First, the family's association with the Farrukhabad nawabs in the eighteenth century was favourable to the process of building an economic and religious base in the Marahra qasba and beyond. Like other religious families in north India, whether Hindu or Muslim, the Barkatiyya Sayyids profited from the political uncertainties of the eighteenth century by virtue of their legitimizing role *vis-à-vis* the local population. Furthermore, by the early nineteenth century, when British control was established over the region, the family must have been sufficiently prominent to be regarded by the administration as 'natural leaders' of the community. While we do not have evidence for contacts between the Barkatiyya Sayyids and

89 *Tazkira-e Nuri*, pp. 25–9.
90 Ibid., pp. 30–46.
91 Ibid., p. 49.
92 Delivered as The Stenton Lecture 1976, University of Reading, 1977, p. 12.

the British Indian government, the British policy of respect and cordiality towards those regarded as 'natural leaders' is well attested.[93] These conditions allowed the religious élites to prosper.

In addition, the institution of the sajjada-nishini, together with all the movable and immovable properties that went with it, played an important role in preserving intact the resources of a line of pirs and ensuring that they were not diffused among a large number of heirs. Although the family properties were legally of a number of distinct categories,[94] each with its own laws of inheritance, some properties were specifically set apart for the upkeep of the dargah, and were not strictly divisible—although, as was illustrated in the case of the Barkatiyya family, mutawallis were not always above selling or pawning such property. On the whole, however, the existence of resources specifically earmarked for the upkeep of the dargah and khanqah must have been effective in ensuring the continuity through time of a line of pirs. To the extent that such resources were not divided, sold, or pawned, the system may be regarded as a special form of primogeniture (or, in exceptional cases, of undivided inheritance by a younger son), which was effective in building an expandable base of land and wealth controlled by successive generations of sajjada-nishins.

Beyond such political and socio-economic factors, the personality of the pirs also accounts in part for the popularity or prominence of the Barkatiyya pirs. The Barkatiyya family appears to have been fortunate (or blessed, they might say) in having had a series of brilliant and devout sajjada-nishins from the eighteenth century right down to the early twentieth, when Nuri Miyan died. Their names and accomplishments have been noted in this chapter: Achhe Miyan the popular eighteenth-century pir, Suthre Miyan the great builder,

[93] See, e.g., Freitag, *Collective Action and Community*, pp. 57–8: 'the British . . . looked for those exercising power through personal, patron-client relationships, whether operating through residential, occupational, caste, ritual, or extended kinship networks . . . the men identified as 'natural leaders' were raises or magnates of high status: in U.P. the term 'rais' was applied equally to prominent traditional 'headmen', commercial men of the urban areas, and to rural large landowners'.

[94] See Gregory C. Kozlowski, *Muslim Endowments and Society in British India* (Cambridge: Cambridge University Press, 1985), p. 132, for a discussion of the differences between *inam*, *madad-maash*, and *waqf*.

and Shah Al-e Rasul the 'alim and revered sufi were some of them. The personal qualities that are mentioned in the sources may perhaps more usefully be seen as a reflection of the attributes that were valued in a pir than as attempts to realistically portray the individuals themselves. The ideal pir was learned, pious, generous with his time and personal wealth, and fond of solitude. He was also a guide to his disciples, and disbursed amulets and other cures to the sick and needy.

Additionally, the pirs' Sayyid ancestry was an important source of authority, being the inalienable heritage of everyone in the family and a constituent part of the baraka or grace of each member. Most of all, however, Peter Brown reminds us of the importance—as Muhammad Miyan, in his family history, did very clearly as well—of holy relics in the lives of the faithful, and the manner in which new ones were constantly being discovered and 'ratified' in festivals. Sixth-century Gaul, Brown says, was 'a world of movement [in which] new things [were] always happening'.[95] Nineteenth century Marahra, at Basti Pirzadagan, appears not to have been very different in this respect, for, as Muhammad Miyan tells us, the family added to its treasure of relics over several generations.[96] As these relics (hairs of the Prophet and of 'Abd al-Qadir Jilani, 'Ali's robe, and others) were on view at times of pilgrimage (the 'urs), the addition of relics over time undoubtedly enhanced the family's baraka in the eyes of followers, and increased the attractiveness of the 'urs pilgrimage itself.

Finally, we must note as important the reformist nature of the 'urs-e Nuri. As mentioned above, sama' and other so-called *be-shar* practices (practices in disregard of shar'i injunctions) were notably absent at the annual 'urs celebrations. Qur'an readings and na't recitals in praise of the Prophet substituted for controversial practices like sama'.

It is instructive to compare the rituals of the 'urs-e Nuri with those at other 'urs as reported in the *Dabdaba-e Sikandari* in the early

[95] Brown, 'Relics and Social Status' p. 12.

[96] Thus, according to Muhammad Miyan, relics came into the family's possession during the lifetimes of Shah Barkat Ullah (1660–1729), his grandson Shah Hamza (1719–83), and Achhe Miyan (1747–1819), Shah Hamza's eldest son.

twentieth century, in order to grasp the full import of the reformist character of the former. At Gangoh (Saharanpur district), the annual 'urs for Shah 'Abd ul-Quddus Gangohi was a very different affair: the sajjada-nishin made his ceremonial way from his house to his pir's tomb on the back of an elephant, accompanied by *qawwali* (devotional singing) and watched by thousands of men and women who lined the route.[97] Women apparently performed the pilgrimage to the tomb as well.

An even greater contrast to the 'urs-e Nuri was the 'urs in Ajmer for Khwaja Mu'in ud-Din Chishti in June 1915. Reporting on that event Muhammad Fazl-e Hasan Sabiri, editor of the *Dabdaba-e Sikandari*, was distressed to find that shops had been set up over a grave, and worse, that in one section of the dargah a group of self-styled *faqirs* spent their time consuming *charas* (marijuana) and drinking alcohol. Fazl-e Hasan was so outraged by this that he demanded a public explanation for such behaviour from the organizers of the 'urs.[98]

While this is undoubtedly an extreme example of be-shar behaviour, the fact that such practices were current at an important all-India shrine, reinforces the point that the participants and organizers of the 'urs-e Nuri were acutely aware of the difference between this 'urs and others. The annual notices put in the newspapers by the sajjada-nishin indicated that the Barkatiyya family prided itself on its faithfulness to the shari'a during the 'urs. It was a sign of their self-consciously 'Sunni' identity, which, in their view and that of their followers, elevated them above, and distinguished them from, other Muslims in the subcontinent.

[97] *Dabdaba-e Sikandari*, 51:26 (May 17, 1915), 5–6.

[98] Ibid., 51:29 (June 7, 1915), 3–4.

Chapter V

Personalization of Religious Authority

Having examined the social and cultural milieu of the Barkatiyya Sayyids we may now return to the world in which Ahmad Riza moved, with increased understanding. His relations with the pirs and 'ulama' of Marahra, Badayun, and other qasba or commercial towns of north India drew him into a network of social, economic, and ritual relations with other learned and pious Muslims, and through them, as in his own capacity as 'alim, into relations with the non-Muslim world of nineteenth-century British India as well. In this chapter, I approach the discussion of religious authority in his life from three perspectives: Ahmad Riza's devotion to his pir, and his views on the nature of a pir's relationship with, and authority over, his disciples generally; his devotion to Shaikh 'Abd al-Qadir Jilani, the founder of the Qadiri order of sufis, with which he identified more closely than with other orders, though he was also affiliated with the Chishti, Naqshbandi, and Suhrawardi orders; and finally, the place of the Prophet as a pivotal figure in his life.

Devotion to the three figures of pir, shaikh,[1] and Prophet was central to Ahmad Riza as believer and to his perception of what it meant to be a 'good Muslim'. Nor were they unrelated to each other in his life: his writings make clear that each is a pathway, and a guide,

[1] I deliberately use the term 'shaikh' to denote the founder of one of the major sufi orders, as distinct from a personal pir, although the two terms are generally used interchangeably. This appears to be the only way of making the distinction between two entirely different levels of belief and ritual practice.

to the next. The culmination of religious authority, in the world of men, is the Prophet.

One of the chief sources I will be drawing upon in this chapter are Ahmad Riza's *Malfuzat*, the collection of orally delivered homilies and responses to questions posed by followers, that was compiled by his son, Mustafa Riza Khan. Important, too, in this context, is Ahmad Riza's diwan, or anthology of poetry, entitled *Hada'iq-e Bakhshish*. The poems, which deal for the most part with the qualities of the Prophet, often have a simplicity and directness that give us additional insight into Ahmad Riza as believer. There is also an extensive collection of fatawa by him on these themes. Indeed, this genre constituted Ahmad Riza's hallmark. I will draw upon some of the fatawa here, though detailed examination of the fatwa literature will not begin until the next chapter.

The Pir in Ahmad Riza's Life

As noted in Chapter II, Ahmad Riza received bai'a, or initiation into discipleship, from Shah Al-e Rasul of Marahra, in 1877, two years before the latter's death. Ahmad Riza's own personal recollections and record of his pir are rather limited in content, which is understandable in the circumstances. Ahmad Riza was about twenty-one at the time; Shah Al-e Rasul, in his eighties. Nor does Ahmad Riza appear to have spent any length of time studying under his direction; indeed, it is related in the *Sirat-e A'la Hazrat* that he was ready for discipleship immediately he met Shah Al-e Rasul, and did not need the forty-day period of instruction which was customary prior to an initiation.[2] The absence of a close personal relationship is also indicated, I believe, by the fact that there is no mention, in Ahmad Riza's *Malfuzat* or in the biographies of him, of

[2] Hasnain Riza Khan, *Sirat-e A'la Hazrat* p. 55. While the hagiographical literature sees this lack of a period of instruction as a sign of Ahmad Riza's high attainments, and gives him centre stage as it were in this event, the decision to seek bai'a from Shah Al-e Rasul was probably made by Naqi 'Ali, Ahmad Riza's father, on Maulana 'Abd ul-Qadir Badayuni's advice. Naqi 'Ali and Ahmad Riza did not know Shah Al-e Rasul personally. Why did 'Abd ul-Qadir, who was also a pir, not make father and son his own disciples? I think it probable that they had expressed a wish to become disciples of a Sayyid, which he, as a descendant of an 'Usmani family, was not.

dreams in which his pir appeared to him, although he reported having seen in his dreams his father, his grandfather, and the Prophet.[3] As an adult, Ahmad Riza was to receive instruction from, and seek the advice of, Nuri Miyan, Shah Al-e Rasul's sajjada-nishin and grandson, who was about fifteen years his senior. Ahmad Riza respected Nuri Miyan as his pir's sajjada-nishin and reportedly had a close personal relationship with him.

Despite the fact that Ahmad Riza did not have such a relationship with Shah Al-e Rasul, the latter held a special place of honour and regard in his life. This is clear from the fact that from about 1905 or 1906, until his death in 1921, Ahmad Riza held an annual 'urs for Shah Al-e Rasul on the latter's death anniversary, at his own home in Bareilly. For three days each year, from the 16th to the 18th Zu'l Hijja, the occasion was commemorated with milad, khatma of the Qur'an, recitation of na't poetry, and sermons by the 'ulama'. The highlight of the proceedings was the sermon (wa'z, bayan) delivered by Ahmad Riza,[4] in which he spoke feelingly and eloquently (so the reports tell us) on a particular *ayat* (verse) of the Qur'an, Shaikh 'Abd al-Qadir Jilani, and the Prophet. Evidently, he was an effective and powerful speaker, for the reports never fail to mention the religious transport and ecstasy of his listeners. One writer reported:

> Everyone was completely captivated [by his wa'z]. Sometimes he makes you laugh, sometimes he makes you cry, sometimes he makes you feel agitated.

He continued:

> If you want to hear the true praises of the Prophet, you must hear them from the lips of A'la Hazrat [Ahmad Riza]. The qualities with which he has been blessed by God make it clear that he is the Mujaddid of the present century . . . . And at a time when such turbid fissures are opening up [among Sunnis], A'la Hazrat is a shield and a chisel.[5]

[3] Ahmad Riza Khan, *Malfuzat-e A'la Hazrat*, vol. 1, p. 83; vol. 3, pp. 68–9.

[4] See, e.g., *Dabdaba-e Sikandari*, 45:50 (January 10, 1910), 9; 46:50 (December 26, 1910), 12–13; 47:51 (December 18, 1911), 3.

[5] Ibid., 46:29 (August 1, 1910), 6. The occasion for this wa'z was an 'urs-e Nuri at Marahra. A mujaddid is a renewer of the religious law, who seeks to ensure that the shari'a is implemented and followed in peoples' lives. The effort of renewal is called tajdid.

Others have reported, as well, on the eloquence of Ahmad Riza's sermons, and the huge crowds he drew.[6]

Even though Shah Al-e Rasul died soon after Ahmad Riza became his disciple, Ahmad Riza did not consider his relationship with his pir, or with the Barkatiyya family, to have ended. His relationship of discipleship appeared instead to embrace the Barkatiyya ancestors of Shah Al-e Rasul, and Nuri Miyan his sajjada-nishin, and to continue in time beyond his death. In a sense Ahmad Riza's relation with Shah Al-e Rasul transcended Shah Al-e Rasul himself, reaching beyond him to the chain of spiritual (and actual) ancestors who were the source of his spiritual authority. The source of their authority, in turn, was in the final analysis their descent from the Prophet. The *shajara* or family tree, in which one's ancestors were listed by name down to oneself, was an important testimonial of authority linking its bearer to the Prophet. Ahmad Riza has a poem in his diwan in which he traces his spiritual descent from the Prophet, through such eminent figures as 'Ali, Husain, 'Abd al-Qadir Jilani, and his pir Shah Al-e Rasul.[7]

In his *Malfuzat*, Ahmad Riza illustrated the point that a person's relationship with his (or her) pir reaches back to the pir's own pir, and so on, with a story about a poor man (faqir) who asked a shopkeeper for alms. When the shopkeeper refused, the faqir began to shout at him, and threatened to turn his shop upside down. This caused a crowd to gather around them. In the crowd was a man of vision who pleaded with the shopkeeper to accede to the faqir's demands. He told the crowd that he had looked into the faqir's heart

> to find out whether there was anything there. I found it empty. Then I looked into his pir's heart, and found that empty as well. I looked at his pir's pir. I found him to be a man of Allah. And I saw that he was standing by and waiting, wondering when the faqir would finally carry out his threat. What had happened was that the faqir was holding on tightly to his pir's garment (*daman*).[8]

[6] See Zafar ud-Din Bihari, *Hayat-e A'la Hazrat*, pp. 97–8, 114, for example.

[7] Ahmad Riza Khan, *Hada'iq-e Bakhshish* (Karachi: Medina Publishing Company, n.d.), Part I, pp. 66–8. I am grateful to Mr. Nigar Erfaney of Karachi for his translation of this shajara.

[8] *Malfuzat*, vol. 3, pp. 29–30. The Urdu original reads 'shaikh' rather than 'pir' as in my translation.

The story conjures up an eloquent picture of a continuous chain of sufi pirs watching over the affairs of their disciples' disciples, many generations removed from them. Clearly, Ahmad Riza did not believe that the relationship of a murid to his pir ended at the latter's death.[9]

On one occassion Ahmad Riza was asked for a fatwa in answer to the question why a Muslim who had grown up in a Sunni home, and had the Qur'an and the hadiṡ to guide him in his daily affairs, should seek a pir.[10] This was an important question, for it raised doubts about the human need for discipleship. Ahmad Riza responded by saying that the Qur'an and hadis contain everything: shari'a, tariqa, and *haqiqa* (truth), the greatest of these being the shari'a. However, knowledge of the shari'a has been handed down from one generation of scholars (mujtahids, those qualified to interpret the shari'a, and 'ulama') to another; had this not been so, ordinary people would have had no way of knowing right from wrong. This being the case with matters related to the shari'a, it was even more vital that there be a similar chain (silsila) for the transmission of gnostic knowledge (*ma'rifa*), which cannot be extracted from the Qur'an and hadis without a teacher (murshid). To try to do so is to embark on a dark road, and be misled along the way by Satan.[11]

But even if one were not seeking gnostic knowledge for its own sake, Ahmad Riza continued, one needed a pir for a different, and more fundamental, reason: without a pir one could not reach Allah. The Qur'an commands one to seek a means (*wasila*) to reach Him. This means is the Prophet. And the means to reach the Prophet are the masha'ikh (pl. of shaikh). It is absurd to imagine that one could have access to Allah without an intermediary; as for the Prophet,

[9] Indeed, it appears that the impending death of a pir causes large numbers of people to seek bai'a from him before it is too late. See below.

[10] *Naqa' al-Salafa fi Ahkam al-Bai'a wa'l Khilafa* (Absorption of the [Teachings of Our] Forebears on the Duties of Discipleship), reprint (Sialkot, Pakistan: Maktaba Mihiriyya Rizwiyya, n.d.), p. 9. The date of the question is 25 Jamadi ul-Awwal 1318/August 1900. Originally published in 1319/1901.

[11] Ibid., pp. 9–11. This is based on a hadis that says, 'He who does not have a shaikh, Satan is his shaikh'. Cf. Annemarie Schimmel, *Mystical Dimensions of Islam* (Chapel Hill: University of North Carolina Press, 1975), p. 103.

access to him was difficult (*dushwar*, though presumably not impossible) without one. Ahmad Riza added that hadis proved that there was a chain of intercession to God beginning with the Prophet interceding with Allah himself. At the next level, the masha'ikh would intercede with the Prophet on behalf of their followers in all situations and circumstances, including the grave (*qabr*). It would be foolish in the extreme, therefore, for one not to bind oneself to a pir and thus ensure help in times of need.[12]

Finally, Ahmad Riza argued that union with the Prophet (through the succession of pirs to whom one was related by means of one's own pir) is a matter of grace (baraka), in itself no small thing. If a chain of transmission was through pirs and masha'ikh of eminence, that was all to the good in terms of the baraka that accrued. In this regard allegiance to Shaikh 'Abd al-Qadir Jilani was better than allegiance to other sufi founders, for he protected the welfare of his murids in no matter what situation.

Ahmad Riza's *Malfuzat* also contain references to the relationship that should obtain between a pir and his murid, and the conditions which should guide a person in choosing a pir. He emphasized the importance of having the right intention or inner desire (*irada*), without which the relationship would be sterile, and 'nothing would happen'. The pir's ability to guide his disciple was thus in part dependent on the disciple's purity of intention and his faith in him. The tie between them was indissoluble and irreplaceable. Ahmad Riza illustrated his point with the following story:

> Bai'a is as Hazrat Yahya Muneri's disciple understood it to be: he was drowning in a river, when Hazrat Khizr (upon him be peace) appeared and asked him for his hand, so that he could pull him out. The disciple replied, I have already given my hand [in discipleship] to Hazrat Yahya Muneri. I can no longer give it to anyone else. Hazrat Khizr (upon him be peace) disappeared, and Hazrat Yahya Muneri appeared and pulled his disciple ashore to safety.[13]

As Ahmad Riza put it memorably on one occasion, 'the fact is that

[12] *Naqa' al-Salafa fi Ahkam al-Bai'a wa'l Khilafa*, p. 12.

[13] *Malfuzat*, vol. 2, p. 41. On the indissolubility of the bond of bai'a, also see *Malfuzat*, vol. 3, pp. 59–60.

the Ka'ba is the qibla of the body, and the pir is the qibla of the soul'.[14]

A disciple attained supreme closeness to his pir in the condition of *fana fi'l-shaikh*, or total absorption in the latter. Thereafter, Ahmad Riza explained, the disciple would never be separated from his pir, regardless of the circumstances. The pir was there to guide and admonish him at all times. Ahmad Riza related the story of one such case to his followers:

Hafiz ul-Hadis Sayyid Ahmad Sijilmasi was going somewhere. Suddenly his eyes lifted from the ground, and he saw a beautiful woman. The glance had been inadvertent [and so no blame attached to him]. But then he looked up again. This time he saw his pir and murshid, Sayyid Ghaus ul-Waqt 'Abd al-'Aziz Dabbagh.[15]

Thus Ahmad Riza advised his followers to choose carefully. A pir should fulfil four exacting standards. He must be a Sunni of good faith (sahih 'aqida). Further, he must be an 'alim or scholar, one who has sufficient knowledge of the Law to solve his own problems and answer his own questions without having to ask someone else to interpret the shari'a for him. Third, the chain of transmission (silsila) should reach back from him, without a single break, to the Prophet. And finally, he should lead an exemplary life, and not be disobedient or wicked in his personal habits.[16]

One sees here, as in other writings by Ahmad Riza, the emphasis on following the shari'a which I argued was also characteristic of the pirs of Marahra. In his *Malfuzat*, he related several stories about ignorant sufis, who have no knowledge of fiqh, mistaking Satan for God:

There was a wali who made large claims for himself. An ascetic heard about him. He called the wali and asked him what he could do. The wali said he saw Khuda [God] every single day. Every day Khuda's canopy ['*arsh*] spread itself on the ocean and Khuda appeared on it. Now, if he had knowledge, he would have known that it is impossible [*muhal*] in this world to see Khuda, that this was something given only to the Prophet. At any rate, the ascetic called

[14] Ibid., vol. 2, p. 65.
[15] Ibid., p. 45.
[16] Ibid., p. 41.

someone and asked him to read the hadis in which the Prophet said that Iblis spreads his throne [*takht*] over the ocean. [When this had been done, the so-called wali] understood that all this time he had mistaken Satan for God, had been prostrating himself before Satan, had been worshipping him. He rent his clothes and vanished into a forest.[17]

Ahmad Riza as Pir

Ahmad Riza himself, while primarily an 'alim, specifically a mufti (jurisconsult) whose opinion was frequently sought on a wide range of issues, was pir to a small number of disciples.[18] He founded the silsila Rizwiyya,[19] and in November 1915 ensured its continuity by appointing his elder son, Hamid Riza Khan, as his sajjada-nishin. The ceremony took place on the last day of the annual 'urs celebration that year for Shah Al-e Rasul.[20] Ahmad Riza placed his robe (khirqa), received from Shah Al-e Rasul, on Hamid Riza's shoulders, and his own turban ('imama) on his head, before reading the authority (sanad) of the sajjada-nishini in Arabic and Urdu. After his death in 1921, his disciples and followers affirmed their allegiance to Hamid Riza as his sajjada-nishin.[21]

In addition to his small circle of murids, Ahmad Riza had a much larger circle of khalifas. Some of them, such as Na'im ud-Din

[17] Ibid., vol. 3, pp. 22–3.

[18] It is virtually impossible to estimate who these were, and how many. In addition to his two sons, Hamid Riza Khan and Mustafa Riza Khan, the names of a few others are known, such as Haji Kifayat Ullah, and Hafiz Yaqin ud-Din Qadiri. The difficulty with identifying Ahmad Riza's disciples is that the individuals named in the literature are often khalifas rather than murids. The difference between them will be discussed below. See *Sirat-e A'la Hazrat*, pp. 124, 132; *Hayat-e A'la Hazrat*, pp. 139–40

[19] By 'silsila' is here meant a chain of discipleship that culminates in a particular pir, not a sufi order. The name Rizwi or Rizwiyya is derived from the 'Riza' in Ahmad Riza's name. A person who wrote 'Rizwi' after his name (probably as part of a string of epithets, written in descending order of importance, such as 'Sunni Hanafi Qadiri Rizwi Barelwi') would be signalling the pir to whom he bore allegiance.

[20] *Dabdaba-e Sikandari*, 51:51 (November 8, 1915), 3.

[21] This occurred in the course of ceremonies marking the fortieth day of Ahmad Riza's death, on December 8, 1921. While I have not seen an account of the event, an announcement that this was intended was made by Hamid Riza and Mustafa Riza in *Dabdaba-e Sikandari*, 58:13 (November 28, 1922), 5.

Muradabadi and Didar ʻAli Alwari, were prominent leaders of the Ahl-e Sunnat wa Jamaʻat in the 1920s.[22] Many came to him from different parts of north India (and central India, in the case of Burhan ul-Haqq Jabalpuri, a murid) toward the end of their course of studies, attracted to him by his growing reputation for scholarship and for the particular point of view he espoused. The term 'khilafat' as it applied to these and other men, did not necessarily denote a relationship of discipleship to Ahmad Riza. It was a loosely applied term, it would appear, usually an honorific bestowed by Ahmad Riza. Granting khilafat was an individual and public act, undertaken from time to time. Thus the *Dabdaba-e Sikandari* reported in January 1910 that on the third and last day of the 'urs for Shah Al-e Rasul at Ahmad Riza's house that year, Ahmad Riza bestowed the title of khalifa on Maulana Zafar ud-Din Bihari by tying a turban (the dastar-e khilafat) on his head. Zafar ud-Din fell at his feet, and Ahmad Riza responded by giving him 'necessary counsel' (*nasihat*).[23]

Ahmad Riza explained the difference between a khalifa and a murid by saying that there are two kinds of khilafat, the ordinary ('amm) and the special (khass).[24] The first kind obtains when a murshid (teacher) chooses to make someone he considers worthy (*la'iq*), whether a student of his or a follower, his khalifa and deputy (*na'ib*). The teacher guides his khalifa in matters related to sufism (*azkar, ashghal, aurad, a'mal*). The 'position' (*masnad*) is of religious (*dini*) significance alone, and there is no limit to the number of khalifas that he may choose to have. This relationship ceases upon the death of the teacher. By contrast, in the second kind of khilafat, the khalifa continues in this role even after his murshid's death. The relationship is special because the khalifa in this case is his murshid's sajjada-nishin, a position to which only one person may be appointed. And here the role carries worldly responsibilities for the maintenance of properties. Ahmad Riza went on to say that this

[22] See Muhammad Masʻud Ahmed, *Neglected Genius of the East: An Introduction to the Life and the Works of Mawlana Ahmad Rida Khan of Bareilly (India) 1272/1856–1340/1921* (Lahore: Rida Academy, 1987), p. 11, for an incomplete list of Ahmad Riza's khalifas.

[23] *Dabdaba-e Sikandari*, 45:50 (January 10, 1910), 9.

[24] *Naqa' al-Salafa fi Ahkam al-Bai'a wa'l Khilafa*, p. 14.

position usually devolves upon the murshid's eldest son, though various shar'i conditions may obtain to alter the situation.[25]

However, this two-fold distinction between the sajjada-nishin on the one hand, and a large number of khalifas on the other, does not convey the diversity of possible relationships between a murshid and his murids or khalifas. On examination it appears that the relationship between a murshid and his murid was not always as close or as intense as has been described above. In Ahmad Riza's own case, shortly before his death a large number of men and women came forward to take bai'a at his hands; so many that he had to deputize his two sons, Hamid Riza and Mustafa Riza, to officiate on his behalf.[26] Obviously not all who became his murids at this time could enjoy a close relationship with him; nor, probably, had they made the careful and thoughtful choice that he had advised. These murids do not fit the picture of one who was giving of him or herself to the pir in the total sense that is described in the literature, including Ahmad Riza's *Malfuzat.* What had probably attracted them to him was the baraka that he, as a learned, upright, and renowned pir (and 'alim), was believed to possess. Nevertheless, the term used in this case is also 'bai'a.

Conversely, Ahmad Riza's relations with his khalifas were not as distant as may appear from his categorization. His relations with them appear to have been rather loosely structured, individual, and diverse. He was their murshid in the informal sense that they respected him greatly, and sought to promote the same ends as he in their own lives; but they did not necessarily live in Bareilly or take instruction from him. Na'im ud-Din Muradabadi (1882–1948), one of Ahmad Riza's khalifas, was a forceful personality. He had already built up a reputation for disputation against 'Wahhabis'[27] and Arya Samajis in Muradabad before he came to Ahmad Riza's attention on account of an article he had written in a local

[25] Ibid., pp. 15–21.

[26] *Sirat-e A'la Hazrat,* p. 124.

[27] A term used by the Ahl-e Sunnat in a loosely-defined sense to include the 'ulama' of the Tariqa-e Muhammadiyya, Deoband, and Ahl-e Hadis, as well as modernist Muslim intellectuals such as Sir Sayyid Ahmad Khan. For detailed treatment of the issue, see Chapter VIII below.

newspaper.[28] He neither studied under Ahmad Riza's direction, nor took bai'a from him, though Ahmad Riza's writings and point of view had influenced his thinking before they met. Once the two men got to know each other, Na'im ud-Din was a frequent visitor at Bareilly, and Ahmad Riza would summon him from time to time to represent the Ahl-e Sunnat wa Jama'at at debates in different parts of the country. For the rest, he was busy writing and debating, and in 1919–20 he set up a madrasa in Muradabad.[29] The relationship between Ahmad Riza and Na'im ud-Din, then, was to a large degree that of intellectual companions, Na'im ud-Din respecting Ahmad Riza as the older and more widely-read 'alim.

Ahmad Riza interacted on a day-to-day basis with a diffuse set of people who sought his advice on all kinds of matters, great and small. Some hours in the late afternoon were set aside for this purpose. We have already seen that Nuri Miyan too allotted some time each day to meeting people and advising them on their problems. As with Nuri Miyan, an important function Ahmad Riza performed for this wide circle of followers was that of curing or healing. A man who came to him asking for a prayer (du'a) because he was beset with problems, was told:

> A Companion [sahabi] went to the Prophet and said, the world has turned its back on me. He said, Don't you remember that tasbih [prayer of praise] praising the angels, by the baraka of which we receive our daily food? Good fortune will come to you after your distress. At the time of the fajr prayer of sunrise, repeat this prayer ('Subhan Allah bi-hamdihi subhan allah al-azim wa bi-hamdihi astaghfir Allah'). Seven days after the Prophet had given the sahabi this advice, the sahabi returned. His fortune had changed so much, he said, that he didn't know how to describe it. You too [Ahmad Riza addressed the man] should repeat this prayer. If you miss the time of sunrise, say it in the morning after joining the congregation at the fajr prayer. And if some day you miss saying it even then, say it before sunrise [of the following day].[30]

The solution to a problem was not always that simple, however. When a man came to him saying that after many years of childless-

[28] Mu'in ud-Din Na'imi, 'Tazkira al-Ma'ruf Hayat-e Sadar al-Afazil', *Sawad-e A'zam*, vol. 2 (Lahore: Na'imi Dawakhana, 1378/1959), pp. 6–7.

[29] Ibid., pp. 7–10, 20.

[30] *Malfuzat*, vol. 1, p. 62.

ness, he had six children only to lose five of them, and that he now had only a three-year old daughter left, Ahmad Riza said:

Next time you are expecting a baby, come here and tell me within two months of conception. Also tell me your wife's and her mother's names. Thereafter, insha'llah, arrangements will be made. Make sure everyone in your household is punctilious in offering namaz, and after every namaz the Ayat al-Kursi should be repeated . . . . And apart from the namaz, the Ayat al-Kursi should be repeated thrice a day—before sunrise, before sundown, and at bedtime. Even women who don't have permission to say the namaz [i.e., are menstruating] should repeat this ayat. But on such days they should say it with the intention not of repeating an ayat of the Qur'an but of praising Allah. And on the days that they are permitted to read the namaz, they should also read the qul three times thrice a day (before sunrise, before sunset, and before sleeping). [Detailed instructions on the position of the hands follow.] There is an elderly man here who makes large lamps (*chiragh*). Get him to make you one, and light it from the time conception takes place right until the time of birth. As for the daughter you already have, if she gets ill, light a lamp for her as well. That lamp will guard against sorcery (*sihr*), misfortune (*aseb*) and disease. And as soon as a new child is born the azan should be repeated in its ear seven times, four times in the right ear and three times in the left. There should be absolutely no delay in doing this. If you delay, Satan enters [the child's body]. For forty days after birth, the child should be weighed against grain, and [the equivalent weight of grain] given in alms. After that, this should be done once a month until it's a year old; once every two months until it is two years old, and once every three months until it is three. In its fourth year, this should be done once every four months, and so too in its fifth year. In its sixth year, it should be done every six months. And from its seventh year on, once a year. Do this for your daughter as well. Since she is in her fourth year, weigh her every four months. Repeat the azan out loud in her ear for seven days at maghrib, seven times on each occasion. And for three evenings, the Surat al-Baqara should be read by a qualified reader (*khwan*) in a loud voice that will reach every corner of the house. At night the door of the house should be shut while saying 'Bism'illah', and the same when opening the door in the morning. When going to the bathroom (*pa-khana*), one should say the Bism'illah outside the door and enter with one's left foot first. And when leaving, one should extend one's right foot first. When taking off one's clothes or bathing, one should say the Bism'illah first. And when approaching one another, both husband and wife should remember to say this first. If you observe all this advice, insha'llah, no harm will befall you.[31]

[31] Ibid., vol. 3, pp. 9–11.

Ahmad Riza's lengthy response shows the seriousness with which he viewed the man's problem. The ingredients of the cure were, essentially, simple: punctiliousness in observing the namaz, repetition of certain verses of the Qur'an (repetition of the Ayat al-Kursi being widespread as a cure), awareness of the details of every personal deed and of the correct way of performing it, and finally, the giving of alms on a large scale. A distinctive feature of his response, which recalls Denny's comment that reciting the Qur'an is in a sense a magical act,[32] was that reciting a verse of the Qur'an repeatedly would ward off the problem at hand.

This was very clear when, on another occasion, Ahmad Riza was asked whether one could receive grace (baraka) only after death or also during one's lifetime. In the course of his reply that grace may accrue both before and after death, Ahmad Riza alluded to the Surat al-Mulk (67),[33] which, he explained, intercedes for the person who prayed to it. The sura was portrayed anthropomorphically in the female gender:

> Nothing exceeds this sura's ability to save [the dead] from the punishment of the grave and to convey peace and tranquillity. If the punishing angels wish to come to the reader of this sura, she [the sura] stops them from doing so. If they try to come from another direction, she hinders them from there. 'He is reading me', she says. The angels say, 'We have come at His command, whose *kalam* [speech] you are'. Then the sura says, 'Wait then, don't come near him until I return'. And the sura puts up such a fight on behalf of the reader at Allah's court, pleading for his pardon . . . . If there is a delay in the pardon being granted, she argues, 'He used to read me, and You haven't forgiven him. If I am not Your kalam, tear me out of Your Book'. The Lord replies, 'Go. I have forgiven him'. The sura immediately goes to heaven. She collects silk cloths, pillows, flowers and perfumes from there, and brings them to the grave. 'I got held up coming here', she explains. 'You didn't get worried, I hope?' And she spreads out the cloths and the pillows, while the angels, commanded by God, go away.[34]

While he attached considerable importance to the 'magical' as a

[32] Denny, 'Islamic Ritual', in Martin (ed.), *Approaches to Islam in Religious Studies*, p. 76.

[33] Referred to in the text as 'Sura Tabaraka', after the first word in the sura. I am grateful to Professor Christian W. Troll for identifying the sura for me.

[34] Ibid., vol. 1, pp. 70–1.

cure to problems, Ahmad Riza also emphasized on numerous occasions the role of individual effort, and of internal 'purity of heart' and purpose in achieving the desired result.[35] Just as a pir could not by himself ensure the progress of the disciple unless the latter had the right 'intention', so also with the removal of obstacles. If the seeker was pure of heart, Allah never failed him. Ahmad Riza cited a hadis qudsi (Divine Saying) in which Allah is reported to have said, '. . . And if he draws nearer to Me by a handsbreadth, I draw nearer to him by an armslength; and if he draws nearer to Me by an armslength, I draw nearer to him by a fathom; and if he comes to Me walking, I come to him running'.[36] Clearly, though, the onus was on the individual to make the first move toward Allah before he could be helped.

In the same vein, Ahmad Riza cautioned his listeners not to undertake the fast or the hajj, or go into seclusion toward the end of Ramazan (*e'tikaf*), for the wrong reasons: they must perform these deeds for Allah, not for themselves, although good would come to them as a result of having done them.[37] And when judging the actions of others, they must be careful not to entertain doubts about others' sincerity as long as a possibility existed that they were well-intentioned.[38] They had constantly to be watchful over the heart, ever given to disobedience (*ma'asi*) and reprehensible innovation (bid'a). A time could come when a person became completely blind to the truth.[39]

The *Malfuzat* reveal the wide range of questions that Ahmad Riza dealt with in these daily conversations. Some related to personal appearance, such as the permissibility or otherwise of dyeing one's

[35] The individual, he explained on another occasion, is composed of *nafs* (the base instincts), *qalb* ('heart' in a metaphoric sense), and *ruh* (spirit). Ibid., vol. 3, p. 63. For a discussion of the background of this tripartite division in sufi thought, see Schimmel, *Mystical Dimensions of Islam*, pp. 191–2. For the importance of 'intention' in sufism, see Padwick, *Muslim Devotions*, pp. 52–4.

[36] *Malfuzat*, vol. 4, p. 33. The translation is by William A. Graham, *Divine Word and Prophetic Word in Early Islam: A Reconsideration of the Sources, with Special Reference to the Divine Saying or Hadith Qudsi* (The Hague, Paris: Mouton, 1977), pp. 127–30.

[37] *Malfuzat*, vol. 1, pp. 29–30.

[38] Ibid., vol. 2, pp. 91, 93.

[39] Ibid., vol. 3, p. 63.

hair black, wearing one's hair long if one were a man, or wearing rings of various metals.[40] Others related to ritual practice, such as the correct manner of performing ablution (*wuzu'*) before prayer, the performance of the prayer itself, or the etiquette (*adab*) to be observed in a mosque.[41] Sometimes conversation turned to marital relations, or to relations with non-Muslims.[42] Beliefs about the dead, their intercession with the Prophet on behalf of the living, the Prophet's knowledge of the unseen, all these and other matters were discussed repeatedly. These daily conversations with people in the neighbourhood, town, and region in and around Bareilly must have been an important factor in Ahmad Riza's growth of influence and stature over the years. Although we have no way of knowing, his audience probably included people who were illiterate, on whom Ahmad Riza's advice and display of learning may have had a particularly powerful impact.[43]

In this examination of the nature of religious authority in Ahmad Riza's life, particularly in reference to the role of the pir that we have looked at so far, it is clear that Ahmad Riza himself exercised considerable personal religious authority over his followers, as did his pir and other scholarly and saintly men over him. What were the likely sources of this authority?

Simon Digby has addressed this question in relation to the Chishti shaikhs in the Sultanate period (twelfth and thirteenth centuries).[44] Digby looks at a range of personal attributes which, as sources of prestige, enhanced the reputation and standing of a pir at that time. These could include 'learning and orthodoxy in conjunction with descent from the Prophet and . . . rank as a Sufi Shaikh', 'poetic sensibility', and 'the ability to construct, extend and organize a

[40] Ibid., vol. 2, p. 102; vol. 3, p. 2.

[41] Ibid., vol. 2, pp. 88–9, 108–12.

[42] Ibid., vol. 2, pp. 86, 97; vol. 3, p. 44.

[43] In this context see Francis Robinson, 'Islam and Muslim Society in South Asia', in *Contributions to Indian Sociology*, 17 (1983), 194–5, wherein he refers to the 'special chemistry of personal contact' as a factor 'spreading Islamic knowledge and bringing about a wider observance of Islamic law'.

[44] Digby, 'The Sufi Shaikh as a Source of Authority', in Marc Gaborieau (ed.), *Islam and Society in South Asia*, pp. 57–8.

Khanqah; to feed, accommodate and attend to the material and spiritual needs of disciples and often numerous dependants; and to accommodate travellers according to Muslim precept and the expectations of hospitality'.[45] Most of these personal attributes (and Digby mentions others), with the exception of Sayyid ancestry, accurately describe Ahmad Riza as pir. Zafar ud-Din Bihari, Ahmad Riza's biographer, enumerates his qualities in the *Hayat-e A'la Hazrat*, including, among others, Islamic equality, kindness to the poor, generosity toward others, depth of learning, and vigilance in the observance of din.[46]

It should be pointed out, however, that these values applied in the particular context of Ahmad Riza's vision of right belief and conduct. Zafar ud-Din sees no contradiction between 'Islamic equality', by which he means that Ahmad Riza treated people of low social status at par with those of high social standing, and Ahmad Riza's proverbial respect for Sayyids, whom he treated with a deference accorded to no one else on account of their descent from the Prophet.[47] A small example of this was that Sayyids were given twice as much food at a milad celebration as other guests at Ahmad Riza's household. Likewise, Ahmad Riza's refusal to have anything to do with Shi'is is interpreted as a sign of his uncompromising attitude in matters related to 'mazhab';[48] Zafar ud-Din comments that people ignorant of din and shar' mistook Ahmad Riza's mazhabi firmness for rudeness or harshness.[49] 'Wahhabis' of various descriptions, whose views Ahmad Riza devoted a lifetime rebutting, were also understood to be outside the circle of those to whom he extended a courteous welcome. In all that Ahmad Riza said and did, he drew a clear line between right and wrong belief and action. This unambiguity, backed by his unquestioned erudition, was perhaps his greatest source of prestige and authority in his followers' eyes.[50]

45 Ibid., pp. 61, 67.

46 *Hayat-e A'la Hazrat*, pp. 40, 46, 50, 131, 181.

47 Ibid., pp. 203–8.

48 Zafar ud-Din Bihari uses mazhab (Ar., madhab) interchangeably with din, the faith.

49 *Hayat-e A'la Hazrat*, pp. 189–92.

50 See, in this context, Katherine P. Ewing, 'Ambiguity and *Shari'at*—A Perspective on the Problem of Moral Principles in Tension', in Katherine P. Ewing (ed.), *Shari'at and*

Shaikh 'Abd al-Qadir Jilani, Founder of the Qadiri Order

The Qadiri order (tariqa) named after Shaikh 'Abd al-Qadir Jilani Baghdadi (d. 1166) is more popular in South Asia than in any other part of the Muslim world apart from Iraq, its place of origin. Ewing writes that 'Abdul Qadir Gilani . . . is regarded as the patron of all the sufi orders in South Asia'.[51] Among pilgrims to his tomb in Baghdad, South Asians outnumber those from other parts of the world.[52] In the late twentieth century Pakistanis (and Iraqis) are the chief source of the authority of the keeper of 'Abd al-Qadir's tomb at Baghdad. The Pakistanis 'periodically send gifts which form the main source of the revenues of his establishment; the members of this family find it worth while to learn Urdu'.[53]

'Abd al-Qadir Jilani, born in Jilan, Iran, migrated to Baghdad as a young man. After several years in solitude as an ascetic he decided in the latter half of his life to become a preacher. As a follower of the Hanbali school, he taught and preached at a madrasa of Hanbali law, and also at a *ribat* or monastery. Both institutions were famous in twelfth-century Baghdad, and 'Abd al-Qadir was by all accounts very popular. His efforts as a preacher gained him the title 'Muhyi ud-Din' or 'reviver of the faith' which, allegedly, had grown weak at the time.[54]

To the Qadiris in the subcontinent, the founder of their order who has over ninety-nine names, is called 'Ghaus-e A'zam', or 'Greatest Helper'.[55] This suggests that he is viewed primarily as one who intercedes with Allah. Padwick explains, 'while the *Shafa'a* [intercession] of the Prophet is his people's great hope for the life of

---

Ambiguity in South Asian Islam (Delhi: Oxford University Press, 1988).

51 Ewing, 'The *Pir* or Sufi Saint in Pakistani Islam', p. 142.

52 Schimmel, *Mystical Dimensions of Islam*, p. 247.

53 D. S. Margoliouth, 'Kadiriyya', in *El2*, p. 382. The article has presumably been updated since Margoliouth's death, though the editor's name is not indicated.

54 See ibid., pp. 380–3. Also, Aftab ud-Din Ahmad's 'Life-Sketch' in his translation of 'Abd al-Qadir's *Futuh al-Ghaib* ('*The Revelations of the Unseen*') (Lahore: Sh. Muhammad Ashraf, 1967), pp. 1–14, for a biographical note on 'Abd al-Qadir Jilani.

55 For a history of the Qadiri order from the fifteenth century, when it was first introduced in the subcontinent, to the late nineteenth, see S. A. A. Rizvi, *A History of Sufism in India* (Delhi: Munshiram Manoharlal, 1983), vol. 2, chapter 2.

the world to come, ['Abd al-Qadir Jilani is one of four] intercessors concerning the life that now is'.[56] He occupies a pre-eminent position in the hierarchy of saints, as we shall soon see; in some of the prayer manuals that Padwick studied, in fact, it is claimed that Allah gave him a seat 'with the spirits of the prophets . . . between this world and the next, between the Creator and the created . . .', which claim, Padwick comments, 'is remarkable, because entrance to that rank [that is, of the prophets] had been regarded as closed since the coming of Muhammad'.[57]

In this respect, Ahmad Riza's views on 'Abd al-Qadir's status *vis-à-vis* the Prophet and the other saints of the sufi hierarchy were very clear. He definitely ranked him below the Prophet, but exalted him above all other saints. In one of his poems he addressed 'Abd al-Qadir with these words:

Except for divinity and prophethood
You encompass all perfections, O Ghaus

(uluhiyyat nubuwwat ke siwa tu
tamam afzal ka qabil hai ya ghaus)[58]

and elsewhere he described how spiritual authority flows from Allah to the Shaikh:

From Ahad to Ahmad, from Ahmad to you
in this order the divine command 'Be' or 'Don't Be' is
followed, O Ghaus

(ahad se ahmad aur ahmad se tujh ko
kun aur sab kun makun hasil hai ya ghaus)[59]

[56] Padwick, *Muslim Devotions*, p. 240. The other three named by Padwick are: Ahmad al-Rifa'i (d. 1183), Ahmad al-Badawi (d. 1276), and Ibrahim al-Dasuqi (d. 1278).

[57] Ibid. In this context, see also S. A. A. Rizvi's comment that 'To all intents and purposes, the Qadiriyyas advocated the deification of their founder and all his descendants'. *A History of Sufism in India*, vol. 2, p. 54.

[58] Ahmad Riza Khan, *Hada'iq-e Bakhshish* (Karachi: Medina Publishing Company, 1976), p. 252. (Note: the reference here is to a different edition from the one cited in footnote 7 of this chapter. This edition is also published by the Medina Publishing Co., Karachi, but it has no date. Unlike the 1976 edition, it has no annotations. It has a slightly different collection of poems, and occasionally gives dates of composition, again unlike the 1976 edition. Hereafter, 'n.d.' or '1976 ed.' will indicate which edition is being cited.)

[59] Ibid., p. 249. *Ahad* = The One, Allah; *Ahmad* = Muhammad.

As this verse suggests, 'Abd al-Qadir was the apex of spiritual authority next only to the Prophet. Echoing the Shaikh's famous saying, 'My foot is on the neck of every saint', Ahmad Riza writes:

Who is to know what your head looks like
as the eye level of other saints corresponds to the sole of your foot
(sar bhala kya ko'i jane ki hai kaisa tera
auliya milte hain ankhen wo hai talwa tera)[60]

For Qadiris he is the Ghaus, or the *Qutb* (Axis or Pole), 'on [whom] the government of the world is believed to depend'.[61] Ahmad Riza explained the invisible hierarchy of saints as follows:

> Every ghaus has two ministers. The ghaus is known as 'Abd Ullah. The minister on the right is called 'Abd ur-Rab, and the one on the left is called 'Abd ul-Malik. In this [spiritual] world, the minister on the left is superior to the one on the right, unlike the worldly *sultanat.* The reason is that this is the sultanat of the heart and the heart is on the left side. Every ghaus . . . [has a special relationship with] the Prophet.[62]

Ahmad Riza went on to name the succession of ghaus and their ministers from the time of the Prophet down to Shaikh 'Abd al-Qadir Jilani. The first ghaus in this list was the Prophet, followed by the four 'rightly-guided caliphs' (Abu Bakr, 'Umar, 'Usman, and 'Ali), each of whom was in turn first the minister of the left hand to the current ghaus, and at the latter's death, replaced him in that position. They were followed by Hasan and Husain, down to Shaikh 'Abd al-Qadir Jilani. The latter was the last occupant of the 'Ghausiyat-e Kubra' (the Great Succour[ship]); those who have followed have been, and will continue to be, deputies (na'ib). Ultimately the Imam Mahdi will receive the Ghausiyat-e Kubra.[63]

[60] Ibid., p. 233. This saying is extremely popular and widely known among Qadiris. For comments see, for example, Schimmel, *Mystical Dimensions*, pp. 247–8.

[61] John A. Subhan, *Sufism, Its Saints and Shrines* (New York: Samuel Weiser Inc., 1970), p. 104.

[62] *Malfuzat*, vol. 1, p. 102.

[63] Ibid., Subhan, *Sufism*, pp. 104–6, gives the details of this hierarchy, which is considerably more complex than this brief summary indicates. Schimmel suggests that the concept of the qutb (or ghaus, for the two terms are interchangeable) as 'the highest spiritual guide of the faithful' bears a structural resemblance to the Shi'i concept of the hidden *imam*. See *Mystical Dimensions*, p. 200.

It is to be noted that in this scheme of things the Prophet and the first four caliphs stand at the head of the spiritual hierarchy which ends in Shaikh 'Abd al-Qadir Jilani. In this way the lines of succession by which spiritual, gnostic knowledge is handed down coincide with the ultimate sources of authority for knowledge of shari'a which, of course, also culminate in the Prophet.[64] Ahmad Riza explicitly made this connection in one of his poems addressing the Shaikh:

You are mufti of the shar', qazi of the community
and expert in the secrets of knowledge, 'Abd al-Qadir
(mufti-e shar' bhi hai qazi-e millat bhi hai
'ilm-e asrar se mahir bhi hai 'abd al-qadir)[65]

'Abd al-Qadir Jilani's relationship with the Prophet was not merely one of spiritual lineage, however. It was also one of genealogical descent, for the Shaikh's mother was a descendant of Husain, and his father of Hasan. This double genealogical link with the Prophet earned the Shaikh one of his many names, 'Hasan al-Husain'.[66] For Qadiri followers this genealogy was of great importance for, as S. A. A. Rizvi notes, 'as a direct descendant of the Prophet Muhammad (through his daughter, Fatima), Shaikh 'Abdu'l Qadir was believed to have inherited every one of his ancestor's spiritual achievements'.[67] Ahmad Riza's poetry is again helpful in understanding the importance of this factor to him personally. In the verses below, Ahmad Riza uses metaphors from nature to describe the Shaikh. It should be understood that the words 'pure', 'beautiful', and 'lovely', stand for Fatima, Hasan, and Husain respectively:

Prophetic shower, 'Alawi[68] season, pure garden
Beautiful flower, your fragrance is lovely

[64] Apparently, Ahmad Riza was here following a scheme outlined by 'Ali al-Hujwiri, the eleventh-century saint popularly known in the subcontinent as Data Ganj Bakhsh. See his *Kashf al-Mahjub*.

[65] *Hada'iq-e Bakhshish*, Part 1, n.d., p. 27.

[66] Subhan, *Sufism*, p. 176.

[67] Rizvi, *A History of Sufism in India*, vol. 2, p. 54.

[68] *'Alawi*: 'of, belonging to, 'Ali'.

Prophetic shade, 'Alawi constellation, pure station
Beautiful moon, your radiance is lovely
Prophetic sun, 'Alawi mountain, pure quarry
Beautiful ruby, your brilliance is lovely
(nabawi menh, 'alawi fasl, batuli gulshan
hasani phul husaini hai mahakna tera

nabawi zil, 'alawi burj, batuli manzil
hasani chand husaini hai ujala tera

nabawi khur, 'alawi koh, batuli ma'adun
hasani la'l husaini hai tajalla tera)[69]

These verses indicate that Ahmad Riza saw Shaikh 'Abd al-Qadir as the repository of the virtues of each one of his illustrious ancestors, not only that of the Prophet. This is the clearest indication we have had so far of his belief that religious authority flows both spiritually and genealogically. Ahmad Riza's choice of a Sayyid as his own pir had already indicated the importance he attached to genealogical descent from the Prophet. Further evidence that spiritual authority is handed down genealogically was his nomination of his own eldest son for the sajjada-nishini.

As with other holders of religious authority, 'Abd al-Qadir Jilani was a very real presence in Ahmad Riza's personal life as lived from day to day. He told his followers of a time when the Shaikh had answered his appeal for help during a visit he had made to Nizam ud-Din Auliya's tomb in Delhi. The tomb was surrounded by musicians and singers, making what seemed to him 'a great commotion' and causing him much distress. Invoking Shaikh 'Abd al-Qadir's help with the words 'Ya Ghaus', he also addressed Nizam ud-Din, saying, 'I have come to your court. Release me from this noise'. As he entered the tomb, silence suddenly reigned. He thought the musicians had gone away, but as soon as he left the tomb, the noise returned in full swing. Then he knew that the Shaikh had answered his prayer.[70]

69 *Haqa'iq-e Bakhshish*, 1976 ed., p. 234.

70 *Malfuzat*, vol. 3, p. 59. Although Ahmad Riza had invoked the help of both Shaikh 'Abd al-Qadir and Nizam ud-Din Auliya, he interpreted this event as a miracle (karamat) of Shaikh 'Abd al-Qadir alone. The latter's miracles are numerous. Many are recorded in the secondary literature in English.

'Abd al-Qadir was also a constant presence in his life in terms of ritual practice. This included saying the Fatiha in the Shaikh's name when a wish was granted, and celebration of the Shaikh's birthdate on the eleventh of every month, a ceremony known as *gyarahwin*. Zafar ud-Din Bihari records an occasion when someone asked Ahmad Riza to read the Fatiha (the opening Sura of the Qur'an) over some food, offered in the Shaikh's name in thanksgiving:

> [Ahmad Riza] first asked all those present to do wuzu' [ritual ablution] and did so himself. The container of halwa was placed in front. Everyone stood facing the direction of the Lord of Baghdad [Shaikh 'Abd al-Qadir] which is eighteen degrees north of the qibla [Mecca]. Ahmad Riza directed everyone to say Bism'illah, and to follow this up with the *durud Ghausia* [prayer calling down God's blessing on Shaikh 'Abd al-Qadir], seven times. Then they were to read *al-hamd* [giving thanks to God] once, the Ayat al-Kursi once, and say '*Qul huwa Allahu*' [Allah is all] seven times. After reading the durud Ghausia thrice, they should offer nazar [the food] to the Sarkar-e Baghdad ['Abd al-Qadir Jilani]. [After completing the reading] [Ahmad Riza] called for a plain table cloth to replace the existing one which had verses written on it here and there, saying that nothing other than the dishes of food should be placed on a table cloth. People clearing up are very careless, he said, as to where they step. Then a bowl and cup containing halwa was placed in front of each person. Everyone said Bism'illah [once more], and sat down to eat. When they had finished, Ahmad Riza told them not to wash their hands immediately, but to line up in rows turning toward Iraq and raise their hands to do du'a [prayer of supplication for 'Abd al-Qadir]. He said, the *sadat* [pl. of Sayyid] should be in the front row, in front of everyone else. He himself stood behind them. After they had said the du'a, everyone washed their hands carefully, as he instructed, and he moved the used water to a safe place, commanding each one to drink a little of it rather than rinse it out.[71]

It remains only to highlight once again the significance of the Qadiri order and its founder, Shaikh 'Abd al-Qadir Jilani, to Ahmad Riza in terms of religious authority. Basically the Shaikh was a means (wasila) of intercession with the Prophet and thence with Allah, and he was seen as a kindly, caring saint who has his petitioners' interests at heart. His Sayyid ancestry made him a perfect intercessionary agent, as religious authority was seen to flow through both spiritual and genealogical lines.

[71] *Hayat-e A'la Hazrat*, pp. 202–3.

Indeed, it appears that we are now in a position to better understand the significance to Ahmad Riza of Sayyid ancestry. In the previous chapter, we saw that Sayyids are generally considered, by a large number of Muslims, to be imbued with baraka or grace, by virtue of their descent from the Prophet, and that this quality may be passed on to others through contact with relics associated with them. When we consider that baraka is itself a source or expression of religious authority, it becomes apparent that Sayyids 'automatically' embody religious authority—though personal spiritual worth is of course also of great importance in determining how a man, or a pir or shaikh, may be judged. According to Zafar ud-Din Bihari Ahmad Riza looked upon Sayyids first as a 'part of the Prophet', and only secondarily saw their personal qualities. Consequently, it was inconceivable to him that a Sayyid could be placed in the socially inferior role of servitor: Sayyids were to be served, regardless of material or social standing.[72]

A second, and rather different, point that emerges from this examination of the role of Shaikh 'Abd al-Qadir Jilani, it appears to me, is that Ahmad Riza saw the Shaikh as uniting within himself both shari'a and tariqa, both the law and the path. Although this point does not emerge as clearly from the literature—which, by its very nature, stresses the tariqa aspect of belief and practice over shari'a, and a more complete documentation of which would require us to examine 'Abd al-Qadir's teachings as they emerge from his own writings—nevertheless, the history of the Qadiri order in the subcontinent indicates that 'reformist' or shari'a-minded sufis have been an important element in the order. Belief in the miraculous, or in the inborn superiority of noble (Sayyid) descent, in no way contradicts emphasis on a 'sober' sufism.[73] The evidence

[72] See *Hayat-e A'la Hazrat*, p. 201. Zafar ud-Din recounts an incident in Ahmad Riza's household when it was discovered that one of the household servants was a Sayyid. Ahmad Riza immediately ordered everyone in the house to serve him instead, to consider the salary he had been receiving as a gift (nazar), and to ensure that he was fed and cared for. After a while the man left of his own accord, made uncomfortable, undoubtedly, by the reversal of roles.

[73] Evidence for the 'reformist' or shari'a-minded orientation of the Qadiris in the subcontinent may be found, for example, in Eaton, *Sufis of Bijapur 1300–1700*, pp. 284–6 Rizvi, *A History of Sufism in India*, also indicates that some famous Qadiri

from Ahmad Riza's own life, his sayings as recorded in his *Malfuzat*, and his writings, together with what we know of the nature of his ritual activities, all indicate (as noted previously) that esoteric beliefs and practices had to be within the bounds of the shari'a, or, as Muslims would say, ba-shar' ('with' shari'a).

The 'Lover of the Prophet' ('ashiq-e rasul)

We have seen how the Prophet was the focal point and apex of religious and spiritual authority for Ahmad Riza, the goal to which devotion to pir and Shaikh lead. All such forms of devotion are undertaken ultimately in order to reach Allah. As he said on one occasion, 'Whoever seeks the help of the saints and the prophets, and of the chief of the prophets [Muhammad] . . . is in reality seeking Allah'.[74] Ahmad Riza's writings on the Prophet are extensive: numerous fatawa deal with the Prophet's attributes, as do his diwan of na't poetry and his *Malfuzat*. I now highlight how the main themes addressed by Ahmad Riza's poetry and *Malfuzat* concern the Prophet. I do not attempt an exhaustive treatment of the subject, for that would be more appropriate to a study of sufism per se.

Veneration of the Prophet has a long history in sufi and popular devotionalism. It goes back to figures like al-Hallaj (d. 922), Sana'i (d. 1131), Ibn al-'Arabi (d. 1240), and Rumi (d. 1273).[75] Ahmad Riza's *Malfuzat* indicate his familiarity with the lives and writings of sufis like Junaid Baghdadi (d. 910), the Persian poet Rumi, the Egyptian poet al-Busiri (d. 1298) who wrote the *Burda* in praise of the Prophet, and the Egyptian 'Abd al-Wahhab Sha'rani (d. 1565).[76] Given his erudition, it is likely that Ahmad Riza's vision of the Prophet and of the latter's place in the life of the believer was shaped

---

sufis such as Shaikh 'Abd ul-Haqq Dehlawi (d. 1642) were devoted to uniting shari'a and tariqa. See pp. 91–4.

[74] *Malfuzat*, vol. 4, p. 18.

[75] Schimmel, *Mystical Dimensions*, discusses the history of the veneration of the Prophet in the Muslim world especially as manifested in poetry, pp. 213–27. The subject receives fuller treatment in her *And Muhammad Is His Messenger: The Veneration of the Prophet in Islamic Piety* (Lahore: Vanguard Books Ltd., Pakistan edition, 1987).

[76] *Malfuzat*, vol. 1, pp. 43, 92–3; vol. 2, pp. 59–60: vol. 3, p. 29.

by this sufi tradition. Schimmel points as well to the popularity of na't poetry in the subcontinent since the Mughal period, written first in Persian and later in Urdu and in regional languages such as Sindhi.[77] Some of this poetry would have been familiar to Ahmad Riza.

The resemblance in the themes of the devotional poetry of the Muslim world generally, and those of Ahmad Riza's writings, indicates that he was, indeed, writing within the context of this larger tradition. Schimmel describes the poets' concerns as follows:

> From earliest times, Muhammad, the messenger of God, had been the ideal for the faithful Muslim. His behavior, his acts, and his words served as models for the pious, who tried to imitate him as closely as possible even in the smallest details of outward life . . . All the noble qualities of his body and his soul were described in terms of marked admiration.[78]

Schimmel places the beginning of a 'genuine Muhammad mysticism' in the early eighth century AD, with the first formulation of the 'Nur-e Muhammadi' concept that Muhammad was created from God's light and preceded the creation of the world and of Adam. In the tenth century Hallaj took the idea a step further, writing that the Prophet is both the 'cause and goal of creation'. Proof of this belief was cited from the hadis, 'If thou hadst not been, I would not have created the heavens'.[79] In subsequent centuries the concept of the 'Muhammadan light' was further developed until the theory of fana fi'l-rasul 'annihilation in the Prophet' emerged in later sufism. The Prophet had by now definitely become an intermediary between man and God.[80]

Ahmad Riza, as a mufti writing fatawa, as a sufi preceptor giving guidance to his followers in his *Malfuzat*, and as a poet expressing his personal longings and passions, held much the same views. One idea worth exploring at this stage is that of the relationship between Allah and the Prophet, for clarification on this point will help us

77 *And Muhammad Is His Messenger*, pp. 207–13.

78 *Mystical Dimensions*, pp. 213–14.

79 Ibid., p. 215. This is a hadis qudsi (Divine Saying). On the Divine Saying, see Graham, *Divine Word and Prophetic Word in Early Islam*.

80 *Mystical Dimensions*, pp. 215–16.

understand one of the major areas of difference between Ahmad Riza and his followers on the one side, and other South Asian Muslims such as the Deobandis on the other. Ahmad Riza's own relationship of 'love' for the Prophet will also become clear.

In his *Malfuzat*, Ahmad Riza says:

> Only the Prophet can reach God without intermediaries. This is why, on the Day of the Resurrection, all the prophets, walis, and 'ulama' will gather in the Prophet's presence and beg him to intercede for them with God . . . . The Prophet cannot have an intermediary because he is perfect [*kamil*]. Perfection is concomitant on [*mutafara'*] existence [wujud]; and the existence of the world is dependent upon the existence of the Prophet [which in turn is dependent on the existence of God]. In short, faith in the pre-eminence of the Prophet leads one to believe that only Allah has existence, everything else is His shadow.[81]

The hierarchy is clear: Allah, the Prophet, the other prophets, the saints, and so on. Within this framework of the Prophet's essentially dependent relationship to Allah, however, there are no limits to the qualities that may be ascribed to him. Ahmad Riza quotes 'Abd ul-Haqq Muhaddis Dehlawi, and the Egyptian poet al-Busiri, in support of his view that

> setting aside the claim that Christians make [about Jesus being divine], you can say whatever you wish in praise of the Prophet for there was no limit to the Prophet's qualities.[82]

This belief in the practically limitless virtues and abilities of the Prophet, given him by God of His own will, is the basis for Ahmad Riza's assertion that the Prophet had knowledge of the unseen ('ilm-e ghaib), a claim denied by the Deobandis. This knowledge was said by Ahmad Riza to include (though by no means to be limited to) the five things specifically said in the Qur'an to be known to God.[83]

[81] *Malfuzat*, vol. 2, p. 58.

[82] Ibid., pp. 58–9.

[83] The kernel of Ahmad Riza's argument with the Deobandis on the 'ilm-e ghaib issue was that 'known to God' did not mean *only* known to Him, and not known to the Prophet. Ahmad Riza believed that Allah gifted such knowledge to the Prophet from time to time, including knowledge of the five things specifically mentioned in Qur'an 31:34. These were: knowledge of the Hour (of Resurrection), of when it would rain, of the sex

In certain respects, however, the Allah–Prophet relationship is not as clear as the above quotations would suggest. In the following passage from the *Malfuzat*, Ahmad Riza made the point that the Prophet is not 'other than God' (*ghair-e khuda*):

[The Prophet had to teach his followers how to recite the Qur'an in the early days of Islam.] After listening to the recitation of a sahabi, Abu Musa Ash'ari, at night [from his own house], he praised his reading the next morning. The sahabi said, O Prophet, had I known that you were listening, I would have read with even greater fervour (*aur zyada bana kar parhta*) . . . . [Ahmad Riza comments] The sahabi himself said he would have recited more forcefully for the Prophet, and the Prophet did not object. This proves that reading for the Prophet was not comparable to reading for one other than God (ghair-e khuda). The Prophet's business (mu'amala) is Allah's business.[84]

Ahmad Riza also gave other examples of the identification of the Prophet and Allah, such as A'isha's (d. 678) statement that she was repenting to Allah and the Prophet.

Once Ahmad Riza was asked whether it was permissible to use lanterns and carpets (and similar expensive decorative items) at a milad function. He responded that it was permissible so long as the purpose of the decoration was to honour the Prophet, rather than some selfish or worldly motive, and reported this story:

Imam Ghazali wrote in his *Ihya' al-'Ulum*, on the basis of a writing by Sayyid Abu 'Ali Rudhbari, that a believer had organized a zikr meeting [remembrance of the Prophet's name]. He had installed a thousand lights in the meeting hall. A guest arrived, and seeing the lights, began to leave [in disapproval of the host's extravagance]. The organizer of the function held him back, took him inside, and said, Any light that has been lit for one other than God should be put out. The man tried to do so, but none of the lights could be extinguished.[85]

The apparent equation of the Prophet with God is at first astonishing. We know, however, from numerous clearly stated passages in Ahmad Riza's works that he did not equate the Prophet with God. What we have here, I think, is evidence of Ahmad Riza's

---

of a child in the womb, of what a person would earn on the morrow, and of where one would die. Ahmad Riza's position on the 'ilm-e ghaib debate is discussed in Chapter VIII.

84 *Malfuzat*, vol. 2, pp. 44–5.

85 Ibid., vol. 1, pp. 99. Rudhbari, d. 934, was a contemporary of Junaid Baghdadi. See Schimmel, *Mystical Dimensions*, p. 54.

unusually strong sense of Muhammad's prophecy, and the uniquely close relationship to God that this implied. In our attempt to understand this we may refer to William Graham, who, in his study of the hadis qudsi or Divine Saying, writes:

> In the Divine Saying one sees perhaps most clearly that aspect of Muhammad's mission that is most often ignored: his genuinely *prophetic* function as the ordinary man who is transformed by his 'calling' to 'rise and warn'—not only through his 'Book', but in all his words and acts . . . . Outside the scriptural Revelation, God's revealing goes on, and most vividly so in the action and speech of His messenger. In terms of religious authority, especially within the realm of personal faith and personal piety, the Qur'an and the varied materials in the Hadith form not two separate homogeneous bodies of material, but one continuum of religious truth that encompasses a heterogeneous array of materials.[86]

Ahmad Riza, like the early umma that Graham describes in his study, appears not to have made any distinction between Muhammad the prophet, recipient and messenger of God's immutable word, and Muhammad the guide or leader, an ordinary mortal like those around him. For him, the Prophet was 'in all his words and acts' prophetic, and thus extra-human. While all believing Muslims see Muhammad as unique among humans in perhaps indefinable ways, by virtue of his calling, Ahmad Riza seems to have had a heightened awareness of Muhammad's 'genuinely prophetic function', causing him to place the Prophet at the centre of his own life as a believer.

As may be expected, these ideas are expressed particularly forcefully in his poetry. In the following verses, the subject is Muhammad's close relationship with Allah:

The two worlds seek to please God
God seeks to please Muhammad

(khuda ki riza chahte hain do 'alam
khuda chahta hai riza-e muhammad)

[86] Graham, *Divine Word and Prophetic Word in Early Islam*, p. 110. Graham argues that the very existence of the hadis qudsi, which is a record of a Divine Saying in the Prophet's words, and which thus straddles the boundaries of Qur'an and hadis, should alert us against making a rigid distinction between the Prophet in his prophetic role and in his personal role. Graham finds evidence to believe that the earliest Muslims did not do so.

Muhammad is the threshold to Allah
Allah is the threshold to Muhammad
(muhammad bara-e janab-e ilahi
janab-e ilahi bara-e muhammad)

A vow was made for all time
to unite Khuda's happiness with Muhammad's
(baham 'ahd bandhe hain wasl-e abad ka
riza-e khuda aur riza-e muhammad)[87]

In the following verse Muhammad is seen as Allah's beloved, completely united with Him:

I will call you only 'Lord', you who are the beloved of the Lord
there is no 'yours' and 'mine' between the beloved and the lover

(main to malik hi kahunga kih ho malik ke habib
yani mahbub o muhibb men nahin mera tera)[88]

On the Prophet's night ascension (*mi'raj*), he became God's bridegroom:

You went as a bridegroom of light
on your head a chaplet of light,
wedding clothes of light on your body
(kya bana nam-e khuda asra ka dulha nur ka
sar pe sihrah nur ka, bar men shahana nur ka)[89]

As for his own relationship to the Prophet, Ahmad Riza made it a conscious object of his life to immerse himself in serving the Prophet in whatever capacity he could. Small details about him say this most eloquently: he used to sign himself as 'Abd al-Mustafa ('Servant of Mustafa', this meaning 'the Chosen' or 'the Elect', being one of Muhammad's names) on all correspondence, fatawa, and other writings. When asked about this at one of his daily meetings, he replied that the name was the sign of good judgment (*husn-e zann*)

[87] *Hada'iq-e Bakhshish*, 1976 ed., p. 47.

[88] Ibid., p. 9.

[89] Ibid., p. 13. A lengthy poem on the mi'raj, adjudged (in a personal communication) to be Ahmad Riza's 'masterpiece' by Professor Muhammad Mas'ud Ahmed, a scholar on Ahmad Riza and his work, again pictures the Prophet's ascension as a wedding. See *Hada'iq-e Bakhshish* (n.d.), Part 1, pp. 106–15. The imagery of a wedding is also central to the notion of 'urs, for, as noted, the word 'urs literally means 'marriage'.

in a Muslim, and cited a hadis in which 'Umar was reported to have said that he considered himself a follower (*banda*) and servant (*khadim*) of the Prophet.[90] On another occasion, he told those gathered about him that if his heart were to be broken into two pieces, it would be found that on one part was inscribed the first part of the *kalima*, 'There is no God but Allah', and on the other was written the second half, 'And Muhammad is His Prophet'.[91]

Just as Shaikh 'Abd al-Qadir Jilani actively intervened on his behalf from time to time, or was perceived to do so, so too did Ahmad Riza experience the Prophet's presence in a very personal way. When he was learning the art of divination (*'ilm-e jafr*), the Prophet appeared to him in a dream giving him permission (*izn*) to proceed with his study.[92] On his second hajj in 1905–6, he spent a month at Medina, the Prophet's birthplace, being present there during the Prophet's birth anniversary celebrations on 12 Rabi' ul-Awwal. He spent this entire period, he said, at the Prophet's tomb, taking time off only once to visit the shrine of one Maulana Daghastani, and another time to go to (ziyarat) the tomb of Hamza, the Prophet's uncle. When he met the 'ulama' of Medina to engage in learned discussions, it was in the precincts of the Prophet's tomb.[93] This was, for Ahmad Riza, the holiest place on earth; he was willing to go so far, indeed, as to say that Medina was better than Mecca, as in this verse:

O pilgrims! come to the tomb of the king of kings
you have seen the Ka'ba, now see the Ka'ba of the Ka'ba

(hajiyo! a'o shahenshah ka rauza dekho
ka'ba dekh chuke ka'be ka ka'ba dekho)[94]

In his belief, the Prophet is very much alive in his tomb, leading 'a life of sense and feeling', as do the other prophets. From his grave

[90] *Malfuzat*, vol. 1, p. 43.

[91] Ibid., vol. 3, p. 67.

[92] However, he gave it up of his own accord after some time. Ibid., vol. 1, pp. 82–3.

[93] Ibid., vol. 2, pp. 34–5.

[94] *Hada'iq-e Bakhshish* (1976 ed.), p. 96. Also see *Malfuzat*, vol. 2, pp. 47–8.

the Prophet helps his 'guests', those who visit his tomb, in whatever way he sees fit.[95]

It was particularly in the hope of being honoured with a vision of the Prophet at his tomb in Medina, Zafar ud-Din Bihari writes, that Ahmad Riza had undertaken this second hajj. While waiting for him to appear Ahmad Riza spent the first night composing a *ghazal*; the next night he presented the ghazal to the Prophet, and it was after this that 'his *qismat* (fortune) awoke. His watchful, vigilant eyes were blessed with the presence of the Prophet'.[96] Unfortunately, Ahmad Riza himself does not appear to have written about this experience.[97]

Ahmad Riza's personal devotion to the Prophet shines through in his poetry. Some poems have become popular nationwide in Pakistan and are recited particularly on the Prophet's birth anniversary. The simplicity, humility in the presence of the awesomeness of the Prophet, and grateful confidence in his forgiveness with which Ahmad Riza addresses the Prophet, are apparent over and over again, as in these verses from the extremely popular poem *Karoron Durud*:

I am tired, you are my sanctuary
I am bound, you are my refuge
My future is in your hands.
Upon you be thousands of blessings

(khastah hun aur tum ma'az basta hun aur tum malaz
age jo shai ki riza, tum pe karoron durud)

My sins are limitless,
but you are forgiving and merciful
Forgive me my faults and offences.
Upon you be thousands of blessings

[95] *Malfuzat*, vol. 3, pp. 28–30.

[96] *Hayat-e A'la Hazrat*, pp. 43–4.

[97] His lengthy ghazal is in the *Hada'iq-e Bakhshish* (n.d.), Part 1, pp. 92–105. I have been unable to find any reference in it to his vision of the Prophet, though this is not surprising given Zafar ud-Din Bihari's information that it was written before he had this experience.

(garche hain behad qasur, tum ho 'afu-e ghafur
bakhsh do jurm o khata tum pe karoron durud)[98]

It was entirely consistent with Ahmad Riza's personal piety and devotion to the Prophet that the latter's birth anniversary on 12 Rabi' ul-Awwal, the *milad un-nabi* (or maulid, both forms being derivatives of the Arabic root *walada*, to give birth), was celebrated on a grand scale. It was a time of rejoicing, eagerly anticipated by Ahmad Riza and his followers. The *Dabdaba-e Sikandari* reported in January 1916 that on the Prophet's birthday 'the Muslims of Bareilly, Rampur, Pilibhit, Shahjahanpur and other towns performed the pilgrimage to A'la Hazrat [Ahmad Riza]', for this was one of the three annual occasions on which he consented to give a sermon.[99] In fact, it appears from Zafar ud-Din Bihari's account that he gave two sermons that day, one in the morning after the first (fajr) prayer, and the second in the evening after the last (*'isha'*) prayer. The sermons were delivered at his ancestral house (the 'Purani Haweli', or 'Old Family Home'), in which his younger brother Hasan Riza lived. In addition to the 'ulama' who came from outside Bareilly, the élite of the city were also invited. People considered it so important to listen to Ahmad Riza on this day, Zafar ud-Din writes, that no one of eminence in the town organized a similar gathering of their own at the same time.[100]

Preparations for the event began around dawn. The townspeople—Ahmad Riza's murids, followers, and admirers—bathed, donned their new clothes, and hurried to the mosque to greet him there at the time of the fajr prayer. After the obligatory prayer (fariza) had been offered, people lined up waiting for him to finish saying his prayers and hoped to get close enough to him to kiss his hand (*dast-bosi*).

Shortly thereafter, and again at night at the 'Purani Haweli',[101]

[98] Ibid. (1976 ed.), p. 195. Although Ahmad Riza did not approve of music and would not have put his verses to music, this poem, as many others he wrote, has a lilt and rhythm that makes it easy to remember and recite.

[99] *Dabdaba-e Sikandari*, 52:11 (January 24, 1916), 3.

[100] *Hayat-e A'la Hazrat*, pp. 96–7. Zafar ud-Din does not tell us to which year his account refers, though I assume the proceedings were more or less standard from year to year.

[101] The text of the *Hayat-e A'la Hazrat* is confusing here. Zafar ud-Din clearly refers to the fajr prayer and the dast-bosi (kissing of the hand) taking place in a mosque, and is

began the recitation by a trained reciter (na't khwan), of na't poetry recalling the Prophet's qualities. Ahmad Riza ascended the pulpit (minbar) exactly at the moment of qiyam (literally 'to stay, to stand') when everyone in the meeting stood up at the remembrance of the Prophet's birth (*zikr-e wiladat*). Ahmad Riza stood in silence for several minutes, for his entrance had caused a tumult among the crowd, which was swelling in numbers and finding it hard to fit into the meeting hall. When the shoving and pushing subsided he rinsed his mouth with water using a spitoon placed next to him, and began his sermon with the words 'Bism'illah ar-rahman ar-rahim'.

In his sermon Ahmad Riza said that Allah, who is intrinsic (*zat*), chose the Prophet as His means of bringing the extrinsic (ghair) world to Him. Everything comes from Allah, and Muhammad distributes what He gives. What is in the one is in the other. The other prophets are a reflection or shadow of Muhammad, like stars reflected in water.

Allah made Muhammad from His light before He made anything else. Everything begins with the Prophet, even existence (wujud). He was the first prophet as Allah made him before He made anything else, and he was the last as well, being the final prophet. Being the first light, the sun and all light originates from the Prophet. All the atoms, stones, trees, and birds recognized Muhammad as Prophet, as did Gabriel, and the other prophets.

The majlis-e milad is held in order to recall God's blessings (*ne'mat*), and to bring Muslims together so as to remember the presence (*tashrif-awari*) and excellent qualities of the Prophet. The collective partaking of food (which follows at the end of a milad meeting), Ahmad Riza said, is not central to the milad's purpose; nor, however, is there any harm in it, for it is an invitation of people 'for a good purpose' (*da'wat ala'l-khair*), and is therefore necessarily

also unambiguous in reporting that the sermons were delivered at the Purani Haweli. However, he then goes on to talk of the na't reciter, and Ahmad Riza, getting up on the pulpit to speak, which suggests that the meetings followed directly after the prayers (fajr and 'isha') at the mosque itself, and that there was no change of venue. He also refers to the people crowding together at the mosque to do the dast-bosi and then getting as close to the minbar as possible. This doesn't sound like a 'by invitation only' event. See *Hayat-e A'la Hazrat*, pp. 96–8, for the entire text concerning the milad meeting.

good.[102] Allah has said, '. . . the bounty of thy Lord rehearse and proclaim!' (93:11, Yusuf 'Ali tr.).

Ahmad Riza reminded his audience that Allah had brought all the prophets together and told them about the future prophethood of Muhammad. All, on Allah's command, bound themselves to believe in his prophecy, and were witness to the fact that the others did so. Thus Allah was the first to speak of the Prophet, and the first majlis to mention the Prophet was this meeting of the prophets. In keeping with this covenant, all the prophets from Adam to Jesus have remembered the Prophet's coming and his birth. Speaking about the circumstances of the birth itself,[103] he recalled its joyous celebration by the angels and the fear with which the event was viewed by the devils (*shayatin*). The meeting ended with a na't calling down Allah's blessings (durud) on the Prophet.

The practice of holding milad meetings, like that of celebrating the 'urs of a saint, reading the Fatiha in thanksgiving over an offering of food, of holding gyarahwin functions in honour of 'Abd al-Qadir Jilani, was a matter of intense debate and argument among the 'ulama' at the turn of the nineteenth century. The Deobandi 'ulama' sought 'to avoid fixed holidays like the maulud of the Prophet, the 'urs of the saints', and other feasts;[104] the Ahl-e Hadis, taking an even more disapproving attitude,

> prohibited 'urs and qawwalli, particularly opposing the giyarhwin of Shaikh 'Abdu'l-Qadir Gilani . . . . They prohibited all pilgrimage, even that to the grave of the Prophet at Medina . . . . In their emphasis on sweeping reform, they understood sufism itself, not just its excesses, to be a danger to true religion.[105]

[102] *Hayat-e A'la Hazrat*, p. 108. Here he was defending his position on the legitimacy of milad functions. See Metcalf, *Islamic Revival*, pp. 300–1.

[103] *Hayat-e A'la Hazrat*, p. 112. Gabriel calmed the fears of Amina, Muhammad's mother, and assumed the shape of a white hen when urging the Prophet to manifest himself. Again the image of a marriage comes up when Gabriel tells Muhammad (not yet born) that the procession (*barat*) of the bridegroom of both worlds is fully adorned and ready to start for the bride's house. (The Prophet, as bridegroom, is awaited before it can set out.) It would appear that in this case the bride is the world rather than Allah.

[104] Metcalf, *Islamic Revival*, p. 151.

[105] Ibid., pp. 273–4.

Like the Deobandis, they too opposed the practice of milad.

In the 1890s, Imdad Ullah Muhajir Makki (1817–99) had addressed the controversy on this matter in his pamphlet *Faisla-e Haft Mas'ala.* In his view, whether a milad was permissible (ja'iz) or not depended on the intention of the participants. If a person equated the details of the milad (such as holding it on a particular date and no other, distributing sweets, lighting incense sticks, or laying carpets) with *ibada* or worship, on a par with namaz and the Ramazan fast (*roza*), then it was reprehensible. It was a reprehensible innovation (bid'a) if a person considered it a religious obligation (*dini farz*), a duty enjoined by the shari'a. But as long as it was viewed as one among several means of honouring and remembering the Prophet, it was permissible.[106]

Apart from the controversy over the permissibility of holding a milad, however, debate also centred over a particular aspect of the milad function itself, namely the practice of standing up (qiyam) during a sermon when the Prophet's birth was recalled, and blessings were called down on him (salat o salam). Ahmad Riza, answering a query about the permissibility of qiyam in a fatwa entitled *Iqamat al-Qiyama,*[107] responded by saying that the practice was viewed as commendable (*mustahsan*) by a majority of 'ulama' throughout the Islamic world—particularly mentioning leading 'ulama' in the Haramain—for two reasons. The first was that it had been practised for hundreds of years, though admittedly not in the first three generations of Islam.[108] Ahmad Riza considered this a valid argument on

[106] *Faisla-e Haft Mas'ala*, pp. 50–76. In the above I have attempted to sum up his position rather than lay it out in all its details.

[107] Ahmad Riza Khan, *Iqamat al-Qiyama 'ala Ta'in al-Qiyam li-Nabi Tihamat il-Jaza' al-Muhya li-Ghalmat Kanhaiyya* (Performing [the Ritual of] Standing Up Despite the Calumny [of Those who Refuse to] Stand for the Prophet . . .), 1299/1881–2 (Karachi: Barkati Publishers, 1986).

[108] This was an important admission, in terms of the argument, for it meant that the practice was an 'innovation' or bid'a. However, as Ahmad Riza argued at some length in this fatwa, it was a bid'at-e hasana or 'good innovation'. The argument was taken even further, and the tables turned on the opponents, when Ahmad Riza quoted an 'alim from the Haramain as saying that because Muslims saw this as a good deed, those who opposed it were *bid'atis!* Ibid., pp. 28–9. I will take up for discussion the Ahl-e Sunnat use of terms such as bid'a and bid'at-e hasana in Chapter VI.

the basis of the hadis that what Muslims consider to be good is good in Allah's sight too, and that a practice which hundreds of 'ulama' have considered to be good over hundreds of years cannot be bad.[109] Second, standing up when the Prophet's birth is recalled, Ahmad Riza argued, was an expression of respect and honour (*ta'zim*),[110] a meritorious act that would earn great reward (sawab).[111] Ahmad Riza did not assert, as Metcalf writes, that the Prophet was actually present (though invisible to the audience) at the time of qiyam,[112] though he cited with obvious approval and concurrence a statement by a Hanbali mufti that the Prophet's spirit is present at this time.[113]

The Importance of Intercession

This chapter has highlighted the importance for Ahmad Riza of intercession on behalf of the believer with God, a role fulfilled most especially by the pir, the shaikh, and the Prophet. However, the power of mediation is accessible to many. 'Not only the dead but the living could be intermediaries',[114] but the intervention or mediation of certain people is more powerful than that of others and that of the Prophet is best of all.

Ahmad Riza believed that such mediatory power (or grace, baraka) inheres most especially in lineal descendants of the Prophet; hence his marked respect for all Sayyids, regardless of social standing. Perhaps this was a significant factor, as well, in his (and his father's) choice of Sayyid Shah Al-e Rasul of Marahra as his pir. It also accounts in part for his devotion to Shaikh 'Abd al-Qadir Jilani.

As Ahmad Riza's attention to birth or death anniversaries such

[109] Ibid., pp. 25–6, 28–9.

[110] Ibid., p. 36. Ahmad Riza offered detailed proofs on both counts, arguing his point of view in about 30-odd pages. The second half of the fatwa was specifically in rebuttal of Maulana Nazir Husain Dehlawi, the Ahl-e Hadis leader.

[111] Ibid., pp. 15–22.

[112] See Metcalf, *Islamic Revival*, p. 301. Ahmad Riza did assert in another context, however, that the Prophet had the ability to be bodily present should he so desire. See section entitled 'Ahl-e Sunnat Prophetology' in Chapter VIII below.

[113] *Iqamat al-Qiyama*, p. 23.

[114] Metcalf, *Islamic Revival*, p. 303.

as 'urs, gyarhawin, and milad, indicates, he believed strongly that the dead continued 'to live' in a spiritual sense, and that they retained an especially close relationship with places that they had been associated with during their lives. Moreover, their spirits were especially alert and their grace heightened on certain days (their birth or death anniversaries). For these reasons supplicants were well-advised to observe the anniversaries and exhibit the greatest respect for tombs. Such behaviour, pleasing to the saint whose intercession was sought, would find favour with him, and therefore be a source of benefit (sawab) to the believer.

While having a pir, or visiting the tombs of saints and 'ulama' in far-flung places were not on a par with the performance of obligatory ritual acts such as prayer or fasting, or substitutes for them, in Ahmad Riza's eyes they could only be a source of good and an aid for the believer. As he said in his fatwa in answer to the question as to why one needed a pir, it was absurd to imagine that one could reach Allah without an intermediary. One senses in all his writings and in his *Malfuzat* the humility of one who believed he needed help in reaching Allah, and in working out his own salvation. Ahmad Riza saw the position taken by the Ahl-e Hadis, or 'Wahhabis', as he called them, rejecting the need for intermediaries, as a sign of their arrogance.

As for the Prophet, his status was so elevated and he was so close to Allah, that for Ahmad Riza the Prophet had in a sense displaced Allah as the centre of his devotions. While Ahmad Riza's writings make clear that the Prophet's qualities and abilities were God-given, and thus contingent, and only God is intrinsic, the fact of prophecy itself had such compelling force in Ahmad Riza's judgment that he viewed love of the Prophet as the best way of showing love of Allah. In all he did or wrote about, love of the Prophet was a motivating factor.

In fact, it was a standard Ahmad Riza consistently applied in drawing boundaries between 'right' and 'wrong' action, and in distinguishing between Muslims who were on the right or wrong track. In my view it would be erroneous to conclude that because Ahmad Riza supported a mediatory, custom-laden 'Islam', he 'made less of a demand for individual responsibility' on himself or his followers than did the Deobandis or others.[115] On the contrary, his whole life was spent defining how a Muslim should conduct him or herself in his or her time and day, and in punctiliously following these standards of conduct and belief in his own life, while at the same time distancing himself from those Muslims of whose beliefs or practice he disapproved. I have also tried to show that he attached great importance to the intention with which an action was undertaken. What emerges, I think, is the distinctiveness of his 'style', caused by the determining role in his life of the Prophet and of his defence of the Prophet against perceived disrespect or slight.

[115] Metcalf, *Islamic Revival*, p. 397.

Chapter VI

Ahmad Riza's Concept of the Sunna

One cannot read far into the Barelwi literature without being struck by the deliberate and repeated use of the term Ahl-e Sunnat wa Jama'at, 'people of the sunnat [customary practices of the Prophet] and the [majority] community', to describe those who shared Ahmad Riza Khan's vision of the faith. The term recurs in a multiplicity of contexts: in fatawa, the malfuzat, debates with other South Asian Muslims, the names given to journals, madrasas, and organizations of 'ulama'.[1] To use this term, with its twin emphases on 'following the Prophet's sunna' and constituting the 'majority community', was to stake a universalistic claim linking its claimants with the Sunni Muslim world beyond the subcontinent. It was also, implicitly, to deny that relationship to other Muslims whose beliefs fell short of standards which Ahmad Riza considered irreducible and uncompromisable.

This spirit of competition with other Muslim groups is sometimes more explicit, as in the following passage by one of Ahmad Riza's followers:

It is recorded in hadis: This umma will split up into seventy-three groups. One

[1] To cite some examples: in 1894–5, a number of 'ulama' from north India created a body called the 'Majlis-e Ahl-e Sunnat wa Jama'at' to counter the influence of the Nadwat al-'Ulama'; in 1904, a madrasa called the 'Madrasa-e Ahl-e Sunnat wa Jama'at Manzar al-Islam' was established in Bareilly; in 1920, Maulana Na'im ud-Din Muradabadi, one of Ahmad Riza's khalifas, started a journal called *Sawad-e A'zam* (The Great Majority); in the 1940s, the 'ulama' of Marahra began a journal entitled *Ahl-e Sunnat ki Awaz* (The Voice of the Ahl-e Sunnat).

group will be jannati [deserving of heaven], the others jahannami [deserving of hell]. [A sahabi asked,] 'Which is that elect group, O Prophet of Allah?' He said, 'Those who follow me and my sahaba, those, that is, who follow the sunna'. There is another *riwayat* [report] which says, 'That [elect group] is the jama'at, that is, the great group of Muslims known as the 'Sawad-e A'zam'. Whoever separates himself from it separates himself in hell. That is why the name of the elect group is 'Ahl-e sunnat wa jama'at'.[2]

In attending here to the Barelwi definition of themselves as the Ahl-e Sunnat wa Jama'at, the focus shifts, as it must (given that the sunna is one of the primary sources for Islamic law), to consideration of the Barelwis as 'ulama': as scholars of Qur'an, hadis, fiqh and related fields. While the central position that the Prophet held for Ahmad Riza is in consonance with the sufi tradition of veneration of the Prophet, Sunni tradition also regards the 'ulama' as 'heirs to the prophets'.[3] Ahmad Riza saw himself primarily as an 'alim rather than a sufi, and was so perceived by his followers. Given his belief in the complementary roles of shari'a and tariqa in a Muslim's life, and his insistence that the shari'a should be accorded precedence over tariqa, we must ask ourselves what sources his prophetology may have had in Hanafi law, the law school (mazhab, Ar. madhab) that he, together with most South Asian Muslims, followed. The answer requires an examination of his fatawa, particularly those in which he defended his views on the Prophet and cited proofs from the classical sources of law (Qur'an, hadis, and fiqh).

Ahmad Riza's fatawa, which later followers of the Ahl-e Sunnat movement have seen as the chief source and guidepost for belief and action in their lives, are available for study in a multi-volume collection (not yet fully published in the 1980s) entitled *Al-'Ataya al-Nabawiyya fi'l Fatawa-e Rizwiyya* (The Gifts of the Prophet in the Fatawa-e Rizwiyya). Although not all Ahmad Riza's fatawa are

[2] The tradition about the seventy-three sects is a classical one to be found in a number of hadis collections. A. J. Wensinck, *A Handbook of Early Muhammadan Tradition* (Leiden: E. J. Brill, 1960), p. 47, lists the following sources under the entry 'Community': Abu Da'ud, Tirmidhi, Ibn Maja, al-Darimi, and Ahmad ibn Hanbal. For Abu Da'ud, see Ahmad Hasan, *Sunan Abu Dawud*, vol. 3, pp. 1290–1.

[3] Wensinck, *Handbook*, p. 234, notes under the entry 'Ulama' that this tradition is recorded in al-Bukhari and Tirmidhi. Also see Ahmad Hasan, *Sunan Abu Dawud*, vol. 3, p. 1034; Friedmann, *Prophecy Continuous*, pp. 92–3.

contained in this collection, it provides an overview of the range of his scholarship and enables the reader to follow his lines of interpretation on various issues and compare them with those of 'ulama' in other movements.

In this chapter I turn to Ahmad Riza's fatawa in order to understand what it meant to him to 'follow the Prophet's sunna'. I have chosen to examine in detail those of his fatawa which deal with a specific issue that engaged him and other 'ulama' of the Ahl-e Sunnat wa Jama'at movement in the early 1900s: the debate over the call to prayer (azan, Ar. adhan). This debate is of particular interest in view of its discussion of the application of the Prophet's sunna in the lives of twentieth-century South Asian Muslims. The views of the 'ulama' who engaged in the debate were printed in the columns of the *Dabdaba-e Sikandari*, the Urdu newspaper published in the princely state of Rampur, over a two-year period (1914–16). Ahmad Riza was at the centre of the controversy, for it was his attempt to 'revive a dead sunna' which had started the discussion.

Before examining this debate, however, I would like to discuss the meaning of the term 'sunna' in a general way, indicating differences amongst scholars regarding when it came to be used and understood as the Prophet's 'way' or 'custom'. The relationship of the sunna to hadis literature, and to sunna's opposite, bid'a (innovation), is pertinent as well, as are the paired opposites of ijtihad (mental effort) and taqlid (adherence to one's law school), and the term tajdid (renewal). These terms were central to the azan debate, and to the Ahl-e Sunnat literature more generally, as they were also to other contemporary South Asian Muslim reform movements. Furthermore, examination of the Ahl-e Sunnat's debates with the Nadwat al-'Ulama' and Deoband in succeeding chapters reveals that there were interpretative differences among the movements as to the scope of the meanings that they assigned to these terms.

The Concept of the Sunna of the Prophet

The Qur'an and the sunna of the Prophet are regarded by Muslims as the two most important sources of authority in determining the beliefs and conduct of a Muslim's life.[4] The word sunna (pl. sunan) is of pre-Islamic origin, signifying 'way, law, mode or conduct of life'.[5] Goldziher writes that 'for the old pagans of the Jahiliyya [pre-Islamic Arabia] . . . sunna was all that corresponded to the traditions of the Arabs and the customs and habits of their ancestors'.[6] In the Qur'an, and in hadis literature, the word has been used to refer to law or practice emanating from sources other than the Prophet, ranging from Allah (Qur'an 33:62) to Companions of the Prophet, Muslims generally, and women. The term also refers on occasion to a religious practice ('the sunna of salat', for instance).[7]

There is disagreement among scholars as to when the term came to be used more specifically to signify the Prophet's 'way' or practice, that is, his words, deeds, and decisions in his personal capacity rather than in his role as prophetic messenger. Joseph Schacht places the beginnings of that usage at the end of the first century AH, and maintains that until this time the Muslim communities in Medina, Syria, and Iraq continued to be guided by their 'living tradition', that is, their pre-Islamic tradition, rather than by traditions of the Prophet. Even after this date, he believes, the 'living tradition' continued to reign, though frequently given prophetic sanction:

> . . . the 'sunna of the Prophet' . . . is not identical with, and not necessarily expressed by, traditions from the Prophet; it is simply the 'living tradition' of the school [in Iraq] put under the aegis of the Prophet.[8]

[4] There are two other sources, ijma' (consensus) and qiyas (analogy), which may be brought to bear on a question in the absence of clear guidance from the Qur'an and the sunna. The means by which the 'ulama' interpret the sources is known as ijtihad, literally '(mental) effort, endeavour'. The 'ulama' have differed with one another as to the weight that may be given to ijma' and qiyas in the exercise of ijtihad. The Ahl-e Hadis in nineteenth-century India, for instance, narrowed the scope of ijma' and qiyas, while others such as Muhammad Iqbal argued for its extension.

[5] M. Mustafa Al-A'zami, *On Schacht's Origins of Jurisprudence* (New York: John Wiley & Sons, 1985), pp. 30–1.

[6] Ignaz Goldziher, *Muslim Studies*, vol. 2, ed. S. M. Stern (Chicago, New York: Aldine, Atherton, 1971), p. 25.

[7] Al-A'zami, *On Schacht's Origins*, pp. 30–4.

[8] Joseph Schacht, *The Origins of Muhammadan Jurisprudence* (Oxford: Clarendon Press, 1950), p. 76. On the concept of the 'living *Sunnah*', see also Fazlur Rahman, 'Social Change and Early Sunnah', *Islamic Studies*, vol. II, no. 2 (Karachi, June 1963), 205–16.

Schacht's view has recently been challenged by scholars writing both from within the Islamic tradition and outside it. Al-A'zami, presenting what he calls the 'Muslim view', argues that the Prophet's sunna (which in several respects was a radical departure from past practice) gained currency during the Prophet's lifetime and was implemented by the early Muslims in large measure.[9] Because 'total obedience' to the Prophet is ordered in several verses of the Qur'an, and Muslims are commanded to regard him as a 'perfect model to be followed',[10] Al-A'zami believes that the Prophet's sunna over-rode existing custom and practice from the very beginning of Islam.

On the basis of recent research in the early history of hadis, Graham also disagrees with Schacht:

> It would . . . be a mistake to see this living *sunnah* of the community of the Companions and early Followers as ever having been consciously set up as a standard different from what was understood to be the *sunnah* of the Prophet . . . . However late the formal development of *sunnat an-nabi* as a conscious legal principle, the community always and ever understood its source of *'ilm* and guidance to lie in the Revelation and the practice of its bearer. The later fabrication of hadiths is not a sign of the late appearance of emphasis on the *sunnat an-nabi.*[11]

Whatever its date of origin, what is of significance to Muslims is that the Prophet's sunna is both an interpretetive guide to the Qur'an, and a source of authority in its own right. It is an interpretive guide because 'the Qur'an cannot answer each and every eventuality; it comes alive and becomes effective through the sunna'.[12] As Graham explains, 'in Islamic terms this is not because of any limitations of the Qur'an, but because of man's limitations. The Qur'an, being the word of God, is too sublime to interpret and decipher without the aid of the Prophet'.[13]

The authority of the prophetic sunna, as several scholars indicate, is perceived as being of divine origin. Goldziher writes, 'Everything

[9] Al-A'zami, *On Schacht's Origins*, pp. 69–95.

[10] Ibid., p. 8. Qur'an 3:32, 3:132, 4:59, 4:80, 33:21, 59:7.

[11] Graham, *Divine Word and Prophetic Word in Early Islam*, p. 12.

[12] Ignaz Goldziher, *Introduction to Islamic Theology and Law* (Princeton: Princeton University Press, 1981), p. 38.

[13] Graham, *Divine Word and Prophetic Word*, p. 33.

that the Prophet ordained in religious matters . . . he has decreed at God's command; it was revealed to him as was the Koran'.[14] And according to Graham: 'the word of the Prophet . . . possessed from the beginning, from the time of the Prophet, a divine authority'.[15] This authority, while secondary to that of the Qur'an, was nonetheless, in practical terms, decisive.[16]

Because the Prophet was a 'perfect model', everything that he (and his Companions) had 'held to be exclusively correct in matters of religion and law', was seen as 'a norm for practical application'.[17] The Prophet's sayings, actions, and decisions, were therefore meticulously memorized, recited, repeated, and ultimately recorded,[18] by his Companions (sahaba) in the form of hadis (literally, 'tale', 'communication').[19] In view of the fact that the sunna of the Prophet is, with the Qur'an, a principally authoritative source, in Islamic legal theory the hadis literature tended to have an authority 'coordinate with that of the Qur'an'.[20]

[14] Goldziher, *Muslim Studies*, p. 31.

[15] Graham, *Divine Word and Prophetic Word*, p. 13.

[16] In Graham's view, the early Muslims had what he calls a 'primarily unitive' view of 'divine word and prophetic word'. Ibid., p. 3. His discussion of the 'hadith qudsi' or 'Divine Saying', which is a record of Allah's speech in the Prophet's words, illustrates his point.

The question of what was to be done in cases where a contradiction arose between the Qur'an and hadis, was dealt with by al-Shafi'i (b. 767) by the rule that 'the Qur'an can only be abrogated by the Qur'an and the *sunna* only by the *sunna*. The *sunna* cannot abrogate the Qur'an because its function is to interpret the Qur'an, not to contradict it'. See N. J. Coulson, *A History of Islamic Law* (Edinburgh: Edinburgh University Press, 1964), pp. 58–9.

[17] Goldziher, *Introduction to Islamic Theology and Law*, pp. 37–8.

[18] The attitude of the Prophet and the early Muslims to committing hadis to writing has been the subject of considerable scholarly debate. See, e.g., Alfred Guillaume, *The Traditions of Islam: An Introduction to the Study of the Hadith Literature* (Oxford: Clarendon Press, 1924), pp. 15–18; Muhammad Zubayr Siddiqi, *Hadith Literature: Its Origins, Development, Special Features and Criticism* (Calcutta: Calcutta University Press, 1961), pp. 37–45.

[19] There are six major collections of hadis, the most authoritative being the *Sahih Bukhari* by al-Bukhari (d. AH 256/AD 870), and *Sahih Muslim* by Muslim (d. AH 261/AD 875). These two collections are jointly referred to as the 'Sahihain', or 'The Two Sahihs', sahih meaning 'correct'. The other four collections are the *Sunan* of Abu Da'ud (d. AH 275/AD 888), al-Nasa'i (d. AH 303/AD 915), al-Tirmidhi (d. AH 273/AD 892), and Ibn Maja (d. AH 273/AD 886). See Goldziher, *Introduction to Islamic Theology and Law*, p. 39.

[20] Graham, *Divine Word and Prophetic Word*, p. 33.

As with the question of when, historically speaking, the Prophet's sunna came to supercede previously existing practices and customs in Muslim-ruled territories, Western scholars have also been critical of several important aspects of Muslim hadis scholarship. Doubts have been raised on the origin of much of the hadis literature, on the reliability of their chains (isnad) of transmission, and on whether the words ascribed to the Prophet had in fact been spoken by him, among other things.[21] The charge of error or deliberate forgery of various kinds is admitted even by Muslim scholars writing from a self-consciously Muslim perspective.[22] This said, it is important to recognize that for the earliest Muslims the repetition of Muhammad's speech or deeds was a pious act, to be performed with great caution: 'Zubayr [a Companion of the Prophet] did not like to relate traditions, because he had heard Muhammad say that he who attributed anything to him falsely would make his seat in hell-fire'.[23] But not all transmitters of traditions were as fearful of committing mistakes, particularly those of later generations. To ensure that false hadis were weeded out, in course of time hadis criticism (known as *al-ta'dil wal-tajrih*) became a fully developed field of scholarship among the 'ulama', each tradition being subjected to a variety of rigorous tests.[24]

Some Basic Legal Concepts

Sunna and Bid'a

Based on the four sources of Qur'an, hadis, ijma' (consensus), and qiyas (analogy), Islamic jurisprudence (fiqh) classifies all human

[21] See, e.g., Guillaume, *Traditions of Islam*, p. 12: 'Our estimate of traditions circulated in their [Muhammad's Companions'] names cannot but be adversely affected by the frequent accusations of forgery levelled against many of the professional traditionists, by the many anachronisms they contain, and the political and sectarian bias they display . . . it is difficult to regard the hadith literature as a whole as an accurate and trustworthy record of the sayings and doings of Muhammad'.

[22] See, e.g., Siddiqi, *Hadith Literature*, who states in his Preface that he is writing in order 'to present . . . the viewpoint of orthodox Islam with regard to Hadith Literature', pp. 52–9; and Al-A'zami, *On Schacht's Origins*, p. 111.

[23] Siddiqi, *Hadith Literature*, p. 36.

[24] On what these tests were, see Al-A'zami, *On Schacht's Origins*, Chapter 7.

actions on a scale of relative religious value, ranging from obligatory acts (farz, Ar. fard) to those which are forbidden (haram).[25] In the legal context the term 'sunna' has a range of specific meanings, being a sub-class that falls under the category of commendable (*mandub*) acts.

The Muslim desire to imitate the Prophet in all spheres of life necessarily meant that any belief, idea, or practice that came into use after the Prophet's lifetime became problematic. The term for the latter is bid'a (literally 'innovation'), that for which 'there is no precedent in the time of the Prophet'. As the opposite of sunna, which is 'old' (*qadim*), it also has the meaning of 'new' (*muhdath* or *hadath*).[26] Goldziher adds that 'in general bid'a is something arbitrary that springs from individual insight and the admissibility of which is not documented in the sources of religious life'.[27] Consequently the term bid'a has the connotation of 'reprehensible'.[28] Thus the hadis: 'May he who introduces new things into this town [Medina] be cursed by Allah, his angels and all men'.[29]

Tracing the history of the use of the term bid'a in Islamic scholarship, Khalid Mas'ud believes that until the sixteenth century the term was used in a 'general and vague' way by traditionalists (*muhaddithun*) and theologians (*mutakallimun*), and was relatively little used in a legal sense by the *fuqaha*. Moreover, it was applied strictly to religious beliefs and practices ('ibada), rather than to social customs in general.[30] In the ninth century al-Shafi'i (767–820) had

[25] The categories are: obligatory (farz), forbidden (haram), commendable (mandub), abominable (*makruh*), and permissible (mubah). Mandub, in turn, is sub-categorized into: *sunna mu'akkada* (omission of act leading to rebuke, but not punishment, e.g. azan); *sunna nafila* (a practice which the Prophet sometimes carried out, but not on every occasion); and *sunna al-mustahab* (a desirable, though not obligatory, practice in imitation of the Prophet, such as his way of walking). See Al-A'zami, *On Schacht's Origins*, pp. 34–5.

[26] J. Robson, 'Bid'a', *EI2*, vol. 1, p. 1199.

[27] Goldziher, *Muslim Studies*, vol. 2, p. 34.

[28] As Robson comments in *EI2*, the term bid'a is to be distinguished from heresy (irtidad).

[29] Quoted by Goldziher, *Muslim Studies*, p. 26.

[30] Muhammad Khalid Mas'ud, 'Trends in the Interpretation of Islamic Law as Reflected in the *Fatawa* Literature of Deoband School: A Study of the Attitudes of the 'Ulama' of Deoband to Certain Social Problems and Inventions', M. A. thesis, Institute of Islamic Studies (Montreal: McGill University, 1969), p. 17.

made a broad distinction between a 'good' and 'bad' bid'a. As Robson says,

a distinction came to be made between a bid'a which was 'good' (*hasana*) or praiseworthy (*mahmuda*) and one which was 'bad' (*sayyi'a*) or blameworthy (*madhmuma*). Al-Shafi'i laid down the principle that any innovation which runs contrary to the Kur'an, the sunna, idjma', or *athar* (a tradition traced only to a Companion or a Follower) is an erring innovation, whereas any good thing introduced which does not run counter to any of these sources is praiseworthy.[31]

In due course Islamic jurisprudence classified bid'a into five classes, ranging from the obligatory to the prohibited, on the basis of the general principle described above.[32]

In the early nineteenth century, however, the Wahhabis in Arabia 'claimed to go back to the early sunna of the Prophet in contradistinction to legal schools'.[33] Goldziher is strongly critical of this development:

Modern Wahhabism follows the pattern of earlier times in striving to brand as bid'a not only anything contrary to the spirit of the sunna but also everything that cannot be proved to be in it. It is known that the ultra-conservative opposed every novelty, the use of coffee and tobacco, as well as printing, coming under this heading.[34]

In nineteenth-century British India the 'ulama' did not all define bid'a the same way. The Deobandi scholars Rashid Ahmad Gangohi (1828–1905) and Ashraf 'Ali Thanawi (1863–1943) regarded 'every new thing . . . in conflict with sunnah [as] bid'ah. According to them the domain of bid'ah [was] only 'ibadat or strictly speaking,

[31] Robson, 'Bid'a', *EI2*.

[32] Goldziher cites the following hadis as one which regards bid'at with favor: 'Anyone who establishes in Islam a good sunna (*s.* hasana) which is followed by later generations will enjoy the reward of all those who follow this sunna, without their losing their proper reward; but anyone who establishes in Islam an evil sunna . . . ' As Goldziher comments, this hadis presupposes the continued introduction of sunna(s) after the Prophet. Goldziher, *Muslim Studies*, p. 37. Although the word 'sunna' is used in this hadis rather than 'bid'a', the manner of its use indicates that here it has the meaning of a 'good' or 'evil' bid'a.

[33] Mas'ud, 'Trends in Interpretation', p. 17.

[34] Goldziher, *Muslim Studies*, p. 34.

religious practices'.[35] Strongly condemning practices such as the 'urs of saints, the giyarhawin of Shaikh 'Abd al-Qadir Jilani, and other customs favoured by the Ahl-e Sunnat, the Deobandis and the Ahl-e Hadis accused the former of being 'bid'atis'. For the Ahl-e Sunnat, by contrast, there was 'good' bid'a and 'bad'. This point will be more fully elaborated in the context of the azan debate below.

Ijtihad and Taqlid

Based on the four sources of Islamic law mentioned above, jurists offer legal opinions on a wide range of questions, as expressed in their fatawa. In the formative period of Islam the process of legal reasoning was known as ijtihad, 'the maximum effort expended by the jurist to master and apply the principles and rules of usul al-fiqh (legal theory) for the purpose of discovering God's law'.[36] According to Joseph Schacht and other Western scholars, the process of ijtihad ceased after the formation of the four law schools (Shafi'i, Maliki, Hanafi, and Hanbali), in the early tenth century. The law schools henceforth provided the basis for legal judgment. This development is frequently described as the 'closing of the gate of ijtihad'.

Wael B. Hallaq has recently argued, on the basis of a re-examination of original sources, that until the twelfth century the presence of mujtahids (those who practised ijtihad) was assumed, and there was no debate about the 'closing of the gate'. However, already by the tenth century ijtihad was practised only within the confines of one of the established schools of law.[37] In the eleventh century, al-Ghazali 'admitted the extinction of independent mujtahids who were able to establish their own school of law', but 'recognized the existence of mujtahids fi al-madhhab [limited to a particular school]'.[38]

Hallaq argues that the debate about the 'closing of the gate of ijtihad' began in the twelfth century, in the context of the Hanbali

[35] Mas'ud, 'Trends in Interpretation', p. 18.

[36] Wael B. Hallaq, 'Was the Gate of Ijtihad Closed?' *International Journal of Middle East Studies*, 16 (1984), 3. My understanding of the concepts ijtihad, taqlid, and tajdid, as set out in this section, are largely based on Hallaq.

[37] Ibid., pp. 10–11.

[38] Ibid., p. 17.

argument that unless there was a mujtahid in every age the shari'a would be in danger of extinction. The Hanafis, Malikis, and some Shafi'is opposed this view. Gradually (by the fifteenth century), the Hanbalis lost ground to their opponents, and the doctrine of taqlid (adherence to one's mazhab) began to gain the support of most jurists.[39]

The perception seems to have grown among the 'ulama' that they were unqualified to undertake the difficult task of ijtihad and to lay claim to the title of mujtahid. In Hallaq's view, however, this perception was not matched by the reality. In the Ottoman empire, for instance, new legal problems relating to cash, coffee, drugs, and tobacco, among other things, arose in the sixteenth and seventeenth centuries and were adjudicated in fatawa: 'In practice, therefore, the methodology of ijtihad continued to be employed but mostly without being recognized under its proper name'.[40]

In the subcontinent, the eighteenth-century scholar Shah Wali Ullah (1703–62) argued in favour of ijtihad, believing that taqlid was a 'bid'ah and *tahrif fi'l-din* (distortion of religion)'.[41] 'He argued that the "door to ijtihad", in the classical phrase, was not closed, and that those skilled in the traditional sciences had the right and indeed the responsibility to consult original sources'.[42] He also maintained that an 'alim 'should know the judgments of all the four law schools and consult them eclectically, using whichever accorded best with *hadis*'.[43]

Unlike Shah Wali Ullah, both the Deobandis and Ahl-e Sunnat in the nineteenth century took a strong stand in favour of taqlid and strict adherence to the Hanafi mazhab. Muhammad Qasim

[39] Ibid., p. 27.

[40] Ibid., p. 32. Also see Mas'ud, 'Trends in Interpretation', pp. 26–7: 'In the technical sense . . . ijtihad continues until today . . . . Only the injunctions existing in the *nusus* (Texts of the law) are theoretically outside the scope of ijtihad . . . . Otherwise the problems which are new, or about which there exists a difference of opinion, or for which the basis of judgement has changed, are mujtahad fih (open for ijtihad)'.

[41] Mas'ud, ibid., p. 24.

[42] Metcalf, *Islamic Revival*, p. 37.

[43] Ibid.; the process of selective combination of different law schools is known as talfiq.

Nanautawi (1833–77), one of the founders of the madrasa Dar al-'Ulum at Deoband, based his argument in favour of taqlid on

> the assertion, self-evident to him, that the world had dramatically declined from the time of the Prophet and that there were simply no people alive today who were as skilled as had been the imams of the classical schools. To consult the learned of today, he suggested, would be like consulting a quack instead of a skilled doctor . . .[44]

Ahmad Riza, likewise, argued in a number of fatawa on the necessity for taqlid, and asserted that there were no 'absolute mujtahids' (*mujtahid mutlaq*) alive in his day.[45] So great was the respect in which he was held by his followers, however, that occasionally one finds the claim that 'if someone were to call [Ahmad Riza] a mujtahid, it would be no exaggeration'.[46] Despite such references, the number of fatawa in favour of taqlid indicate clearly that the Ahl-e Sunnat position was the classical Hanafi one indicated by Hallaq.

Among nineteenth-century 'ulama' in British India, the Ahl-e Hadis, on the other hand, took a position strongly denouncing taqlid based on the schools of law. They were known, for this reason, as the ghair-muqallid (non-adherers, those who accepted only the Qur'an and hadis as a basis for law), a term used in a pejorative sense in the Ahl-e Sunnat literature.[47]

Tajdid

The concept of tajdid (renewal) differs from that of ijtihad in that, rather than denoting a jurist's opinion on a newly arising situation, or a restatement on a new basis of an old problem, it describes the attempt by the 'ulama' to restore the Prophet's sunna when the Muslim community has become negligent (ghafil) in implementing something the Prophet had instituted. The Muslim belief that this state of neglect recurs every century is based particularly on the hadis

[44] Ibid., p. 144.

[45] *Fatawa-e Rizwiyya*, vol. 6 (Mubarakpur, Azamgarh: Sunni Dar al-Isha'at, 1981), p. 70 (on there being no mujtahids).

[46] Zafar ud-Din Bihari, *Hayat-e A'la Hazrat*, p. 163. The comment is made in the context of his knowledge of 'ilm-e taksir (the making of numerical charts for amulets).

[47] On the Ahl-e Hadis, see Metcalf, *Islmaic Revival*, pp. 268–96.

from Abu Da'ud which says: '[o]n the eve of every century Allah will send to this community a person who will renew its religion'.[48] The one who emerges each century to renew the faith is the mujaddid or renewer.

Hallaq observes, in the context of his study of ijtihad, that 'mujaddids . . . were, *inter alia*, mujtahids'.[49] The status of mujaddid was therefore the higher of the two. Yet while the claim to be a mujtahid ceased to be made around the fifteenth century, mujaddids were recognized (sometimes more than one at a given time) every century.[50]

Hallaq's observation that because the Hanafis had embraced the idea of taqlid, believing that ijtihad had ceased, they 'did not even participate in the race for tajdid',[51] does not hold true for the Indian subcontinent. The majority of Sunni Muslims here are Hanafis, and tajdid has been a major theme—as it has in other parts of the Muslim world—of a number of Islamic reform movements since the eighteenth century.[52] The leaders of these movements, identified by their followers as the mujaddids of their centuries, have been 'ulama', 'men of learning and piety who symbolize the aspirations of the community and who come to the fore in what are seen as times of crisis'.[53] In early nineteenth-century British India, this claim was made on behalf of Sayyid Ahmad Barelwi (1786–1831), leader of the jihad against the Sikhs, by his followers. It was also made by Rashid Ahmad Gangohi (1829–1905), one of the founders of the

[48] The translation is by Yohanan Friedmann, *Prophecy Continuous*, p. 95. As Friedmann notes, the tradition occurs in the context of a description of the calamities expected to occur just before the Day of Judgment; the idea of tajdid, thus initially associated with eschatological expectations, came in time to be associated with the idea of revival every hundred years. See Friedmann for discussion, pp. 94–101. The tradition is recorded in Ahmad Hasan's translation of Abu Da'ud as follows: 'Allah will raise for this community at the end of every hundred years the one who will renovate its religion for it'. Ahmad Hasan, *Sunan Abu Dawud*, vol. 3, p. 1194.

[49] Hallaw, 'Was the Gate of Ijtihad Closed? p. 28.

[50] The question of timing, including the dates of birth and death of a potential candidate, was in fact subject to considerable argument and debate. See Chapters VII and VIII below for a discussion.

[51] Ibid.

[52] Metcalf, *Islamic Revival*, p. 4.

[53] Ibid., p. 6.

madrasa Dar al-'Ulum at Deoband.[54] And at the end of the nineteenth century, it was made by Ahmad Riza's followers on his behalf; although he did not advance the claim himself, he was probably not unwilling to accept the title. The Ahl-e Sunnat did not, of course, accept the claims of Sayyid Ahmad and Rashid Ahmad, and vice versa.

That there was no consensus among nineteenth-century Ahl-e Sunnat and Deobandi 'ulama' as to the identity of mujaddids in centuries close to their time[55] is a significant indication of their interpretative differences on other issues. As a first step toward understanding what these were, and to assessing their significance, we must attend to Ahmad Riza's concept of the sunna of the Prophet as reflected in his fatawa.

The Fatawa of Ahmad Riza Khan

When Ahmad Riza was approaching death in 1921, he reportedly told Hamid Riza Khan, his eldest son, that by Allah's grace, for more than ninety years the writing and sending out of fatawa (to those who had requested them) had been a continuous activity in his house. The task had been started by his grandfather, handed over after many years to his father, and passed on in turn to him when he was a mere lad of fourteen. He had continued the work throughout his life. Now he, in his turn, was entrusting it to his two sons and nephew, as part of his bequest. If they all worked together, by Allah's grace they would be successful.[56]

Ahmad Riza could not have indicated more forcefully than he did in this statement from his deathbed the importance to him of writing fatawa. He regarded it as a religious service he had rendered

[54] Metcalf discusses the claims of Sayyid Ahmad Barelwi and Rashid Ahmad Gangohi in ibid., pp. 60–1, 138–9.

[55] Disagreement among the 'ulama' on the identity of the mujaddid goes back even earlier, as Friedmann's discussion in *Prophecy Continuous*, pp. 98–100, suggests. According to Hallaq, 'after Sirhindi [seventeenth century] the practice of choosing a mujaddid seems to have lost some importance'. Hallaq, p. 28.

[56] Hasnain Riza Khan, *Wasaya Sharif*, p. 5, in *Rasa'il-e Rizwiyya*, vol. 5 (Faisalabad, 1984).

the Muslims of the subcontinent uninterruptedly for about fifty years. In his view, so great was the volume of questions received that it would require the joint efforts of three 'ulama' dedicated to the task, to accomplish what he had done singlehanded.

Elsewhere he had suggested that the volume of fatawa he wrote was so great that 'it exceeds the work of ten muftis'.[57] In a fatwa dated Zu'l Hijja 1331/November 1913, he wrote:

> Questions come from the town [of Bareilly], from other cities, and from all Hindustan: Bengal, Panjab, Malabar, Burma, Arakan, [as well as countries such as] China, Ghazni, America, and Africa; so much so that they come even from the Haramain. At any one time there are about five hundred questions (*istifta*). If there is delay in answering any of them, or if some go unanswered, then [I will be] to blame. 'On no soul doth Allah place a burden greater than it can bear'. [Qur'an 2:286][58]

Ahmad Riza was not without assistance in handling this vast correspondence, however. Zafar ud-Din Bihari, his disciple and biographer, offers glimpses of how it was done. Each day's mail was gathered and opened occasionally during the late-afternoon public audience Ahmad Riza held every day at his home. Zafar ud-Din Bihari would read the letters out one by one, and, depending on their subject matter, each was assigned to different students or disciples of Ahmad Riza for reply. Thus

> if the letter dealt with tasawwuf [sufism], A'la Hazrat [Ahmad Riza] would respond to it himself. If it asked for a ta'wiz [amulet], he would pass it on to me [Zafar ud-Din] or to Maulana Hamid Riza Khan [Ahmad Riza's eldest son]. If it was an istifta [request for a fatwa], he would give it to [one of several assistants] or to me, . . . or to Maulana Amjad 'Ali [a disciple of Ahmad Riza, whose title was 'Sadr ul-Shari'at'], depending on the complexity of the question. If the question was a particularly complex one, he would answer it himself.[59]

Questions which had not come up before, and for which there was no precedent in Ahmad Riza's fatawa, were also answered by him.

Ahmad Riza's students received their training in the writing of

57 A mufti is an 'alim who issues fatawa.

58 *Fatawa-e Rizwiyya*, vol. 4, problem 123 (Ramnagar, Nainital: Riza Dar al-Isha'at, 1986), p. 149.

59 *Hayat-e A'la Hazrat*, p. 68.

fatawa chiefly by making copies of his fatawa, so that he retained a record of them before they were sent out. A Dar al-Ifta had been created sometime before 1904–5.[60] It was a centre to which aspiring students like Zafar ud-Din came to learn by assisting in the daily writing of fatawa. Over time they came to learn Ahmad Riza's style of fatwa-writing, and to be able to write their own on his model. As Zafar ud-Din Bihari's biography indicates, once they became proficient he entrusted some of his daily correspondence to them. The student Ahmad Riza regarded as most skilled in the art of fatwa-writing was Amjad 'Ali A'zami, author of the *Bahar-e Shari'at.*[61]

The Dar al-Ifta was much closer to Ahmad Riza's heart, in fact, than was teaching. As indicated earlier, the Madrasa Manzar al-Islam founded by Ahmad Riza in 1904 in fact owed more to Zafar ud-Din Bihari's interest and initiative than it did to Ahmad Riza's. Ahmad Riza's time was devoted chiefly to answering, in the form of fatawa, the questions he received in the mail and by other means. It is said that, despite help from students at the Dar al-Ifta, he personally replied to the bulk of the questions in the privacy of his personal library or his household living quarters (*zenana-khana*). The work took up most of his day, and as a follower of his recalled, he kept it going even when he fell sick.[62] Regarding it as a shar'i duty, he was offended when someone offered payment for a fatwa he had written.[63]

It is probable that the first two volumes of the *Fatawa-e Rizwiyya*

[60] This was the date when Zafar ud-Din first came to Bareilly, and the Dar al-Ifta was already in existence. Muhammad Ahmad Qadiri, 'Malik ul-'Ulama' Maulana Muhammad Zafar ud-Din Bihari aur Khidmat-e Hadis', *Ashrafiyya* (Mubarakpur, April 1977), p. 29.

[61] Ahmad Riza used to recommend that others learn the art of writing fatawa under Amjad 'Ali's direction. *Hayat-e A'la Hazrat*, p. 214.

[62] There is a remarkable story related in *Hayat-e A'la Hazrat*, pp. 36–7, about how Ahmad Riza was once seen dictating twenty-nine fatawa to four scribes, when sick in bed. While one scribe wrote down his response to one question, he dictated the answer to another to a second person, and so on—in continuous relay, as it were—until all twenty-nine questions had been answered.

[63] Maulana Yasin Akhtar Misbahi, *Imam Ahmad Riza aur Radd-e Bid'at o Munkarat* (Mubarakpur: Al-Majma' al-Islami, 1985), p. 75. I have been unable to trace Maulana Yasin Akhtar's source.

were published during Ahmad Riza's lifetime, perhaps at the Hasani Press at Bareilly owned by Ahmad Riza's brother, Hasan Riza Khan.[64] Evidently the intention was to publish the full collection, projected to be a twelve-volume work. For reasons that are not clear, but that may have stemmed from financial difficulties at the Hasani Press and disarray in the leadership of the Ahl-e Sunnat after Ahmad Riza's death, publication of the remaining volumes was not undertaken until the late 1950s. It began at the behest of Mustafa Riza Khan, Ahmad Riza's younger son, under the direction of Maulana 'Abd ur-Ra'uf of the Dar al-'Ulum Ashrafiyya at Mubarakpur, in district Azamgarh.[65] Because the volumes have since been published in a variety of locations, under different editors and over a time span of about three generations, they are of uneven length and have a varied format.

More troubling, though, is that when 'Abd ur-Ra'uf began the process of publication, he found that the manuscripts (themselves copies of copies at fourth remove, rather than originals) were in poor condition, or incomplete, and frequently had to be verified. Where he and his associates were able to trace an incomplete reference, they inserted it themselves. Where they were not able to do so, they left it as it was. The process entailed laborious checking of hand-written materials, and considerable expense, apart from difficulties with printers.[66]

From our point of view, however, the most troublesome aspect of all about the collection is that it omits a number of important

[64] On this press, see Chapter III. Unfortunately only the most sketchy outlines of its operations are known. I thank Mr. Muhammad Mustafa 'Ali Rizwi, an advocate in Bareilly, for kind permission to photocopy original works published at the Hasani Press, and elsewhere, from his personal collection of Ahmad Riza's writings.

[65] He was Deputy Shaikh al-Hadis at the Dar al-'Ulum Ashrafiyya. The publication of the *Fatawa-e Rizwiyya* was not undertaken under the auspicies of the Ashrafiyya, however, but under a separately constituted body called the 'Sunni Dar al-Isha'at' of which 'Abd ur-Ra'uf was the head. When he died in 1971, only volumes 4 and 5 had been published. The remaining volumes were published by other 'ulama' at Mubarakpur, as also at Bareilly. See Introduction to *Fatawa-e Rizwiyya*, vol. 7, for details.

[66] An interesting aspect of the publication problems encountered was that the printers occasionally turned out to have Deobandi views! Publication of volume 5 languished for five years with the Na'imi Press, Lucknow, for this reason, until it was finally repossessed by the 'ulama' at Mubarakpur and assigned to another printer. See ibid.

fatawa by Ahmad Riza. This may be due to the loss of some risalas (treatises) intended for incorporation in the collection; in addition, the *Fatawa-e Rizwiyya* may have been intended as a comprehensive guide to Ahmad Riza's opinions rather than sole reference on specific matters. Consequently it is necessary to refer to fatawa published separately in addition to the *Fatawa-e Rizwiyya.* Such publications appeared in the course of the late nineteenth and early twentieth centuries from the Hasani Press at Bareilly, and from presses in other small towns in the United Provinces, as well as Patna, Bihar.

The *Fatawa-e Rizwiyya* are organized in the traditional manner into a number of books (*kitab*), some of which are further broken down into chapters (*bab*). Matters relating to ritual and the so-called 'pillars'—purification (*taharat*), prayer (salat), alms-giving (zakat), fasting (sawm), and the pilgrimage (hajj)—appear first and in that order, in the first four volumes. The remaining volumes deal with marriage (*nikah*), regulations concerning infidels, apostates; and rebels (*sair*), economic issues such as partnership (*shirkat*) and sale (*bai'*), and bequests (*rahn*), among other things.[67]

Encompassed within this handful of topics are a host of important, though subsidiary, issues. Thus in a lengthy chapter (of 377 pages) on funerals (*janaza*), itself a part of the book entitled *Salat*, are fatawa detailing beliefs about the dead, the performance of death rituals such as fatiha, and offering food to faqirs in memory of the dead.[68] Similarly in the book dealing with infidels, apostates, and rebels, are fatawa relating to the Khilafat movement of the 1920s, on learning the English language, and on whether India was dar al-harb or dar al-Islam. And so, although there is no separate treatment of sufi-related or political themes in the two instances cited, these are enmeshed, as it were, in the primary classification of the fatawa into

[67] I was unable to make a complete listing of the kitabs, on account of inability to find volumes 8, 9, and 12, which perhaps have not yet been published. The order of the kitabs is similar to that of the *Hidaya* by al-Marghinani (d. 1195) and of the *Fatawa-e A'lamgiri* (composed 1664-72). See J. H. Harington, 'Remarks upon the Authorities of Mosulman Law', in *Asiatic Researches*, 10 (1811), 511.

[68] This is only a small number of the subjects covered by the fatawa in this chapter. The details are set out in the list of contents to volume 4.

those dealing with funeral prayers or treatment of apostates and non-Muslims.

A not dissimilar issue is that the question that called up a fatwa in the first place could and often did consist of a cluster of distinct questions, such that the fatwa responding to it could be classified under more than one head.[69] Thus, a question as to whether a Sunni who had become an Ahmadi ('Qadiyani') was an apostate, and if so, what injunctions applied to his wife and children,[70] was one that related both to the treatment of apostates, and to marriage. It appears in the book on apostasy rather than that on marriage, however, because in his response Ahmad Riza concentrated on that aspect of the question, treating the second half relatively briefly.

This fatwa is a good illustration of Ahmad Riza's style of argumentation, his citation of a number of sources to support his opinions, and his clear judgment on the question at hand. The question had originally been asked of an 'alim in Amritsar by a resident of that city in 1902–3, soon after Ghulam Ahmad first made his claim to be a 'shadowy' prophet. The fatwa given by this 'alim was certified by a number of other 'ulama' from Amritsar. The first 'alim then sent his fatwa and the certifications to Ahmad Riza, requesting his opinion on the matter.

Ahmad Riza responded with a comprehensive review of Ghulam Ahmad's writings, as he interpreted them. Citing these, and giving complete references to each book and page he was quoting, he found Ghulam Ahmad guilty of kufr on ten distinct grounds. He found the first kufr, for instance, in

[69] This was also the case with the Deobandi fatawa. Metcalf, discussing Rashid Ahmad Gangohi's fatawa, writes: 'Any categorization of the topics covered in his pronouncements is necessarily crude, for a single fatwa could often illustrate at once a variety of issues concerning belief, practice, jurisprudential principles, and attitudes toward other religious groups'. Metcalf, *Islamic Revival*, p. 148.

[70] The Ahmadis are followers of Mirza Ghulam Ahmad (*c.* 1835–1908). A number of Muslims, including the Ahl-e Sunnat, consider them to be non-Muslims. For a recent interpretation of the Ahmadi movement, see Friedmann, *Prophecy Continuous*.

The question and the fatwa that was its response are in *Fatwa-e Rizwiyya*, vol. 6, pp. 297–307, in the form of a risala (tract) entitled *Al-Su' wa'l E'qab 'ala'l Masih il-Kazzab* (Punishment of the False Claimant to Prophethood). This risala has also been published separately, in a collection entitled the *Majma'-e Rasa'il: Radd-e Mirza'iat* (Karachi: Idara-e Tasnifat-e Imam Ahmad Riza, 1985), pp. 23–45.

a risala entitled *Ek Ghalti ka Izala* [The Annulling of a Mistake]. On page 673 of this, he writes 'I am Ahmad', and quotes from [Qur'an 61:6] [in which Jesus gave] 'glad tidings of an apostle whose name shall be Ahmad'. [In saying this, Ghulam Ahmad implies that] he, and not the Prophet Muhammad, was the Prophet about whom Jesus spoke.[71]

After quoting from other books by Ghulam Ahmad in this way, Ahmad Riza then examined Ghulam Ahmad's claim that he was using the word nabi (prophet) in a different sense from the one ordinarily understood. Ahmad Riza poured scorn on this statement. Citing authorities from fiqh, he demonstrated that such arguments had not been accepted in the past. Nor would they be acceptable to people in the present: for instance, if a man told his wife that she was 'free' (taliq), it would be understood that he was divorcing her, not that he was giving her permission to go wherever she wished.[72] Indeed, if such reversals of meaning were accepted, there would be chaos (*darham barham*) in all religious and worldly affairs (*din o duniya*).[73]

After arguing in this detailed, point-by-point manner that Ghulam Ahmad was a kafir, Ahmad Riza asserted that it was incumbent on Muslims who knew of Ghulam Ahmad's claims and statements to pass the verdict of kufr on him. Those who did not do this (he specifically mentioned the Nadwa), became kafirs themselves. Again a number of authorities from fiqh were cited in support of this view. Finally, addressing the related question about the validity of the marriage between an Ahmadi man and his wife, he said that the wife was released from her marriage bond, with all the consequences that this entailed with respect to rights over the *mahr* (marriage settlement) and children.

While the Deobandi 'ulama' did not always bolster their opinions with a citation of sources,[74] it was characteristic of Ahmad Riza to cite authorities from Qur'an, hadis, and fiqh when writing a fatwa.[75]

71 *Fatawa-e Rizwiyya*, vol. 6, p. 299.

72 Ibid., pp. 300–1.

73 Ibid., p. 302.

74 See Mas'ud, 'Trends in Interpretation', p. 71, where he shows that the number of fatawa that did not cite a source outnumbered those that did.

75 To give some examples from the fatwa examined above, in dismissing Ghulam

His appeal to logic was characteristic as well. In the fatwa cited, he made his opponent's position appear foolish, and the unassailability of his own view self-evident, by showing that the (seemingly) arbitrary change in the meaning of a word would lead to chaos in everyday life. Finally, he argued that not only was Ghulam Ahmad's claim foolish; much worse, it was an act of infidelity. Muslims must recognize this fact, and denounce it unequivocally; else they too would be guilty of kufr.

At a time when a variety of conflicting opinions were being expressed through different Muslim movements, the combined effect of Ahmad Riza's erudition, logical argument, and decisiveness must have had a considerable impact on those he addressed. As the above fatwa illustrates, his judgments were as much a guide to belief and action as a clear injunction and warning about what should *not* be done or believed. The lack of ambiguity in his judgments was thus joined by a call for action in the believer's personal life, even if this entailed taking a stand on controversial issues. As the next few chapters will make clear, this call for action was not limited to his condemnation of Ghulam Ahmad (in which he was joined by the Deobandi 'ulama' and others), but was made in relation to his opinions on other 'ulama' and other issues also. He firmly believed that it was the shar'i duty of Muslims not only to follow the Qur'an and sunna but also to condemn those who failed to do so, regardless of the consequences.

It can be said about Ahmad Riza's fatawa, as Metcalf notes regarding the Deobandi fatawa, that while they focused on 'belief and ritual, 'aqa'id and ibadat, . . . they explored [these areas] with remarkable depth and range. Indeed, . . . the fatawa reflect not a narrowing of concerns but an expansion, for they treated issues earlier fatawa had not even considered'.[76] Reflecting problems of concern to a number of Muslims in his day, Ahmad Riza addressed issues as diverse as the correct attitude toward Hindus, on whether

---

Ahmad's claim to be using the word nabi in a special way, Ahmad Riza cited the *Fusul-e Imadiyya, Fatawa-e Hindiyya* (presumably the same as *Fatawa-e Hind*, an Urdu[?] translation of *Fatawa-e 'Alamgiri*), Qazi Iyaz's *Al- Shifa'*, vol. 3, and Maulana Rumi, among others.

[76] Metcalf, *Islamic Revival*, p. 148.

Muslims should join the anti-British non-cooperation movement launched by Gandhi in the 1920s, on the monetary value of bank notes, on whether news on the sighting of the moon during Ramazan could be acted upon if conveyed by telegraph, and so on.

A remarkable feature is Ahmad Riza's appeal to the 'ulama' of the Haramain for sanction and approval on a number of controversial issues.[77] One such case was the debate about bank notes, mentioned above, that began around 1877 (AH 1294).[78] While both Ahmad Riza and Rashid Ahmad Gangohi agreed that notes were a valid form of money and that zakat must be paid on them, they disagreed on whether transactions involving exchange in unequal amounts was similar to interest (*riba*), which is forbidden to Muslims. Gangohi held such transactions to be unlawful in that they resembled interest, whereas Ahmad Riza argued that they were not comparable to interest and were permissible. Another mufti, 'Abd ul-Hayy Firangi Mahali, also opposed Ahmad Riza's judgment. This debate had political implications for the stand the 'ulama' took on British rule in India, as will be discussed in Chapter IX.

While the details of the jurisprudential arguments made on each side are undoubtedly important, also significant is the fact that Ahmad Riza wrote his definitive fatwa on the subject, *Kafl al Faqih*, in Mecca in 1906 in response to questions by two 'ulama' in that city on the monetary value of the bank note.[79] Here we see him in the role of mufti to other 'ulama' of the Haramain, which must surely have been exceptional. His admirers view this (with under-

[77] I am grateful to Khalid Mas'ud for drawing my attention to this in a personal communication.

[78] My summary of the debate is based on Mas'ud, 'Trends in Interpretation', pp. 40–3, for the Deobandi view; and, for the Ahl-e Sunnat side, *Fatawa-e Rizwiyya*, Introduction to vol. 7, pp. 9–10, and Ahmad Riza's fatwa, *Kafl al-Faqih al-Fahim fi Ahkam Qirtas al-Darahim* (Guarantee of the Discerning Jurist on Duties relating to Paper Money), in that volume, pp. 126–95.

[79] They were Maulana 'Abd Allah Ahmad Mirdad, imam at the Masjid al-Haram, and Maulana Hamid Ahmad Muhammad Jaddawi, his teacher. These and other details are in another fatwa by Ahmad Riza entitled *Kasir ul-Safih il-Wahim fi Ibdal Qirtas al-Darahim* (Foolish Breaking and Misleading Notions on the Exchange of Paper Money), AH 1329/AD 1911, in *Fatawa-e Rizwiyya*, vol. 7, p. 228. At the beginning of this fatwa, Ahmad Riza explains that the word 'foolish' in the title refers to Rashid Ahmad Gangohi, and the 'misleading notions' to 'Abd ul-Hayy Firangi Mahali. Ibid., p. 199.

standable pride) as evidence of Ahmad Riza's high reputation, already established in the course of a previous judgment relating to the Nadwat al-'Ulama'.[80] In that debate, as in the one concerning Deoband (both shortly to be examined in Chapters VII and VIII), Ahmad Riza sought confirmation and approval by the 'ulama' of Mecca and Medina of a fatwa written in Bareilly.[81] In this instance, unlike the case of the bank note debate, he was seeking ratification by a higher authority on a matter on which the 'ulama' in British India were divided. Approval would not only confirm his position, but could also be expected to discomfit his opponents. That several 'ulama' of the Haramain did ratify his fatawa on a variety of issues, over a span of roughly twenty years, including his 1915 judgment on the azan debate (to be examined below), and that his relationship with them was one of reciprocity, can be understood to have considerably bolstered his personal standing in India.

The Call to Prayer: From Inside the Mosque or Outside?

The 'azan debate' (Ahl-e Sunnat sources also call it the 'Badayuni affair', for reasons that will shortly become clear) invites our attention because for three years (1914 to 1917) Ahl-e Sunnat 'ulama' engaged with one another in fierce controversy in newspapers and pamphlets, questioning and defining terms such as sunna and bid'a in different ways. The issues at stake were far wider than the specific subject under discussion. The debate ended on a rather dramatic note in 1917, in a British magistrate's court in Badayun where a charge of libel had been brought against Ahmad Riza the preceding year. Indeed, a full analysis of the azan debate, whose participants gradually drew in an audience not only of 'ulama' but also of educated 'lay' Muslims, takes us beyond questions of ritual to issues of a public and political nature. For the present I shall focus on the discussion as reported in the Urdu press and led by the 'ulama'.

[80] See, for example, Muhammad Mas'ud Ahmed, *Fazil Barelwi 'Ulama'-e Hijaz ki Nazar Men*, 6th edition (Mubarakpur, Azamgarh: Al-Majma' al-Islami, 1981), pp. 90–2.

[81] The success of the Wahhabis in establishing their rule over the Arabian peninsula in 1924 may be the reason Ahmad Riza does not seem to have sought confirmatory opinions from the 'ulama' of the Haramain after 1906.

The debate had apparently already generated considerable heat and argument (probably orally) when the *Dabdaba-e Sikandari*, the weekly Urdu newspaper published in Rampur, addressed a series of ten questions to the 'ulama' at Bareilly's Dar al-Ifta. These appeared in the section of the paper entitled *Chashma-e Dar al-Ifta-e Bareilly* (Fount of Bareilly's Dar al-Ifta), which (as described in Chapter III) had been started by Munshi Muhammad Fazl-e Hasan Sabiri, the sub-editor, in November 1910, at the request of some of its readers. Now and then, Munshi Muhammad Fazl-e Hasan himself asked the questions which occasioned the fatawa printed therein. In 1913, thus, he asked about an unusual practice he said he had noticed in the mosque near Ahmad Riza's house at Bareilly. This was the act of blessing (salat o salam) the Prophet thrice aloud after the azan, just before the start of the prayer. Since the practice was unusual in the country, was it a bid'a? On what authority could it be said to be valid, he asked.[82]

Ahmad Riza, responding himself on this occasion, asserted that the practice of blessing the Prophet after the azan was followed in Arabia, Egypt, Syria, and other countries of dar al-islam; and indeed also in the Holy Mosque at Mecca, and in Medina, at all times except during the maghrib (evening) prayer. It had been an accepted practice for more than five hundred years. 'Holy remembrance of [the Prophet] is the faith of the Muslim at every instant, at all times. It is the life of faith, the tranquillity of life, and the source of repose'. Citing a work of fiqh[83] in support of the practice, Ahmad Riza went on to say that it was a bid'at-e hasana, a good bid'a, which had started in AH 781/AD 1379–80. This was one of those new (*taza*) things which was 'good and praiseworthy' (*nek o mahmud*).

The questions and corresponding fatwa about the azan appeared in the *Chashma-e Dar al-Ifta-e Bareilly* section in January 1914.[84] Unlike the usual brief question and answer, however, the questions in this case were detailed and lengthy, as was the response. The tone

[82] *Dabdaba-e Sikandari*, 50:2 (December 8, 1913), 7.

[83] *Al-Durr al-Mukhtar*, a seventeenth-century work by a mufti of Damascus.

[84] *Dabdaba-e Sikandari*, 50:9 (January 26, 1914), 3–5. The questions were asked by one Maulawi Muhammad Jamil ur-Rahman Khan, of Bareilly, of whom nothing is known. This fatwa also appears in the *Fatawa-e Rizwiyya*, vol. 2, pp. 488–94.

suggests that the issue had already been debated and that disagreement was known to be strong in certain circles. Moreover, the style of the questions seems to indicate that the questioner himself had a position on the questions he was asking, and that he expected the mufti concerned to take a stand in sympathy with his view, although this is nowhere stated.[85] The central question was whether the second call to prayer (azan-e sani),[86] should be given from inside the mosque (facing the pulpit, minbar), or from outside it. Among the related questions were the following: What was the practice of the Prophet Muhammad and the four 'rightly-guided' caliphs and what did the books of fiqh say on the matter? Should one act on the practice of the Prophet and the first four caliphs, and on the command of fiqh, or on customary practice, when the latter differed from the former, and what was the current practice of the 'ulama' of the Haramain? Do the hadis command one to revive the sunna, and do they promise a reward equal to that received by a hundred martyrs to the person who does so? Is it obligatory (lazim) on the 'ulama' to revive a dead sunna, or not?

In his response Ahmad Riza[87] wrote that in the time of the Prophet, Abu Bakr, and 'Umar, the azan had been given from the door of the mosque, which he interpreted to be 'outside' rather than 'inside'. Citing a hadis from the *Sunan* of Abu Da'ud, he said that the (key, though controversial) words *bain yad* ('a hand's breadth') were followed by the words *'ala'l bab al-masjid* ('at the door of the mosque').[88] Moreover, the books of Hanafi fiqh (of which he cited

[85] I owe this insight to a comment by Khalid Mas'ud, made in an unpublished paper.

[86] This second azan is given only at the start of the Friday congregational prayer; thus the debate concerned only this particular prayer.

[87] The name of the writer of the fatwa, given at the end, is Hamid Riza Khan, Ahmad Riza's eldest son. Ahmad Riza has confirmed it, along with other 'ulama' from the Dar al-Ifta. However, both the style of the fatwa, and later references to it as Ahmad Riza's fatwa, reveal that it was he, rather than his son, who wrote it. Perhaps the controversial nature of this fatwa had prompted Ahmad Riza to ascribe it to his son, as a precautionary measure. Questions about the authorship of a tract later written on this very issue were similarly raised in the course of the Badayun libel case.

[88] In Ahmad Hasan's translation, the relevant passage in this hadis reads: 'The call to the (Friday) prayer was made at the gate of the mosque in front of the Apostle of Allah (may peace be upon him) when he sat on the pulpit, and of Abu Bakr and 'Umar'.

several) have forbidden the practice of calling the azan from within the mosque. Replying to the other questions, he said that obviously Muslims must never cling to custom when this goes against hadis and fiqh, that one must distance oneself from that which is contrary to the sunna of the Prophet and the caliphs, that the practice in Mecca and Medina was in accordance with the sunna, and that several hadis promised great reward to the one who revived a dead sunna. He ended on a note of appeal to all Muslims:

> Muslim brothers! This is din. It is not some worldly quarrel. See what your Prophet's sunna is, what is written in the mazhabi books. It [this fatwa] is submitted (*ma'ruz*) to the 'ulama' of the Ahl-e Sunnat . . . . Revival of the sunna is your task. Don't say to yourselves that a small person among you has started it. It is for you to do it too. Your lord has commanded [you to] 'strengthen piety and faith' (*ta'wana 'ala'l birr wa'l-taqwa*). If you think my opinion on this matter is wrong, do not get angry. Without hesitation, give your opinion as to what is right.[89]

He also added five new questions to the ten already asked and said that whoever dissented with his opinion must include in his response an answer to the fifteen questions raised.

The note of challenge thus sent out was reinforced, on the same page, by Mustafa Riza Khan, who as muhtamim (manager) of the Dar al-Ifta, issued an 'important request (*zaruri guzarish*) to [our] Muslim brothers'. He asked that whoever came across the above fatwa make every effort to publicize it among his fellows, by reading it out loud to friends and in the mosque, and that the names and addresses of all those who revived this sunna be sent to him, Mustafa Riza, so that they could be published at some future date in the paper. He asked, further, that those 'ulama' who agreed with the opinion should say so in writing, and send their approval to him with the signatures of as many people in their town as possible. Finally, the names of twenty-odd men, who had already revived this sunna in their mosques, were listed.

The second round of the azan debate (insofar as the *Dabdaba-e Sikandari*'s pages reveal) followed about six weeks later. On March

---

Ahmad Hasan, *Sunan Abu Dawud*, vol. 1, p. 280.

[89] *Dabdaba-e Sikandari*, 50:9 (January 26, 1914), 4–5.

16, 1914, the paper reproduced an istifta (request for a fatwa) from some 'ulama' of Pilibhit, which they had sent to an 'alim of Rampur for reply. Both the question and the response, which had been confirmed by four other Rampur 'ulama', condemned the fatwa of the 'ulama' of Bareilly. The istifta argued that the practice of saying the second azan from inside the mosque was in force in places such as Mecca, Medina, Hindustan, Turkistan, Iran, and Egypt, among others, and had been so for 1,300 years. Muslims were agreed that this was a lawful (*masnun*) azan. For an 'alim to say that it was a great sin (*gunah kabira*) was to accuse all Muslims of perpetrating a grave offence. At best, his judgment could be said to be his ijtihad, not one on which all Muslims must act. What was the opinion of the 'ulama' of Rampur on this?

In their fatwa and confirmatory opinions, the 'ulama' of Rampur agreed with those of Pilibhit that saying the second azan from within the mosque was, and had been, the practice of Muslims all along, in keeping with the original practice of the Prophet and of the ancestors (*salaf*). There was consensus (ijma') among Muslims on this point, and 'ijma' is regarded by the Ahl-e Sunnat as proof (*hujjat*)'. It was also pointed out that the second azan had been started by the caliph 'Usman, not by the Prophet, and that it was evident from the *nusus* (clear verses of the Qur'an), as from hadis and fiqh, that unlike the first azan, which was given outside the mosque, the second azan was to be given 'in front of the imam', and 'near the *khatib*'. One Rampur 'alim wrote: 'Brothers! This is not to make a dead sunna come alive, but to kill a living sunna. And far from getting a reward, you will be punished'.

To this, Ahmad Riza gave a detailed, three-part rebuttal, printed in the pages immediately following the above fatwa. In the first part of the rebuttal, aimed at 'ordinary Muslims', he made two major points. First, he charged that the Arabic fiqh texts quoted by the Rampur 'alim nowhere commanded that the azan be given inside the mosque, and that by failing to give an Urdu translation of the texts, he was misleading those (in effect, most Indian Muslims) who could not read Arabic. Second, he challenged the interpretation by the Rampur 'ulama' of the phrase which was key to the whole discussion, namely, bain yad. He argued that this phrase, 'a hand's breadth', did not imply that the muezzin had to be contiguous to the pulpit when making the call to prayer, but only that he face the pulpit. In addition, he challenged the nature of the Rampur 'alim's sources, pointed to the range and large number of his own, and accused the Rampur 'ulama' of committing a list of twenty wrongs in their fatwa.[90]

An interesting aspect of this discussion, which emerged in the open letter Ahmad Riza wrote to the Rampur 'alim who had opposed his fatwa (also printed in this issue of the *Dabdaba-e Sikandari*), was his citation of the writings of Shaikh Ahmad Sirhindi, founder of the Naqshbandi Mujaddidi sufi order. A note at the end of this letter, apparently by the newspaper editors, indicated that all those who had opposed Ahmad Riza's fatwa were followers of the Shaikh Mujaddid.

Digressing for a moment from the substance of the arguments made on each side, it is important that we pay attention to the source of the opposition. The fact that the 'ulama' of Pilibhit and Rampur were (primarily) Naqshbandi Mujaddidis in their capacity as sufis, while Ahmad Riza and his supporters were primarily Qadiris, had no doctrinal significance. The occurrence of multiple affiliation, by the nineteenth century, had decreased the difference in religious styles between orders.[91] (In fact, the editorial note rejoiced at the fact that Ahmad Riza was citing Shaikh Ahmad Sirhindi's writings in his support, for that was a source which his opponents would have to accept.) The manner in which the difference in sufi affiliation of the various 'ulama' impinged on this debate would seem to have been social, rather than religious. For, as Metcalf points out in a different context, what the orders did define were 'different spiritual networks'.[92] It was the operation of these different spiritual networks, it seems to me, that explains the strong opposition to the 'ulama' of Bareilly that emerged in subsequent months from the Naqshbandi Mujaddidi khanqah at Ganj Muradabad, near Awadh [93]

90 For the details, see *Dabdaba-e Sikandari*, 50:16 (March 16, 1914), 3–8.

91 See Metcalf, *Islamic Revival*, p. 158.

92 Ibid., p. 164.

93 See *Dabdaba-e Sikandari*, 50:20 (April 13, 1914), 9, article entitled 'A Voice from Ganj Muradabad on the Second Azan of Friday'; *Dabdaba-e Sikandari*, 50: 21 (April 20,

and still later from the Sabiri Chishti khanqah at the shrine of Mu'in ud-Din, at Ajmer.[94]

There was opposition from other quarters as well. In his open letter to the Rampur 'alim who had opposed his fatwa Ahmad Riza suggested that its author had been encouraged by certain 'Wahhabis' to openly disagree with him when a personal letter would have enabled them to discuss their differences in private.[95] That Ahmad Riza was probably referring to some 'ulama' from Deoband is indicated by another open letter in the paper a week later, by Maulana Amjad 'Ali A'zami (author of the *Bahar-e Shari'at*, as noted above) and addressed to an 'alim of Deoband. This accused the Deobandi 'alim of misquoting certain sources on the question of the second azan being said from inside the mosque. Amjad 'Ali offered a fifty-rupee prize if the claim could be substantiated from the sources.[96]

This extended, many-sided, and strong disputation, together with the deep sense of anguish created in some by the prolonged uncertainty surrounding a prayer ritual of central importance to Muslims, provided the context for the fatwa that appeared in the February 15, 1915 issue of the *Dabdaba-e Sikandari* by certain 'ulama' of the Haramain. It had been requested by a Muslim of Pilibhit, who wrote to one Maulana Muhammad Karim Allah of Medina. Enclosing a copy of Ahmad Riza's fatwa, he said:

> Here people have raised a huge uproar (*shor o ghul*) on account of [Ahmad Riza's fatwa], saying that the [second Friday] azan should be said inside the

---

1914), 'Voices from Sirhind on the Question of the Second Azan on Friday: A Very Urgent Appeal to Hazrat Shah Ahmad Miyan Ganj Muradabadi'; *Dabdaba-e Sikandari*, 50:24 (May 11, 1914), 5–6, 'Janab Shah Ahmad Miyan Sahib Ganj Muradabadi's Answer to the Appeal'; and *Dabdaba-e Sikandari*, 50:25 (May 18, 1914), 4–5, 'Second Appeal to Shah Ahmad Miyan Ganj Muradabadi'.

[94] See *Dabdaba-e Sikandari*, 53:6 (December 4, 1916), 3–5, 'An Interesting Conversation between Maulawi Na'im ud-Din Muradabadi and Maulawi Mu'in ud-Din Sahib Ajmeri, on the Question of the Second Friday Azan'; and *Dabdaba-e Sikandari*, 53:26 (April 23, 1917), 4–6, 'Investigation into the Question of the Second Azan, and its . . . Answer'.

[95] Ibid., 50:16 (March 16, 1914), 5.

[96] Ibid., 50:21 (March 20, 1914), 'An Open Letter in the Name of Mufti 'Azi ur-Rahman Deobandi, and a Promise of a Fifty-Rupee Prize'.

mosque. Kindly, therefore, send your reply to this istifta, with the confirmation of the 'ulama' there, very quickly, so that the discord may be repelled. In writing this, kindly think deeply. The Wahhabis have raised a great tumult here. The answer of *Shahab-e Saqib* [The Brightly Shining Star, a tract by an opponent of Ahmad Riza] has been published.[97]

In a letter dated Zu'l Qa'da 1332/October 1914, Muhammad Karim Allah replied that requests for a fatwa on the azan question had been received by a number of 'ulama' in Mecca and Medina, from Muslims resident in places as diverse as Karachi, Bhopal, Bareilly, and Badayun (via a resident of Bombay). He explained that he had circulated this particular istifta in Medina, and that the replies of two 'ulama' were included in the letter.

All the three 'ulama' who replied to the question endorsed Ahmad Riza's position strongly.[98] Praising Ahmad Riza's erudition and his devotion to the Prophet, Muhammad Karim Allah wrote:

I would urge upon you that at this time there are few who equal A'la Hazrat Barelwi. The 'ulama' of the Haramain, of Arabia, of the East, of Syria, and of Egypt, have acknowledged (*qa'il*) A'la Hazrat, and have accepted him as their imam . . . . [The 'Wahhabis'] burn from head to foot in the fire of wretchedness, asking why A'la Hazrat has become so famous in the whole Islamic world . . . . Don't pay attention to other people. Soon *Daulat al-Makkiyya* [Ahmad Riza's 1906 fatwa, written in the Haramain] will be published, and you will [gauge] A'la Hazrat's quality from its study.[99]

Addressing the issue itself, Ahmad al-Jaza'iri al-Husain, the Mufti al-Malikiyya, wrote in his fatwa that the second azan had been instituted by the caliph 'Usman, and since his time, the residents of the cities of the Maghrib, and of the countryside, had given this azan from the minaret. He added:

. . . and that is correct (saba) . . . . there is no advantage to giving the azan in

[97] *Dabdaba-e Sikandari*, 51:13 (February 15, 1915), 3–6, 'Fatawa by the 'Ulama of the Haramain on the Azan Question'. The writer of the istifta was one Sayyid Muhammad 'Umar, of Pilibhit, Muhalla Ahmad Za'i.

[98] They were: Maulana Muhammad Karim Allah of Medina, the addressee of the istifta, Maulana Ahmad al-Jaza'iri al-Husain, Mufti al-Malikiyya, and Maulana Sayyid Muhammad Taufiq Afendi al-Ayubi al-Ansari al-Hanafi, teacher (*mudarris*) at al-Haram al-Nabawi al-Sharif, the mosque of Medina.

[99] Ibid., p. 4.

(fi'l) the mosque. Those people who are outside the mosque [are alerted, by the azan, that they] should strive after the rememberance of Allah, and leave off selling, and whatever is forbidden. There is no need for an azan for those who are [already] inside the mosque.

Imam Malik considered it makruh to say the azan inside the mosque. He said, 'Some have [called it a] *bid'at madi'at* [a useless bid'a]'.[100]

In addition to the points already made by various 'ulama' in support, or rejection, of Ahmad Riza's position on the second azan on Fridays, there was considerable discussion of the reliability that was to be placed on hadis which some regarded as weak (*za'if*). The main hadis to be cited in the course of this extended debate was from the *Sunan* of Abu Da'ud. Opponents of Ahmad Riza's position argued that this hadis was weak, while supporters (including Muhammad Taufiq Afendi, of Medina) claimed that it was included in the universally accepted *Sahih* of al-Bukhari, and in other collections.[101]

It might have been expected that the strong endorsement of Ahmad Riza's position by the 'ulama' of the Haramain in 1915 would have ended the matter. This was not the case. That opposition to his fatwa continued is indicated by continued correspondence in the *Dabdaba-e Sikandari*, such as the report of a debate between Na'im ud-Din Muradabadi, Ahmad Riza's khalifa, and the sajjada-nishin of Mu'in ud-Din Chishti's khanqah at Ajmer, mentioned above. It is also evident that at some point the matter began to be debated in tracts (risala), rather than in the newspapers. It was this 'war of the risalas' (which calls to mind the 'fatwa war' of about ten years before, to be discussed in Chapter VIII), which led to the

100 Ibid., p. 5. The mention of 'leaving off selling' is a reference to Qur'an 62:9: 'O ye who believe! When the call is proclaimed to prayer on Friday (the day of assembly), hasten earnestly to the remembrance of God, and leave off business (and traffic). That is best for you if ye but knew!' (Yusuf 'Ali tr.). I am grateful to Professor Muhammad Mas'ud Ahmed for bringing this Qur'anic verse to my attention.

101 However, one writer, while saying that the phrase bain yad did not appear in any sahih hadis other than the one by Abu Da'ud, nevertheless argued that it be accepted. His reason was that 'among Hanafis, the position is that in matters relating to worship ('ibada) it is fitting and better to act on a weak hadis. In worship, a weak hadis cannot be given up'. *Dabdaba-e Sikandari*, 51:21 (April 12, 1915), 6–7. One wonders whether the Hanafi 'ulama' of the subcontinent would have concurred with this position.

institution of a court case against Ahmad Riza, probably in 1916, by a resident of Badayun. The charge was that of libel.

According to the magistrate who heard the case, and who delivered his judgment on it in early 1917, the origins of the dispute between the 'ulama' of Bareilly and Badayun lay in a fatwa opposing Ahmad Riza's stand on the azan, written by one Maulana Muhammad Ibrahim, and confirmed by Maulana 'Abd ul-Muqtadir Badayuni.[102] Whether in response to this, or somewhat earlier, Ahmad Riza had stated his position in a risala entitled *Ta'bir-e Khwab* (Interpretation of a Dream). The magistrate's account of subsequent events is as follows:

> Now the discussion of this question began in earnest, and [more] risalas . . . began to be published. Efforts were made to hold a [verbal] debate, but were unsuccessful. In the series of risalas published, one was *Jawab-e Shafi* [A Decisive Answer], published from Badayun. This was the incentive for *Sad al-Firar* [Fleeing a Hundred Times]. This debate had generated a great deal of anger, which is reflected in the writings.[103]

It was *Sad al-Firar* which apparently gave the most offence. The prosecution alleged that in it, Ahmad Riza had libelled Maulana 'Abd ul-Muqtadir, recently deceased. One of the subsidiary charges was that this risala, though allegedly by Hamid Riza Khan, had in fact been written by Ahmad Riza.

The Hindu magistrate who passed judgment on the case rejected the Badayuni plaint that *Sad al-Firar* was libellous, while accepting that, in his view, Ahmad Riza rather than his son had probably written the book. The decision was seen as a great victory for Ahmad Riza, who had refused to testify in the court when summoned, and a loss of prestige for the 'ulama' of Badayun. In Ahl-e

[102] Muhammad Ibrahim (1876–1956) was a khalifa of Maulana 'Abd ul-Muqtadir Badayuni (1866–1915). The latter was a well-known and greatly-respected 'alim in Ahl-e Sunnat circles, and belonged to the famous line of 'Usmani 'ulama' and pirs, whose Madrasa Shams al-'Ulum was a scholarly centre for the Ahl-e Sunnat. It was Maulana 'Abd ul-Muqtadir's father, 'Abd ul-Qadir Badayuni, who in 1877 had directed Ahmad Riza and his father to Shah Al-e Rasul of Marahra, that they may become his disciples.

[103] *Dabdaba-e Sikandari*, 53:20 (March 12, 1917), 7–10, 'Decision on the Famous Libel Case between Badayun and Bareilly'.

Sunnat sources, the judgment was seen as a landmark vindicating their position.[104]

Wider Significance of the Azan Debate

Despite the court judgment in Ahmad Riza's favour, his 'victory' was in fact inconclusive. Three years after the issue first arose much opposition still remained. Although some Muslims did change their practice of calling the second Friday azan from inside the mosque as a result of the debate, the majority appear to have continued their old practice.[105]

A number of assertions had been made during the debate, several of them contradictory. Proponents of the change, couching their argument in terms of reviving a dead sunna, had defended their position by claiming to be following the Prophet's sunna, which in this case had died out in the subcontinent, though it was in use in various parts of the Islamic world, including Mecca and Medina. Their opponents, recasting the debate in terms of the consensus (ijma') of the Ahl-e Sunnat 'ulama', had argued that the second azan only came into currency during the reign of 'Usman, the third caliph (and by extension, therefore, no sunna could be traced back on this issue to the Prophet himself, only to one of the 'rightly-guided' caliphs). Moreover, the practice in other parts of the Islamic world, they held, was to say it as they did, inside the mosque.

Both sides had cited textual sources in their support. Indeed, most of the attention was directed to citing texts in support of the respective positions, and to faulting the manner in which sources had been quoted by the opposition. As the magistrate commented in his judgment, 'In the risalas, the kinds of arguments that were made were: Some books had been wrongly quoted; or, their

104 The importance of this case is indicated in Ahl-e Sunnat sources by the fact that past events are sometimes dated in reference to this judgment, such as 'when the Badayuni case was going on', or 'soon after the Badayuni case was won'. Such usage illustrates the landmark nature of the event in the subsequent oral tradition of the movement. See Zafar ud-Din Bihari, *Hayat-e A'la Hazrat*, pp. 150 and 190, for examples.

105 Apparently this continues to be the current practice in the subcontinent. This was conveyed to me by Maulana Yasin Akhtar Misbahi, author of *Imam Ahmad Riza aur Radd-e Bid'at o Munkarat*, in a private communication in 1987.

meaning had been misrepresented; or, does a particular word have only one meaning, or several?'[106] This textual orientation was a distinctive feature of other debates between the Ahl-e Sunnat and their fellow Muslims as well.

But the azan debate differs from earlier ones in one important respect: to a large extent those who opposed Ahmad Riza's stand perceived themselves as Ahl-e Sunnat wa Jama'at (rather than Nadwi, Deobandi, or Ahl-e Hadis, for example). Indeed, this is the first major internal debate that we can reconstruct through written sources. Most striking is the fact that Ahmad Riza was opposed by 'ulama' in Badayun, whose elders (as we shall see more fully in the next two chapters) had been partners in debate with Ahmad Riza in opposing the Nadwat al-'Ulama', affirming belief in the Prophet's knowledge of the unseen, and trying to counter Shi'i influence in their midst, among other things. Prior to this, there had been no hint of a difference of opinion between Ahmad Riza and 'Abd ul-Qadir Badayuni (d. 1901), while his son 'Abd ul-Muqtadir had reportedly held Ahmad Riza is such esteem that he called him 'Mujaddid' in a meeting attended by the Ahl-e Sunnat leadership in 1900. The same 'Abd ul-Muqtadir now signed his name to a fatwa opposing Ahmad Riza on the azan issue. That this was a significant new development is confirmed by 'Abd ul-Muqtadir's further opposition to Ahmad Riza in the course of the Khilafat movement of the early 1920s.

The azan debate was, historically, the last of its kind insofar as the early history of the Ahl-e Sunnat movement is concerned. Freitag's comment that in the early twentieth century 'the dynamic of debate' was moving from the personal to the public sphere[107] is apposite to this case. The azan debate marked, in a sense, a watershed. From a past in which the Ahl-e Sunnat had only defined themselves against those Muslims they perceived as 'other'—Nadwis, Deobandis, Ahmadis, Sir Sayyid's 'Aligarh school', and Shi'is—they were now also debating one another, thereby making internal distinctions in

[106] *Dabdaba-e Sikandari*, 53:20 (March 12, 1917), 8.

[107] Sandria B. Freitag, 'Ambiguous Public Arenas and Coherent Personal Practice: Kanpur Muslims 1913–1931', in Ewing (ed.), *Shari'at and Ambiguity*, p. 146.

leadership and future direction. The political implications of this emerge more fully in Chapter IX.

Another change—a dramatic one—was that, apparently for the first time insofar as Ahl-e Sunnat debates are concerned, a party to the debate had signalled its willingness to take its differences with its fellow Muslims to court.[108] As the Hindu magistrate in the case wrote, 'Muslims of the same belief ('aqida) were engaged in a trial of strength (*zor-azma'i*) with one another'.[109] This had considerably intensified hostile feelings. More importantly, the act of taking one's internal differences of opinion to a British Indian court was to completely change the terms of the debate. By choosing an outside arbiter, the differences of opinion no longer remained internal, of concern to the Muslim umma alone, and which it could iron out in self-sufficient wholeness. Conceptions of authority and tribunal, it seems, were in process of change within the movement.

But before we try to understand these larger issues thrown up by the azan debate, in the next couple of chapters I would like to continue to explore definitions of sunna and related terms by attending to the attitudes of Ahmad Riza and the Ahl-e Sunnat toward fellow Indian Muslims, both Sunni and Shi'i. In so doing, I take a step backward in time, to debates that preceded that about the Friday azan.

108 Note that the circumstances in which the Badayun libel case began were in this sense very different from those of the Kanpur mosque incident of 1913, which Freitag describes in 'Ambiguous Public Arenas'. In the latter case, a dispute with an outside group—the British Indian government itself—was involved.

109 *Dabdaba-e Sikandari*, 53:20 (March 12, 1917), 7.

Chapter VII

The Ahl-e Sunnat and Other Muslims, Late Nineteenth Century

Not infrequently, religious reformers exhibit in their life and work a sense of deep moral outrage against those guilty, in their view, of moral laxity and weakening of faith. In late nineteenth-century British India—which saw the rise of several movements of religious reform, both Muslim and non-Muslim—a number of reformers spoke and wrote with dismay about the moral condition of their communities, and saw an urgent need for self-correction. In the writings of Nawab Siddiq Hasan Khan, the Ahl-e Hadis leader, for instance, 'there [was] a pervasive pessimism, a fear of the end of the world, and an emotional commitment to the need for dramatic reform'.[1] Mirza Ghulam Ahmad, founder of the Ahmadi movement, likewise 'was convinced that Islamic religion, Islamic society, and the position of Islam vis-a-vis other faiths [had sunk] in his times to unprecedented depths'.[2] On the Hindu side of the religious spectrum, Swami Dayanand, founder of the Arya Samaj movement in the 1860s, attacked Hindu orthodoxy for weakening Hinduism from within, and causing it to fall before the challenges of 'invading Islam and the Christian British'.[3]

Ahmad Riza Khan's writings also convey a sense of pessimism

[1] Metcalf, *Islamic Revival*, p. 269.

[2] Friedmann, *Prophecy Continuous*, p. 105.

[3] Jones, *Arya Dharm*, p. 33.

about the condition of Islam in his day and age, while urgently calling upon Muslims to reform their ways. As with most nineteenth-century Muslim reformers in British India, he blamed his fellow Muslims, rather than others, for their situation. He denounced the views of Sir Sayyid Ahmad Khan and his 'modernist' Aligarh school, and of 'ulama' such as the Ahl-e Hadis, the Deobandis, the Nadwat al-'Ulama', and the Ahmadis. In addition, the Shi'is came under attack.[4] The Hindu reform movement of the Arya Samaj was also a concern, though debates and writings rebutting it arose later than those against other Muslims, and were largely the work of Ahl-e Sunnat leaders who followed Ahmad Riza.

It is essential to examine the Ahl-e Sunnat's opposition to the Muslim movements mentioned above in order to understand what they meant by the sunna and the way in which they sought to apply it in their lives. In a broad sense, their opposition to their Muslim contemporaries in the late nineteenth-and early twentieth-century period stemmed from the argument that there is a constellation of beliefs, the *zaruriyat-e din* ('essentials of the faith'), which includes the main creed of Islam but is wider than it in scope, and which must be embraced if one is to 'be' a Muslim. Failure to believe in even a single one of these 'zaruriyat' made one a kafir. Thus,

> whoever denies any of the zaruriyat-e din is a kafir, and whoever doubts his kufr and punishment is a kafir.[5]

> Does a man become a Muslim . . . merely by saying the kalima and bowing before the qibla? Until he believes in the zaruriyat-e din, he is not entitled to call himself a Muslim. Nor will he be saved from the eternity of the fire . . .[6]

[4] It was a measure of the Ahl-e Sunnat's strong disapproval of these movements that the terms used in their writings to describe them are implicitly derogatory: Sir Sayyid and his school are referred to as *nechari* (nature lovers); the Ahl-e Hadis are ghair-muqallid (followers of none of the four Sunni mazhabs, or schools of law) or wahhabi, a term also used to describe Deobandis; all Ahmadis, without distinction, are *qadiyani*s (after the town of Qadiyan, where the movement first began); Shi'is are referred to as *rafizi* (Ar. *rafidi*; lit., dissenters), the name of a Shi'i group in early Muslim history. The Ahl-e Sunnat's opponents, of whom there were many, responded in kind with terms such as 'Barelwi', 'bid'ati', and 'mushrik' ('innovators', 'idolators').

[5] Ahmad Riza Khan, *Fatwa al-Haramain bi-Rajf Nadwat al-Main* (Bareilly:Matba'e-Ahl-e Sunnat wa Jama'at, 1317/1900), reply to question 2, pp. 29–31.

[6] Haji La'l Khan, *Darbar-e Sarapa-e Rahmat* (Patna:Matba' Hanafiyya, c. 1902), p. 5.

What exactly is meant by the apparently vague term zaruriyat-e din becomes clearer when we examine Ahl-e Sunnat opposition to groups such as the Shi'is and the Nadwat al-'Ulama'. More specifically, Ahl-e Sunnat differences with other Muslims, which surfaced particularly in debates with the Deobandis, but also in anti-Ahmadi writings, were based on their prophetology. This will form the subject of Chapter VIII.

THE ZARURIYAT-E DIN AND CATEGORIES OF 'FALSE' BELIEF

In 1896 (Shawwal 1313), Ahmad Riza Khan wrote a series of fatawa in response to several (self-generated) questions about contemporary Muslim groups such as Sir Sayyid Ahmad of Aligarh and his followers, the Shi'is, the Ahl-e Hadis, the Deobandis, and the Nadwat al-'Ulama'. Four years later, in 1900 these fatawa received the approval of leading 'ulama' of the Haramain, and were published in a risala entitled *Fatawa al-Haramain bi-Rajf Nadwat al-Main* (Fatawa from the Haramain [causing] the Falsehood of the Nadwa to Shudder). Twenty of the twenty-eight questions in the risala dealt with the Nadwat al-'Ulama', one of the most recent Sunni Muslim movements to have arisen.

Taking the groups in turn, Ahmad Riza concluded that each, in one way or another, was guilty of 'false' belief, thereby becoming *bad-mazhabs* (people with 'wrong' or 'bad' beliefs) and *gumrah* ('those who had lost their way'), or kafirs and *murtadds* (apostates).[7] The terms occur in pairs. A group was described as either 'bad-mazhab' and 'gumrah', or as 'kafir' and 'murtadd'. Sir Sayyid Ahmad and his followers were said, in the first question, to deny the corporeal existence of the angel Gabriel, the other angels, the jinn, Satan, heaven, and hell, as well as the resurrection of the dead on the Last Day, and the occurrence of miracles. In their view, all these stood for moral states such as good and evil, and did not 'actually exist'.

[7] The distinction between these terms is discussed below. It should be noted at the outset, however, that in this and other texts where the discussion is confined to Muslims, the terms kafir and murtadd are treated as a single category, i.e. 'those who have become kafirs by apostasy from Islam'. Non-Muslims, while kafirs, cannot be apostates unless they had earlier been Muslims.

Moreover, the question said, they believed 'that all books of hadis and tafsir are false; they have all been created by 'ulama' from their own heads . . . . Only the Qur'an is true'.[8] In view of such beliefs, were they to be considered to be Muslims, as they claimed to be? In response, Ahmad Riza wrote:

the *nechariyya* [Sir Sayyid Ahmad and his followers] have no relation to Islam. They are kafirs and murtadds, as they deny the zaruriyat-e din. Although they read the kalima, and accept the qibla of the Muslims, this is not sufficient to make them ahl-e qibla and Muslims. There is no room for alternate interpretation (*ta'wil*) of the zaruriyat-e din. This has been the judgment of the 'ulama' in their books of 'aqa'id and fiqh, as stated in clear expositions (*tasrih*).[9]

In that case, the next question asked, what was Ahmad Riza's judgment on those who, being acquainted with their views, nevertheless called them Muslims and considered them to be celebrated leaders of Muslim opinion (*namwar ahl-e ra'e*)? To this, Ahmad Riza replied that 'approval of kufr is kufr . . . if one advances and promotes that kufr [by publishing the views of persons holding beliefs that qualify as such, for instance], then the kufr is even greater'.[10]

About the Ahl-e Hadis Ahmad Riza further said they were bid'ati (i.e., they had introduced reprehensible innovations), and jahannami (deserving of hell) on account of their rejection of taqlid and their exclusive reliance on Qur'an and hadis:

Sayyid Allama Tahtawi . . . writes, 'Those who separate themselves from the collectivity of the people of fiqh and 'ilm (knowledge), and from the great majority, separate themselves in that which will take them to Hell. O, you Muslims! It is imperative (lazim) on you, the group that will receive salvation, that you follow the ahl-e sunnat wa jama'at, because Allah's help, guidance, and favour are with those who agree with the ahl-e sunnat, while those who oppose the ahl-e sunnat, leave Allah and make Him angry. This salvation-attaining group is today divided into four mazhabs: Hanafi, Shafi'i, Maliki, and Hanbali. Whoever is outside these four, is bid'ati, jahannami.[11]

[8] *Fatawa al-Haramain bi-Rajf Nadwat al-Main,* pp. 27–8.

[9] Ibid., p. 29

[10] Ibid., pp. 29–31. This second question, and its reply, referred to the Nadwat al-'Ulama', discussed further on in this chapter.

[11] Ibid., p. 35. Al-Tahtawi was (apparently) a nineteenth-century Egyptian who wrote

Being 'bid'ati', they could not be among the Ahl-e Sunnat, the terms 'bid'a' and 'sunna' being mutually contradictory and opposed. In another fatwa, Ahmad Riza said clearly that 'it is farz qat'i (a definitive obligation) to recognize all groups other than the Ahl-e Sunnat as bid'ati'.[12] It did not follow, however, that all bid'atis had denied the zaruriyat-e din (and were therefore kafirs). The Ahl-e Hadis were among those who 'are not kafirs, but have been declared to be gumrah on account of their opposition to the Ahl-e Sunnat'.[13] They were 'bad-mazhab' and 'gumrah', and it was 'necessary by the mazhab of the Ahl-e Sunnat' to 'show contempt for them and to oppose them . . . it is forbidden to show love for them or to unite with them'.[14] In the *Fatawa al-Haramain* he wrote: 'How can it be permitted (ja'iz) to honour bad-mazhabs? . . . The Prophet said, "Whoever attempts to honour a bad-mazhab, is helping in the destruction of Islam".'[15]

The company of Ahl-e Hadis, and of bad-mazhabs generally, was to be shunned lest they mislead ignorant Muslims, and cause wrong belief to spread further:

> Continually, hadis and the words of the imams [here, the founders of the four Sunni law schools] have come down, saying that it is forbidden to mingle with bad-mazhabs and that it is imperative to stay away from them . . . . the Prophet said, 'Stay away from them, lest they lead you astray, and cause turmoil (fitna) [among you]' . . . . [He also said,] 'If they fall ill, don't ask about them, if they die, don't join their funeral'. [And,] 'When you meet them, don't salute them'. 'Don't sit near them, don't drink or eat with them, don't marry them'. 'Don't read the namaz with them'.[16]

---

one of the earliest biographies of the Prophet in that country. See Schimmel, *And Muhammad Is His Messenger*, p. 234.

[12] Ahmad Riza Khan, *Fatawa al-Qudwa li-Kashf Dafin al-Nadwa* (Exemplary Fatawa to Reveal the Nadwa's Secret), 1313/1895–96, p. 6. (Publication details not legible.)

[13] Ahmad Riza Khan, *Fatawa al-Sunna li-Iljam al-Fitna* (Fatawa on the Sunna to Rein in Discord), (Bareilly: Matba' Ahl-e Sunnat wa Jama'at, 1314/1896–97), p. 14.

[14] Ibid. Ahmad Riza cited sources from Ghazali's *Ihya al-'Ulum*, Shaikh Ahmad Sirhindi's *Maktubat*, and Shah 'Abd ul-'Aziz's *Tafsir 'Azizi*, among other things, in support of his view.

[15] *Fatawa al-Haramain bi-Rajf al-Main*, p. 37.

[16] Ibid., p. 43. These and other comments below about relations with bad-mazhabs were made in the context of the Nadwat al-'Ulama', whose members were also described

More positively, they were to be openly denounced and rebutted, and their wrongdoing and false belief made known, particularly by the 'ulama':

> When bad-mazhab things are published, by the ijma' of the *ummat-e din* (the religious community), it is one of the important duties [of the 'ulama'] to rebut them, and to make their baseness apparent.[17]

If the 'ulama' did not do so, people would begin to respect them, they would listen to what they had to say, and soon they would be misled. 'Then the work of din would fall into the hands of those who have broken their faith into many pieces . . . and become a separate group'.[18]

In Ahmad Riza's interpretation 'bad-mazhabi' and 'gumrahi' differed from kufr and irtidad (apostasy) in terms of degree, the latter being of course the worst category for a Muslim. For instance, he said if the Shi'is (referred to as 'rafizis' in the literature) elevate 'Ali, the Prophet's son-in-law and fourth caliph in the Sunni view, above Abu Bakr and 'Umar, the first and second caliphs respectively, this is merely 'bad-mazhabi' according to the jurists. Categorical denial of the caliphate of either or both of the latter, however, is kufr, at least in the eyes of the jurists. Theologians (mutakallimin) are more cautious, preferring to call this too 'bad-mazhabi' rather than 'kufr'.[19] Ahmad Riza, who saw himself as a jurist, based his contention that a Muslim became a kafir murtadd if he denied any of the 'essentials' of the faith, the zaruriyat-e din, on an array of Sunni juridical sources. In practical terms, a Muslim may offer the namaz behind a bad-mazhab, even though this is undesirable, but if he does so behind a kafir, his prayer will be rendered invalid.[20]

What, then, were these 'essentials', in Ahmad Riza's definition? In an early work, written in 1880–81,[21] he devoted a brief chapter

---

as 'bad-mazhab'.

17 Ibid., pp. 39–41; also see p. 65.

18 Ibid., p. 39.

19 Ibid., p. 31.

20 Ahmad Riza Khan, *Radd-e Rafaza* (1320/1902–3), in *Majmu'a-e Rasa'il: Radd-e Rawafiz* (Lahore: Markazi Majlis-e Raza, 1986), pp. 47, 49.

21 Ahmad Riza Khan, *E'tiqad al-Ahbab fi'l Jamil wa'l Mustafa wa'l Al wa'l Ashab* (Faith

to the zaruriyat-e din, describing them as those beliefs which are based on the clear verses (nusus) of the Qur'an, on accepted and unbroken (*mashhur wa mutawatir*) hadis, and the consensus (ijma') of the community.[22] He then listed a number of beliefs founded on these sources, which the Ahl-e Sunnat wa Jama'at therefore uphold. Starting with the unity of Allah and the prophethood of Muhammad, the list includes belief in heaven and hell, the delights and punishments of the grave, the questioning of the dead, the reckoning on the Day of the Resurrection, and the heavenly river (Kausar) and bridge.[23] The other chapters in the book describe in some detail the qualities of Allah, the Prophet, the angels, the Prophet's Companions, his family, and the relative ranking of the first four caliphs. This organization suggests that the topics treated in the rest of the book fall outside the rubric of the zaruriyat-e din, which in this case seem to relate more to Ahl-e Sunnat cosmology than to its belief system as a whole.

In later writings, however, Ahmad Riza clearly indicated that the term zaruriyat-e din had the widest application. Based on (or deduced to be based on) the three sources of clear verses of the Qur'an, unbroken and accepted hadis, and the consensus of the community, they included everything that falls under the term 'aqa'id (articles of faith), which were central to the identity of a Muslim. The Ahl-e Sunnat wa Jama'at were defined, in fact, as those who faithfully followed and believed in the zaruriyat-e din. As long as one did not deny these, one was a Muslim.

Not all Muslims, however, were necessarily of the Ahl-e Sunnat. As we have seen, some groups, perceived to be opponents of the Ahl-e Sunnat, were described as bid'ati, gumrah, and bad-mazhab, though not kafir. I turn now to the Ahl-e Sunnat wa Jama'at's use of these terms in relation to some specific groups.

---

of the Dear Ones, Consisting of the Beautiful, the Prophet, the Family, and the Companions), reprinted with translation and annotations by Mufti Muhammad Khalil Khan Barkati (Lahore: Hamid and Company Printers, n.d.).

22 Ibid., p. 77.

23 Ibid., pp. 77–8.

The Ahl-e Sunnat and Shi'ism

Anecdotes from Ahmad Riza's life illustrate his complete refusal to have any social relations whatever with Shi'is.[24] He is reported to have refused to meet, or to accept any gifts from, Hamid 'Ali Khan (ruled 1896–1930), the Shi'i Nawab of Rampur.[25] He admonished a follower for wearing a black cap during the month of Muharram, when Shi'is observe mourning rituals to commemorate Husain's death at Karbala.[26] In addition, he is reported to have challenged a group of Tafzilis (Shi'is who accord pre-eminence to 'Ali over the Prophet's other Companions, but do not deny the legitimacy of the first three caliphs) to debate with him, though the challenge was allegedly not taken up.[27]

The Ahl-e Sunnat's objections to Shi'i doctrines are probably not in their general outline significantly different from those of other Sunni Muslim movements,[28] though they appear to differ on matters of detail from the Deobandi 'ulama' in regard to certain Shi'i ritual practices. Doctrinally, Ahmad Riza distinguished between Shi'is on the basis of how 'extreme' (*ghali, tabara'i*) their beliefs were. At the

[24] Zafar ud-Din Bihari, *Hayat-e A'la Hazrat*, pp. 189–90.

[25] Ibid., pp. 191–2. Perhaps Ahmad Riza was influenced by the reported refusal of Maulana Nur of Firangi Mahal to greet the Shi'i minister of the Nawab of Awadh. Maulana Nur, who had taught Ahmad Riza's sufi preceptor, Shah Al-e Rasul, would have commanded respect with Ahmad Riza for that reason. See *Malfuzat*, vol. 1, p. 81.

[26] *Hayat-e A'la Hazrat*, p. 194. Ahmad Riza is reported to have said that green, red, and black were the three colours to be avoided during the first ten days of Muharram—green was the colour of the Shi'i standard-bearers; red was the colour worn by the Kharijis, who celebrated Husain's death; and black is worn by the Shi'is as a sign of mourning.

[27] Ibid., pp. 12–13, 197. This event dates to 1882–83. Tafzili 'ulama' from Badayun, Rampur, and Sambhal sent a representative to Bareilly, hoping that Ahmad Riza, then physically weakened by a digestive disorder, would be easy to defeat. But Ahmad Riza sent the representative a set of thirty questions, seeing which the latter left Bareilly without attempting to reply. Zafar ud-Din Bihari alleged that Ahmad Riza's personal doctor had conspired with the opposition.

[28] For a general treatment of Sunni-Shi'i differences, see, e.g., Anwar A. Qadri, *Islamic Jurisprudence in the Modern World*, 2nd. rev. ed. (Lahore: Sh. Muhammad Ashraf, 1973), pp. 159–73; and Moojan Momen, *An Introduction to Shi'i Islam: The History and Doctrines of Twelver Shi'ism* (Delhi: Oxford University Press, 1985). For a Shi'i perspective, see Sayyid Muhammad Husayn Tabataba'i, *Shi'ite Islam* (Albany: State University of New York Press, 1975).

'mild' and therefore less objectionable end, were Tafzili Shi'is, who were merely bad-mazhabs. But in his view most Shi'is in his day were 'extreme', being guilty of kufr on one or more grounds, such as belief that the Qur'an in its existing state is defective; that 'Ali and the other imams are superior to the non-legislative prophets (*anbiya*); or denial of the legitimacy of the first three caliphs before 'Ali.[29] Belief in the perfection of the Qur'an, in the superiority of prophets over the imams, and acceptance of the caliphate of the first three caliphs were all among the zaruriyat-e din. Hence Shi'is holding beliefs to the contrary were kafirs and apostates.[30]

Turning to Shi'i ritual practices, such as the making of *ta'ziyas* (replicas of Hasan and Husain's tombs) during Muharram, or the reading of *shahadat-namas* (elegaic poetry dealing with Husain's martyrdom), Ahmad Riza was, however, more equivocal. When asked for his judgment on *ta'ziyadari* (rituals associated with the re-enactment of Husain's martyrdom), Ahmad Riza responded that in principle there was no harm in keeping a reproduction of Husain's tomb as a tabarruk (sacred relic). It was like keeping pictures of the Ka'ba, or of the Prophet's tomb, or reproductions of the Prophet's shoes. These were all sources of baraka, or grace, and the making and keeping of reproductions of inanimate objects is permitted in Islam.[31] So long as people kept faithful reproductions of Husain's tomb, and transferred the reward (isal-e sawab) accrued by reading the Qur'an to the spirits of the martyrs, this was permissible (ja'iz).

However, ta'ziyadari as currently practised was completely haram as it contained a number of bid'a. These included the fact that the ta'ziya bore no resemblance whatever to Husain's tomb. The excessive display of grief, bowing before the image, circumambulating it, making a wish on it, and the mingling of men and women, were also bid'a and haram. Sunnis should avoid associating them-

[29] *Fatawa al-Haramain bi-Rajf Nadwat al-Main*, pp. 31–3; *Radd-e Rafaza*, pp. 47–50.

[30] Ibid., pp. 53–7.

[31] Ahmad Riza Khan, *A'la al-Ifada fi Ta'ziya al-Hind wa Bayan al-Shahada* (Great Benefit in the *Ta'ziya* of Hind, and Discourse on the *Shahadat[nama]*), (1321/1903–4), in *Majmu'a-e Rasa'il: Radd-e Rawafiz*, p. 74.

selves with such acts, for not to do so would be to convey the impression of similarity (*mushabeh*) with Shi'is.[32]

Ahmad Riza's judgments on other Shi'i practices were similar. On the reading of the shahadat-nama, in which the martyrdom of Husain and his army at Karbala are recalled, he said that if the events of that battle were accurately portrayed, and if the grief and mourning that takes place on such occasions were replaced by recollection of the martyrs' qualities and their patience under duress, there would be no harm. But as currently practised, the participation of Sunnis in a shahadat-nama was forbidden. In addition, recollection of the martyrs of Karbala should never take place in a majlis-e milad, in which the Prophet's birth is narrated or recited, and which is an occasion for happiness.[33]

Likewise, Ahmad Riza, apparently differing from the 'ulama' of Deoband, saw no intrinsic harm in the practice of offering food to the poor on 'Ashura (the tenth day of Muharram). If food or water were offered 'with the right intention, purely for the sending of reward (sawab) to the good spirits of the imams, then without a doubt this is good and pleasing'.[34] But he warned against wastefulness in offering *langar* (food offerings for religious purposes), and lack of respect toward either food or money: 'Allah has made everything for the fulfillment of man's needs, and it should not be thrown [on the ground]'.

Ahmad Riza emphasized several times the importance of having the right intention. Not only were the bid'a associated with many of the rituals of Muharram to be avoided, but their performance had to be accompanied by the right *niyya* (purpose, intention). Sometimes he advised that a ritual act, even when not objectionable in itself, be avoided because of the possibility that others may imitate the act with the wrong intention. Thus he advised a questioner against eating food offered to Husain's spirit, because 'even if one's intention is good, in the eyes of ignorant people a forbidden

32 Ibid., pp. 74–6. In the same risala, Deobandis ('Wahhabis') are said to consider ta'ziyadari shirk (associating another with Allah). See p. 88.

33 Ibid., pp. 76–9.

34 Ibid., pp. 82–4.

(na-ja'iz) matter [i.e., eating the food with the wrong intention] will acquire respect'.[35]

Despite the careful manner in which Ahmad Riza weighed his opinions and judgments, hedging his approval of certain Shi'i practices with conditions, particularly the requirement that all such practices be within the limits of the shari'a (as he interpreted it), he has been accused of holding views sympathetic to Shi'i thought.[36] These criticisms centre, most importantly, on Ahmad Riza's 'belief concerning the knowledge of the unseen possessed by the prophets, and the doctrine of will [and predestination] . . .'[37] Critics charge that he quoted Shi'i traditions with approval, and that the personal names of his parents and ancestors betray a Shi'i background.

The personal charge against Ahmad Riza, that he 'belonged to a Shi'i family' which passed off as Sunni in order to undermine the Sunnis from within,[38] is easily dismissed. His Sunni Pathan background is well documented, and has already been mentioned in Chapter II. However, we have seen (Chapter IV) that Ahmad Riza's sufi preceptor, Shah Al-e Rasul, belonged to a renowned Sayyid family which had migrated from Bilgram, in Awadh, in the seventeenth century, but continued until the early twentieth century to maintain marriage links with the Shi'i branch of the family which had remained in Bilgram. The fact that different branches of a single extended family could have Sunni and Shi'i affiliations was not in itself unusual or remarkable in the eighteenth century. Shah 'Abd ul-'Aziz, eldest son of the famous Shah Wali Ullah, himself had Shi'i in-laws, and is said to have 'complained that in most households one or two members had adopted Imam [Twelver] Shi'ism'.[39] In the nineteenth century, the Barkati Sayyids of Marahra, to which family Shah Al-e Rasul belonged, engaged vigorously in

[35] Ibid., p. 86.

[36] See, e.g., Ehsan Elahi Zaheer, *Bareilavis: History and Beliefs*, tr. Dr. Abdullah (Lahore: Idara Tarjuman al-Sunnah, 1986), pp. 42–6.

[37] Ibid., p. 42.

[38] Ibid.

[39] Cole, *Roots of North Indian Shi'ism in Iran and Iraq*, p. 230.

countering Shi'i influence in their midst. To the extent that this affinal connection of his pir influenced Ahmad Riza, it seems probable that it strengthened his anti-Shi'i attitudes.

However, one must take more seriously the charge that some of Ahmad Riza's 'beliefs and ideas . . . were borrowed from the Shi'a'.[40] While the term 'borrowed' seems misplaced, one does find on examination that the views of Ahmad Riza and the Ahl-e Sunnat are close to Shi'i doctrine in some aspects of the concept of prophecy.[41] Like Shi'is, he believed in the sinlessness of all the prophets preceding and including Muhammad.[42] Extreme respect for the Prophet Muhammad's family was another feature shared by Ahmad Riza and Shi'is; in an earlier chapter I noted Ahmad Riza's belief that baraka or grace is inherent in Sayyids, those genealogically related to the Prophet through his daughter Fatima and her descendants.

Moreover, there is a remarkable similarity between the Shi'i concept of the 'divine light' and that revealed in Ahmad Riza's writings on the Prophet. Ahmad Riza attached considerable importance to the concept of the pre-eminence of the Prophet's light, which was created before Allah created the spiritual or material universe, and before the creation of Adam, the first prophet.[43] In some Shi'i traditions, the Prophet and 'Ali were said to have been

[40] Zaheer, *Bareilavis*, p. 42.

[41] Ahmad Riza's views on Muhammad's prophethood are further examined in Chapter VIII, in the context of his differences with Mirza Ghulam Ahmad, founder of the Ahmadi movement, and leading early twentieth-century Deobandi 'ulama'.

[42] On the Shi'i view, see Tabataba'i, *Shi'ite Islam*, pp. 144–5; for Ahmad Riza's view, see *E'tiqad al-Ahbab*, pp. 40–1.

[43] In his risala, *Silat al-Safa fi Nur al-Mustafa* (The Rewards of Internal Purity in Discourse on Muhammad's Light), 1329/1911, included in *Majmu'a-e Rasa'il: Masa'il Nur aur Saya* (Karachi: Idara-e Tahqiqat-e Imam Ahmad Raza, 1985), p. 8, Ahmad Riza cites the following (Sunni) hadis on the authority of 'Abd al-Razzaq (d. AH 211): 'The Prophet told the *sahabi* Jabir b. 'Abdallah that Allah had created the light of Muhammad from His own light, prior to all things . . . . When Allah wanted to create the world He divided the light of Muhammad into four parts. From the first He created the pen (*al-qalam*), from the second He created the tablet (*al-lawh*), from the third the throne. The fourth part was subdivided into four. From the first of the four parts He created . . . ' The above translation is by U. Rubin, who cites the hadis in full in 'Pre-Existence and Light: Aspects of the Concept of Nur Muhammad', *Israel Oriental Studies*, V (1975), 115.

created before Adam, their light being the source for all other things.[44] Other traditions include Fatima in the light from which Allah created all else:

> 'When Allah created paradise', says a [Shi'i] tradition, 'He created it from the light of His face. Then He took the light and dispersed it. One third hit Muhammad, one third hit Fatima, and another third hit 'Ali. All people whom this light reached found the right path of loyalty to Muhammad's family; those who missed it—went astray'.[45]

Prior to Muhammad's birth, according to Shi'i tradition, the light was transferred through successive generations of men, each 'the most excellent of mankind', until Muhammad was born.[46] Here Ahmad Riza's views were identical to Shi'i belief. He wrote that the divine light had been transferred from generation to generation by Muhammad's ancestors, through 'pure backs [i.e., loins] and pure wombs' until his birth. 'All [Muhammad's] male ancestors were noble, and his female ancestors pure'.[47]

Because they were always the best of their generation, and were pure bearers of the divine light, it followed that they could not have been kafirs: 'Allah always chose the prophethood to pass through the best qaums. And what could be worse, more base, and more impure, than kufr and shirk?'[48] Ahmad Riza cited a hadis from 'Ali, said by him to be sahih (based on a sound chain of transmission), to the effect that there had never been less than seven Muslims on the face of the earth; Muhammad's ancestors had been among these.[49] Finally, he based his opinion, as do Shi'i interpretations, on a Qur'an

[44] Momen, *An Introduction to Shi'i Islam*, p. 148: 'The following Tradition is attributed to the Prophet: "God created 'Ali and me from one light before the creation of Adam. . . then He split (the light) into two halves, then He created (all) things from my light and 'Ali's light".'

[45] Rubin, 'Pre-Existence and Light', pp. 65–6.

[46] Ibid., pp. 72–6, 92–5.

[47] Ahmad Riza Khan, *Shumul al-Islam li-Usul al-Rasul al-Karam* (Inclusion in Islam of the Doctrines of the Noble Prophet), (Bareilly: Hasani Press, 1315/1897–98), pp. 5, 20.

[48] Ibid., p. 17.

[49] Ibid., pp. 3, 4.

verse (26:219) in which Muhammad is told to put his trust in 'the worshippers' (*sajidin*).[50]

Similarities between Shi'i thought and Ahmad Riza's views on Muhammad's prophecy, including the *nur Muhammadi* concept, can be traced further. For instance, Shi'i tradition holds that

> the entire world was created [for the purpose of] Muhammad's prophetic emergence at a predestined time and place . . . . Allah revealed to Adam that Muhammad was the only cause for his own creation, as well as for the creation of heaven, earth, paradise and hell.[51]

This idea is readily found in Ahmad Riza's work. In his collection of poems, for instance, one finds the following:

The earth and the heavens are for you
The master and the house are for you
    This and that, it's all for you
    The two worlds were made for you[52]

Or again:

The world gets its life from you
Because of you the world came into being
    The real is bound to its shadow
    Upon you be thousands of blessings[53]

According to another Shi'i tradition, 'Muhammad and the imams, created from the divine light, were believed not to cast shadows'.[54] Here too one find parallels in Ahmad Riza's writings: there are

[50] As Rubin explains in 'Pre-Existence and Light', p. 77, the term sajidin is interpreted by Shi'is as standing for Muhammad's ancestors. 'Sajidin', 'worshippers', is understood by extension to mean 'believers' or Muslims. Ahmad Riza's opinion is in *Shumul al-Islam*, p. 20.

[51] Rubin, ibid., p. 95.

[52] zamin o zaman tumhare li'e makin o makan tumhare li'e
    chunin o chunan tumhare li'e bane do jahan tumhare li'e

Ahmad Riza Khan, *Hada'iq-e Bakhshish* (Karachi: Medina Publication Co., 1976), p. 374.

[53] tum se jahan ki hayat tum se jahan ka sabat
    asal se hai zill bandha tum pe karoron durud

Ibid., p. 426.

[54] Rubin, 'Pre-Existence and Light', p. 112.

several fatawa in which he argued that the Prophet, being made of light, had no shadow.[55]

It is unnecessary to search the literature for further similarities, which undoubtedly exist, particularly in relation to the Prophet. One must, however, be careful not to interpret this as a 'borrowing' of Shi'i concepts by Ahmad Riza and his followers. First, and most obviously, there are important differences of detail. The fact that in Ahmad Riza's interpretation the Prophet Muhammad's light was not passed on, differs significantly from Shi'i belief that the infallible imams inherited it from Muhammad through 'Ali.[56] As noted in Chapter V, Ahmad Riza considered Muhammad's spiritual descendants to be the sufi 'helpers' or ghaus, culminating in Shaikh 'Abd al-Qadir Jilani. The ghaus, and the auliya, inherited or achieved grace (baraka), but the light was Muhammad's alone. And again, in the case of Muhammad not having a shadow, for Ahmad Riza this quality was unique to the Prophet Muhammad, and was not shared by the imams.

The larger point that emerges, however, is that one has to attend seriously to the insistent claim made by Ahmad Riza and his followers that they were the Ahl-e Sunnat wa Jama'at, people of the Prophet's 'way', whose belief system and self-identity centred around the Prophet. Paradoxical though this may seem, the resemblance between aspects of Ahl-e Sunnat prophetology and Shi'i concepts regarding the Prophet appear to have arisen from the centrality of the figure of the Prophet and desire to faithfully follow his sunna in Ahmad Riza's thought, rather than any direct influence derived from Shi'ism. To the extent that Muhammad and the *ahl-e bait* (members of [his] house) occupied centre-stage for both Ahmad Riza and the Shi'is, they reached similar positions. However, they did so along different paths, coming from different traditions.

An important measure of the fact that Ahmad Riza was writing very much from within the Sunni tradition is the fact that his sources were entirely Sunni. Even when he cited a tradition from 'Ali, or

55 Several of these are collected in *Majmu'a-e Rasa'il: Mas'ala Nur aur Saya.*

56 See Rubin, p. 108, for the Shi'i tradition: 'It is related that before his death, Muhammad transmitted to 'Ali his divine light, together with the rest of the heritage that was handed down to him through the preceding prophets'.

interpreted a Qur'an verse as Shi'i tradition does, he did so on the basis of Sunni sources. Thus, when citing the hadis that says that all of creation proceeded from the Prophet's light, he named the Sunni authorities who had accepted this hadis, Ahmad bin Muhammad al-Qastallani (d. 1517), a Shafi'i authority on tradition and theology in Cairo, and 'Abd ul-Haqq Dehlawi (d. 1642), the well-known hadis scholar from Mughal India.[57] Other prominent sources for hadis and fiqh cited by him were Muhammad al-Zurqani, a Maliki scholar; Jalal al-Din al-Suyuti (d. 1505), a scholar of Mamluk Egypt; al-Tirmidhi, the Sunni traditionist; Ibn al-Jauzi; and 'Abd ul-'Aziz Dehlawi. Occasionally sufi sources were cited, such as Shaikh Ahmad Sirhindi.[58] In another work, in which Ahmad Riza argued that 'Ali, the fourth caliph, had been a believer (*mu'min*) from the earliest years of his life, the sources used were largely Ash'ari and Maturidi, both Sunni theological schools—not Shi'i, as one may have expected given the subject matter.[59]

To sum up, then, while there are some important conceptual similarities between Shi'i thought and aspects of Ahmad Riza's prophetology, the evidence indicates that his writings were based on Sunni sources, most of them well-known works of fiqh, hadis, and collections of fatawa. In his works, he indicated clearly that he regarded the Shi'is of his day as kafirs. Given this unequivocal judgment and the lack of evidence that Ahmad Riza was acquainted with Shi'i literature, one has to discount the suggestion that he was influenced by Shi'ism.

[57] See *Silat al-Safa fi Nur al-Mustafa*, p. 9.

[58] These names are a selection of those cited in Ahmad Riza's *Nafy al-Fay' 'Amman Anara bi-Nurihi Kulla Shay'* (Negation of the Shadow from Him who Illuminated Everything by His Light [i.e., the Prophet]), 1296/1878–9, reprinted in *Majmu 'a-e Rasa'il: Mas'ala Nur aur Saya*, pp. 51–69.

[59] Ahmad Riza Khan, *Tanzih al-Makanat al-Haidariyya 'an Wasma 'Ahd al-Jahiliyya* (Discussion of the Purity of 'Ali's Dignity from the Blemish of the *Jahili* Era), 1312/1894–95, reprinted under the title *Bara'at-e 'Ali az Shirk-e Jahili* ('Ali's Innocence of *Jahili* Associationism), (Muhammadabad, Azamgarh: Madrasa Faiz al-'Ulum, n.d.), 40 pp.

The Ahl-e Sunnat and the Nadwat al-'Ulama'

The Nadwat al-'Ulama' (Council of 'Ulama') was first conceived in 1892 by a group of 'ulama' who had assembled at Kanpur's Madrasa Faiz-e 'Amm to attend the school's annual graduation (dastar-bandi) ceremonies.[60] Senior teachers at the school, such as Maulana Lutf Ullah Aligarhi (the madrasa's *sadr mudarris*, or principal), Sayyid Muhammad 'Ali Mungeri (the Nadwa's first nazim, or administrator), and Ahmad Hasan Kanpuri, were in the forefront of the leadership. More importantly, the early leaders of the Nadwa were united by the fact that several of them had either studied under, or were disciples of, Shah Fazl-e Rahman Ganj Muradabadi (1797–1895/96). Maulana Fazl-e Rahman had taught hadis to Maulanas Muhammad 'Ali Mungeri, Ashraf 'Ali Thanawi, Ahmad Hasan Kanpuri, and Sayyid Zuhur ul-Islam Fathpuri, among others, all of whom were leaders of the Nadwa in its early years. Muhammad 'Ali Mungeri and Wasi Ahmad Muhaddis Surati (a close friend of Ahmad Riza's and a supporter of the Nadwa at this time) were, in addition, disciples of Shah Fazl-e Rahman Ganj Muradabadi. Indeed, according to one writer, the latter was the 'spiritual centre' uniting the founders of the Nadwa.[61]

These leaders were soon joined by others, notably Maulana Shibli Nu'mani, then teacher of Arabic at the Muhammadan Anglo-Oriental College founded by Sir Sayyid Ahmad. Their chief aims were twofold, to improve the system of madrasa education by establishing one of their own, based on a new curriculum, and to promote unity among the 'ulama', settling disputes between them internally.[62] By improving on the existing madrasa system of education, of which the founders were highly critical, they hoped to train a new generation of religious leaders who would be respected both within the Muslim community and by the British Indian government: 'They would act as spokesmen for Muslims to the government

[60] Sayyid Muhammad Al-Hasani, *Sirat-e Maulana Sayyid Muhammad 'Ali Mungeri Bani-e Nadwat al-'Ulama'* (Lucknow: Shahi Press, 1962), p. 115.

[61] Khwaja Razi Haidar, *Tazkira-e Muhaddis Surati* (Karachi: Surati Academy, n.d.), p. 102, quoting Sayyid Suleiman Nadwi's *Hayat-e Shibli.*

[62] Al-Hasani, *Sirat-e Maulana Sayyid Muhammad Mungeri*, pp. 119–20.

. . . . They called for improved communications among the 'ulama, and, in the style of the Congress and the Educational Conference [of Sir Sayyid Ahmad], annual meetings at which they would assemble'.[63]

By one account—Al-Hasani's—, the proposal to start such a 'council' was greeted with enthusiasm by a large number of 'ulama'. Support for the idea was expressed by 'ulama' from Deoband, Rampur, Patna, Aligarh, Bhopal, and Bombay, among other places,[64] and two 'ulama' whose views were close to Ahmad Riza's, Wasi Ahmad Surati and 'Abd ul-Qadir Badayuni, attended the Nadwa's 1893 annual meeting.[65]

Serious opposition to the Nadwa, however, was not long in coming. At their 1894 annual meeting, held at Kanpur, statements made by one Maulana Ibrahim Arwi of the Ahl-e Hadis, and by the Shi'i 'alim Ghulam Hasnain Kantori, upset the Sunni Hanafi 'ulama'. The Ahl-e Hadis speaker used the Nadwa platform to talk about the shortcomings of taqlid, concluding that logically the founders of each of the four major schools of law (mazhabs) were bound to declare each other to be kafirs. As for the Shi'i 'alim, he addressed the Sunni 'ulama' at length on 'Ali as the Prophet Muhammad's successor 'without any separation' (*bila fasl*), implying thereby that the caliphate of Abu Bakr, 'Umar, and 'Usman (the first three caliphs, in the Sunni view) was invalid. However, having previously agreed that there would be no argument (radd o qadh) at the meeting, the 'ulama' reportedly remained silent.[66]

At the same meeting, Shibli also spoke, saying, 'We recognize both muqallids and ghair-muqallids as muwahhid (professors of Allah's unity) and mu'min (believers, Muslims), and we regard it as a grave fault (gunah) to call any believer a mushrik and bid'ati'.[67] The namaz would be considered valid if read behind another Muslim, regardless of distinction, because 'whoever has faith in the kalima-e tauhid is a Muslim'. At the next annual meeting held at

[63] Metcalf, *Islamic Revival*, p. 336. Metcalf's brief account of the Nadwa, on pp. 335–47, is one of the few available in English.

[64] Al-Hasani, *Sirat-e Maulana Sayyid Muhammad Mungeri*, p. 118.

[65] Khwaja Razi Haidar, *Tazkira-e Muhaddis Surati*, pp. 101–2.

[66] Ibid., pp. 103–4.

[67] Ibid., p. 105.

Lucknow in 1895, Maulana Muhammad 'Ali Mungeri, the chief administrator (nazim), is reported to have expressed similar sentiments minimizing internal differences between Muslims. He said, for example, that the differences between muqallids and ghair-muqallids were like the minor differences, relating to matters of detail, that existed between the four Sunni law schools.[68]

Ahmad Riza had supported the Nadwa initially, in the hope, he wrote, that 'in this era full of misfortune, in which the affliction of bad-mazhabi surrounds us and the plague of freedom [*azadi* (religious 'free thinking'?)] has conquered the world, the Nadwat al-'Ulama' . . . would strengthen the Ahl-e Sunnat, and dispel turmoil'.[69] In January 1896 (Sha'ban 1313), however, he wrote a private letter to Maulana Muhammad 'Ali Mungeri to persuade the Nadwa's leadership to adopt certain 'reforms' (islah) he viewed as essential.[70] These included, most importantly, the exclusion of all but 'Sunni' 'ulama' (the Ahl-e Hadis, as noted earlier, were not in the category of 'Sunni') from the Nadwa's leadership, and a public repudiation of statements which were objectionable from the Sunni point of view. Muhammad 'Ali replied that the Nadwa's aims had been misrepresented and misunderstood, that the differences between Ahmad Riza and the Nadwis were not as wide as appeared, and that the reforms Ahmad Riza wanted the Nadwa to undertake could best be carried out if he joined the new organization. Muhammad 'Ali also felt that lengthy written rebuttal of each others' arguments was pointless, and that they could sort out their differences verbally at the forthcoming Nadwa conference in Bareilly.[71]

As the exchange of letters continued, however, it became clear

[68] Ibid.

[69] Muhammad Hasan Riza Khan, *Sawalat Haqa'iq-Numa ba-Ru'asa Nadwat al-'Ulama'* (Truth-Showing Questions Addressed to the Leaders of the Nadwat al-'Ulama'), (Badayun: Victoria Press, 1313/1895–96), p. 2. The questions were asked by Ahmad Riza, not by his brother Hasan Riza as suggested by the title page.

[70] Both sides of this correspondence were published in *Murasalat-e Sunnat wa Nadwa* (Correspondence of the [Ahl-e] Sunnat and the Nadwa), published by Hamid Riza Khan (Bareilly, 1313/1895–96), 23 pp. Ahmad Riza's letters are also available in a new edition, *Maktubat-e Imam Ahmad Riza Khan Barelwi*, ed. Mahmud Ahmad Qadri (Lahore: Maktaba Nabuwwa, 1986), pp. 88–102.

[71] *Murasalat-e Sunnat wa Nadwa*, pp. 3–5.

that the positions were irreconcilable. Muhammad 'Ali argued that while he himself had no sympathy for 'Nechari' (Sir Sayyid Ahmad's) or Ahl-e Hadis or Shi'i views—and he was taking steps to ensure that the Shi'is did not make statements distressing to Sunni members, as they had done in previous meetings—the inclusion of all these different Muslim groups within the Nadwa was nevertheless 'necessary' or 'expedient'. In his view, new groups such as the Ahl-e Hadis would not have become as numerous or as influential as they were if the 'ulama' had simply ignored them at the outset, when they were but a handful. By opposing them, the 'ulama' had merely helped to publicize their beliefs, and thereby helped spread their movement. In saying this, he implied that Ahmad Riza's opposition, too, was counterproductive, and that quiet persuasion would be more effective. Second, present disputes with other Muslim groups were distracting the 'ulama' from the more important task of 'erasing the dishonour' with which they were regarded by the 'kafir rulers'.[72] Given the appalling state into which Muslims had fallen, when 'our enemies laugh at us and at our pure mazhab, . . . [our] disgraceful quarrels should be set aside'. In short, it was against their best interest (*khilaf-e maslahat*) to exclude any Muslim group from the Nadwa, because they needed to unite and strenghen their position against the British government.

Ahmad Riza completely rejected this interpretation of maslahat, or 'benefit', 'interest'. In his view, by bringing Sunnis and 'bad-mazhabs' under one platform, the Nadwa was engaged in that which was absolutely contrary to the Muslims' best interest as spelt out in Qur'an, hadis, and the writings of the founders of the law schools. Quoting Shaikh Ahmad Sirhindi from the *Maktubat*, to the effect that 'the harm done by a single mubtadi' (innovator, heretic) is greater than that done by a hundred kafirs', he asked: 'Maulana, do you . . . and the leaders of the Nadwa know the best interest in din and mazhab better, or does the Shaikh Mujaddid?'[73] And, cataloguing a long list of statements by which the Ahl-e Sunnat had been 'slandered' at past meetings of the Nadwa, he asked rhetorically: 'In

[72] Ibid., pp. 11–15.

[73] *Maktubat-e Imam Riza Khan*, pp. 90–1.

which direction does the benefit lie (*maslahat kis taraf hai*)?'[74] In fact, the Nadwa was no longer entitled to its name, 'Nadwa' or 'Council' of 'ulama', given its opposition to the 'ulama' of the Ahl-e Sunnat. It was now better suited to be a meeting seeking (religious?) freedom, as so many others were, in association with the followers of Sir Sayyid Ahmad ('nechari sahib[s]').[75]

By the time the Nadwa held its next annual session at Bareilly some months later, a veritable 'storm of opposition' had broken out. Ahmad Riza alone is said to have written approximately two hundred anti-Nadwa works over the next few years.[76] Several were collections of fatawa, circulated to 'ulama' around the country and printed with their confirmatory opinions and seals at the end. Statements were taken from one or other of the Nadwa's annual reports, and posed as a question (istifta). An influential set of fatawa was one entitled *Fatawa al-Qudwa li-Kashf Dafin al-Nadwa* (Exemplary Fatawa to Reveal the Nadwa's Secret), which was signed by more than fifty 'ulama' from places as far apart as Bombay, Allahabad, and Delhi, apart from smaller towns like Bareilly, Muradabad, and Rampur. A number of the questions dealt with relations between different Muslim groups. For instance, was it correct to say that Shi'i–Sunni differences were exaggerated, given that both groups agreed on love of the Prophet, his family, and the Companions?[77] Was it true, as the Nadwa claimed, that the person with the greatest *taqwa* (religious fear) was closest to Allah, regardless of his or her mazhab (group affiliation)?[78] Or again, should Muslims

[74] Ibid., pp. 93–4.

[75] Ibid. This comment probably points to the fact that large numbers of 'ulama' had begun to leave the Nadwa, as a result of the aggressive anti-Nadwa initiative of leaders like Ahmad Riza. As we shall see, several were soon to form an organization of their own.

[76] Al-Hasani, *Sirat-e Maulana Sayyid Muhammad Mungeri*, p. 175.

[77] This was answered, here and elsewhere, in the negative. Ahmad Riza said that the Shi'is denied some of the zaruriyat-e din and were therefore kafirs. *Fatawa al-Qudwa li-Kashf Dafin al-Nadwa*, pp. 6–7. Also see Muhammad 'Abd ur-Razzaq Makki Haidarabadi's *Fatawa al-Sunna li-Iljam al-Fitna*, p. 8.

[78] Taqwa had nothing to do with 'aqa'id, came the reply. If there was *fisq* (falsehood) in one's 'aqa'id (or mazhab, the same thing in Ahmad Riza's usage) no amount of pious conduct could alter the fact that one was a bad-mazhab, gumrah, and bad-din. *Fatawa al-Qudwa li-Kashf Dafin al-Nadwa*, pp. 3–4.

of one group desist from characterizing those of another group as mushrik, bid'ati, gumrah, or fasiq?[79]

As the signatures at the end of Ahmad Riza's fatawa indicate, he was by no means alone in his denunciations of the Nadwa. Maulana 'Abd ul-Qadir Badayuni was also most forcefully opposed. Among the many publications of this period is one in which 'Abd ul-Qadir is reported to have met Maulana Lutf Ullah Aligarhi, who had chaired the Nadwa's Bareilly meeting, and got his signature to an anti-Nadwa fatwa. Charges were later made that the fatwa had been wrongly represented to Lutf Ullah, to which 'Abd ul-Qadir eventually replied, among other things, by challenging Lutf Ullah Aligarhi to a mubahala.[80] Apparently Ahl-e Sunnat leaders and representatives continued to communicate with Lutf Ullah even after he left for Haidarabad to serve under the Nizam shortly thereafter. According to Ahl-e Sunnat sources, Lutf Ullah indicated to them that while Ahmad Riza's opinions were essentially 'correct' (from a jurist's point of view), they were 'against the exigencies of the times' (*muqtaza-e waqt ke khilaf hain*).[81]

The high point of Ahl-e Sunnat writing against the Nadwa (which included posters, poems, and risalas, in addition to fatawa) was, undoubtedly, Ahmad Riza's *Fatawa al-Haramain bi-Rajf Nadwat al-Main* which was published in 1900 (AH 1317) with the *tasdiq* (confirmatory opinions) of sixteen 'ulama' from Mecca, and seven from Medina. In this fatwa, Ahmad Riza had argued that the Nadwis were 'bad-mazhabs', who were misleading ordinary Muslims and creating yet another group in opposition to the Ahl-e Sunnat.[82] Among the 'ulama' who confirmed his opinions were two muftis

[79] Ahmad Riza's reply to this was that no Muslim should call another a mushrik; but all groups apart from the Ahl-e Sunnat were bid'ati. Ibid., p. 6.

[80] Yohanan Friedmann, in *Prophecy Continuous*, pp. 197–8, explains that the literal meaning of mubahala is 'an act of cursing each other', and defines it as 'a procedure in which two opponents in a debate invoke the curse of Allah on the person who is wrong'. Sayyid Ikhlas Husain Sahaswani Chishti Nizami, *Hadis-e Jankah Mufti Lutf Ullah* (A Heart-Rending Calamity concerning Mufti Lutf Ullah), especially pp. 13–14. As Lutf Ullah refused to respond to the challenge, the mubahala never took place.

[81] *Fatawa al-Qudwa li-Kashf Dafin al-Nadwa*, pp. 17–19.

[82] See discussion earlier in this chapter, in the context of the concept of 'zaruriyat-e din', for more detailed treatment of this fatwa collection.

of Mecca (one of them Shafi'i, the other Hanafi) and several teachers at the Haram mosque. In this fatwa, Ahmad Riza set a pattern to be followed some years later in a more dramatic fashion, with a bitter 'fatwa war' against the Deobandis culminating in his getting confirmatory opinions from the Haramain, thereby considerably bolstering his authority at home.

If the Ahl-e Sunnat's anti-Nadwa efforts had been confined to writing and publication, that alone would have remarkable. By the end of the nineteenth century, however, a new phase in the movement's history was inaugurated with the creation of the 'Majlis-e Ahl-e Sunnat wa Jama'at', a forum for the annual gathering together of 'ulama' much the same way as the Nadwat al-'Ulama' was. Its sole purpose was opposition to the Nadwa.

Although the Ahl-e Sunnat organization appears to have first met at Bareilly (perhaps in the immediate aftermath of the Nadwa meeting in that town in 1896), its centre of activity soon shifted to Patna in the state of Bihar. To have an eastern centre rather than a western one based in Bareilly, was in fact a logical choice, given that the Nadwa itself was centred in places such as Lucknow (where it had established a Dar al-'Ulum in 1898), and Kanpur (at the Madrasa Faiz-e 'Amm). The Nadwa's influence could thus be understood to be strong in the eastern region. Or, as one Ahl-e Sunnat source had it, the 'plague' of the Nadwa had reached such proportions in Patna and its environs that a collective effort by the 'doctors of the shari'a and the physicians of din and millat' became necessary in order to eradicate it. In June 1897 (25 Muharram 1315) the Ahl-e Sunnat 'ulama' of Patna met for the first time.[83] This meeting was a forerunner to the first major meeting of the Majlis-e Ahl-e Sunnat wa Jama'at, in Rajab 1318/October 1900, attended by 'ulama' from all over the country.

The creation of the Majlis-e Ahl-e Sunnat was itself part of a larger multi-faceted organizational effort mounted by Qazi 'Abd ul-Wahid Azimabadi of Patna to promote Ahl-e Sunnat interests.[84]

[83] *Makhzan-e Tahqiq*, more commonly known as *Tuhfa-e Hanafiyya*, vol. 1, no. 1, Jamadi al-Awwal 1315/September 1897, pp. 9–10.

[84] Few biographical details appear to be available about Qazi 'Abd ul-Wahid, whose name is absent from Rahman 'Ali's *Tazkira-e 'Ulama'-e Hind* (Karachi, 1964), as well as

It coincided with his founding of the Madrasa Hanafiyya (the formal opening of which probably took place on the occasion of the Majlis-e Ahl-e Sunnat meetings in October 1900). Qazi 'Abd ul-Wahid was the school's first muhtamim (manager). Wasi Ahmad Muhaddis Surati was its sadr mudarris (principal) for the first two years, leaving his own madrasa in Pilibhit in order to set up this new one on a sound footing. Qazi 'Abd ul-Wahid had also started the monthly journal *Tuhfa-e Hanafiyya* in 1897, in which anti-Nadwa writings figured prominently. This paper continued to be published until about 1910.[85] Early lists of the buyers of the *Tuhfa-e Hanafiyya* indicated that it enjoyed the support of a number of the local landowning and government-employed Muslim élite of the North-Western Provinces and Oudh, and Bihar.[86]

From the first, the Majlis-e Ahl-e Sunnat wa Jama'at adopted the aggressive strategy of holding its annual meetings (generally lasting about a week) at the same time as, and in the same town as, the Nadwa. Its first meetings, held in Patna in 1900, thus took place side by side with those of the Nadwa. A list of participants attached to its published report shows that this first Majlis was attended by all the leading 'ulama' of the Ahl-e Sunnat: 'Abd ul-Qadir Badayuni, Ahmad Riza Khan Barelwi, Wasi Ahmad Surati, and 'Abd us-Salam Jabalpuri, among others. The total number was about a hundred; the sadr, or 'chair', was taken by 'Abd us-Samad Sahaswani.[87]

Mahmud Ahmad Qadri's *Tazkira-e 'Ulama'-e Ahl-e Sunnat* (Muzaffarpur, Bihar: Khanqah Qadiriya Ashrafiyya, 1391/1971). Brief mention may be found in Hasnain Riza Khan, *Sirat-e A'la Hazrat*, p. 113. Qazi 'Abd ul-Wahid was a ra'is ('person of authority', notable) of Patna, at those home Ahmad Riza stayed when attending the Majlis meetings in 1900.

[85] Khwaja Razi Haidar, *Tazkira-e Muhaddis Surati*, pp. 78–9. The *Tuhfa-e Hanafiyya* lasted until shortly after Qazi 'Abd ul-Wahid's death in 1908. The last volume I have been able to trace is vol. 13, dated Safar 1327/February 1910.

[86] *Tuhfa-e Hanafiyya*, vol. 1, nos. 4–5, Sha'ban-Ramazan 1315/Dec. 1897–Jan. 1898, last 4 pages of journal. Of the 119 persons listed, 43 were styled 'ra'is' or 'ra'is-e 'a'zam'; some had government titles such as 'wakil', 'honourary magistrate', 'station master', 'municipal commissioner', or 'tahsildar'; finally there were several imams of mosques. See Chapter III.

[87] Unfortunately, I have not been able to see the report. Brought out by 'Abd ul-Wahid Azimabadi, it was entitled *Darbar-e Haqq o Hidayat* (Patna: Matba' Hanafiyya, 1318/1900), and was approximately 160 pp. long.

Ahmad Riza addressed the gathering in a sermon (wa'z) on the Prophet's light, and the meaning of faith (iman).[88] Faith had two pillars, he said: Allah was the first pillar and the Prophet the second. Allah had created the jinn, and men, that they may worship Him. But He himself neither benefited by their worship, nor was diminished by their failure to do so. He had commanded it because it was a measure of people's obedience to the Prophet. Worship of Allah strengthened love of the Prophet, as exemplified by 'Ali who once missed saying his prayer because the Prophet had fallen asleep on his lap, and Abu Bakr, who allowed himself to be bitten by a snake rather than wake the Prophet.[89] 'Such respect and love were the self-sacrificing devotion of the moth for the candle of prophethood'.[90]

Ahmad Riza then spoke of Muhammad being the distributor of Allah's bounty:

> The Prophet said, 'I am the distributor, and Allah is the giver'. From the first day until today, and from today until the last day, . . . whatever blessings have been received, or will be received, were and will be distributed by the hand of Mustafa. Din and millat, Islam and sunna, virtue and prayer, devotion and purity, knowledge and gnosis, all these dini blessings have been distributed by him; in the same way, the worldly blessings of wealth and property, cure and health, respect and dignity, power and rulership, and children, were also received from him.[91]

Such blessings cannot be reciprocated. One can only be grateful, devoted and humble. And this in turn invites further blessings, as were received by Abu Bakr and 'Ali.[92]

Ahmad Riza had been discoursing at length on Abu Bakr's

[88] Reprinted in full in Zafar ud-Din Bihari's *Hayat-e A'la Hazrat*, pp. 113–31.

[89] Ibid., pp. 118–20. These two incidents are based on hadis. The Prophet rectified the damage. In 'Ali's case, he ordered the sun, which had set by the time he awoke, to return, so that 'Ali could offer his prayer; and in Abu Bakr's, he spat on the snake-bite and made him well.

[90] Ibid., p. 120.

[91] Ibid., p. 121.

[92] Abu Bakr's behaviour (*suluk*) toward the Prophet was said to be superior to that of all others—consequently he received the honour of becoming the Prophet's father-in-law; 'Ali received the blessing of being brought up by the Prophet in his childhood and later married the Prophet's daughter, Fatima. Ahmad Riza insisted, however, on Abu Bakr's superiority to 'Ali. Ibid., p. 123.

superiority over 'Ali when he learned that some Nadwis had joined the audience. From then on he spoke along now-familiar lines of argument against the Nadwa. He also rebutted the latest Nadwi charges that his own anti-Nadwa fatwa, ostensibly approved by 'ulama' of the Haramain, had in fact been signed by Indian 'ulama' on hajj. The sermon, which had started at eight in the evening, continued well past midnight.[93]

The efforts of the 'ulama' of the Ahl-e Sunnat to weaken the Nadwa continued forcefully for several years. In December 1901, the Majlis-e Ahl-e Sunnat met at Calcutta, again in conjunction with the Nadwa's annual meeting there.[94] The persistent opposition it represented was at least partially responsible for the loss of the influence of the Nadwa, and the withdrawal of the Shi'is, and those from Aligarh, from its membership.[95]

Ahmad Riza as the Mujaddid of the Hijri Fourteenth Century

It was during the debates surrounding Ahl-e Sunnat differences with the Nadwis that a number of Ahl-e Sunnat 'ulama' made the remarkable claim that Ahmad Riza was the mujaddid (renewer) of the Hijri fourteenth century. In the course of the Ahl-e Sunnat meeting at Patna in 1900, Maulana 'Abd ul-Muqtadir Badayuni, the sajjada-nishin of the Khanqah-e Qadiriyya at Badayun, referred to Ahmad Riza in his sermon as the 'mujaddid of the present [i.e., fourteenth Hijri] century'.[96] Zafar ud-Din Bihari wrote that all those

[93] See ibid., pp. 124–31.

[94] A report of the Ahl-e Sunnat meeting, entitled *Darbar-e Sarapa-e Rahmat*, was published by Muhammad Zia' ud-Din, muhtamim of the *Tuhfa-e Hanafiyya* at Patna, in 1319/1901.

[95] See Metcalf, *Islamic Revival*, pp. 342–4, for the many reasons for the Nadwa's loss of support.

[96] Not having been able to locate the report of this meeting, 'Abd ul-Muqtadir's sermon was not available to me, nor were the reactions of other participants. Secondary sources refer to the event, however. My source here is Zafar ud-Din Bihari, *Chaudhwin Sadi ke Mujaddid* (Lahore: Maktaba Rizwiyya, 1980), p. 66. (Although recently published, the work must have been written before the early 1950s, the time of Zafar ud-Din's death. In view of Zafar ud-Din's close association with Ahmad Riza Khan, I regard it as a reliable source.)

present at the meeting accepted the title, and that later thousands of others, including several 'ulama' of the Haramain, did so. Thus there was ijma' (consensus) among the Ahl-e Sunnat wa Jama'at on the question.[97]

The proclamation of Ahmad Riza as the mujaddid of the Hijri fourteenth century at this meeting occurred at a time when 'ulama' who identified themselves as Ahl-e Sunnat were strongly united in condemnation of the Nadwat al-'Ulama'. Ahmad Riza had written extensively in its rebuttal, and it was not surprising that his personal influence should have grown considerably as a result. The formation of the Majlis was also a major new development, lending coherence to previously individual and uncoordinated opinions on the Nadwa. Each of these factors seems to have played a part in Ahmad Riza's emergence at this time as the intellectual centre of the new movement.

As he and his followers saw it, of course, their movement was not new: their main purpose being to revive the Prophet's sunna, they were following in the footsteps of the Prophet and his Companions, and thereby reviving the 'old' way. For the same reason, the term 'founder' was—as it is today—rejected as a way of describing Ahmad Riza's relationship to the movement. To the 'ulama' attending the Ahl-e Sunnat meetings, the term 'mujaddid', on the other hand, must have seemed to perfectly describe the role Ahmad Riza had come to play, while at the same time being a means of commenting on all that they collectively found wrong with the Muslim community of their day.

The concept of the mujaddid is based, as Zafar ud-Din Bihari indicated, on the hadis from Abu Da'ud in which the Prophet is reported to have said, 'on the eve of every century Allah will send to this community a person who will renew its religion'.[98] As is well known, the need for renewal is premised on the Muslim belief that

[97] Ibid., pp. 68–71. Zafar ud-Din Bihari cited the opinions of some 'ulama' of the Haramain who certified Ahmad Riza's 1906 fatawa, *Husam al-Haramain* and *Daulat al-Makkiyya*. These fatawa will be discussed in Chapter VIII.

[98] Zafar ud-Din Bihari, *Chaudhwin Sadi ke Mujaddid*, p. 33; for an analysis of the concept of tajdid (renewal), see Friedmann, *Prophecy Continuous*, pp. 94–101. Also see discussion on the relationship between tajdid and ijtihad in Chapter VI above.

'an almost unarrestable process of decline' set in immediately after the death of the Prophet Muhammad, in whose lifetime 'divine will [had been] embodied in the most perfect fashion'.[99] The process of decline could, however, be temporarily reversed by the appearance, once every hundred years, of the renewer or mujaddid who would 'reviv[e] the beliefs and customs of the prophetic age'.[100]

Among the conditions necessary for one to qualify as mujaddid, Zafar ud-Din wrote, were that the man (it could not be a woman) be a Sunni of sound belief, an 'alim who combined in himself all the sciences and skills (*'ulum o funun ka jami'*), that he be well known ('the most famous among the celebrated of his age'), a protector of din unfettered by fear of going against prevailing 'innovations', and learned in shari'a and tariqa (sufism). He also had to satisfy the technical requirement that he be well known by the end of the century in which he was born, and at the beginning of that in which he was to die.[101] In fact, failure to appear at the right time disqualified an otherwise acceptable person. According to Zafar ud-Din, Shah Wali Ullah (1115–76/1703–62) could not be a mujaddid because he was born and died in the Hijri twelfth century, thus failing to span two centuries. Sayyid Ahmad Barelwi (1201–47/1786–1831) was disqualified for the same reason.[102] Ahmad Riza, on the other

[99] Friedmann, *Prophecy Continuous*, p. 95.

[100] Ibid., p. 100. Friedmann indicates that the concept of tajdid was initially associated with the eschatological expectation of the end of the world and Judgment Day, in that the appearance of the mujaddid was instrumental in postponing Judgment Day. However, the two ideas gradually became dissociated. In his view, Shaikh Ahmad Sirhindi, known as the 'Renewer of the Second Millenium', restored the eschatological connection of the concept of the mujaddid. For Sirhindi, see Friedmann, *Shaykh Ahmad Sirhindi*, pp. 13–21. There is no evidence in Ahmad Riza's writings, as far as I can tell, of his having associated the concepts of Judgment Day (qiyamat) and the coming of the mujaddid.

[101] Zafar ud-Din Bihari, *Chaudhwin Sadi ke Mujaddid*, p. 34. On this last issue, Friedmann writes: 'Considerable attention is devoted to the question of exactly when the mujaddid should appear in order to qualify for the title . . . . It has become accepted that the mujaddid should be a well-known scholar at the end of a century and should die in the first years of the next one. Doubts were cast on the status of persons who were suggested as mujaddidun if their death occurred later than the second decade'. Friedmann, *Prophecy Continuous*, pp. 98–9.

[102] Zafar ud-Din Bihari, pp. 39, 41. It should be noted, however, that the Ahl-e Sunnat had serious differences with Sayyid Ahmad's vision of Islam, and in particular with that

hand, did span two Islamic centuries, having been born in 1272/1856, and died in 1340/1921.[103]

The Ahl-e Sunnat saw Ahmad Riza as having succeeded Shah 'Abd ul-'Aziz, Shah Wali Ullah's eldest son, as mujaddid. Shah 'Abd ul-'Aziz, as mujaddid of the Hijri thirteenth century, was said to have had all the necessary qualities of learning, piety, and fame among the 'ulama' both in India and in the Arab lands. He was a brilliant teacher of hadis, and writer of fatawa. Moreover, he had dissociated himself from the movement of Sayyid Ahmad Barelwi and Shah Muhammad Isma'il. When Muhammad Isma'il wrote the book *Taqwiyat al-Iman* (Strengthening the Faith), he was unable to write a rebuttal to it, being then a blind man in old age. However, had he not been so weak it is said that he would have done so.[104]

Zafar ud-Din recognized (as does the classical theory of tajdid) that there could be more than a single mujaddid in any one century. Sometimes there was no consensus on any one person. This was, indeed, the situation in late nineteenth-and early twentieth-century British India, in which different Muslim groups looked to different people as the mujaddid of the century. The Deobandis looked to Rashid Ahmad Gangohi (though he himself apparently suggested that the term could be applied to a group of 'ulama' rather than a single individual), while the founder of the Ahmadi movement claimed that he was the mujaddid.[105]

Disputation about the validity of rival claims to the mujaddid title, however, arose to some degree from the very commonalities shared by the movements of the period. While their vision of the ideal society differed, movements such as the Deobandi and the Ahl-e

---

of Muhammad Isma'il, who was Shah Wali Ullah's grandson and Sayyid Ahmad's disciple. They would thus have refused to accept Sayyid Ahmad as a mujaddid on other grounds. With regard to Shah Wali Ullah too, they had reservations, saying, for instance, that his writings could not be relied upon as they had been changed by others since his death. See 'Introduction' to Zafar ud-Din Bihari's *Chaudhwin Sadi ke Mujaddid*, p. 18.

[103] His death would have been considered 'late', however, in accordance with classical theory. See note 101 above.

[104] Zafar ud-Din Bihari, *Chaudhwin Sadi ke Mujaddid*, pp. 50–5. For the Ahl-e Sunnat interpretation of Sayyid Ahmad's movement, and their view of Muhammad Isma'il's *Taqwiyat al-Iman*, see Chapter VIII.

[105] Metcalf, *Islamic Revival*, pp. 138–9; Friedmann, *Prophecy Continuous*, pp. 107–8.

Sunnat were at one in their desire to bring about a morally self-conscious society, guided by the Prophet's sunna and other sources of Islamic law.[106] Despite differences of opinion about Shah Wali Ullah's contribution to the task of tajdid, both movements revered his successor Shah 'Abd ul-'Aziz and adopted aspects of his teaching. Paradoxically, then, these common roots and purposes were perhaps responsible to some degree for the sense of deep divide that separated the Ahl-e Sunnat and Deobandi 'ulama'. In the following chapter, I turn to examination of the nature of their differences.

[106] See Metcalf, *Islamic Revival*, p. 314: 'In fact, [despite their differences] . . . these groups were concerned with the Law and with devotion to the Prophet; and . . . expressed their beliefs in a self-conscious oppositional style'.

Chapter VIII

The Ahl-e Sunnat on Deobandis and 'Wahhabis'

In 1906, Ahmad Riza Khan addressed some Meccan 'ulama' in his fatwa *Husam al-Haramain 'ala Manhar al-Kufr wa'l Main* (The Sword of the Haramain at the Throat of Kufr and Falsehood), as follows:

> Tell me clearly whether you think these leaders of heresy are as I have portrayed them . . . , and if so, whether the judgment [of kufr] that I have passed on them is appropriate . . . some ignorant people, in whose hearts faith has not lodged itself, claim that because they are 'ulama' and maulawis the shari'a calls upon us to respect them—even though they are Wahhabis, and even though they insult Allah and the Prophet.[1]

The 'leaders of heresy' referred to in the above passage were well-known 'ulama' in early twentieth-century British India: Mirza Ghulam Ahmad of Qadiyan, the first on Ahmad Riza's list of kafirs, was the founder of the Ahmadiyya movement. The others—Rashid Ahmad Gangohi, Muhammad Qasim Nanautawi, Ashraf 'Ali Thanawi, and Khalil Ahmad Ambethwi—were leading figures at the Dar al-'Ulum at Deoband or in affiliated institutions. In this fatwa, originally written in 1902, all but Mirza Ghulam Ahmad were described as 'Wahhabis', a word frequently encountered in the then current literature of the Ahl-e Sunnat in reference to 'ulama' with Deobandi or Ahl-e Hadis affiliations.

[1] Ahmad Riza Khan, *Husam al-Haramain 'ala Manhar al-Kufr wa'l Main* (Lahore: Maktaba Nabawiyya, 1985), p. 10. Originally written in 1323/1905–6.

The judgment of kufr passed in *Husam al-Haramain* in 1906 [2] was a highly public one, delivered in Mecca while Ahmad Riza was on his second hajj. Despite Ahmad Riza's unrelenting opposition to numerous groups of Muslims, among them the Twelver Shi'is and the organization of 'ulama' known as the Nadwat al-'Ulama' examined in the previous chapter, it was only in 1902, and again in 1906 when *Husam* was written, that he had accused specific persons of kufr. Hitherto he had written in general terms of various groups of Muslims being either bad-mazhab (those whose beliefs were 'wrong'), or gumrah ('lost', on the wrong path), or murtadd (apostates from Islam), based on whether or not they had, as he interpreted it, denied any of the 'fundaments' of belief (zaruriyat-e din). Though he had used the term kafir in this context, it had not been personally directed. There was no specific takfir (declaration of someone as kafir) involved.

It was thus of some consequence that Ahmad Riza should have accused the 'ulama' named in *Husam al-Haramain* of kufr, and have presented this fatwa to certain 'ulama' in Mecca and Medina for their seals and signatures (*tasdiqat*), whereby they signalled approval of his opinion.[3] He himself regarded the takfir of another Muslim with great seriousness. Experts in the law (fuqaha), he wrote, had enjoined restraint in making a charge of kufr as long as any possibility existed that a statement that seemed on the face of it to involve kufr may not have been intended that way, that another, perfectly 'Islamic' (as opposed to kufr-laden) interpretation of the statement may have been meant.[4]

Nevertheless, and on the face of it in contradiction of the above principle (in fact not so, seen in Ahl-e Sunnat terms), Ahmad Riza wrote that when confronted with one who 'ascribes lies to Allah or decreases the glory of the leader of prophets', such search for

[2] In fact, *Husam al-Haramain* was written in 1902, in the form of a commentary (sharh) on Fazl-e Rasul Badayuni's *Al-Mu'tamad al-Muntaqid*. Originally in Arabic, entitled *Al-Mu'tamad al-Mustanad*, it was probably not widely known before its reissuance in Mecca in 1905–6.

[3] Some of these 'ulama' had previously signed Ahmad Riza's earlier fatwa against the Nadwat al-'Ulama'. See *Malfuzat-e A'la Hazrat*, vol. 2, p. 7.

[4] Ahmad Riza Khan, *Tamhid al-Iman ba-Ayat al-Qur'an* (Bombay: Raza Academy, n.d.), pp. 33–5. Originally written in 1326/1908.

intended meaning was unnecessary, for this was a clearcut case of kufr. Failure to acknowledge such a person as kafir, or doubt of such a person's kufr, resulted in the denier or doubter of kufr becoming a kafir as well.[5] Because offences of this nature (denigrating Allah or the Prophet Muhammad) were against the 'fundaments' of religion, even if a person's faith ('aqida) was within the bounds of Islam in every other respect, in Ahmad Riza's view the person was a kafir. As he put it rather graphically, 'If you put one drop of urine in nine hundred and ninety-nine drops of rose water, it will all become urine. But these ignorant people say that if you put one drop of rose water in nine hundred and ninety-nine drops of urine it will all become pure'.[6] Seen in this light, everything hinged on whether or not a statement constituted denial of a 'fundament' of belief.

The Deobandis and others, however, saw their faith in different terms. After *Husam* was written in 1905–6, the Deobandis countered Ahmad Riza's fatwa with fatawa of their own, collecting signatures from 'ulama' in the three north Indian princely states of Tonk, Bhopal, and Bahawalpur, as well as British north India, testifying that the Deobandis were Sunni Hanafi Muslims.[7] The Ahl-e Sunnat likewise gathered signatures from other 'ulama' in support of their position. In short, there was a 'fatwa war'.

Detailed analysis of *Husam* provides a useful entrée into the nature of the Ahl-e Sunnat's differences with Deoband. It also enables us to approach related issues such as the Ahl-e Sunnat use of the term 'Wahhabi', and, most important, Ahl-e Sunnat prophetology. As preceding chapters have suggested, it was the Prophet who really held the key to the Ahl-e Sunnat perspective on what it was to be a 'good' Muslim. And it was differing conceptions of the Prophet, as well, that lay at the heart of Ahl-e Sunnat denunciation of the Deobandis.

[5] Ibid., p. 35. Although Ahmad Riza does not explicitly say this, the other side of the same coin is that a person who wrongly accuses another of kufr himself becomes a kafir, as in the following hadis: 'If a Muslim charges a fellow Muslim with kufr, he is himself a kafir, if the accusation should prove untrue'. There no discussion in this fatwa of types of kufr, but see W. Bjorkman, 'Kafir', in *EI2*, pp. 407–8.

[6] *Tamhid al-Iman*, p. 33.

[7] Metcalf, *Islamic Revival*, p. 310.

The Charges of Kufr in Husam al-Haramain

Mirza Ghulam Ahmad, founder of the Ahmadiyya movement, was in a category all by himself in *Husam al-Haramain*. Condemned as the Antichrist (*dajjal*) inspired by Satan, his kufr was believed to be greater than that of the other 'ulama' mentioned. Ahmad Riza's opinion was based on a number of claims made by Ghulam Ahmad, among them the fact that he was 'like the Messiah' (Jesus Christ), and that, having received revelations from Allah, he was a kind of prophet:

> In the beginning, he claimed to be 'like the Messiah'. Allah, in this he spoke the truth, because he is like the Antichrist, the liar. Then he began to elevate himself still more, and claimed to have received revelation. And Allah, in this too he is truthful, because Allah says that in the assembly of devils there is one among them who is inspired by Satan, whose inspiration is false and deceptive . . . . Then he made an unambiguous claim to prophecy (*nabuuwat*) and messengership (risalat), writing that Allah is He who sent His messenger to Qadiyan, and asserted that a verse had been revealed to him that says, We sent him to Qadiyan, and sent him with the truth. He also asserted that he was the Ahmad whom Jesus had predicted would come [after him as the next prophet] . . . Then he began to say that he was better than all the other prophets and messengers: forget about Ibn-e Maryam [Jesus], Ghulam Ahmad is better than he.[8]

Of all the claims made by Mirza Ghulam Ahmad (and there were others, such as his declaration that he was the mujaddid or renewer of the fourteenth Hijri century[9]), the one that incensed Ahmad Riza and other Indian 'ulama' the most was his assertion that he was a 'shadowy' (*zilli*) prophet.[10] This appeared to a large number of Sunni 'ulama' to directly deny the Muslim belief that Muhammad was the 'seal of the prophets' (*khatam al-nabiyyin*). (Much later, it was on the basis of this alleged denial that under the terms of a constitutional

[8] Ahmad Riza Khan, *Husam al-Haramain*, p. 12.

[9] For more on this and other claims advanced by Mirza Ghulam Ahmad, see Friedmann, *Prophecy Continuous*, pp. 107–17.

[10] As Friedmann explains in *Prophecy Continuous*, Ghulam Ahmad's interpretation of prophecy was deeply influenced by Ibn al-'Arabi's belief in the continuous existence of prophecy in the Muslim community. Ibid., pp. 72–5, and passim.

amendment in Pakistan in 1973 Ahmadis were declared to be non-Muslims.)

In addition to his prophetic claim, Ghulam Ahmad had also angered Ahmad Riza (and other 'ulama') by offering an interpretation of Jesus which was at variance with the Sunni mainstream. He denied the prevailing Muslim belief that Jesus was alive in heaven and would return to earth at the end of days as the Mahdi to defeat the Antichrist (dajjal), thereby inaugurating a kingdom of justice on earth. Against this, Ghulam Ahmad maintained that Jesus was dead, and that it was he, Ghulam Ahmad, who had been sent by Allah and Jesus's spirit to restore the Muslim community to its former glory.[11] For Ghulam Ahmad, to believe in Jesus's second coming was to acquiesce in Christianity's claimed superiority to Islam, which it was one of his principal aims to deny.[12] Ironically, the image he evoked to described Christianity—'the most perfect manifestation of Satan'[13]—was the same one called up by Ahmad Riza in *Husam al-Haramain* to describe Ghulam Ahmad: the Antichrist inspired by Satan. The fact that the Qadiyani Ahmadis were subsequently led by the logic of their position to pronounce the judgment of kufr on non-Ahmadi Muslims was also of course the mirror opposite of the Ahl-e Sunnat stance in relation to those they believed to be deviating from the 'Sunni' path.[14]

Ahmad Riza's *Husam* turned next to those described as 'Wahhabis': four different groups of 'Wahhabis' were identified, each guilty of

[11] Ibid., pp. 111–18. As Friedmann explains, Ghulam Ahmad's prophetic claim and his claim that he bore absolute affinity to Jesus were linked aspects of his prophetology.

[12] Ibid., p. 117.

[13] Ibid., p. 118.

[14] It is fascinating that the Ahmadi interpretation of Islam thus led to a logical end point similar to that of the Ahl-e Sunnat. In the following passage quoted by Friedmann, the Qadiyani Ahmadis assert that if persons 'who are called Muslims' deny 'a person sent by Allah to reform the world' after the Prophet Muhammad, 'they are . . . included among the ill [the infidels] because they do not fulfil one condition [in order to become true believers] . . . '. This stand closely resembles Ahmad Riza's assertion that a Muslim who denies even one of the 'fundaments' of the faith is not a Muslim. Friedmann's remark about the Ahmadis that 'Faith is, thus, indivisible: even the rejection of one essential article places the person outside the pale' (ibid., p. 160) applies equally well to Ahmad Riza and his followers.

denigrating Allah or His Prophet in some specific way. The 'Wahhabiyya Imsaliyya' and the 'Wahhabiyya Khawatimiyya' believed, according to Ahmad Riza, that there exists a prophet like Muhammad in every one of the six levels of the earth beside this one,[15] and that each of these prophets is a Last and Final Prophet as was Muhammad. He suggested that these groups thereby denied that Muhammad was the best prophet of all and that he was unique in his capacity as the last prophet. Ahmad Riza then charged Maulana Qasim Nanautawi (1833–79), a leading sufi and a founder of the Dar al-'Ulum at Deoband, with denial of the finality of Muhammad's prophethood in a recent work. Nanautawi was quoted to the effect that although the ignorant were under the impression that Muhammad is the last prophet in time, the discerning knew that prophetic superiority (fazilat) was unrelated to being either first or last in time.[16] Ahmad Riza's response to this was that belief in the temporal finality of Muhammad's prophethood was among the 'fundaments' of belief. Consequently, those who belonged to this group were 'followers of Satan the rebel (against God)' (*sarkash shaitan ke chele*).[17]

The third group of 'Wahhabis' were those Ahmad Riza called

[15] Debate on this particular issue, known as imkan-e nazir (the possibility of an equal)—or, alternatively, as imtina'-e nazir (the impossibility of an equal)—derived from questions about the transcendence of Allah, and His ability to produce another prophet equal in every respect to Muhammad. Isma'il Dehlawi (d. 1831), founder of the Tariqa-e Muhammadiyya (on which see below), had argued that this was within Allah's power, while Fazl-e Haqq Khairabadi (d. 1862) had denied that even Allah had such power. Ahmad Riza's father Naqi 'Ali Khan, arguing in favour of Fazl-e Haqq's position, had participated in the debate a generation later, against one Amir Ahmad Sahaswani, of the Ahl-e Hadis. See Rahman 'Ali, *Tazkira-e 'Ulama'-e Hind*, p. 531. The debate as set out by Ahmad Riza in *Husam al-Haramain* differs from that framed by Isma'il Dehlawi and Fazl-e Haqq in that Allah's transcendence is not mentioned. Instead, the issue is seen from the vantage point of the Prophet alone.

[16] Friedmann, in his excellent discussion of the historical changes in the Muslim interpretation of the term khatam al-nabiyyin, writes 'even in the mainstream of Sunni literature one can find passages that reflect a certain measure of uneasiness caused by the belief that Muhammad was the last prophet and that the Muslims are the last community to receive divine revelation'. *Prophecy Continuous*, p. 78. Perhaps it was in the context of such a concern that Nanautawi's statement was made.

[17] *Husam al-Haramain*, p. 14.

the 'Wahhabiyya Kazzabiyya', who believed that Allah can lie.[18] The leader of this group was said to be Rashid Ahmad Gangohi (d. 1905), a founder and patron (sarparast) of the Dar al-'Ulum at Deoband. Ahmad Riza alleged that he was a follower of Isma'il Dehlawi, founder of the Tariqa-e Muhammadiyya movement. Ahmad Riza's argument against this group was that if one believed that Allah can lie, one would be inclined to doubt even the first half of the profession of faith (the kalima).

Ahmad Riza's fourth group, which he called the 'Wahhabiyya Shaitaniyya', were explicitly described as followers of Satan. Led once again by Rashid Ahmad Gangohi, this group, he said, believed that Satan's (Iblis's) knowledge was more vast than that of the Prophet Muhammad, and that Muhammad's knowledge of the unseen ('ilm-e ghaib) was only partial. The question of the Prophet's knowledge was one that interested Ahmad Riza deeply. He devoted the greatest part of *Husam* to rejection of what he viewed as slights on the Prophet's knowledge, and wrote extensively in other fatawa (one of these, *Daulat al-Makkiyya bi'l Madat al-Ghaibiyya*, was written during the same 1905–6 hajj as *Husam*) in defence of his views on the matter. Two more Deobandi 'ulama', Khalil Ahmad Ambethwi[19] and Ashraf 'Ali Thanawi,[20] were singled out and accused of kufr for statements they had made in recent writings.

18 This too, like the imkan-e nazir debate, was ultimately about Allah's transcendental power, which, some maintained, included His ability to lie, though He voluntarily refrained from exercising the power to do so. Ahmad Riza wrote a lengthy rebuttal to this position in *Subhan al-Subuh 'an 'Aib Kizb Maqbuh* (Praise to the Glorified One [in denial of] the Repulsive Blemish of Lying), in *Fatawa-e Rizwiyya*, vol. 6, pp. 212–71. Originally written in 1307/1889–90.

19 Khalil Ahmad Ambethwi was at the time principal of the Mazahir-e 'Ulum madrasa at Saharanpur, linked to Deoband. He was a disciple (murid) of Maulana Rashid Ahmad Gangohi. The book for which Ahmad Riza attacked him in *Husam al-Haramain* was *Barahin-e Qati'yya*, in which he allegedly said that there was no *nass* (clear verse of the Qur'an), to support the belief that Muhammad had 'vast knowledge' (*wus'at-e 'ilm*), though such evidence does exist with regard to the knowledge of Iblis (Satan).

20 Ashraf 'Ali Thanawi was sarparast of the Dar al-'Ulum at Deoband for several years, and was a leading sufi. See Metcalf, pp. 157, 203 passim. The book for which Ahmad Riza took issue with him in *Husam* was *Hifz al-Iman*, in which Ashraf 'Ali had purportedly said that 'the sort of knowledge of the unseen ('ilm-e ghaib) that the Prophet has, every child, madman, animal and four-footed creature has'. *Husam al-Haramain*, p. 18.

Apart from the space and level of detail entered into by Ahmad Riza on the 'ilm-e ghaib issue, his citation of sources also indicates how important it was to him to defend the Prophet on this score. Central to his argument that Allah had gifted knowledge of the unseen to the Prophet[21] was this verse from the Qur'an (72:26, 27): 'He (alone) knows the Unseen, nor does He make any one acquainted with His mysteries, except an apostle whom He has chosen' (Yusuf 'Ali tr.). As Ahmad Riza considered the Prophet Muhammad to be the most beloved of Allah's prophets, it followed that Muhammad must have been one of the messengers referred to in these verses. He defended his view, in addition, with quotation from works of fiqh, and rejection of a hadis in which the Prophet is reported to have said that he didn't even know what lay behind a wall.[22]

It is evident from this somewhat simplified summary of Ahmad Riza's takfir of Mirza Ghulam Ahmad and the Deobandi 'ulama' named in *Husam* that the grounds for the charges related largely (though not wholly, given the debates centred on Allah's transcendence) to the Prophet Muhammad. Specifically, Ahmad Riza interpreted the various statements quoted to imply denial of Muhammad's superiority to all other prophets, denial of the finality of Muhammad's prophethood, belief in the superiority of Satan's knowledge to Muhammad's, and denial of the fact—indisputable to Ahmad Riza—that Muhammad had been granted knowledge of the unseen by Allah. For these reasons, Ahmad Riza regarded the above 'ulama' as kafirs and apostates from Islam (murtadds), followers of Satan rather than of Allah.

The satanic imputation was in fact frequent throughout the fatwa. The words most used to describe Satan were 'liar', 'false', and

[21] The word 'gifted' ('ata) was important to Ahmad Riza, for, as he argued at length in *Daulat al-Makkiyya*, it had never been his position that the Prophet had acquired it on his own. It was failure to make this distinction, he maintained, that led his opponents to argue as they did.

[22] The sources cited were 'Allama Khafaji's *Nasim al-Riyaz* and Shihabuddin Ahmad b. Hajar Makki's (d. 1565/66) *Afzal al-Qura*. The hadis in question was apparently mentioned in *Barahin-e Qati'yya* in defence of the view denying that Muhammad had 'ilm-e ghaib. Ahmad Riza maintained that this hadis was baseless (*be-asl*) and had been declared to be so by 'Abd ul-Haqq Muhhadis Dehlawi (d. 1642) in his *Madarij al-Nubuwwa*.

'deceitful'. It comes as no surprise that such epithets should have been used to describe Mirza Ghulam Ahmad, whom Ahmad Riza regarded as the worst kafir then living in India.[23] It does surprise one, however, to find that Maulana Qasim Nanautawi, accused of denying the temporal finality of Muhammad's prophethood, was a follower of Satan: 'Satan has planted deceit in their hearts', Ahmad Riza wrote of those who accepted Nanautawi's leadership.[24] Maulanas Rashid Ahmad Gangohi and Khalil Ahmad Ambethwi were similarly described, for their alleged belief that Satan's knowledge exceeded that of the Prophet. In fact, they were said to go so far as to associate Iblis with Allah.[25]

Ahmad Riza's portrayal of Satan as engaged in artfully luring the believer away from obedience to Allah and His Prophet toward disobedience and hence kufr[26] appears to have been largely based on hadis literature. As Awn explains in his study of the Satan motif in Islamic literary sources, hadis literature depicts him as 'evil, cunning, and wily; his delight is to lead mankind astray'.[27] Mankind experiences Satan as a constant presence throughout life, for he is 'part of man's very lifeblood'.[28] One has therefore to be watchful at all times, waking and sleeping, against Satan's snares. As Ahmad Riza saw it, the fact that the 'ulama' mentioned in *Husam* had taken the positions they had, in alleged denigration of Allah and the Prophet,

[23] As with the mujaddid issue examined in the last chapter, Ahmad Riza's condemnation of Mirza Ghulam Ahmad as the dajjal or Antichrist, whose arrival signals the approach of the Last Day, raises the interesting question as to whether he believed the approaching end to be locally or globally pertinent. There is no discussion of this in the literature, to my knowledge. It seems fair to say, however, that since we are dealing here with the perception of spiritual and moral crisis, such issues are perhaps beside the point.

[24] *Husam al-Haramain*, p. 14.

[25] Ibid., p. 16.

[26] Such portrayals are also to be found in the *Malfuzat*. In one instance, Ahmad Riza says that if one eats or drinks without saying 'Bism'illah', Satan will enter the food. Or again, Satan and his followers are portrayed exchanging news with one another at the end of the day as to the number of people they were able to lead astray that day. See *Malfuzat*, vol. 2, pp. 92–3; vol. 3, pp. 22–4.

[27] Peter J. Awn, *Satan's Tragedy and Redemption: Iblis in Sufi Psychology* (Leiden: E. J. Brill, 1983), p. 46.

[28] Ibid., p. 47.

was proof that they had fallen victim to Satan's wiles. And because following Satan was the antithesis to following Allah and the Prophet, they were necessarily kafirs.

The Term 'Wahhabi' in its Indian Context

Before we can attempt to understand the Ahl-e Sunnat's use of the term 'Wahhabi' in *Hasam al-Haramain* and other writings, it is necessary to briefly consider the wide application of this term to a variety of nineteenth-century renewal movements in India. The term 'Wahhabi' had its origins, as is well known, in a movement of the Muwahhidun led by Muhammad ibn 'Abd al-Wahhab (1703–92) in eighteenth-century Nejd.[29] With patronage and military support from Muhammad ibn Sa'ud (d. 1765), the tribal leader of Dir'iya, the Muwahhidun were gradually able to establish territorial control over large parts of the Nejd.

The basic teachings of the Muwahhidun are well known. Briefly, as described by Voll,

> Muhammad ibn 'Abd al-Wahhab . . . vigorously rejected the whole structure of the Sufi devotional practices as being unwholesome innovations. He proclaimed that veneration for any human, however saintly, constituted shirk or polytheism.... [He] replaced the pantheistic style of Sufi theology with a renewed emphasis on the interpretation of tawhid, the oneness of God, that stressed God's transcendence. In that interpretation, there was emphasis on strict obedience to the word of God and on the full responsibility of the individual believer . . . . Implicit in that position is a rejection of the unquestioning acceptance of the medieval scholarly authorities, and blind taqlid or imitation was rejected in examining the importance of the Quran and the Sunnah.... [T]he Wahhabi position insisted on the right of an informed independent analysis of the fundamental sources of the faith (ijtihad).[30]

As Rahman comments, the rejection by Muhammad ibn 'Abd al-Wahhab and his followers of the authority of the law schools and

[29] For an interpretive essay on the unhelpfulness of the uncritical use of the term 'Wahhabi' to describe diverse Muslim movements, see William R. Roff, 'Islamic Movements: One or Many?' in Roff (ed.), *Islam and the Political Economy of Meaning*, pp. 31–52.

[30] John Obert Voll, *Islam: Continuity and Change in the Modern World* (Boulder, Colorado: Westview Press, 1982), p. 61.

even of qiyas, the use of analogy to interpret the Qur'an and sunna, gave rise to two 'diametrically opposed' tendencies, one toward 'ultra-conservatism and almost absolute literalism', and the other toward the encouragement of the exercise of independent reasoning (ijtihad).[31]

Numerous nineteenth-century renewal movements in India were named 'Wahhabi' by rival Muslim groups. These included, in Bengal, the Fara'idi movement of the 1820s, and, in Delhi, the Tariqa-e Muhammadiyya as well as the Ahl-e Hadis, intellectual heirs to Shah Wali Ullah. Indian Muslim hostility to 'Wahhabis' was largely a response to the Muwahhiduns' record of uncompromising opposition to popular practice, especially in connection with their demolition of the tomb over the Prophet's grave at Medina. Additionally, in the aftermath of 1857, the term came to be associated in British circles with 'sedition'. The Tariqa-e Muhammadiyya leaders Shah Muhammad Isma'il and Sayyid Ahmad Barelwi, whose concept of reform will be discussed shortly, began a jihad in the 1820s which subsequent leaders had kept alive. In the climate of suspicion of Muslim loyalty that dominated British thinking in the years after 1857, the Muhammadiyya leaders' 'continuation of the *jihad* on the frontier . . . associated them in the minds of the British with unrelenting Muslim discontent'.[32] Through the 1860s, therefore, the British conducted the so-called 'Wahhabi trials', finally convicting certain individuals in 1871.[33]

The assertion by opponents that one or other group was 'Wahhabi' has generally been denied by the group concerned. Unfortunately, relatively little has been done thus far to establish direct and substantive connections between the Muwahhidun movement in Arabia and the Fara'izis, Shah Wali Ullah, the Tariqa-e Muhammadiyya, or the Ahl-e Hadis. One contribution in this direction is John Voll's study of an eighteenth-century intellectual group in Medina, centred on the scholar Muhammad Hayya

[31] Fazlur Rahman, *Islam*, 2nd ed. (Chicago and London: University of Chicago Press, 1979), p. 198.

[32] Pearson, 'Islamic Reform', p. 213.

[33] Ibid., pp. 215–20.

al-Sindi.[34] An indirect intellectual link between Shah Wali Ullah and Muhammad ibn 'Abd al-Wahhab is provided by al-Sindi, a scholar of hadis who was in sufi terms a Naqshbandi (as was Shah Wali Ullah). One of al-Sindi's teachers, Ibrahim al-Kurani, is known to have taught Shah Wali Ullah, while al-Sindi himself taught hadis to Muhammad ibn 'Abd al-Wahhab, among others. While there is no suggestion that Shah Wali Ullah met, or was influenced by, Muhammad ibn 'Abd al-Wahhab,[35] each can be understood to have been influenced, in his own way, by the scholarly circle of al-Sindi.

As Voll elaborates elsewhere, however, participation in a scholarly network does not imply that there was 'some form of either hidden or manifest agreement in doctrine or teachings beyond the basic common factors of faith that unite all Muslims'.[36] To the extent that there was any unifying vision shared by members of the network, Voll suggests that it was in a common concern for 'sociomoral reconstruction'. Yet, the direction and consequences of the reforms of Muhammad ibn 'Abd al-Wahhab and Shah Wali Ullah were clearly different, shaped by their particular local circumstances.[37] Knowledge of these circumstances is thus centrally important, as Roff points out, to our appreciation of the understanding which different reformers, in historical time and place, have brought to their chosen task.[38]

In addition to the connection which scholars, and some Muslim

[34] John O. Voll, 'Muhammad Hayya al-Sindi and Muhammad ibn 'Abd al-Wahhab: An Analysis of an Intellectual Group in Eighteenth-Century Madina', *Bulletin of the School of Oriental and African Studies*, 38 (1975), 32–9.

[35] Ibid., pp. 35, 39.

[36] John O. Voll, 'Linking Groups in the Networks of Eighteenth-Century Revivalist Scholars: The Mizjaji Family in Yemen', in Nehemiah Levtzion and John O. Voll (eds.), *Eighteenth-Century Renewal and Reform in Islam* (Syracuse: Syracuse University Press, 1987), p. 81.

[37] Ibid., pp. 70, 71.

[38] Of the Muwahhidun, for instance, Roff writes: 'The Wahhabi-Sa'udi conquest of Arabia was, of course, to a considerable degree a matter of warfare and submission, but it was warfare invested with moral argument, that made moral claims, and carried moral teaching . . . . *How* this teaching meant is likely to elude us unless we can apprehend both the circumstantial context in which it operated and the discourse that accompanied its contestation and acceptance'. 'Islamic Movements', p. 36.

renewers themselves, have assumed to obtain between the Wahhabis and Shah Wali Ullah, they have also posited a link between the Muwahhidun and the Tariqa-e Muhammadiyya on the one hand, and the former and the Fara'izi movement of Bengal on the other. Ahmad Khan, in his study of the Fara'izi movement, has discussed the similarities and differences between each of these movements at some length. He concludes that while there is undoubtedly 'a remarkable similarity' between the Muwahhidun emphasis on tauhid and that of the Tariqa-e Muhammadiyya, 'there is no historical evidence of any contact [between the] *Tariqah-i-Muhammadiyah* with Wahhabism of Arabia in its formative stage'.[39] As to the Fara'izis, the differences in teaching between them and the Muwahhidun are sufficiently numerous and important, in his view, as to preclude the conclusion that the Fara'izis were an offshoot of the Arabian Wahhabis.[40]

While the historical connection between the Muwahhidun and the above renewal movements in nineteenth-century India is therefore dubious, or unclear at best, the term 'Wahhabi', as far as one can tell, has come to stay. As Rahman writes,

> Wahhabism...is a kind of umbrella term—the 'Wahhabi-Idea'—covering analogous rather than identical phenomena in the Muslim world. It may be summed up as a reassertion of monotheism and equality of men combined with varying degrees of reinterpretation of the actual positive legacy of the Islamic tradition for the reconstruction of Muslim society.[41]

It was undoubtedly in the sense of a 'positive legacy . . . for the reconstruction of Muslim society' that Sir Sayyid Ahmad Khan regarded the term Wahhabi. He considered the Tariqa-e Muhammadiyya leader Muhammad Isma'il 'the founder of Wahhabeeism in India', and on occasion even described himself as a 'friend' and 'well-wisher' of 'Wahhabeeism'.[42]

For the Ahl-e Sunnat, by contrast, the name 'Wahhabi' was pejorative. I turn below to detailed consideration of their use of the

[39] Mu'in-ud-Din Ahmad Khan, *History of the Fara'idi Movement in Bengal*, pp. xlv–xlvi.

[40] Ibid., p. li.

[41] Rahman, *Islam*, 2nd ed., p. 199.

[42] Pearson, 'Islamic Reform', pp. 265, 269.

label, particularly in relation to the Tariqa-e Muhammadiyya and the Deobandi 'ulama'.

The Ahl-e Sunnat and 'Wahhabis'

As we have seen, Ahmad Riza used the term 'Wahhabi' to describe the kinds of kafirs that he believed some Deobandi 'ulama' to be. He looked upon them as the latest in a line of kafirs that went all the way back to the Prophet's and 'Ali's own time. When asked whether Wahhabis had existed during the (golden) age of the first four caliphs, he responded in the affirmative, relating a number of hadis in support of his view. The Kharijis who had seceded from 'Ali's army after he agreed to submit his battle against Mu'awiya to arbitration (37/657) had been among the first.[43] Thereafter one group (of kafirs) followed another, generation after generation, assuming new shape and a new name in each age. In the present time, they were known as 'Wahhabis'.[44]

Ahmad Riza depicted these and other people considered to be kafir as superficially devout, though in fact not so: 'You will consider your namaz contemptible in comparison with their namaz, and so also with your fast and your [pious] acts. They will read the Qur'an, but it[s words] will not go further than their throats'.[45] On another occasion he related a story about the 'father of the Wahhabis', illustrating at the same time the Prophet's knowledge of future events:

> One day [some] Companions entered into the Prophet's presence. A man came and, after standing at the edge of the group, went into the mosque. [The Prophet] asked, 'Which of you will kill that man?' Abu Bakr got up and went [toward him]. He saw that the man was saying the namaz with great humility. Abu Bakr's hand did not come up, for to kill such a worshipper in the very

[43] Ahmad Riza did not refer to the Kharijis by name on this occasion, though it is evident that it was they that he meant in his recounting of hadis. *Malfuzat,* vol. 1, p. 57.

[44] Ibid., vol. 1, p. 56.

[45] Ibid. This image of the Qur'an as spiritual food which is indigestible to kafirs is interesting in view of the sufis' portrayal of Iblis's 'presence in man [as] analogous to, and . . . mythically symbolized by the ingestion of food, one of the most concrete of human processes'. Awn, *Satan's Tragedy and Redemption,* p. 61. See also note 26.

act of praying [seemed wrong]. He returned, and related all that had happened. [The Prophet] asked, 'Who is there who will kill him?' 'Umar got up and the same thing happened with him. The Prophet again asked who would kill the man. 'Ali rose and said, 'O Prophet of Allah, I shall'. He said, 'Yes, you. If you can find him. But you will not be able to find him'. And so it happened. By the time 'Ali reached [the mosque] the man had finished his namaz and left. The Prophet said, 'If you had killed him a great calamity (fitna) would have been lifted from the community'. This was the father of the Wahhabis, whose external and intrinsic (*ma'anawi*) heirs are making the world dirty today.[46]

Despite his humble demeanour, Ahmad Riza went on, in truth he was haughty. For, while standing at the edge of the crowd of Companions surrounding the Prophet, he had said to himself that none among them was as good as he. This pride nullified all his pious deeds. Without respect (ta'zim) for the Prophet there could be no faith (iman), and without faith prayer had no efficacy. 'The true servant of Allah (*'abd allah*) is he who is the servant of the Prophet (*'abd mustafa*); if not he will be the servant of Satan (*'abd shaitan*)'.[47]

The concept of fitna, tumult, or moral and social chaos, evoked in conjunction with the description of the 'father of the Wahhabis' in the above passage, and in the opening paragraphs of *Husam*, recurs frequently in the literature. It is seen as the result, experienced in worldly life, of pride, deceit, and refusal to repent (to do tauba). Ultimately of course it would lead to punishment in hell after judgment on the Last Day. In the meantime, in the here and now of late nineteenth-century British India, Muslims were witnessing the realization of the prediction in the classical hadis recorded by Abu Da'ud that a time would come when the community of believers would be split into seventy-three groups, only one of which (the jama'at or majority) would be destined for heaven (jannat).

The Ahl-e Sunnat movement itself was ultimately predicated on this view of the world: For them, the 'Wahhabis' (not to mention Mirza Ghulam Ahmad, seen as Antichrist) were Satanic and hell-bound in contradistinction to themselves, who were true followers of Allah and the Prophet. Once again the similarities between the Ahl-e Sunnat view of the world around them and the image of Satan/Iblis

[46] *Malfuzat*, vol. 1, p. 58.

[47] Ibid.

in the Qur'an and hadis literature are striking. The themes of Satan's refusal to bow before Adam despite Allah's command that he do so (Qur'an 2:34, 7:11), his lack of penitence (7:12, 13), his responsibility for spreading fitna among men and women (7:16, 17; 15:39), and his ultimate punishment (17:63; 38:77, 78)[48] are echoed in Ahmad Riza's discussion of kafirs, Wahhabi or otherwise, acquiring resonance and force through constant reiteration.

The Wahhabis were depicted not merely as proud and disrespectful to the Prophet, as in the story related by Ahmad Riza above, but as people who refused to repent. If a Wahhabi repents, Ahmad Riza once said, he was not one to begin with.[49] Moreover, they practised dissimulation (taqiyya) to an even greater degree than did Shi'is, for purposes such as raising—among the Deobandis—money for their madrasa from supporters of the Ahl-e Sunnat.[50] A terrible punishment awaited them—and other alleged apostates, such as Shi'is, Ahmadis, and Sir Sayyid Ahmad's followers—on the Last Day in hell:

> Every kafir will be made to drink boiling water, so hot that the mouth will melt when it touches it. And when the water reaches the stomach, it will reduce the intestines to pieces. And they will drink this water like a camel suffering from great thirst. They will be faint from hunger. They will be fed thorny cactus . . . which, on reaching their stomachs, will cause them to be in a great frenzy just as the boiling water did and will in no way alleviate their hunger . . . . Death will come from all directions, but they will not die. Nor will there ever be any let up in their punishment.[51]

[48] For the Iblis theme in the hadis literature, see Awn, *Satan's Tragedy and Redemption*, pp. 33–4, 36, 38, 53–4, passim.

[49] *Malfuzat*, vol. 3, p. 39. The comment was made in the context of the uselessness, in Ahmad Riza's view, of supplicating Allah (saying du'a) on a Wahhabi's behalf.

The tauba theme occurs on several occasions. In reference to Deobandis, the following examples are of interest: in 1906, Khalil Ahmad Ambethwi reportedly fled Mecca one night after having requested an 'alim to arrange for the presence of a translator so that he could do tauba for his book *Barahin-e Qati'yya*. *Malfuzat*, vol. 2, p. 14; in 1911, Ahmad Riza wrote to Ashraf 'Ali Thanawi inviting him to repent of statements made in his *Hifz al-Iman* in which Ashraf 'Ali had allegedly denigrated the Prophet. The latter presumably did not respond. *Maktubat-e Imam Ahmad Riza Khan Barelwi* (Lahore: Maktaba Nabawiyya, 1986), p. 130.

[50] *Malfuzat*, vol. 2, p. 60.

[51] Ibid., vol. 1, p. 78. In this instance food and drink are a means of punishment, rather than of nourishment. The contrast with the Qur'an as spiritual food is clear. There are

When one asks how the Ahl-e Sunnat defined a 'Wahhabi', and which of the 'ulama' groups of the late nineteenth century were so labelled, Ahmad Riza's use of the term initially appears confusing. In one fatwa, he disagreed with a questioner who said that in India there were three kinds of Muslims: Shi'is, Sunni muqallids (followers of one of the four main Sunni law schools) and Sunni ghair-muqallids (those who were unaffiliated with any school). His disagreement was not with this three-fold classification, but with the use of the word 'Sunni' to describe the ghair-muqallids. He regarded them as bid'ati. He then went on to say that the Wahhabis were one of three ghair-muqallid groups (though they called themselves Ahl-e Hadis and Muhammadi, not Wahhabi).[52] The Deobandis were not mentioned as 'Wahhabi' in this fatwa. This was logical in the context of the definition of Wahhabis as ghair-muqallids, because the Deobandis insisted on taqlid within one of the four Sunni schools of law, as did the Ahl-e Sunnat.

We have seen, however, that certain leading Deobandi 'ulama' were called 'Wahhabi' in Ahmad Riza's 1905–6 fatwa, *Husam al-Haramain.* The explanation for this inconsistency can only be that by this time Ahmad Riza had redefined the term in his mind, and was now using the word 'Wahhabi' to describe the leaders of the Tariqa-e Muhammadiyya movement, notably Sayyid Ahmad Barelwi and Muhammad Isma'il Dehlawi, and 'ulama' he considered to be their followers, among them many Deobandis. The connection is indicated (though not spelled out) in *Husam* by Ahmad Riza's assertion that Rashid Ahmad Gangohi was a follower of Muhammad Isma'il, and by a derisive reference to the latter as Rashid Ahmad's *pir-e ta'ifa* ('sufi master of musicians and dancing girls').[53] The

---

numerous Qur'anic passages about the torments that transgressors will suffer from food and drink in hell. Thus, 14:16–17: ' . . . and he is given, for drink, boiling fetid water. In gulps will he sip it, but never will he be near swallowing it down his throat: Death will come to him from every quarter, yet will he not die . . . ' (Yusuf 'Ali tr.) Also see 17:62–5, 44:43–6, and 56:52–5. For details on the association of Iblis with food and drink, see Awn, *Satan's Tragedy and Redemption*, pp. 61–3.

[52] Ahmad Riza Khan, *Fatawa al-Sunna li-Iljam al-Fitna*, p. 3. The 'necharis' (Sir Sayyid Ahmad Khan and followers) were said to make up the remaining group of ghair-muqallids.

[53] Rashid Ahmad's real pir had been Haji Imdad Ullah Muhajir Makki (1815–99),

literature also offers more conclusive evidence that Ahmad Riza and the Ahl-e Sunnat movement generally considered Deoband an intellectual and spiritual heir of the Tariqa-e Muhammadiyya, and that (going backwards in time) they saw an intellectual link between the Arabian Muwahhidun of the eighteenth century and the Tariqa-e Muhammadiyya. Indeed, *Husam al-Haramain* was first written in 1902 as part of a longer commentary (sharh) on a work by Fazl-e Rasul Badayuni (d. 1872) in which the latter had explicitly linked the beliefs of the 'Nejdis' with those of Muhammad Isma'il, both of which he condemned.[54] In a later work, Muhammad Isma'il was condemned by Ahmad Riza on some of the same grounds as the Deobandi 'ulama' named in *Husam* had been.[55]

The Ahl-e Sunnat thus used the term Wahhabi primarily to indicate a perceived commonality of views between the Tariqa-e Muhammadiyya and some later Muslim movements in the subcontinent, with the implication that the ultimate source for the opinions they purportedly shared was the Muwahhidun movement of eighteenth-and early nineteenth-century Arabia. The term as used in the Ahl-e Sunnat literature is therefore something of a catch-all, in which Deobandis, Ahl-e Hadis, and sometimes Sir Sayyid Ahmad and his followers as well, were included. As the Ahl-e Sunnat saw it the founders of the early nineteenth-century Tariqa-e Muhammadiyya movement and their followers constituted the first wave of Indian Wahhabis (and consequently those most directly responsible for the fitna that they, the Ahl-e Sunnat of the late nineteenth-century, had to root out). In order to understand Ahl-e Sunnat differences with Deoband I start therefore by examining Ahl-e Sunnat writings on the Tariqa-e Muhammadiyya.

---

revered by the Ahl-e Sunnat and Deobandis alike. Ahmad Riza must have been aware of Rashid Ahmad's discipleship to Haji Imdad Ullah, and should be understood in this context to be implying an intellectual affinity between Isma'il Dehlawi's vision of Islam and Rashid Ahmad's. On Haji Imdad Ullah, see Metcalf, *Islamic Revival*, p. 79.

54 Fazl-e Rasul's 1854 work, entitled *Al-Mu'tamad al-Muntaqid* (Trustworthy Critic) written in Arabic, dealt with 'aqa'id (belief). In it, the properties and characteristics of Allah and the Prophet were discussed. Ahmad Riza's commentary, approving this work, was entitled *Al-Mu'tamad al-Mustanad* (Dependable Reason). *Husam al-Haramain*, published separately in 1906, had originally been a part of this 1902 work.

55 Ahmad Riza Khan, *Tamhid al-Iman ba-Ayat al-Qur'an*, pp. 42–3.

The Tariqa-e Muhammadiyya in Ahl-e Sunnat Perspective

The Tariqa-e Muhammadiyya movement, led by Sayyid Ahmad Barelwi and inspired by the reformist teachings of Shah Wali Ullah and Shah 'Abd ul-'Aziz, has been frequently mentioned in this study. Its purposes do not therefore need repetition. The Ahl-e Sunnat literature dealing with the Tariqa leaders Sayyid Ahmad Barelwi and Muhammad Isma'il Dehlawi, referred to as 'Wahhabi', focuses on certain key texts of their movement. As was his wont when it came to rebuttal of those with whom he disagreed, Ahmad Riza wrote a number of books in which he set out, point by point, what he found objectionable in these texts. In one of these, written in 1894 (AH 1312), he enumerated seventy different grounds for the takfir of Muhammad Isma'il and other writers of the Tariqa-e Muhammadiyya, but declared at the end that in his view it was prudent to 'stop the tongue' (*kaff-e lisan*) and refrain from doing so.[56] It appears that here as in other books on the subject he chose to give the leaders of the Tariqa-e Muhammadiyya the benefit of the doubt regarding their faith, as he had said a faqih ought if possible to do. Yet in view of his takfir of the Deobandi 'ulama' named in *Husam al-Haramain*, whom he regarded as followers of the 'Wahhabi Isma'iliyya' (as he called followers of Muhammad Isma'il), this restraint is curious.[57]

Among Tariqa-e Muhammadiyya writings, one work by Muhammad Isma'il was particularly influential in spreading the ideas of the movement and creating a mass following. This was *Taqwiyat al-Iman* (Strengthening the Faith), originally written in Arabic but soon translated and printed in Urdu.[58] *Sirat al-Mustaqim* (The Straight

[56] Ahmad Riza Khan, *Al-Kaukab al-Shihabiyya fi Kufriyat Abi al-Wahhabiyya* (Brightly-Shining Star among the Blasphemies of the Father of the Wahhabis) (Lahore: Nuri Book Depot, 1375/1955–6). Originally published in 1312/1894–5.

[57] One can only speculate as to the reason for this. Perhaps he refrained because by this time the Tariqa leaders whose books he referred to were all dead, and therefore unable to defend themselves. Mirza Ghulam Ahmad, and the Deobandi 'ulama' mentioned in *Husam al-Haramain*, by contrast, were alive at the time of the original takfir in 1902. (Rashid Ahmad Gangohi died in 1905, a year before the takfir was presented to the 'ulama' of the Haramain. However, Ahmad Riza claimed that he had refused for several years before his death to respond to Ahmad Riza's questions. The latter interpreted this as an admission of guilt.)

[58] Apparently *Taqwiyat* was translated into Urdu a bit at a time. Pearson, 'Islamic

Path), written in Persian in 1818, was intended for an élite audience and dealt with Sayyid Ahmad Barelwi's qualities as a leader.[59] Passages from these and other books by Muhammad Isma'il were found objectionable by the Ahl-e Sunnat.

The central theme of *Taqwiyat al-Iman* and other popular works was that Muslims should live their lives in accordance with the kalima or profession of faith—'There is no God but God and Muhammad is His Prophet'. The first clause of the profession, Muhammad Isma'il wrote in *Taqwiyat*, required strict adherence to the monotheistic belief in Allah's unity (tauhid), and consequent abhorrence of polytheism or shirk. He distinguished between three different types of shirk, each the subject of an extended discussion in the text. The second part of the kalima, belief that Muhammad is Allah's prophet, called upon Muslims to act in keeping with the Prophet's sunna, as preserved in (sound) hadis, and reject bid'a, defined as innovations not validated by hadis.[60]

Muhammad Isma'il went to great lengths in *Taqwiyat al-Iman* to stress the importance above all else of acknowledgement of Allah's transcendental power, and avoidance of shirk or associationism. Referring to the shirk of associating others with Allah's knowledge

Reform', p.81, says that the second chapter of the work was 'not translated . . . until 1834 A.D., and, therefore, was probably less important (than the first]'. The first chapter had presumably been published some time in the 1820s.

[59] Ibid., pp. 79, 106. English translations of extracts from these works, or essays discussing them, appeared in the first half of the nineteenth century, a reflection no doubt of the importance the British attached to the perceived 'Wahhabi' problem. See 'Notice of the Peculiar Tenets held by the Followers of Syed Ahmed, taken chiefly from the "Sirat-ul-Mustaqim",' *Journal of the Asiatic Society of Bengal* (Calcutta), 1 (January-December 1832), 479–98; Mir Shahamat 'Ali, 'Translation of the Takwiyat-ul-Iman, Preceded by a Notice of the Author, Maulavi Isma'il Hajji', *Journal of the Royal Asiatic Society*, 13 (1852), 310–72.

[60] The foregoing is based on Pearson, pp. 80–1. In the following pages, I focus on Muhammad Isma'il's views on shirk rather than bid'a. The bid'a he indicates in *Taqwiyat al-Iman* and *Sirat al-Mustaqim* overlap considerably with the types of shirk to be discussed below, thereby making it unnecessary to go into the matter separately. It may be noted, briefly, that he indicated three distinct sources of bid'a: practices arising from association with people who appeared to be sufis, but were not; practices arising from association with Shi'is; and practices arising from the imitation of corrupt usages generally. For greater detail, see 'Notice of the Tenets held by the Followers of Syed Ahmed', 488–93.

(*ishrak fi'l 'ilm*), the first of the three, he denied that anyone but Allah had 'ilm-e ghaib, or knowledge of the unseen:

the prophets, angels, pirs, martyrs, imams, devils, or fairies, are not endowed with power to discover the concealed things that God has been pleased to hide from them; but He occasionally discloses any such thing to any one of His servants, in a twinkling; yet this is done with His free will, and not at their supplication, as we are led to believe. It has often happened that the Prophet himself several times desired to know things, the truth of which he could not discover until voluntarily apprised of them by God.[61]

Notwithstanding this admission of the possibility that Allah sometimes apprised the Prophet Muhammad of things he had not known, Muhammad Isma'il went on to argue that the Prophet definitely did not have knowledge of the 'five things' mentioned in Sura Luqman.[62] Anyone who maintained that the Prophet had been told about them by Allah but had abstained from revealing it was a liar.

As the discussion earlier in this chapter suggests, Ahmad Riza's position on this issue was diametrically opposed to that set out here by Muhammad Isma'il. In a work devoted exclusively to the subject of the Prophet's knowledge, to be discussed below, he argued that knowledge of these five things had been gifted by Allah not only to the Prophet but also to the seven *aqtab* (pl. of qutb), the pivots of the world of whom there is only one in existence at any given time.[63]

In *Taqwiyat al-Iman*, Muhammad Isma'il proceeded to attack a second kind of shirk, that of associating others with Allah's power (*ishrak fi'l tasarruf*) His concern here was with the dangers of intercession:

It is customary for many, in the time of difficulty, to call for aid on the pirs, religious guides, apostles [prophets], imams, martyrs, angels, and fairies, and beg them to comply with their wishes; and to propitiate them, vows and

[61] *Taqwiyat al-Iman* (Mir Shahamat 'Ali tr.), p. 331.

[62] Qur'an 31:34, 'Verily the knowledge of the Hour is with God (alone). It is He who sends down rain, and He who knows what is in the wombs. Nor does any one know what it is that he will earn on the morrow. Nor does any one know in what land he is to die. Verily with God is full knowledge and He is acquainted (with all things)'. (Yusuf 'Ali tr.)

[63] On Ahmad Riza's description of the hierarchy of saints culminating in the qutb, see Chapter V.

offerings are made in their names. Moreover, children are named after them; for instance, 'Abd-un-nabi (servant of the apostle), 'Ali Bakhsh (granted by 'Ali) . . . Further, many perform other similar rites for their respective saints . . . : one keeps a . . . lock of hair on his head: others wear . . . woven thread round their necks . . . , and others again invoke the saints . . . and take oaths in their names. In short, what the Hindus do towards their idols, the Mussulmans do for them, and yet they call themselves Muhammadans![64]

In reality, Muhammad Isma'il argued,

. . . it is evident that there is none, either in heaven or in earth, who can be mediator with God, or by invoking whom any profit or hurt can be produced. Nay, the apostles and saints can only intercede with God, by His permission. So there is no advantage in invoking them.[65]

Muhammad Isma'il went on to say that 'both angels and men were equally [Allah's] servants', and that Allah had not delegated any power to one other than Himself.

Intercession was to be understood, Muhammad Isma'il wrote, as nothing more than 'recommendation' (sifarish). Comparing Allah to a 'King of kings', Muhammad was said to be like a minister whose intercession was acceptable to Allah only because it was undertaken 'to please his master, and with his tacit permission'. Allah's power was so great that

in a twinkling, solely by pronouncing the word 'Be!' he can, if he like[s], create crores [tens of millions] of apostles, saints, genii, and angels, of similar ranks with Gabriel and Muhammad, or can produce a total subversion of the whole universe, and supply its place with new creations.[66]

Here, then, embedded in an argument on Allah's transcendental power was the statement which was to give rise to subsequent debate as to whether or not denial of the finality of Muhammad's prophethood was implied. Some seventy years after this was written, Ahmad Riza, in his fatwa *Husam al-Haramain*, was to argue that there could not be another prophet like Muhammad in any of the six levels of the earth believed to exist beside this one, and that it was kufr to hold otherwise.[67]

64 *Taqwiyat al-Iman* (Mir Shahamat 'Ali tr.), pp. 319–20.

65 Ibid., p. 320.

66 Ibid., p. 339.

67 As noted previously, in his treatment of this issue (known as imkan-e nazir, the

In addition to disagreement with Muhammad Isma'il on this issue, Ahmad Riza and the Ahl-e Sunnat could not accept his general attitude to intercession. In their view, to say, for instance, that 'none . . . can be mediator with God', or have the power to profit or hurt anyone, went much too far in denying Muhammad's and other prophets' powers of intercession. In a work devoted to rebutting Muhammad Isma'il, Ahmad Riza argued that occasionally he contradicted the very word of Allah, thereby making Allah Himself appear to be a mushrik, or polytheist:

> In . . . the *Taqwiyat al-Iman* is written that the giving of health, of well-being, fulfillment of desires, etc. are all part of Allah's glory. It is not in the power of any prophet or wali (saint) to fulfill someone's wishes, or to help them. If someone asks for help from any of these he is a mushrik, whether he believes that they have this power in and of themselves or whether [he believes] they have received it from Allah. This statement is tantamount to accusing everyone of shirk, including Allah, because the Qur'an says Allah and Allah's prophet have made you prosperous out of their bounty (*tumhen daulatmand kar diya allah aur allah ke rasul ne apne fazl se*). No one, neither the saints nor the prophets, nor Allah Himself, would be devoid of shirk in Isma'il Dehlawi's [Muhammad Isma'il's] interpretation. Another verse would also become shirk: (3:49) 'I [Jesus] heal those born blind, and the lepers, and I quicken the dead, by God's leave'. [Yusuf 'Ali.][68]

In other words, prophets intercede with Allah on behalf of human beings, and have in addition an independent God-given ability to change human destinies for good or ill by performing miracles. Muhammad Isma'il had not in fact denied that prophets can intercede with Allah's 'permission' (*izn*). But he had clearly discouraged the practice, arguing that there was 'no advantage' in invoking the help of saints and prophets. This merely encouraged people to worship them and make them their patrons, thereby distancing themselves from Allah rather than getting close to Him.

Muhammad Isma'il also objected to a third kind of shirk, which he called *ishrak fi'l 'ibada*, or association in worship. This included practices such as

---

possibility that Muhammad could have an equal), there was no discussion of Allah's transcendental power, solely of belief in the finality of Muhammad's prophethood.

68 Ahmad Riza Khan, *Al-Kaukab al-Shihabiyya*, pp. 40–1.

prostration [to a tomb, or another person], bowing down, standing with folded arms, spending money in the name of an individual, fasting out of respect to his memory, proceeding to a distant shrine in the peculiar dress of a pilgrim, and calling aloud his name while going along . . . Also, to avoid slaying cattle purposely while on pilgrimage, to go round the shrine, . . . to make vows, to cover the grave with a sheet . . . as well as on leaving the shrine to walk backwards, with the face towards it, and hold the jungle around in respect, refraining from slaying any animals found therein . . . or from cutting trees or grass situated there. God hath ordained all these ceremonies of worship to be performed by His servants for Himself alone. Should any one in any way observe these or other similar honors towards apostles [prophets], he shall certainly be guilty of associating them with God.[69]

The practices Muhammad Isma'il criticized here were associated with the veneration of shrines, including the annual 'urs of saints centred on their tombs. As this study of the Ahl-e Sunnat has shown, respect for such tombs or graves, in which several of the practices listed above were carried out, was part of Ahl-e Sunnat ritual. This followed from their belief, based on the classical hadis, 'Allah, the exalted, has prohibited the earth from consuming the bodies of [p]rophets',[70] that the bodies of prophets, saints, and martyrs remained in a state of perfect preservation after death. The afterlife of such persons being both corporeal and spiritual, veneration of their tombs was a sign of the respect they were due.[71] As for the area surrounding the Prophet's tomb, Ahmad Riza cited a hadis from al-Bukhari in which the Prophet is reported to have said that he would make the land between Medina's two mountains haram (sacred), just as Abraham had made Mecca haram.[72] From the Ahl-e Sunnat point of view, thus, to say as Muhammad Isma'il did that it was shirk to venerate Muhammad's tomb was yet another sign of his lack of respect toward Muhammad, and consequently of kufr.[73]

69 *Taqwiyat al-Iman* (Mir Shahamat 'Ali tr.), pp. 323–4.

70 Ahmad Hasan, *Sunan Abu Dawud*, vol. 1, p. 269; also Schimmel, *And Muhammad Is His Messenger*, p. 284, n. 56.

71 Ahmad Riza Khan, *Ihlak al-Wahhabiyyin 'ala Tauhin Qubur al-Muslimin* (Ruin to the Wahhabis for Disrespect toward Muslim Graves), 1322/1904–5, pp. 2–7.

72 Ahmad Riza Khan, *Al-Kaukab al-Shihabiyya*, p. 42.

73 Though, as noted above, Ahmad Riza refrained from making a formal charge to this effect.

It thus comes as no surprise that Muhammad Isma'il's image of the Prophet Muhammad was radically different from that of the Ahl-e Sunnat. Muhammad Isma'il's prophet was a perfect but essentially human model for behaviour, while the Ahl-e Sunnat's prophet was—and is—not. Muhammad Isma'il spoke of the prophets, imams, pirs, and martyrs as 'brothers' who ought to be honoured as 'human beings, not as God'.[74] In the same vein, he wrote that the Prophet had discouraged his followers from seeing him as more than a 'servant' of Allah who 'one day . . . would die, and return to the dust; and [who] could not therefore be worthy of worship'.[75] As the following section on prophetology will underline, this egalitarian portrayal of the prophet and other purveyors of religious authority was at odds with the Ahl-e Sunnat view. Whatever Muhammad was, he was not an 'elder brother', nor an ordinary person whose body would disintegrate after death. To suggest otherwise was, once again, to show extreme disrespect.

Ahl-e Sunnat Prophetology

Much has already been said herein about the Ahl-e Sunnat concept of the Prophet. I now wish to pull the pieces together in order to present a coherent picture of Ahl-e Sunnat prophetology. Insofar as Ahl-e Sunnat beliefs about the Prophet were in line with the standard Sunni view, such as belief in the finality of Muhammad's prophethood, this does not tell us a great deal about the Ahl-e Sunnat. But there was much in their prophetology that was distinctive: belief that the Prophet had knowledge of the unseen; that he was made of light and had no shadow; that Allah can only be approached through the intermediacy of Muhammad and none other; and that, because the Prophet lives on in corporeal as well as spiritual form in his grave at Medina, he continues to 'exist' and to be. In prayer ritual, Ahmad Riza defended the distinctive practice of kissing the thumbs of both hands and touching them to the eyes at designated moments when the Prophet was mentioned.[76]

[74] *Taqwiyat al-Iman* (Mir Shahamat 'Ali tr.), p. 362.

[75] Ibid., pp. 362–3.

[76] These moments were: during the azan (call to prayer) when the words '*ashhadu anna Muhammadan rasul Allah*', 'I testify that Muhammad is the apostle of Allah', during iqamat

The most important element of Ahl-e Sunnat prophetology, around which everything else seems to revolve, was the belief in Muhammad's intercessionary role with Allah on behalf of mankind. In *Daulat al-Makkiyya*, a work devoted primarily to defence of the Prophet's knowledge of the unseen, Ahmad Riza wrote as follows on the Prophet's intercessionary powers:

> Our Prophet received the gift of intercession. The Prophet says in the *Sahih Muslim*, 'I have been given the gift of intercession'. The 'Wahhabis' say that the Prophet hasn't yet been given this ability, that he will receive it only on the day of the resurrection. They say this so as to dissuade people from seeking the Prophet's help in times of distress . . . . Not only is it true that the Prophet's intercession is best in Allah's regard, but furthermore, no one can approach Allah without the Prophet's intermediacy. All have to approach the Prophet, for he alone can intercede for them with Allah. The Prophet said, 'I am the owner (malik) of the intercession of all the prophets'.[77]

In this passage, Ahmad Riza alluded to several characteristics believed by the Ahl-e Sunnat to inhere in the Prophet as intercessor: his ability to intercede was a gift from Allah; it was not a gift held in abeyance until the day of the resurrection, but was exercised in the present time in the interests of those who supplicated him for help; his intercessionary powers were superior to those of all other prophets, also believed to possess such influence with Allah (through the Prophet Muhammad, who alone had direct access to Him).

The Prophet's intercessionary role, in addition, was believed to have existed from the very beginning of his prophetic calling. This is illustrated by a story, recounted below, which was based, Ahmad Riza said, on sahih (sound) hadis recorded in al-Nasa'i, al-Tirmidhi, and Ibn Maja. In this hadis, importantly, the Prophet himself was reported to have taught someone of the efficacy of his intercession with Allah:

(the second call to prayer at the beginning of the namaz, when everyone stands up), and every time the Prophet's name is mentioned. Ashraf 'Ali Thanawi wrote a fatwa disapproving of the practice, while Ahmad Riza wrote a contrary opinion. Ahmad Riza Khan, *Fatawa-e Rizwiyya* (Muradabad: Maktaba Na'imiyya), vol. 2, pp. 517–648.

[77] Ahmad Riza Khan, *Daulat al-Makkiyya bi'l Madat al-Ghaibiyya* (The Bounty of Mecca on That which is Hidden), (Karachi: Maktaba-e Rizwiyya, n.d.), p. 137.

The Prophet taught a blind man a du'a (supplication) to be said after the namaz which went as follows: 'Allah! I ask you and turn toward you through the intermediacy (*ba-wasile*) of your prophet Muhammad who is a compassionate (*mehrban*) prophet. O Prophet of Allah (*ya rasul allah*)! By means of the prophet I turn toward my lord in my need that my need may be fulfilled. Allah, accept his intercession in my favour'.[78]

The man was cured of his blindness immediately after saying the prayer as instructed by the Prophet.[79]

This hadis was cited in defence of the argument that it is permissible to address the Prophet directly by saying 'Ya rasul allah', 'Muhammad ya mansur' (O Muhammad, Victorious One), or words to that effect, and ask for his help. The expression 'Ya rasul allah' was in fact so closely associated with the Ahl-e Sunnat that it came to be thought of as a sort of emblem of identification.[80] As seen above, Ahmad Riza said that one could address the Prophet in this way in the form of a du'a after the namaz, or at any other time. As in the case of the blind man cited above, such supplication was considered to have immediate effect.

Not only did Allah gift the Prophet the power of intercession from the very beginning of his prophethood, the Ahl-e Sunnat believed, but this power continued after death. This is an important dimension of Ahl-e Sunnat prophetology, for it meant in effect that the Prophet is a continuous presence in the lives of Muslims at all times, intervening when called upon. It is for this reason that Ahmad Riza always spoke, and wrote, of the Prophet in the present tense. He was believed to be *hazir o nazir*, present and seeing.

This presence could be either spiritual or physical, and was unlimited in terms of space or time. The Prophet could go anywhere any time. His spiritual presence and therefore grace (baraka) were likely to be particularly strong on particular occasions such as the

78 Ahmad Riza Khan, *Anwar al-Intibah fi Hill Nida Ya Rasul Allah* (The Lights of Vigilance Concerning the Permissibility of the Call 'Ya Rasul Allah'), (Karachi: Bazm-e Qasimi Barkati, 1986), p. 7. Originally written in 1304/1886–7.

79 Ibid., pp. 7–10. This hadis, and a refutation of the Ahl-e Sunnat argument just noted, were discussed in Ibn Taimiyya's *Kitab Iqtida' as-Sirat al-Mustaqim Mukhalafat Ashab al-Jahim*. See Muhamad Umar Memon, *Ibn Taimiya's Struggle Against Popular Religion* (The Hague, Paris: Mouton, 1976), pp. 308 and 371, n. 415.

80 Metcalf, *Islamic Revival*, p. 301.

celebration of his birth anniversary (majlis-e milad). It was a mark of respect to his presumed spiritual (and perhaps even physical) presence to stand up at the end of the ceremony when the salat o salam (prayer calling down Allah's blessings on him) was read.[81] No one could know whether the Prophet was physically present at such a time: the decision to be so or not was in his hands, a matter of choice (ikhtiyar) on his part.[82]

Baraka or grace was particularly associated, in the Ahl-e Sunnat view, with the graves which marked the last earthly home of exalted spiritual beings, whether it be Muhammad, the best of all created beings, or other prophets, or saints. This was because prophets and other spiritually eminent persons inhabit their graves in a state of perfect physical preservation, and lead afterlives devoted to prayer. The Ahl-Sunnat insisted therefore that graves are places worthy of the greatest respect. In a fatwa discussing the impermissibility of demolishing a grave and building some other structure over it, Ahmad Riza wrote:

> It is not permitted to any Muslim to break up and demolish another Muslim's grave and put up a building on that spot. As far as the Ahl-e Sunnat are concerned, the prophets (anbiya), saints (auliya), and martyrs (shuhada) are alive. They have sense perception (ihsas). Although an ordinary person's body decays after a few months or years of burial, the bodies of prophets, saints and martyrs don't decay. They remain in a state of perfect preservation, because Allah made it haram for any decay to take place.[83]

He quoted approvingly a work in which the prophets' afterlives were said to take place on both a material and a spiritual plane. Another writer was quoted as saying that the spirits of the saints became so powerful after their deaths that they acquired bodies (*jism*) which roamed the earth and the sky. Inside their graves, in addition, they read the namaz, and performed devotional exercises (zikr and tilawat).[84] Ahmad Riza's *Malfuzat*, likewise, contains

81 Ahmad Riza Khan, *Iqamat al-Qiyama* (Karachi: Barkati Publishers, 1986), pp. 17–29. Originally written in 1299/1881–2.

82 Ahmad Riza Khan, *Fatawa-e Rizwiyya* (Mubarakpur, Azamgarh: Sunni Dar al-Isha'at, 1981), vol. 6, p. 147. In Urdu, *tashrif awari huzur ke ikhtiyar hai.*

83 Ahmad Riza Khan, *Ihlak al-Wahhabiyyin*, p. 3.

84 Ibid., p. 4.

references to the ability of saints to be physically present in several places at the same time.[85]

If prophets and saints shared in some respects in the Prophet Muhammad's qualities, they were in no way his equal. Ahmad Riza and other Ahl-e Sunnat 'ulama' tirelessly and repeatedly taught that the Prophet Muhammad was the most exalted being of all creation, to whom Allah had gifted unimaginable powers. The reason this was so, Ahmad Riza frequently explained, was that Muhammad was Allah's beloved (*habib*). So beloved was he, in fact, that Allah had created the world for him. As we saw in Chapter VII, Muhammad was believed to have been both the first and the last prophet to be created; his ancestry was of the purest, never having been tainted by the existence of any kafirs in his genealogical history; and, finally, he transmitted and was a part of Allah's own light.

In Ahl-e Sunnat interpretation, therefore, the Prophet was a being exalted by Allah above imagining, because of Allah's love for him. Nonetheless, all the qualities he possessed had been gifted him by Allah. Herein lay the crucial difference between Allah and His Prophet: Allah was unconditional, uncreated, necessary (wajib), while the Prophet was a created, contingent (mumkin), and limited being. Ahl-e Sunnat prophetology is characterized by this duality, in which the Prophet is at once very close to Allah, such that there can be no true faith if the believer has no 'love' for him, and yet is distinct from Allah and subject to Him. All that he knows and has power over, is a gift from Allah. The issue of Muhammad's knowledge was for Ahmad Riza a perfect illustration of this central fact.

Ahmad Riza's interpretation, as presented in *Daulat al-Makkiyya*, was that there are some verses in the Qur'an denying that he had knowledge of the unseen, and others affirming that he did. It was therefore necessary to recognize that both are true, and to understand the underlying sense of the Qur'anic references.

Ahmad Riza made a distinction between two basically different kinds of knowledge:

> One is the *masdar* or source, from where knowledge emanates, and the other is dependent upon it. In the first case, knowledge is *zati*, that is, it is complete

[85] E.g., *Malfuzat*, vol. 1, p. 101.

and independent in itself, not dependent on any outside source. In the second case, it is 'ata'i, that is, 'gifted' by an outside source. Zati knowledge is exclusively Allah's; it would be absurd to claim it for anyone else. Whoever attaches such knowledge in no matter how small a degree to anyone on earth, is a mushrik. The second kind is peculiar to Allah's creatures. It is not for Allah.[86]

Further on, Ahmad Riza made the following distinctions between Allah's knowledge and that of created beings:

Allah's knowledge is intrinsic while man's is gifted; Allah's knowledge is necessary (wajib) while man's is contingent (mumkin); Allah's knowledge is pre-existent, everlasting, ancient and true, while man's knowledge is recent (hadis) since all created beings are themselves recent . . . . Allah's knowledge is uncreated, while man's knowledge is created. Allah's knowledge is omnipotent, while man's is in Allah's power and subject to Him. While Allah's knowledge has to be perpetual, man's could be extinguished. While Allah's knowledge never changes in any way, man's is changing all the time. Given these differences, there can be no suspicion of equality.[87]

Within the ambit of the limitations spelled out above, the knowledge possessed in Ahmad Riza's view by man and by the prophets was nevertheless vast. To begin with, some knowledge of the unseen is possessed even by ordinary people, Ahmad Riza argued. This was proved by the fact that Muslims believe in the resurrection, heaven, hell, and other unseen things commanded by Allah. This belief was itself a confirmation of the existence of these and other things.[88] As for the knowledge of prophets,

[it] is [but] a small part of Allah's knowledge; yet it is like an ocean beyond counting, for the prophets know, and can see, everything from the First Day (*roz-e awwal*) until the Last Day (*roz-e akhir*), all that has been and all that will be.[89]

Muhammad's knowledge, though, was even greater than that of other prophets because 'the Qur'an was revealed to him, in which

[86] Ahmad Riza Khan, *Daulat al-Makkiyya*, pp. 15, 17, 19.

[87] Ibid., pp. 45, 47.

[88] As he argued, 'Our faith is confirmation [that heaven, hell, etc.] exist, and confirmation is knowledge. If someone doesn't know the unseen, how can he confirm it? And if he can't confirm it, how can he believe in it?' Ibid., p. 39.

[89] Ibid., pp. 57, 59.

everything was explained'. Because the Qur'an was revealed bit by bit, the Prophet's knowledge kept growing over time until, at the end of the revelation, it was complete. Qur'anic verses which speak of the Prophet's lack of knowledge about something refer to the time when the revelation, and consequently his knowledge, was still incomplete. By the end of the period of revelation, the Prophet's knowledge went beyond the Last Day,

> to the tumult of the resurrection (*hashr o nashr*), the accounting (hisab o kitab) and the reward and punishment (sawab o iqab). So much so that he will see everyone arriving at their proper places, whether heaven (jannat), or hell (*dozakh*), or whatever else Allah may tell him. Undoubtedly, the Prophet knows this much, thanks to Allah, and Allah alone knows how much besides. When He has given his beloved (mustafa) so much, then it is apparent that knowledge of everything in the past and the future, which is recorded in the Tablet (*lauh-e mahfuz*) is but a part of his knowledge as a whole.[90]

The Prophet also had knowledge of people's internal mental states:

> In the view of the Ahl-e Sunnat, every single thing that exists is . . . known to the Prophet: all that exists between the sky and the earth, from East to West, everything pertaining to people's selves, their states, their movements, their moments of rest. He knows the movement and glance of the eyelid, the fears and intentions of the heart, and whatever else exists.[91]

Finally, Ahmad Riza addressed himself to the 'five things' referred to in 31:34, which were widely interpreted as known to Allah alone.[92] Ahmad Riza argued that contrary to Deobandi interpretation, these were but minor things in the vast store of the Prophet Muhammad's knowledge. With the exception of the resurrection, they were not very important in themselves, compared to the nature and attributes of Allah, hell, heaven, and such matters. They had merely been singled out by Allah because the age in which Muhammad lived was the age of the *kahins*, the soothsayers, who believed they could predict these things. Allah wanted them to know that

[90] Ibid., p. 77. See pp. 59, 72 for reference to the Qur'an being revealed to Muhammad bit by bit, and his knowledge growing accordingly.

[91] Ibid., p. 93.

[92] These were: knowledge of the Hour of resurrection, of when it would rain, of the sex of a yet unborn child, of what one would earn on the morrow, and of the land where one would die.

without His telling someone about the 'hidden' (al-ghaib), none could know it. The Prophet was favoured with knowledge of these things, including the Hour, but was commanded not to reveal it.[93]

All this, Ahmad Riza wrote in a variety of contexts, was gifted to Muhammad by Allah because of Allah's love for him. This concept of the love between Allah and the Prophet as the ultimate cause for creation has a distinctly sufi flavour. So does the argument that Muhammad, being made of light, had no shadow. It is important, therefore, to note that such arguments were defended in Ahmad Riza's writings largely, indeed overwhelmingly, by citation of works of hadis and fiqh.[94] Asked whether Muhammad had a shadow, for instance, Ahmad Riza replied:

> Undoubtedly the Prophet did not have a shadow. This is clear from hadis, from the words of the 'ulama', of the ai'ma [founders of the four main Sunni law schools], and *fuzala* (learned men) . . . 'Allama Ibn-e Saba', Imam Qazi 'Iyaz, Imam 'Arif Bi'llah, . . . 'Allama Jalal al-Din Suyuti, Imam Ibn-e Jauzi, . . . Imam Ahmad bin Muhammad Qastallani, Muhammad Zarqani Maliki, Shaikh Muhaqqiq Dehlawi, Shaikh Mujaddid-e Alf-e Sani, . . . Shah 'Abd ul-'Aziz Dehlawi, etc. Today's unsound claimants ['Wahhabis'] claim to be their pupils, but they don't understand the words of the masters.[95]

Ahmad Riza cited numerous hadis illustrating the luminous quality of Muhammad's face and body, including accounts of the light that was shed on cities far and wide at his birth. In another fatwa,

[93] *Daulat al-Makkiyya*, pp. 119–35, 175–91.

[94] This is not to say, however, that sufi sources are entirely absent. Among sufi authors encountered in Ahmad Riza's works are Shaikh Ahmad Sirhindi ('Mujaddid-e Alf-e Sani'), and al-Ghazzali, Sirhindi being comparatively frequent.

[95] Ahmad Riza Khan, *Nafy al-Fay' 'Amman Anara bi-Nurihi Kulla Shay'* (Negation of the Shadow from him who Illuminated Everything by his Light), in *Majmua'-e Rasa'il: Mas'ala Nur aur Saya*, pp. 51–2.

I have not been able to identify all the writers mentioned in this quotation here. Some of them are: Qazi 'Iyaz (d. 1149), a Maliki theologian and judge in Ceuta and Granada, whose *Kitab al-Shifa'* is one of the most frequently used handbooks on the Prophet; Jalal al-Din al-Suyuti (d. 1505), scholar of Mamluk Egypt; Ibn al-Jawzi (d. 1256), famous preacher and historian in Damascus; al-Qastallani (d. 1517), authority on tradition and theology in Cairo; 'Abd ul-Haqq Dehlawi (d. 1642), authority on hadis in Mughal India; Shaikh Ahmad Sirhindi (d. 1624), the Naqshbandi shaikh who was imprisoned by Emperor Jahangir for heresy; and Shah 'Abd ul-'Aziz Dehlawi (d. 1824), Shah Wali Ullah's eldest son and well-known hadis scholar.

al-Suyuti was cited to the effect that flies did not settle on the Prophet's body, Fakhr al-Din al-Razi was cited as saying that mosquitoes didn't suck his blood, and al-Suyuti, again, was reported to have written that once the Prophet had ridden on an animal, that animal never aged any further. One hadis, acknowledged to be weak but nevertheless accepted, was quoted to prove that the Prophet could see in the dark.[96]

Such views were by no means new, or unknown at the time. As Schimmel indicates, there was a whole genre of popular literature based on hadis in Sindhi, among other languages, the object of which was to venerate the Prophet down to the smallest details of his life.[97] Ahmad Riza himself contributed to this *shama'il* and faza'il literature, in praise of the Prophet's lofty qualities and outward beauty, with his Urdu poems. In addition, it was his distinctive contribution to give this existing popular veneration authority by defending such an image of the Prophet in erudite fatawa, and making it acceptable to some sections of the 'ulama'.

In short, Ahl-e Sunnat prophetology inclined toward a view of Muhammad as a miraculous, extra-human being the like of whom could not be equalled, nor imagined. Allah had created an unparallelled individual in Muhammad, due to His love for him. There could never, even hypothetically, be another like Muhammad.

The crowning event in Muhammad's life, which bore witness to his unique place in Allah's sight, was Allah's revelation of Himself to Muhammad on the occasion of the mi'raj or night ascension. Ahmad Riza wrote that this event was both spiritual and physical (*ruh ma'a al-jasad*).[98] As he put it in a memorable verse:

How could anything whatsoever be hidden from you
When Khuda Himself did not conceal Himself from you
On you be thousands of blessings![99]

[96] Ibid., pp. 62–5; Ahmad Riza Khan, *Qamar al-Tamam fi Nafi al-Zill 'an Sayyid al-Anam* (The Full Moon of Denial of a Shadow for the Leader of Mankind), pp. 79–84. Acknowledging that some of the hadis cited were weak, Ahmad Riza challenged would-be opponents of these views to produce proof bearing on a contrary position.

[97] Schimmel, *And Muhammad Is His Messenger*, pp. 32–5.

[98] *Malfuzat*, vol. 4, p. 23; vol. 3, p. 51. Also see *Fatawa-e Rizwiyya*, vol. 6, p. 170.

[99] Ahmad Riza Khan, *Hada'iq-e Bakhshish* (Karachi: Medina Publishing Company,

This was the ultimate act of love, not given even to the angel Gabriel.

Schimmel writes that the stories of Muhammad's miracles and accounts of his natural beauty have been recounted by generations of Muslims, who find 'nothing . . . wonderful and beautiful enough to give an adequate impression of the personality of the beloved Prophet'.[100] So it was with Ahmad Riza, who called himself 'Abd al-Mustafa and taught that faith and belief could only be true if it placed devotion to the Prophet above all human ties.

Conclusion

Friedmann, in his study of Ahmadi religious thought, has shown the difficulty experienced by certain Muslim thinkers with the dogma of khatam al-nubuwwa, cessation of prophecy. To Ibn al-'Arabi, he writes, 'the idea implies that the link between man and the object of his worship has been put asunder; this is the most bitter experience to which a devout Muslim can be subjected'.[101] Ibn al-'Arabi found compensation for the spiritual loss represented by the Prophet's death in the transmission of Qur'an and hadis scholarship, and in the idea that prophecy never ceases, though it takes on new forms. As Friedmann explains, Ahmadi prophetology is indebted to Ibn al-'Arabi's concepts of prophecy.

While the Ahl-e Sunnat denied, of course, the possibility that there could be any prophet after Muhammad (even one with a mission to enforce the law instituted by Muhammad), in a sense they too have grappled with the problem of the spiritual loss to the Muslim community caused by the Prophet's death. Their answer is that Muhammad continues to 'be', that he continues to intervene in human affairs, and to guide those who seek to follow him.

n.d.), p. 425. The reference to God revealing Himself to the Prophet is of course to Muhammad's night ascension. (I was also told orally by Maulana Yasin Akhtar Misbahi, a contemporary authority on the Ahl-e Sunnat, that there are hadis in which it is recorded that when the Prophet arrived at Allah's threshold, he saw the other prophets who had preceded him seated around Allah's throne, and taught them the namaz. This would not have been possible, Maulana Yasin Akhtar pointed out, if they had not had bodies.)

100 Schimmel, *And Muhammad Is His Messenger*, p. 76.

101 Friedmann, *Prophecy Continuous*, p. 72.

Muhammad's intercessionary role, therefore, is crucial. Without it, the community would be thought to be bereft. Ahmad Riza's denial of the belief that Muhammad intercedes for his community only on the day of the resurrection confirms this. Prophetic intercession is a constant process: ultimately, it is man's link with Allah. The hierarchy of saints, the appearance of the mujaddid (renewer) once in a hundred years, and the presence of 'ulama' who keep the Prophet's sunna alive—all these are further links in the 'rope of God'.

The concept of hierarchy is inseparable from this view of the Prophet Muhammad and other spiritually exalted persons. The measure is 'closeness to Allah': the Prophet Muhammad, Allah's beloved who saw Him face to face and for whose sake Allah created the world, is of course the closest to Him. Then follow the ghaus, pivot of the world, the auliya or saints, and ultimately the 'ulama'. Although much further from Him, the latter are securely linked as long as they follow the Prophet. The believer's proper response, in turn, is to humbly respect and obey, which means that he or she should strive at all times to follow the Prophet's sunna, as enunciated by the 'ulama'.

But if obedience is called for, it is loving obedience. All through his writings, and in the living out of his own life, Ahmad Riza stressed both respect and love for the Prophet to an equal degree. For the Prophet, like Allah Himself, is ultimately a source of forgiveness. Ahmad Riza frequently pointed out to his opponents that if they repented their lack of respect and love for the Prophet, all would be forgiven and they could start out afresh with a clean slate. Thus the notions of hierarchy and love, seemingly contradictory, co-exist harmoniously in Ahl-e Sunnat prophetology, reinforcing one another to create an attitude of religious devotion that is quite consistent.

For the Ahl-e Sunnat, it followed that if one loved the Prophet, one must hate his enemies and do all one could to rebut them. Ahmad Riza regarded it as one of his most important tasks as an 'alim to devote every effort in this direction. He once said that he was happy that people attacked his writings as frequently as they did because in the process they forgot to denigrate Allah and the Prophet.[102] Consequently, Ahl-e Sunnat leaders wrote voluminous

[102] *Malfuzat*, vol. 2, p. 50.

fatawa, risalas, poetry, and posters against the perceived insults, misinterpretations, or false beliefs of these and other 'enemies of the Prophet'. Thanks to the easy availability of printing presses in north India at the time, the message got around quickly and loudly that the Prophet was being insulted by Deobandis, 'Wahhabis', and others, and that the Prophet's sunna, correctly interpreted, indicated a different course of action. Ahl-e Sunnat writings, guided by Ahmad Riza, were marked by a remarkable tone of certainty throughout, regardless of which group of Muslims was being rebutted.

The literary sources for Ahl-e Sunnat prophetology, as we have seen, were interpretation of Qur'an, hadis, and fiqh works for the most part. In hadis, weak traditions were not rejected if they elevated the Prophet's stature, for nothing that did this was considered unacceptable, and authorities could be cited in their defence just as easily as they could for rejecting them. In addition, there was a large corpus of medieval fiqh scholarship to draw on, which Ahmad Riza did with skill.

These arguments mirrored popular conceptions of the Prophet as reflected in poetry, oral tradition and legend throughout the Islamic world. As examined in this study, the Ahl-e Sunnat also had a strong sufi dimension, in affiliation particularly with the Qadiriyya order. Many of the leading lights of the Ahl-e Sunnat leadership in the late nineteenth and early twentieth centuries were caretakers of sufi shrines, and belonged to a world in which the intercessionary power of saints and family ancestors was taken for granted. Ahmad Riza's conceptions about the Prophet's role as mediator with Allah and his miraculous achievements were in line with sufi concepts of spiritual authority and power.

Finally, it must be noted that the deep-rooted sense of hierarchy implicit in Ahl-e Sunnat prophetology, as well as the underlying spirit of devotion noted above, were in harmony with social and religious conceptions held by South Asians who were not Muslim. Ahl-e Sunnat sources seldom refer to the Hindus amidst whom they lived, and when they do, the purpose is to distance themselves from the beliefs and customs of these 'polytheists'. This is as one would expect from the followers of a movement which wanted to stress its universalistic Sunni roots and ties to the umma (religious community) beyond South Asia. Nevertheless, it would not be out of place, nor in contradiction of the larger Islamic roots of the Ahl-e Sunnat movement, to note that the simultaneous emphasis on hierarchy and intimacy (religious 'love') is not alien to South Asian (that is to say, chiefly Hindu) religious conceptions as expressed in, for instance, the devotionalism of *bhakti* saints or in Hindu religious poetry.

There was, one might say, a similarity of 'religious styles' between aspects of Ahl-e Sunnat belief and ritual and that of other South Asian religious traditions which made the Ahl-e Sunnat movement seem so distinctly subcontinental. Indirectly, the Ahl-e Sunnat literature itself indicates an awareness of this, though the suggestion is rejected because it comes from hostile detractors. Thus, the Deobandis compared the rituals surrounding the Prophet's birth anniversary (majlis-e milad) to Hindu celebrations of the birth of Lord Krishna ('Kanhaiyya'). Muhammad Isma'il had likewise compared Muslim devotions and ritual surrounding saints' tombs with Hindu idol worship. The point here is not that the Ahl-e Sunnat 'resembled' Hindus in any way—they certainly denied any such similarity—but that the spirit of reverential devotion with which they regarded the Prophet, their manner of expressing this love through poetry, and their use of rose water, incense and so on on ritual occasions, would have been familiar and comprehensible to the Hindus among whom they lived.

The Ahl-e Sunnat themselves, however, were no more compromising toward their Hindu neighbours than they were toward their fellow Muslims. In the 1920s, the focus of debate began to shift away from internal questions toward definition of boundaries with non-Muslims. At first there was concern over the conversion of Muslims to Hinduism, resulting from the Shuddhi movement launched by the Arya Samaj. But soon political questions loomed: should Muslims participate with Hindus in the Khilafat movement? And what should be their attitude to the British Indian government? In the chapters ahead, I turn to Ahl-e Sunnat debate and perspective on these issues.

Chapter IX

Perspectives on the Khilafat, Hijrat and Non-Cooperation Movements

Indian Muslims were deeply affected by political events after 1910. These were years of enormous political change in the world, and in British India specifically. Abroad, the Ottoman empire collapsed after World War I, various European nations claiming parts of its territory. In India, the nationalist movement gained momentum in reaction to unpopular British policies, becoming more broadbased particularly after Gandhi's return from South Africa. In 1919–20, Muslims took their stand on the Khilafat and Hijrat movements.

Despite the crowded political landscape of the period, from the Indian Muslim perspective the issues at stake were at bottom quite small in number. One problem, called into question after decades of acceptance of the status quo, was the religious status of India under British rule. The early twentieth century saw a revival of debate among the 'ulama' on whether British India was dar al-harb (the land of war) or dar al-islam (the land of Islam, and of peace). Although the Khilafat movement of 1919–20 arose out of a different concern—the role and significance to twentieth-century Muslims in the subcontinent of a pan-Islamic caliph—the two questions were, at least to some Indian Muslims, related. The connection is apparent from the fact that the Hijrat movement of 1920, in the course of which thousands of Indian Muslims emigrated to Afghanistan, followed immediately on the heels of the Khilafat movement. Evidently some 'ulama', looking upon British India as dar al-harb at this time, gave the call for migration (hijra) in accordance with classical Islāmic theory and in pursuance of the historical precedent of the Prophet's migration from Mecca to Medina.

A third issue, also related to the status of British India and to the structure of Muslim political relations, was what kind of relationship Indian Muslims should seek with Hindus. While for some 'ulama' the current political situation seemed to call for Muslims joining with Hindus in common cause against the British, others looked upon Hindus as *harbis* (those with whom one was at war), co-operation with whom could have no legal Islamic (shar'i) sanction. Both sides, it should be said, argued as they did on the basis of shari'a and the historical model of the Prophet's example.

In what follows, I shall try to elucidate Ahl-e Sunnat views on the issues outlined above, seeking connections to the extent possible between these and the more theologically oriented debates dealt with earlier in this study. Ahmad Riza's writings will again be my main guide, though I shall also note dissenting voices within Ahl-e Sunnat circles. Ahmad Riza's death in October 1921 (Safar 1340) occurred soon after the collapse of the Hijrat movement (in 1920). The Khilafat movement collapsed in 1923–4. The disarray within the Indian Muslim political leadership that followed upon these events coincided with a period of profound change in the Ahl-e Sunnat movement, which split into opposing camps in the 1930s and 1940s under new leadership. These events and the debates that they generated form part of a new phase in the movement's history, dealt with briefly in the Epilogue.

Debate on the Religious Status of British India

The ambivalence of the 'ulama' in the United Provinces toward the British, across the entire 'reformist' spectrum, was illustrated in the course of the nineteenth century by the debate that had started in the early 1800s about whether British India was dar al-harb or dar al-islam. The question was raised not once but several times. Throughout the nineteenth century, most 'ulama' appear to have agreed, albeit with reservations, that British India was dar al-islam.

The debate began immediately after the British conquered Delhi from the Marathas in 1803 (in the Third Maratha War). Shah 'Abd ul-'Aziz Dehlawi wrote a fatwa, the first on the subject as far as one can tell, that has been widely interpreted as an unequivocal declaration of British India as dar al-harb, implying a call for jihad or hijrat.[1] According to this interpretation, the jihad movement led by Sayyid Ahmad Barelwi against the Panjab kingdom of Ranjit Singh was a direct outcome of Shah 'Abd ul-'Aziz's earlier fatwa.[2]

However, several scholars have challenged this interpretation.[3] Mushir ul-Haqq's detailed analysis of Shah 'Abd ul-'Aziz's fatawa on this issue was perhaps the first to do so.[4] He argues that although in his 1803 fatwa Shah 'Abd ul-'Aziz did say that British India was dar al-harb, this was not intended as a call for either jihad or hijrat. There was no move in either of these directions after the issuing of this fatwa, nor any significant discussion in the literature of these courses of action.[5] Indeed, Shah 'Abd ul-'Aziz defended his decision not to emigrate from British India, and advised 'Abd ul-Hayy, his

[1] See, e.g., M. Mujeeb, *The Indian Muslims* (Lahore: Mustafa Waheed, n.d.), pp. 390–1; I. H. Qureshi, *The Muslim Community of the Indo-Pakistan Subcontinent* (Karachi: Ma'aref, 1977), pp. 220–3. Which option is chosen (jihad or hijrat) depends on the likelihood of success against the opponent. In the classical theory, jihad may only be undertaken if it is deemed likely to succeed. A noteworthy study of the doctrine of jihad is in Rudolph Peters, *Islam and Colonialism: The Doctrine of Jihad in Modern History* (The Hague: Mouton, 1979), particularly Chapter 2.

[2] Ibid. For example, Qureshi writes (p. 223): 'It seems legitimate to draw . . . the conclusion that Shah 'Abd ul-'Aziz had played an important role in preparing the Saiyid for the leadership of the new [jihad] movement'. Aziz Ahmad, *Studies in Islamic Culture in the Indian Environment* (Oxford: Clarendon Press, 1969), p. 215, is not as categorical in making this connection, but nevertheless writes that Shah 'Abd ul-'Aziz 'encouraged Muslims to migrate to other Muslim lands'.

[3] Among them: Pearson, 'Islamic Reform', p. 97; Metcalf, *Islamic Revival*, pp. 46, 50–1; Friedmann, *Prophecy Continuous*, p. 169. All these interpretations accept the arguments of Mushir ul-Haqq, discussed below.

[4] Mushir ul-Haqq, 'Unniswin Sadi ke Hindustan ki Hai'at Shar'i: Shah 'Abd ul-'Aziz ke Fatawa-e Dar al-Harb ka Ek 'Ilmi Tajzi'a' (The Shar'i Condition of Nineteenth-Century India: A Scholarly Examination of Shah 'Abd ul-'Aziz's Fatawa [on the issue of] Dar al-Harb), *Burhan*, 63:4 (October 1969), 221–44.

[5] Ibid., p. 222, and passim. Mushir ul-Haqq points out that this fatwa was cited by early twentieth-century Muslim nationalists in defence of their own struggle against the British. It suited them, according to him, to make the argument that Shah 'Abd ul-'Aziz's fatwa proved that jihad against the British was a shar'i duty.

nephew and son-in-law, to accept an offer of employment by the East India Company.[6]

Mushir ul-Haqq demonstrates convincingly that Shah 'Abd ul-'Aziz's fatawa must be viewed in the context of the economic conditions of Muslims of the time, not political considerations. He argues that the controversial 1803 fatwa had been written in response to a set of questions about the shar'i injunction relating to the giving and taking of interest (*sud*, Ar. *riba*) on loans in a land that had been adjudged to be dar al-harb.[7] He believes that Shah 'Abd ul-'Aziz, well aware of the economic problems and contraints of his fellow Muslims, issued a fatwa that rendered their economic activities legally acceptable, while refraining from drawing any political implications therefrom.[8] If this interpretation of Shah 'Abd ul-'Aziz's fatwa is correct, it is unlikely that he would have looked upon the jihad movement of the Mujahidin favourably.[9] As he died in 1824, shortly after Sayyid Ahmad and his followers returned from hajj prior to launching their jihad, he may not have been in sufficiently fit condition to pass judgment on the issue.[10]

In Bengal, another movement arose under the leadership of Haji Shari'at Ullah (d. 1840), which interpreted British occupation of

[6] Ibid., pp. 235, 237.

[7] In view of Muslims' right to engage in interest-bearing loans in such a situation, it was important for those Muslims already weighed down by debt, Mushir ul-Haqq argues, to know whether their new subjection to the British had rendered their land a dar al-harb. If so, they could draw some comfort in the knowledge that their involvement in interest-paying loans, forbidden in a dar al-islam but entered into by them with other Muslims nevertheless (a practice regarded particularly negatively in a dar al-islam), due to adverse circumstances, now had shar'i sanction. In short, the question showed an interest in Muslim 'rights' rather than 'duties' in the new situation. Ibid., pp. 228, 231–3.

[8] Barbara Metcalf summarizes the position cogently: 'Abdu'l-'Aziz thus appears to have wanted Muslims to behave politically as if the situation were *daru'l-islam*, for he gave no call to military action, yet he wanted them to recognize that the organization of the state was no longer in Muslim hands'. Metcalf, *Islamic Revival*, p. 51.

[9] Metcalf suggests that Shah 'Abd ul-'Aziz may have been opposed to the jihad. See ibid., p. 55.

[10] For details on the jihad, see Pearson, 'Islamic Reform', pp. 49–53. Apparently, despite his initiation of the jihad movement, Sayyid Ahmad Barelwi 'indicated that British territory was not *dar al-harb* but was temporarily occupied and needed to be liberated'. Ibid., p. 49, n. 3. Also see Peters, *Islam and Colonialism*, pp. 44–9.

India as transformation of a dar al-islam into a dar al-harb.[11] Returning to Bengal in 1821 after more than twenty years in the Haramain, Haji Shari'at Ullah forbade the performance of the jum'a (Friday congregational) prayer and the 'id (holiday) prayers in the absence of duly functioning qazis and amirs (governors) in towns and villages. In a situation of extreme economic distress caused by the destruction of local industry by indigo planters and others, he concentrated his efforts on religious reform and economic uplift among Bengal peasants, rather than a call for jihad.[12]

The popular uprising of 1857 was the last occasion in the nineteenth century when the banner of jihad was raised.[13] In the aftermath of this cataclysmic event, W. W. Hunter's book *The Indian Mussalmans: Are They Bound in Conscience to Rebel Against the Queen?* (published in 1871) provoked an outpouring against his thesis that 'the fanatical masses' of Muslim peasants and artisans were bound by their faith to rebel against British rule.[14] Muslim thinkers such as Maulawi Karamat 'Ali of Jaunpur (1800–73), Sir Sayyid Ahmad Khan (1817–98), Chiragh 'Ali (1844–95), Maulawi Nazir Ahmad (1833–1912), and others, responded with counterarguments of their own. Some, such as Karamat 'Ali, argued that British India was dar al-islam because 'the three conditions laid down by Abu Hanifa for the conversion of a dar al-islam into a dar al-harb were not satisfied'.[15] The fact that Muslim law was in force in matters such as

[11] Peter Hardy, *The Muslims of British India* (Cambridge: Cambridge University Press, 1972), pp. 55–7. The most comprehensive study of the Fara'izi movement is Muin-ud-din Ahmad Khan, *History of the Fara'idi Movement in Bengal (1818–1906)* (Karachi: Pakistan Historical Society, 1965).

[12] Hardy, *Muslims of British India,* pp. 55–7.

[13] See, e.g., Eric Stokes, *The Peasant Armed: The Indian Rebellion of 1857*, ed. C. A. Bayly (Oxford: Clarendon Press, 1986), pp. 86–7. Although Bahadur Shah Zafar, the Mughal Emperor, refused to turn 'the rebellion into a predominantly Islamic crusade' against 'white *kaffir* rule', some local leaders such as Bakht Khan saw the fight as a jihad and raised local support on that basis. Another well-known figure, Rahmat Allah Kairanawi (1818–90), 'endorsed the jihad against English rule and escaped to Mecca with a price on his head following the collapse of the Mutiny'. Martin Kramer, *Islam Assembled: The Advent of the Muslim Congresses* (New York: Columbia University Press, 1986), p. 5.

[14] For a discussion of Hunter's book, see Lelyveld, *Aligarh's First Generation,* pp. 10–12.

[15] Hardy, *Muslims of British India*, p. 111. The three conditions were: '(1) the law of the

marriage, divorce, and inheritance, and that Muslims enjoyed complete freedom of worship, Karamat 'Ali said, made it unlawful to declare British India to be dar al-harb. Others, including Sir Sayyid Ahmad Khan and Chiragh 'Ali, argued that British India was neither dar al-Islam nor dar al-harb 'but something of both' (in Sir Sayyid's words), or 'simply British India' (in Chiragh 'Ali's).[16]

It is in this context of post-1857 debates about the shar'i status of British India amid increasing changes under colonial rule, that fatawa on the dar al-harb question by north Indian 'ulama such as Ahmad Riza must be seen. Asked in 1880–81 whether British India was dar al-harb or dar al-Islam, and whether the Jews and Christians of the time should be regarded as kitabi ([people] of the book), Ahmad Riza's reply (to the first question) was essentially in agreement with the views of Karamat 'Ali and others, who had maintained that there was no basis in Hanafi law for declaring British India to be dar al-harb.[17] As to the second question, he cited conflicting opinions from fiqh literature on whether belief that Jesus was God rendered a person a mushrik (polytheist) and thus deprived him or her of the privileged status of a kitabi; then advised that in view of the lack of consensus it was best for a Muslim not to eat meat slaughtered by a Jew or Christian, or marry among them.[18]

On the dar al-islam issue, Ahmad Riza cited disagreement within the Hanafi school on whether fulfillment of all three conditions was required for a dar al-islam to become dar al-harb, or whether

---

unbelievers replaces that of Islam; (2) the country in question directly adjoins the dar al-harb; (3) Muslims and their non-Muslim *dhimmis* no longer enjoy any protection there. The first of these conditions is the most important'. A. Abel, 'Dar al-Harb', in *EI2.* There is disagreement within the Hanafi school as to whether all three conditions have to be met to render a place dar al-harb, or whether the existence of even one of these conditions is sufficient to do so.

[16] Hardy, *Muslims of British India*, pp. 112–13.

[17] Ahmad Riza Khan, *I'lam al-A'lam bi-anna Hindustan Dar al-Islam* (Notification of the Notables that Hindustan is Dar al-Islam), (Bareilly: Hasani Press, 1306/1888–89), 20 pp. Reprinted in *Do Ahamm Fatwe* (Lahore: Maktaba Qadiriyya, 1977).

[18] This opinion was significant in light of the later charge (on which, see below) that Ahmad Riza had pro-British sympathies. His defenders never cited this part of the fatwa, however.

fulfillment of the first alone was sufficient to do so.[19] His own judgment was as follows:

In Hindustan . . . Muslims are free to openly (*'ala al-a'lan*) observe the two 'ids, the azan [call to prayer], iqamat [standing up at start of the prayer], *namaz ba-jama'at* [congregational prayer] . . . which are the signs of the shari'a, without opposition. Also the fara'iz [religious duties], nikah [marriage ceremony], *raza'* [fosterage], . . . There are many such matters among Muslims . . . on which . . . the British government also finds it necessary to seek fatawa from the 'ulama' and act accordingly, whether they [the rulers] be Zoroastrian or Christian . . . . In short, there is no doubt that Hindustan is dar al-islam.[20]

In his judgment, the first condition was the decisive one. Because Muslims were free to fulfill their religious duties, and to conduct their personal lives in accordance with Muslim law, British India was dar al-islam. Ahmad Riza charged that anyone who ruled differently was doing so merely in order to permit Muslims to engage in interest-bearing debt (an analysis, one might note in passing, substantially similar to Mushir ul-Haqq's interpretation of Shah 'Abd ul-'Aziz's fatwa of 1803). They had no intention of either waging jihad, or doing hijrat, Ahmad Riza said, as they ought to do if they were sincere in holding India to be dar al-harb.[21]

The opinion that British India was dar al-islam was, as noted above, in agreement with the generally prevailing view at this time among leading Muslim thinkers. The same judgment was delivered by Deobandi 'ulama' such as Ashraf 'Ali Thanawi and Rashid Ahmad Gangohi,[22] and by Maulana 'Abd ul-Hayy of Firangi

[19] On these three conditions, see note 15 above.

[20] Ahmad Riza Khan, *I'lam al-A'lam*, p. 2.

[21] This may or may not have been a charge against a hypothetical opinion contrary to Ahmad Riza's. The only 'alim who expressed a contrary opinion at this time was Muhammad Qasim Nanautawi, of Deoband, who, according to Ashraf 'Ali Thanawi, 'gave preference to (*tarjih*) [British India being] dar al-harb'. *Do Ahamm Fatwe*, p. 55.

[22] See *Do Ahamm Fatwe*, pp. 38–55 for Ashraf 'Ali's fatwa, entitled *Tahzir al-Ikhwan* (Warning to [our] Brothers). Unlike the istifta (question) addressed to Ahmad Riza, in which the question about British India's religious status was followed by questions about the status of Jews and Christians, and whether Shi'is were innovators (mubtadi') or not, the questions asked of Ashraf 'Ali related to the use of bank promissory notes, and the giving and taking of interest. Ashraf 'Ali said that although there was disagreement within the Hanafi school as to the precise conditions under which a dar al-islam becomes

Mahal, Lucknow.[23]

However, after about 1910 the political climate in north India changed dramatically from that of the 1880s, turning progressively anti-British. Although it would be an oversimplification of a complex political process to assign a single date or event to this ongoing change, the partition of Bengal in 1905 is generally acknowledged to have been a significant turning point for both Hindus and Muslims.[24] For Muslims, events in the international arena were equally important in changing their attitude: their single greatest cause for discontent was the European dismemberment of the Ottoman empire, a process that began in the last decades of the nineteenth century, and was renewed in 1911–12.[25] By 1912–13, influential Urdu journals such as *Al-Hilal* owned by Abu'l Kalam Azad (1888–1958) and English-language papers such as Maulana Muhammad 'Ali's (1878–1931) *Comrade* were advocating helping the Turks. The British rightly interpreted these and other signs of pro-Ottoman feeling as evidence of a growing pan-Islamic movement.[26]

It was in this climate of growing Muslim opposition to the British

---

dar al-harb, he considered it impermissible to give or take interest-bearing loans in India, even from Hindus who had been *zimmis* (people for whose security one was responsible, *zimme-dar*) since Mughal times. Ibid., p. 45. Gangohi's reply also appears to clearly imply that British India was dar al-islam. Judging by this fatwa, Hardy's statement that Rashid Ahmad Gangohi 'refused to give a clear answer when bluntly asked for a *fatwa*' seems mistaken. See Hardy, *Muslims of British India*, pp. 115, 174.

23 Hardy, *Muslims of British India*, p. 114. On p. 174, however, Hardy suggests that 'Abd ul-Hayy left it to his audience to decide whether British India was dar al-harb or dar al-islam. According to Hardy, he merely set out Abu Hanifa's conditions in his fatwa, but did not address the question of whether those conditions obtained in India.

24 Though, for Muslims, it was the 1911 revocation of the partition, not the 1905 act of partition, that they objected to. For a general survey of the political events of early twentieth-century British India, see, e.g., Stanley Wolpert, *A New History of India* (New York: Oxford University Press, 1982), 2nd ed., Chapters 19–21. For a specifically Muslim perspective on these events, see Hardy, particularly Chapters 6–7.

25 See Hardy, *Muslims of British India*, pp. 176, 182.

26 Ibid., pp. 175, 177. For British fears of a pan-Islamic movement in Southeast Asia, see Anthony Reid, 'Nineteenth-Century Pan-Islam in Indonesia and Malaysia', *Journal of Asian Studies*, XXVI:2 (1967), 267–83. For discussion of the pan-Islamic character of the Khilafat movement, see below.

Indian government that in 1914 the azan debate was sparked off by Ahmad Riza's attempt to change an aspect of the ritual practice of the congregational prayer. As noted in Chapter VI above, by 1916 the debate had become unusually acrimonious and public when a follower of Maulana 'Abd ul-Muqtadir Badayuni charged Ahmad Riza with libel. Although Ahmad Riza was vindicated by the court in 1917, the events surrounding the case reveal important fissures within the Ahl-e Sunnat movement. It is significant that 'Abd ul-Majid Badayuni,[27] a close disciple of 'Abd ul-Muqtadir Badayuni, opposed Ahmad Riza's position in court despite his family's long-standing friendship with Ahmad Riza and his family. Following Benedict Anderson's analysis, one might say that by 1916–17 a younger generation of Ahl-e Sunnat leaders was emerging, shaped by the availability of 'print capitalism' and the development of mass communications generally. This leadership no longer defined the 'religious' realm as an internal, apolitical one, but as one which was infused with political meaning, which meaning could appropriately be negotiated in a public arena (such as a British Indian courtroom). Thus, while Ahmad Riza defined issues such as the azan debate in narrowly 'religious' terms (which were private and outside the purview of the state), by 1916 Ahl-e Sunnat leaders such as 'Abd ul-Majid were enlarging the scope of such issues. This also led 'Abd ul-Majid into a range of political activities and alliances on the wider stage of Indian Muslim concerns related to the Khilafat movement.

In 1919, a large number of 'ulama' lent their support to leaders such as Azad and Muhammad 'Ali in creating an organization called the Jam'iyyat al-'Ulama'-e Hind. Its declared purposes were:

> to protect the Hijaz and the Arabian peninsula [from non-Muslim encroachment] and to defend Islamic nationality (qaumiyyat) from all ills; to obtain and protect the religious and patriotic (*watani*, i.e. relating to their homeland India) rights and interests of Muslims; to bring the 'ulama together at one centre; to

[27] Though earlier associated with the Ahl-e Sunnat leadership, 'Abd ul-Majid's (1886/7-1931) career represents a clear break from the path advocated by Ahmad Riza and other Ahl-e Sunnat leaders. Following the leadership of his pir, Shah 'Abd ul-Muqtadir Badayuni (1866/7–1915/16), he played a leading role in the Khilafat movement and Congress politics. See Mahmud Ahmad Qadiri, *Tazkira-e 'Ulama'-e Ahl-e Sunnat* (Muzaffarpur, Bihar: Khanqah-e Qadiriyya Ashrafiyya, 1391/1971), pp. 146–9.

organize the Muslim community (millat) on a shari'a footing and to establish shari'a courts; to bring about [the] complete freedom of the country (mulk) in accordance with shari'a objectives; to seek the religious, educational, moral, social and economic welfare of Muslims and to propagate Islam inside India so far as they are able in terms of Islam; to strengthen the bonds of brotherhood and unity with the Muslims of other lands; and to establish in conformity with the mandates of the shari'a co-operative and comradely relations with their non-Muslim brothers living in their common homeland (watan).[28]

Among the leaders of this new organization were Maulanas 'Abd ul-Bari Firangi Mahali, Abu'l Kalam Azad, 'Abd ul-Majid Badayuni, and Shabbir Ahmad 'Usmani of Deoband. In outlining the ambitious list of objectives above—particularly in the declaration that they would seek to bring about the complete freedom of the country—the 'ulama' of the Jam'iyyat sent out a clear signal that they were no longer inclined to acquiesce in British rule or issue fatawa declaring British India to be dar al-islam. Indeed, they were prepared, as their declaration of objectives shows, to co-operate with non-Muslims in this endeavour.

The names of Ahmad Riza and other important leaders of the Ahl-e Sunnat movement, such as Na'im ud-Din Muradabadi and Muhammad Miyan Aulad-e Rasul Marahrawi, were however conspicuously absent from the list of supporters of the Jam'iyyat al-'Ulama'.[29] In the late summer of 1920, some leaders of the Jam'iyyat (notably Maulanas 'Abd ul-Bari Firangi Mahali and Abu'l Kalam Azad) launched the Hijrat movement. Shortly thereafter, in October 1920, a fatwa by Ahmad Riza was published in *Dabdaba-e Sikandari*, Rampur, on the dar al-islam/dar al-harb issue.[30] It was the same

[28] Peter Hardy, *Partners in Freedom—and True Muslims: The Political Thought of Some Muslim Scholars in British India 1912–1947* (Lund: Scandinavian Institute of Asian Studies, 1971), pp. 31–2.

[29] Other well-known 'ulama' also stood apart, among them Ashraf 'Ali Thanawi of Deoband. After 1921, however, the Jam'iyyat appears to have come under Deobandi domination. See Gail Minault, *The Khilafat Movement: Religious Symbolism and Political Mobilization in India* (New York: Columbia University Press, 1982), p. 80; Thursby, *Hindu–Muslim Relations in British India,* p. 154.

[30] *Dabdaba-e Sikandari*, 57:5 (October 18, 1920), 4–6. Only the first part of the fatwa, dealing specifically with the question as to whether British India was dar al-harb or dar al-islam, was published.

fatwa that had been written in 1880–81. It made clear his refusal to declare British India dar al-harb, and his condemnation of the Hijrat movement.

The publication of this fatwa evidently raised an outcry among fellow Muslims, for in January 1921 the *Dabdaba-e Sikandari* published a lengthy rebuttal of charges that Ahmad Riza had pro-British sympathies.[31] The paper reported that Ahmad Riza had been accused (possibly by the Jam'iyyat's United Provinces wing[32]) of opposing assistance to the Ottoman sultan, and of not considering it necessary to protect the holy places (Mecca and Medina) from European occupation. Moreover, it was said that he had met the Lieutenant-Governor of the United Provinces (Sir James Meston) while on retreat in the hill station of Naini Tal,[33] that he wrote fatawa on lines pleasing to the government, and that he was in its pay. The article reported a conversation between Ahmad Riza, Maulana Muhammad Miyan of Marahra and one Ahmad Mukhtar Siddiqi of Bombay, in which Ahmad Riza verbally answered each charge.

Debate on How Best to Help the Turks, 1912–1920

Several scholars of twentieth-century subcontinental history have noted the important effect that loss of territory by the Ottoman empire to European countries such as Britain, France, and Italy had on the politicization of the Indian Muslim intelligentsia and literate

[31] Ibid., 57:20 (January 31, 1921), 4–6.

[32] Maulanas Nisar Ahmad Kanpuri and Riyasat 'Ali Khan Shahjahanpuri, representatives of the U.P. branch of the Jam'iyyat, had sought Ahmad Riza's participation in a forthcoming meeting. (No date is indicated for this meeting.) He told them that if they agreed to give up unity (ittihad) with Hindus, and not associate Deobandis and 'Wahhabis' with it, he would consider himself a khidmatgar (servitor) of the Jam'iyyat and send a paper (tahrir) to be read at the meeting. Illness and weakness prevented him from attending personally, he said. Although they reportedly agreed to these conditions, the Jam'iyyat's stand on participation with Hindus, among other things, undoubtedly did not change. See ibid., p. 5.

[33] For the last two or three years of his life (from 1918–19 to 1921, the year of his death), Ahmad Riza had been going to Bhawali, near Naini Tal, to observe the Ramazan fast there. His poor health made it difficult for him to fast in the heat of the plains, while in the foot hills of the Himalaya at Bhawali it was relatively easy to do so. Hasnain Riza Khan, *Sirat-e A'la Hazrat*, pp. 123–4.

public.[34] As they note, internal events such as revocation of the partition of Bengal in 1911, which many Muslims interpreted as a setback to their economic interests in terms of competition with Hindus, and the government's refusal to grant the Muhammadan Anglo-Oriental College at Aligarh university status in 1912, added to anti-British feeling caused by developments in the international arena.[35] Even the pro-government Muslim League, founded in 1906, had become anti-British a decade later as a result of these and other events.

The role of the press was most important in creating across-the-board awareness of these matters and widening the range of discontent. As noted above, Muslim journalists such as Muhammad 'Ali and Abu'l Kalam Azad advocated through their respective papers measures against European encroachment on Ottoman territory. In Panjab, Zafar 'Ali Khan, like Muhammad 'Ali an alumnus of MAO college, Aligarh, was equally influential in Urdu-speaking circles through his paper, *Zamindar.* These men were influential not only among élite Western-educated Muslims (MAO college alumni, for the most part) but also among the 'ulama'. This was particularly the case with Muhammad 'Ali and his brother Shaukat 'Ali (1873–1938) who became disciples of Maulana 'Abd ul-Bari Firangi Mahali sometime after 1913.[36] 'Abd ul-Bari had been independently involved in efforts to raise money for Turkish relief prior to his meeting with the brothers in December 1912. At this meeting, he proposed the setting up of an association 'dedicated to the cause of preserving the holy places [Mecca and Medina] from harm', to be called the Anjuman-e Khuddam-e Ka'ba (Society of the Servants of the Ka'ba).[37] The brothers approved the idea, and actively supported

[34] See, e.g., Hardy, *Muslims of British India*, pp. 175–82; I. H. Qureshi, *Ulema in Politics: A Study Relating to the Political Activities of the Ulema in the South-Asian Subcontinent from 1556 to 1947* (Karachi: Ma'aref, 1974), 2nd ed., pp. 229–32; Minault, *The Khilafat Movement*, pp. 22–4.

[35] See, e.g., Minault, *The Khilafat Movement*, pp. 10, 22–3.

[36] Minault, relates the circumstances in which the brothers met Maulana 'Abd ul-Bari, in ibid., pp. 34–5.

[37] Organization of assistance to Mecca and Medina of course also signalled support of the Ottomans, who controlled Arabia until 1916.

'Abd ul-Bari and other 'ulama' in their efforts.[38]

During 1913 'Abd ul-Bari was busy recruiting members and seeking funds for the Anjuman.[39] Over eight thousand Muslims were enrolled in the course of the year as a result of extensive tours, public meetings, and circulation of leaflets.[40] Ahmad Riza was prominent among those whose patronage was sought. The two 'ulama' exchanged a series of letters on the subject in the course of which Ahmad Riza expressed his objection to the Anjuman on two major grounds: first, the language of the Anjuman's constitution (dastur-e amal) which might, he felt, lead to 'impermissible opposition' (na-ja'iz mukhalafat) to the government, for such opposition was not beneficial but harmful to the Muslims.[41] The reference was (apparently) to a suggestion that jihad might (in the future) be undertaken against the British government. Ahmad Riza wanted these words to be changed. As we saw earlier, his stand on the religious status of British India was that it was dar al-islam. He had not changed his mind on this despite the spate of international and domestic events that had so angered fellow 'ulama', and could not therefore countenance the idea of jihad.

His second objection was to the presence of Deobandis and bad-mazhabis (those whose faith he thought to be wanting) in leadership roles in the Anjuman, and their taking on teaching and preaching.

[38] Co-operation in Anjuman affairs between Western-trained Muslims and 'ulama' was apparently quite wide-ranging. Among others, prominent 'traditional' Muslims included Hakim Ajmal Khan (1863–1928), son of an old family of *tabibs* (Yunani medical practitioners) in Delhi, who later rose high in the ranks of the Indian National Congress. Dr. M. A. Ansari (1880–1936), also a 'nationalist Muslim' (i.e., one who supported Congress rather than Muslim League policies), had a European education but belonged to a family in which two brothers practised tibb. One of these was for a time a disciple of Maulana Rashid Ahmad Gangohi of Deoband. See Minault, pp. 30, 36.

[39] This was also the year of the 'Cawnpore Mosque Affair', as Muslim agitation over destruction by municipal authorities of a washing area attached to the Machhli Bazaar Mosque in Kanpur was known. 'Abd ul-Bari and the 'Ali brothers were involved in anti-government protests over this incident as well. For details on the event, see Freitag, 'Ambiguous Public Arenas', in Ewing, ed., *Shari'at and Ambiguity in South Asian Islam*, pp. 143–53; See also Minault, *The Khilafat Movement,* pp. 46–8, for 'Abd ul-Bari and the 'Ali brothers' role in the affair.

[40] See ibid., pp. 36–8.

[41] *Dabdaba-e Sikandari*, 49:35 (August 11, 1913), 5–6.

'Their islam is not islam in our regard, and their introduction as teachers of din will be extremely harmful'.[42] He proposed that the Anjuman have a small select leadership, such that its inner 'circle is confined to the Ahl-e Sunnat'—meaning, in this instance, not only those 'ulama' who were part of his close circle of followers, but also 'ulama' such as 'Abd ul-Bari himself, whom he regarded as a good but currently misled, 'Sunni'. Subject to these conditions, he would gladly become a member and patron.[43]

As with Ahmad Riza's previous correspondence with Maulana Muhammad 'Ali Mungeri, who had played a leading role in founding the Nadwat al-'Ulama' in Lucknow in the 1890s,[44] the outcome of this exchange was a stalemate. On Ahmad Riza's part, there was consistency in his arguments on these two occasions, particularly in his insistence that the 'ulama' of the Ahl-e Sunnat could not join with 'ulama' he considered bad-mazhab on a common platform in defence of any religious cause, no matter how laudable. To do so, Ahmad Riza argued, was to be responsible for the ruin of din itself.

Refusal to join the Anjuman-e Khuddam-e Ka'ba did not however mean that he opposed helping the Ottomans. Asked, in February 1913, what (Indian) Muslims should do in their present circumstances, and how they could help, Ahmad Riza gave a fatwa outlining a plan for internal reform, to be undertaken by Indian Muslims in their own communities, as well as assistance to the Turks.[45] Expressing his sympathy for the plight of the Turkish people, Ahmad Riza's central message was encapsulated in Qur'an 13:11, quoted at the beginning of his fatwa: 'Verily never will God

[42] Ibid., p. 6.

[43] Ibid.

[44] For discussion of this correspondence, and Ahl-e Sunnat arguments in that connection, see Chapter VII above.

[45] Ahmad Riza Khan, *Tadbir-e Falah wa Najat wa Islah* (Means of Prosperity, Salvation, and Reform), (Bareilly: Hasani Press, 1331/1913), 15 pp. The question was posed by Munshi La'l Khan Madrasi, a khalifa of Ahmad Riza who lived in Calcutta. He was a wealthy merchant (personal communication with Maulana Yasin Akhtar Misbahi, of Delhi), and was active in directing important Ahl-e Sunnat activities in the early twentieth century.

It should be noted that both the question and the fatwa given in response refer to the Turks rather than the Ottomans.

change the condition of a people until they change it themselves (with their own souls)' (Yusuf 'Ali tr.).[46] Essentially, both Turks and Indian Muslims must help themselves, rather than wait to be helped. However, the Indian Muslims could help the Turks as well as themselves if they would but 'open their eyes'.

Indian Muslims did not have the resources to enable them to leave their homes, possessions, and families, and travel thousands of miles to help their Turkish brethren on the battlefield, Ahmad Riza wrote. But they could help by giving money (mal). If every Muslim wage-earner donated a month's salary, living for twelve months on eleven months' income, tens of thousands of pounds could be gathered for Turkish relief without causing excessive hardship.[47] What had been achieved so far in assistance was but a pittance of what was needed.

Ahmad Riza was highly critical of the manner in which the Muslim leadership, both 'ulama' and Western-educated Muslims, had gone about the task of Turkish relief. In his view they had merely frittered money away in meaningless activities:

> The Muslims there [in Turkey] are going through grave hardship. But here there are the same meetings, the same colour, the same theatre, the same entertaining performances (*tamashe*), the same forgetfulness (*ghaflaten*), the same useless expense. Nothing is lacking. Just the other day a man donated fifty thousand rupees to some worldly cause . . . . When it comes to helping the poor of Islam, the enthusiasm expressed is sky high; [but] the actions which accompany it are at floor level.[48]

In passages such as this throughout the fatwa, Ahmad Riza indicated his disdain for the populist efforts of 'Abd ul-Bari and others then active in Muslim public affairs. None of their meetings, associations, or colleges accomplished anything for the welfare of Muslims, in his view. It was all a waste of money.[49]

[46] Ibid., p. 3.

[47] Ibid., p. 14.

[48] Ibid., pp. 5–6.

[49] In 1921, answering the Jam'iyyat al-'Ulama'-e Hind's charge that he had done nothing to help either the Turks or the holy places, Ahmad Riza countered by saying that they had accomplished nothing in that direction either. In fact, he said, they had taken money from ordinary Muslims and spent it on their travels, meetings, and

Ahmad Riza's answer to the related question of what should be done by Indian Muslims in the midst of prevailing anti-British sentiment, was to propose a four-fold course of action. Dismissing a proposal by other 'ulama' for a boycott of European goods as impractical on account of a widespread love by Indians of foreign goods, he suggested instead that Muslims seek means to be legally and economically self-sufficient, dependent on help from neither the British nor the Hindus. First, excepting those limited matters on which the government had the right to intervene, Muslims should refrain from taking their disputes to the courts.[50] They should make their own judgments, thereby saving large sums of money on stamp duties and legal fees. Second, Muslims should buy whatever they needed from other Muslims, thus keeping money within the community, giving a fillip to Muslim traders, and being self-reliant. Third, wealthy Muslims in large cities such as Bombay, Haidarabad, and elsewhere should open interest-free banks for their fellow Muslims. This would benefit the Muslim bankers in the long run if not immediately, as well as their brethren. Moreover, the wealth currently being lost to Baniyas would remain in Muslim hands. Finally, the most important thing that Muslims had was their din. They had neglected it in pursuit of other goals, and reduced it to its current weak state. They should go back to acquiring 'ilm-e din, knowledge of their faith, and act on it.[51]

This is one of the few fatawa known to me in which Ahmad Riza proposed a course of action to address current Muslim problems, rather than purely theological concerns. Its interest lies both in what it does and does not say. Focusing chiefly on economic reform to be carried out individually and collectively by Muslims themselves, it is silent on the need for political action. The problem, Ahmad

festivities. See *Dabdaba-e Sikandari*, 57:20 (January 31, 1921), 4.

50 This suggestion was by no means novel, of course. The Deobandi 'ulama' had been discouraging Muslims from using the British-run courts since the late nineteenth century, even setting up a court of their own under Maulana Qasim Nanautawi. See Metcalf, *Islamic Revival*, pp. 146–7. For his part, Ahmad Riza had followed this policy of avoiding the courts in his own life, refusing in 1917 to answer a court summons. For details, see Chapter VI.

51 *Tadbir-e Falah*, pp. 6–8.

Riza argued, was internal to the Muslim community—the Muslims were so engrossed in mutual quarrels, the pursuit of pleasure, and the quest for a university education so as to get government jobs that they had neglected din and allowed the non-Muslims to get ahead of them in worldly affairs as well. Ahmad Riza's criticism of the Muslim leadership, on grounds that it was wasting time and money on selfish and self-promotional activities (including meetings, associations, and educational programmes), is indicative of his distance and isolation from the leading 'ulama' and Muslim intellectuals of his day on issues of public concern. His vision of reform remained an internal one, as that of many other 'ulama' had been in the late nineteenth century. But while others had begun to explore new alliances and organizational avenues for improving the political situation of the Muslims *vis-à-vis* the British and the Hindus, Ahmad Riza's position that British India was a dar al-islam, coupled as we shall see with his objections to a Muslim-Ḥindu political alliance, caused him to be resolutely opposed to the course advocated by the Jam'iyyat leadership.

On the Turkish question, however, Ahl-e Sunnat leaders did more than advise fellow-Muslims to donate a month's salary to help the Turks. Several years later, in Sha'ban 1339/April–March 1921, shortly before Ahmad Riza's death, they created their own association called the 'Ansar al-Islam'[52] one of the main purposes of which was to help the Turkish state and the holy places.[53] Resolutions were adopted to this end, as also to promote the economic reforms proposed by Ahmad Riza in his 1913 fatwa. Ahmad Riza's closest followers were in the forefront of the leadership: Muhammad Miyan Marahrawi, Zafar ud-Din Bihari, Na'im ud-Din Muradabadi, Didar 'Ali Alwari, and others. However, the new organization could not escape the accusation that it had been appointed by the British and

[52] In choosing the word 'Ansar', Helpers, they were undoubtedly invoking the Prophet's own lifetime, when the Ansar of Medina gave Muhammad shelter from his enemies in Mecca and enabled him and his fellow companions (the Muhajirs, or Emigrants) to set up the first state run in accordance with Muslim prescriptions. See Chapter III for more detailed treatment of the Ansar al-Islam.

[53] *Al-Sawad al-A'zam* (Muradabad), 2, 5 (Sha'ban 1339/April-May 1921), 2-8.

was a 'government meeting'. Opposition to it was apparently strong, coming this time from supporters of the Khilafat movement.

Ahl-e Sunnat Opposition to the Khilafat Movement, 1919–20

The Jam'iyyat al-'Ulama'-e Hind, formed in November 1919 in response to a strong tide of anti-British feeling, was the first 'political' party of 'ulama' in British India. Its decision to co-operate with the Hindu-dominated Indian National Congress, made on the basis of shar'i interpretation,[54] coincided with an agreement forged between the purely political parties of the Muslim League and Congress in 1916, under the terms of the famous Lucknow Pact.[55] The Khilafat movement arose in 1919 in the context of this internal political climate of anti-British feeling, Hindu-Muslim unity,[56] and post-World War I events abroad.

The Indian movement must also be seen in light of a broader trend, namely pan-Islamic sentiment centred around loyalty to the Ottoman ruler who became, for many Muslims, a rallying point against European colonial expansion in the nineteenth century. As Kramer points out, threat of 'an expanding West' had made many Muslims 'anxious to exchange professions of allegiance for whatever military, diplomatic, or moral aid the Ottomans could spare them'.[57] For his part, the sultan-caliph 'Abd al-Hamid II (r. 1876–1909), no longer able to defend the empire against European encroachment,

[54] For an analysis of the Jam'iyyat's attitude to the Indian nationalist movement down to 1947, the year of India's independence and Pakistan's creation, see Yohanan Friedmann, 'The Attitude of the Jam'iyyat-i 'Ulama'-i Hind to the Indian National Movement and the Establishment of Pakistan', *Asian and African Studies*, 7 (1971), 157–80. Also see Hardy, *Partners in Freedom*.

[55] These events are well-documented in the scholarly literature. Judith M. Brown, *Gandhi's Rise to Power: Indian Politics 1915–1922* (Cambridge: Cambridge University Press, 1972), gives a vivid account from the point of view of Gandhi's political role during this period. For a Muslim perspective, see Hardy, *Muslims of British India*; Stanley Wolpert, *Jinnah of Pakistan* (New York: Oxford University Press, 1984).

[56] Minault argues in *The Khilafat Movement*, pp. 1–3, that it is primarily in this context of Indian nationalist interest—what she calls a quest by Indian Muslims for a 'pan-Indian Islam'—that the Khilafat movement should be viewed, not in terms of pan-Islamic sentiment (discussed below).

[57] Kramer, *Islam Assembled*, p. 5.

was in need of outside sources of support himself.[58] When war broke out in 1914, the then Sultan, Mehmet V Resad, declared a holy war against Russia, France, and England, and asked all Muslims worldwide to rally to the Turkish cause.[59]

Whether Khilafatists came to the movement primarily out of sympathy for pan-Islamic ideals, or whether they did so in order to 'reconcile Islamic identity with Indian nationality',[60] there can be no doubt that they all opposed British rule in India. This was true of all the Khilafat leaders, whether 'ulama' or 'modernist' intellectuals. Leaders as diverse as Abu'l Kalam Azad, the Deobandi 'ulama' 'Ubaid Ullah Sindhi and Mahmud al-Hasaṇ, Shi'is such as Chiragh 'Ali, and other Muslim scholars, shared in the primary goal of opposing British rule.[61] In this respect, they may be said to have been the heirs of Jamal al-Din al-Afghani (1838–97), seen by many as the first to have spread and popularized pan-Islamic ideas in India, who had himself been fiercely anti-British.[62]

Before we move on to Ahmad Riza's views on the Khilafat question and related issues, it is worth noting that Sir Sayyid Ahmad Khan, standing apart from most of his late nineteenth-century contemporaries—both in India and in other parts of the Muslim world—had been hostile to the idea of a universal Muslim caliphate. Aziz Ahmad suggests that the determining factor in his attitude was

[58] Ibid., p. 6. Indeed, Hourani writes that 'Abd al-Hamid promoted the concept of the Ottoman caliphate with an eye particularly to gaining the support of Muslims outside the Ottoman empire against the colonial powers. See Albert Hourani, *Arabic Thought in the Liberal Age, 1798–1939* (Cambridge: Cambridge University Press, 1983), reprint, pp. 106–7.

[59] Kramer, *Islam Assembled*, p. 55. On this, also see Peters, *Islam and Colonialism*, pp. 90–4.

[60] Minault, *The Khilafat Movement*, p. 2.

[61] Aziz Ahmad, *Studies in Islamic Culture in the Indian Environment*, pp. 62–5; Kramer, *Islam Assembled*, pp. 59–61, on 'Ubaid Ullah Sindhi; Ian Henderson Douglas, *Abul Kalam Azad: An Intellectual and Religious Biography*, ed. Gail Minault and Christian W. Troll (Delhi: Oxford University Press, 1988), pp. 176–8; Hardy, *Partners in Freedom*, pp.-22–3, 32, 38, and passim.

[62] For al-Afghani's influence on Indian Muslims in the nineteenth and twentieth centuries, see Aziz Ahmad, 'Afghani's Indian Contacts', *Journal of the American Oriental Society*, 89, 3 (1969), 476–504. Aziz Ahmad points out that Afghani was not in fact the first to have popularized pan-Islamic ideas in India.

his loyalty to the British, rather than theoretical concern about the institution of the caliphate:

> In 1870 Sayyid Ahmad Khan had been as pro-Turkish as any other educated Muslim . . . . he had complimented Sultan 'Abdul-'Aziz as one 'who graces and defends the throne of the Caliph'. He had praised the *tanzimat* and the subsequent Turkish reforms . . . . In fact everything was perfect as long as the British, to whom he had pledged his own and his community's loyalty, and the Turks, towards whom his community felt an emotional attachment were on good terms.[63]

When, in the 1890s, British and Turkish interests clashed, however, Sayyid Ahmad declared that the Indian Muslims were 'devoted and loyal subjects of the British government . . . We are not the subjects of Sultan 'Abdul Hamid II; . . . He neither had, nor can have any spiritual jurisdiction over us as Khalifa'.[64]

Ahmad Riza, contrary to Sayyid Ahmad Khan, refused to make a connection between support for the Turkish ruler and opposition to British rule in India. In a 1920 fatwa dealing specifically with his views on the caliphate in light of shar'i considerations, he criticized the Khilafat leaders for using the issue of the caliphate as an 'excuse for working toward their real goal of freedom [from the British]'.[65] In another fatwa, he criticized 'Abd ul-Bari for saying that he considered the fight for Indian independence to be an 'Islamic duty' (farz islami).[66] The political goal of freedom from British rule was for Ahmad Riza an entirely separate matter from support of a shar'i institution.

Ahmad Riza's conception of the caliphate, as set out in his 1920 fatwa *Dawam al-'Aish*, corresponds to Islamic theory as formulated by medieval jurists, particularly Mawardi (d. 1058), a famous jurist

63 Aziz Ahmad, *Studies in Islamic Culture*, p. 60.

64 Ibid., p. 64.

65 Ahmad Riza Khan, *Dawam al-'Aish fi'l Ummat min Quraish* (Permanence of the Quraish Community's Way of Life), (Lahore: Maktaba Rizwiyya, 1980), p. 95. Originally written in 1339/1920.

66 Ahmad Riza Khan, *Al-Mahajjat al-Mu'tamana fi Ayat al-Mumtahana* (The Trusted Way with Regard to the Ayat al-Mumtahana), 1339/1920, in *Rasa'il-e Rizwiyya*, vol. 2 (Lahore: Maktaba Hamidiyya, 1976), p. 155.

in Baghdad at the end of the 'Abbasid era.[67] The arguments, supported by illustrative examples from Muslim history, are, briefly, that the caliph is the Prophet's deputy (na'ib) and is therefore owed absolute obedience by the Muslim community. Furthermore, there can only be one caliph at any one time, though there may be several sultans or kings (badshah). The caliph's authority over these sultans has frequently been unrelated to his command over physical resources or power (for the sultans have often been more powerful than he), yet has been acknowledged to be superior to theirs. The reason for this, Ahmad Riza wrote, is that the caliph has always been required to be—and has historically been—a member of the Quraish tribe, and therefore a descendant of the Prophet himself. Accordingly, 'Among the Ahl-e Sunnat it is a condition of the shar'i caliphate that the caliph be a Quraish'.[68] The genealogy of 'worldly' rulers such as sultans was immaterial to their exercise of power.[69] The institution of the caliphate had ceased to exist after 132/749 (the beginning of the 'Abbasid caliphate), and all Muslim rulers since then had been, and presently were, rulers or sultans, but not caliphs. The next caliph would be the Mahdi.[70]

The theological basis for the above theory of the caliphate is the hadis literature.[71] Ahmad Riza cited several hadis in his fatwa,

[67] See Hourani, *Arabic Thought in the Liberal Age*, Chapter I, on Mawardi's, as well as later thinkers' theoretical writings on the khilafat and the Islamic state more generally. Also see Mahmud O. Haddad, 'Rashid Rida and the Theory of the Caliphate: Medieval Themes and Modern Concerns', Ph.D. dissertation, Columbia University, 1989, pp. 42–8. Ahmad Riza did not mention Mawardi as a source, though he quoted later works such as Jalal al-Din al-Suyuti's (1445–1505) *Tarikh al-Khulafa'* and *Husn al-Muhadarah*, a biographical work. See, e.g., *Dawam al-'Aish*, pp. 51, 52.

[68] *Dawam al-'Aish*, p. 46.

[69] Ibid., pp. 47–56. The requirement of Quraish ancestry was not the only one, Ahmad Riza went on to say. There were seven requirements in all: That he be Muslim, free (*hurriyat*), male (*zukurat*), intelligent (*'aql*), mature (*bulugh*), and powerful (qudrat) were the other six. Ibid., pp. 46, 50. This is similar to (though differs in some respects from) Mawardi's list, for which see Thomas W. Arnold, *The Caliphate*, reprint (Lahore: Oxford University Press, 1966), pp. 71–2.

[70] This argument is based on a hadis in which the Prophet is reported to have said that after the caliphate had come to the Bani 'Abbas, it would not be given to anyone until the appearance of the Mahdi. *Dawam al-'Aish*, p. 74.

[71] See Wensinck, *Handbook of Early Tradition*, entry 'Imam', p. 109, for a hadis from al-

including some from al-Bukhari and Muslim, all bearing on the requirement that the caliph be of Quraish descent.[72] Responding to an argument by 'Abd ul-Bari Firangi Mahali on the view of Ibn Khaldun (d. 1406) that Quraish descent was not a necessary condition for a caliph, Ahmad Riza said that Ibn Khaldun, a historian rather than an 'alim, was outnumbered by the authorities he (Ahmad Riza) had cited. Ibn Khaldun's importance had been exaggerated; furthermore, he 'smelled of' one who was a Mu'tazila, and sometimes of a 'Nechari'.[73]

Ahmad Riza's fatwa was simultaneously an exposition of a theory of the caliphate and an attack on the views of 'Abd ul-Bari Firangi Mahali and Abu'l Kalam Azad. At the time, the latter were actively engaged in promoting the cause of the Khilafat movement in British India, through political association with the Indian National Congress and their journalistic writings. Of the numerous arguments Ahmad Riza made in *Dawam al-'Aish* and elsewhere against their views, I would like to turn in particular to two specific points.

First, Ahmad Riza referred to Abu'l Kalam's argument that limiting the choice of caliph to a member of the Quraish tribe contravened the principle of equality that it had been Islam's original purpose to uphold, and that such a rule did not in fact exist.[74] Ahmad

---

Tayalisi's *Musnad* (Haidarabad, 1321) which indicates that the imam must be of Quraysh descent. Arnold, *The Caliphate*, cites variant versions of the same hadis on p. 47. Also see Malcolm H. Kerr, *Islamic Reform: The Political and Legal Theories of Muhammad 'Abduh and Rashid Rida* (Berkeley: University of California Press, 1966), for an extended discussion of the issue, particularly with reference to Rashid Rida.

72 *Dawam al-'Aish*, pp. 65–8.

73 Ibid., pp. 78–80. Arnold, *The Caliphate*, discusses Ibn Khaldun's theory of the caliphate on pp. 74–6. Arnold writes that Ibn Khaldun defended the principle of Quraish descent being a necessary condition for a caliph. Also see Hourani, *Arabic Thought*, pp. 22–4. On Ibn Khaldun's views on the caliphate, see Kerr, *Islamic Reform*, pp. 45–6, 174–5.

74 Hardy writes of Azad's argument: 'He [Azad] rejects the classical ijma' that the caliph must be chosen from among the male members of the Prophet's clan, the Quraysh, with the rhetorical question whether it was likely that Islam the religion of equality and human brotherhood would have permitted the caliphate to become the preserve of any one kin-group, with the claim that reports in favour of the Quraysh qualification in Tradition are advisory rather than mandatory and with a denial that there had been an ijma' of the Companions of the Prophet that the caliph must be Quraysh'. Hardy, *Partners in Freedom*, pp. 26–7.

Riza, in his fatwa, explicitly repudiated the claim that equality was a principle of din. In one instance, he wrote, the Mamluk king Baybars I (r. 1260–77) installed the uncle of the last 'Abbasid king as caliph, despite the fact that he, Baybars, enjoyed great power while the caliph, al-Mustansir (d. 1261), did not. Ahmad Riza argued that this showed that Baybars considered the ascribed status of Quraish descent more important than his own achievements.[75] Elsewhere in the fatwa, Ahmad Riza again affirmed his acceptance of the inequalities caused by high birth:

> The Ahl-e Sunnat argued [against the Kharijis, who had favoured the principle of equality] that kinship definitely had some bearing on the matter, for when Muslims know that the ruler belongs to the Prophet's family, they will pay greater attention. And there is none to equal the Quraish in nobility (sharif) . . . .
>
> And in marriage (nikah) everyone must know, even the ignorant . . . what the place of equality (*kafa'a*) is in the shar'i view. All the books of fiqh are full of it, and there are also ahadis on the matter [defending the principle that marriages not take place between people of distinct social class.][76]

These sentiments, defended on the authority of fiqh and the hadis literature, confirm the importance to the Ahl-e Sunnat worldview of the principle of hierarchy based on genealogical descent, to which earlier chapters have alluded. We also see that Ahmad Riza highlights the fact that the Quraish, as kin of the Prophet, are by virtue of this alone superior to all other people. This argument is of course consistent with Ahmad Riza's Prophet-centred vision of the faith.

Another significant, and decisive, difference between Ahmad Riza's position and that of Abu'l Kalam Azad and 'Abd ul-Bari in the course of the Khilafat movement—but also in other areas—was his view that Muslims may not seek the help of kafirs in pursuit of shar'i goals.[77] Ahmad Riza's criticism of these two 'ulama' and of Jam'iyyat al-'Ulama'-e Hind leaders generally for their leadership of

75 *Dawam al-'Aish*, p. 51. The fact that the Mamluks treated the caliphs with scant regard, seeing them merely as a means of legitimizing their own rule, does not invalidate Ahmad Riza's argument.

76 Ibid., pp. 96–7.

77 The fatwa *Dawam al-'Aish* does not deal with this aspect of Ahmad Riza's differences with Khilafat leaders. He discussed it at length in his *Al-Mahajjat al-Mu'tamana*, also dating to 1920, which was written in the context of the Non-Cooperation movement.

the Khilafat movement (which, as we saw, had in his view nothing at all to do with protection of the shar'i caliphate), was based in part on the fact that they had welcomed the co-operation of Hindus in the movement. At one level, this can be viewed simply as objection to certain tactical aspects of the movement; but Ahmad Riza's use of the term harbi (those with whom one is at war) to describe the Hindus of his day indicates that his objection went much deeper.

To understand what was at issue here we need now to broaden the discussion. For this related but nevertheless distinct debate on Hindu-Muslim relations took place in the context of other major political events such as the Hijrat and Non-Cooperation movements as well as the Khilafat movement. Additionally, of course, arguments between the 'ulama' about relations between Hindus and Muslims were simultaneously arguments about Muslims' relations with the British. In the remaining section of this chapter, I shall try to delineate Ahmad Riza's, and thereby the Ahl-e Sunnat's, perspective on the Muslim-Hindu-British relationship, such that we may find coherence in the wide range of arguments examined thus far.

Muslim, Hindu, British: Ahl-e Sunnat Perspectives

It is well known that when the Khilafat movement began to lose momentum in 1920 in response to the publication of the Peace Treaty of Sevres,[78] some prominent Muslim leaders raised the cry of hijrat, and encouraged the migration to Afghanistan of several thousands of Indian Muslims on the grounds that British India was

[78] 'Under its terms the Sultan would keep Constantinople as the capital of the Turkish state, but would lose Eastern Thrace to Greece, while Armenia, Syria, Mesopotamia and Palestine were to become independent states. This meant that two of the three claims made by Indian Khilafat leaders were not granted: the Jazirat-ul-Arab [Arabian peninsula] would not remain under Muslim sovereignty, and the Khalifah would not remain warden of the Muslim sanctuaries'. Brown, *Gandhi's Rise to Power*, p. 217. The only claim to have been recognized was that the 'personal centre of Islam, the Khalifah, should retain his empire with sufficient temporal power to defend the faith'. Ibid., p. 192. Even this, of course, was to become a part of history when the caliphate was abolished altogether in 1924 by Turkish nationalists.

In saying, on p. 217, that the 'Jazirat-ul-Arab would not remain under Muslim sovereignty', Judith Brown seems to overlook the fact that the Arabian Peninsula, although no longer under Ottoman rule, was under the authority of the Sharif of Mecca.

dar al-harb. 'Abd ul-Bari and Abu'l Kalam Azad were among those who spoke in favour of hijrat, while Ahmad Riza, predictably, spoke against.[79] He said that in a place that was dar al-islam it was prohibited (haram) for Muslims to do hijrat and go elsewhere.[80]

Although the Hijrat movement still awaits careful scholarly study,[81] there are indications that among those who responded to the call for hijrat were peasants suffering economic hardship in parts of the United Provinces, Sind, and the North-West Frontier Province.[82] Attracted by the promise of land in Afghanistan by the Amir of that country, several thousands gave up their possessions in British India only to find on arrival that the situation in Afghanistan was even worse than the one they had left behind.[83] While Ahmad Riza and other opponents of the movement blamed fellow 'ulama' for having encouraged people to migrate, one returnee to British India also blamed the Urdu press for having magnified the scale of the economic help promised on the other side of the border.[84]

In 1920, leaders of the Jam'iyyat such as 'Abd ul-Bari and Abu'l Kalam Azad were engaged in anti-British activities on yet another

[79] Details of statements made by these and other 'ulama' at various meetings or in their writings, as reported in the Urdu press of the time, may be found in Raja Rashid Mahmud, *Tahrik-e Hijrat (1920) Ek Tarikh, Ek Tajziya* (Lahore: Maktaba 'Aliyya, 1986).

[80] However, if a particular individual was unable for one reason or another to perform his ritual duties in his current place of residence, it was his duty to migrate elsewhere, whether this meant moving to a different house, neighbourhood, or town. The distinction between the two situations was that between the general ('amm) and the particular (khass), the latter being unrelated to the larger question of a politically delimited area being dar al-islam or dar al-harb. Ahmad Riza Khan, *Fatawa-e Rizwiyya* (Azamgarh: Sunni Dar al-Isha'at, 1981), vol. 6, p. 2. Also reprinted in Raja Rashid Mahmud, *Tahrik-e Hijrat*, p. 72.

[81] In addition to brief references to it in larger histories, there exist only a handful of articles in English, among them: F. S. Briggs, 'The Indian Hijrat of 1920', *Muslim World*, 20, II (April 1930), 164-8; M. Naeem Qureshi, 'The 'Ulama of British India and the Hijrat of 1920', *Modern Asian Studies*, 13, 1 (Cambridge, 1979), 41–59; Lal Baha, 'The Hijrat Movement in the North-West Frontier Province', *Islamic Studies*, XVIII, 3 (Autumn 1979), 231–42. Interesting parallels and differences, yet to be investigated, must exist between the internal debates that occurred during this hijrat and the one that led to the creation of Pakistan in 1947.

[82] Qureshi, 'The 'Ulama of British India', p. 52.

[83] Raja Rashid Mahmud, *Tahrik-e Hijrat*, pp. 90–2.

[84] Ibid., p. 90.

front, the Gandhi-led Non-Cooperation movement. This movement, which grew out of the Khilafat movement,[85] adopted a plan of progressively escalating non-violent non-cooperation with the government, starting with the return of titles previously awarded and accepted.[86] Gandhi believed that independence could be achieved by these means, provided the movement remained faithful to his ideal of non-violence.[87]

Throughout the second decade of the twentieth century, then, we see large sections of the Muslim leadership, both 'ulama' and 'modernist', engaging in a series of anti-British initiatives in concert with the Indian National Congress (the Muslim League being at this time still a fledgling organization). This culminated in August 1920 in the issuing of a fatwa by the Jam'iyyat al-'Ulama'-e Hind supporting the Congress-proposed boycott of courts, legislative councils, schools and foreign goods, among other things.[88]

Ahmad Riza, looking at this alliance of Hindus and Muslims against the British in shar'i terms rather than 'nationalist' or 'political' ones, could see no justification for it. His fatwa, *Al-Mahajjat al-Mu'tamana*, written in 1920, makes a strong and clear argument for the view that the Muslim leadership had lost its sense of balance between relations with the British, which it wanted to cut off completely, and those with Hindus, which it wanted to be of the closest. In shar'i terms, it had pronounced that which was mubah (indifferent) to be haràm, and that which was haram to be *farz qati'* (an absolute duty).[89] Moreover, he argued that even from a political standpoint, far from throwing off the yoke of dependence, the Muslims had merely allowed themselves to become more dependent—for

[85] See Brown, *Gandhi's Rise to Power*, pp. 216–18, and passim.

[86] This was to be followed by: '(2) Resignation from government service; (3) Resignation from the police and the military; and (4) Nonpayment of taxes'. Minault, *The Khilafat Movement*, p. 98. Gandhi visualized the last two stages, which constituted acts of civil disobedience and not merely of non-cooperation, as distant goals.

[87] In fact he called it off abruptly in February 1922 after violence at Chauri Chaura, U.P. The movement was into its civil disobedience phase in some parts of the country at the time. See Brown, *Gandhi's Rise to Power*, pp. 319–28.

[88] Qureshi, *Ulema in Politics*, p. 269.

[89] *Al-Mahajjat al-Mu'tamana*, p. 197.

unlike the British, who had refrained from interfering in the Muslims' ritual observances, the Hindus were beginning to do that as well.[90]

Criticizing the Muslim leadership bitterly for its pro-Hindu stance, he wrote:

What din is this which goes from its [previously] incomplete subservience to the Christians to completely shunning them, and immerses itself wholly in following the mushriks [i.e., Hindus]? They [the Muslims] are running from the rain only to enter a drainpipe.[91]

Ahmad Riza described the Hindus as *muharib bi'l fi'l* (active belligerents), and as *qatilin zalimin kafirin* (killers, oppressors, infidels).[92] He reminded his fellow Muslims of recent Hindu atrocities committed against them:

Did they [the Hindus] not fight with us over din? Has their extremely oppressive viciousness (*sakht zalimana fasad*) [already] grown old? Have the impure and terrifying tyrannies of Katarpur, Arrah and elsewhere, still fresh [in the mind], been obliterated from the heart? Innocent Muslims were sacrificed with great cruelty. They were set alight with petroleum. Those impure people demolished our pure masjids and tore and burnt the pure pages of [our] Qur'an, and did other things the mention of which makes one sick.[93]

Responding to the Non-Cooperation leaders' argument that responsibility for violence of this sort lay with only a few individuals rather than with Hindus as a whole, he argued that on the contrary this was a case of the Hindu qaum (community) fighting the Muslims. The individual aggressors had acted as representatives of the Hindu community. For even if only a few committed the actual

[90] A reference to the friction between Hindus and Muslims over the Muslims' right to slaughter cows during Baqr-e 'Id. See below for details.

[91] *Al-Mahajjat al Mu'tamana*, p. 94.

[92] Ibid., p. 136 and passim.

[93] Ibid., p. 116. Also on p. 137, and passim. The reference to Katarpur in this passage is to a riot that occurred in Katarpur village, Saharanpur district. Of its approximately 800 residents a third were Muslim. The riot originated from the Hindus' 'unwillingness to settle for anything less than a total ban' on the sacrifice of cows during the 'Id festivities. It left thirty or more Muslims dead (burned alive in many cases), and several houses and a mosque demolished. Thursby, *Hindu-Muslim Relations in British India*, p. 82.

deed, others helped behind the scenes with money, or by their writings, or in other ways. At the very least, they acquiesced in it.[94]

As for the British, social relations (mu'amalat) with them were permitted (ja'iz) under the shari'a as long as kufr was not promoted thereby, nor any disobedience to the shar' involved. Here, Ahmad Riza was arguing particularly in the context of a speech made in October 1920 by Abu'l Kalam Azad at Lahore, in which he had said that the local Islamiyya College must cease to accept government grants-in-aid, and disaffiliate itself from Panjab University.[95] Ahmad Riza, however, maintained that these steps should only be taken if shar'i reasons so warranted. He wondered, further, why Muslim leaders advocating steps such as these continued to use facilities like the railways, the telegraph, and the postal system, all of which benefitted the government revenues:

> Are these not also mu'amalat? The difference is that in taking aid [from the British] one is taking wealth in, while in using [the services they provide] one is giving it away. How strange that in [this] boycott (muqata'a) it is halal to give money away but haram to take it in . . . . What remedy is there for this inverted logic? But then what is one to say of this qaum which has not only turned shari'a on its head but the essence (nafs) of Islam as well?[96]

The argument between the two sides revolved, essentially, around the definition of non-cooperation itself,[97] as well as the conditions in which different degrees of friendship between Muslims and non-Muslims were permitted. Ahmad Riza maintained that his opponents had failed to make a vital distinction between two completely different sorts of relationship between Muslims and non-Muslims:

[94] *Al-Mahajjat al-Mu'tamana*, p. 117. He went on to say, furthermore, that if one accepted the Non-Cooperation movement's argument that only a small number of Hindus were aggressing against the Muslims, then one must also argue, on the same principle, that only a certain limited number of Englishmen had aggressed against the Turks or against the Indian Muslims. Ibid., p. 118.

[95] Ibid., pp. 80, 96–7. Azad's speech must of course be seen in the context of the Non-Cooperation movement's programme under which Indians were to refuse to participate in government-run institutions.

[96] Ibid., pp. 85–6.

[97] In Urdu, the term non-cooperation is generally translated as *tark-e muwalat*, 'the giving up of friendly relations'. See Qureshi, *Ulema in Politics*, pp. 268–71, for more on this debate.

those of 'mere human relations' (*mujarrad mu'amalat*) which were permitted with all non-Muslims under the shari'a (though forbidden with a murtadd or apostate), and those of friendship or intimacy (*muwalat*), which Muslims may enter into only with other Muslims.[98] He believed that the relationship between Hindus and Muslims being advocated by the non-cooperators was one of love, intimacy, even unity, all of which, being forms of muwalat, were forbidden; while, on the other hand, worldly or social relations with the British were being forbidden although they had shar'i approval.

Both sides based their respective cases on quotation from the Qur'an. The non-cooperators cited two verses of the Qur'an (60:8,9), in which Muslims were told that they might enter into friendly relations with non-Muslims so long as the latter were not warring against them.[99] Ahmad Riza countered by saying that these verses had been abrogated by a historically later (though sequentially earlier) one (9:73) which advocated taking stern measures against 'unbelievers' and 'hypocrites'.[100]

As Qureshi says, however, Muslim public opinion was so overwhelmingly anti-British at the time that dissenting voices such as Ahmad Riza's were not heard, regardless of the merits of their argument.[101] Indeed, Ahmad Riza's views on the Khilafat and Non-Cooperation movements were not unanimously accepted even within the Ahl-e Sunnat leadership. The rift occurred, interestingly, along the same lines as those of the internal controversy

[98] *Al-Mahajjat al-Mu'tamana*, p. 95.

[99] The title of Ahmad Riza's fatwa contains the name of this sura, *al-Mumtahana*. The verses are (Yusuf 'Ali tr.): '8. God forbids you not, with regard to those who fight you not for (your) faith nor drive you out of your homes, from dealing kindly and justly with them: For God loveth those who are just.

9. God only forbids you, with regard to those who fight you for (your) faith, and drive you out of your homes, and support (others) in driving you out, from turning to them (for friendship and protection). It is such as turn to them (in these circumstances) that do wrong'.

[100] Verse 73 of this sura, called *al-Taubah* or *al-Bara'at*, reads (Yusuf 'Ali tr.): 'O Prophet! Strive hard against the unbelievers and the hypocrites, and be firm against them. Their abode is hell, an evil refuge indeed'.

[101] Ahmad Riza and other Ahl-e Sunnat leaders were not the only opponents to Non-Cooperation. Apparently Maulana Ashraf 'Ali Thanawi of Deoband also wrote a long fatwa along similar lines of argument. See Qureshi, *Ulema in Politics*, p. 270.

within Ahl-e Sunnat circles over the azan debate in 1914–16, which had reached the British courts as a suit for libel. As noted earlier in this chapter, one of the founding members of the Jam'iyyat al-'Ulama'-e Hind was Maulana 'Abd ul-Majid Badayuni. His pir 'Abd ul-Muqtadir Badayuni (d. 1915) had been supportive some years earlier of 'Abd ul-Bari's efforts through the Anjuman-e Khuddam-e Ka'ba to protect the Hijaz from Western encroachment. He had encouraged 'Abd ul-Majid to involve himself in its affairs.[102] In 1916, the libel case against Ahmad Riza had been initiated by another of 'Abd ul-Muqtadir's disciples, and had centred around a work by 'Abd ul-Muqtadir, then recently deceased. Opposition by Badayuni 'ulama' to Ahmad Riza on the Khilafat and other issues appears therefore to have stemmed in part from their refusal to accept his leadership of the Ahl-e Sunnat movement. Given the political situation in the 1920s, they disagreed with him in his insistence that the movement continue to define itself in narrowly 'religious' and apolitical terms as before.

AMHAD RIZA: PRO-BRITISH, ANTI-HINDU?

The accusation that he was pro-British was frequently levelled at Ahmad Riza. Indeed, the positions he took on major national issues facing Indian Muslims in the period 1910–21, such as the Khilafat, the Hijrat, and the Non-Cooperation movements, were all consistently opposed to the anti-British positions of the Jam'iyyat al-'Ulama'-e Hind. While this proves that he opposed the Jam'iyyat, it does not, in and of itself, prove that he was 'pro-British'.

I would argue that Ahmad Riza was uninterested in the nationalist movement and the question of political self-determination as long as Muslims were free to practise their faith unhindered. Freedom to fulfill the dictates (ahkam) of the shari'a was, to Ahmad Riza, what made British India dar al-islam. His concern as an 'alim lay in guiding and teaching the Muslims around him as to how (in his view, which he believed to be the only 'correct' view) the shari'a should be interpreted and practised. For this reason, he was deeply interested

102 Mahmud Ahmad Qadiri, *Tazkira- e 'Ulama'-e Ahl-e Sunnat*, p. 147.

in—and often critical of—what other Muslims in India and elsewhere were saying, writing, and doing. He acquiesced in the British presence. He did not actively oppose it, choosing instead to distance himself from it, and to carve out an identity removed from its concerns.

Ahmad Riza indicated his distance from the British Indian state in a number of small but nonetheless significant ways. He himself cited some of these. He had written anti-British poems, he said, in some works he named; he had spoken out against the Nadwa, which enjoyed British support; he had opposed 'Abd ul-Bari's fatwa on the Kanpur mosque affair of 1913, in which 'Abd ul-Bari had said that the demolition (by the British civil authorities) was permissible as it had taken place outside the mosque proper, and so on.[103] When mailing a postcard he would deliberately affix the stamp (which had a picture of Queen Victoria on it) upside down as a mark of disrespect to the Queen.[104] More importantly, his refusal to attend a British-run court in 1916 showed that he did not acknowledge its authority over himself. But he never made the British a target of his writings—as he did numerous contemporary Muslim movements and even, to some extent, Hindus—because they did not really matter to him. Had the British had an active anti-Muslim policy in terms of interference in 'religious' affairs, however, Ahmad Riza would undoubtedly have become very anti-British.

Ahmad Riza's distance from political concerns is also apparent in some of his conversations with his followers, as recorded in the biographical literature. Typically, the questions asked of him related to matters of ritual and belief or to social relations with one's fellows.[105] In the context of Muslim political concerns in the 1920s, however, he was occasionally asked about the shape of things to come rather than a currently existing situation. One such discussion, reported by a close follower (khalifa) of his, is of great interest, and is pertinent to my argument here.

[103] See *Al-Mahajjat al-Mu'tamana*, pp. 142–4.

[104] I am grateful to Professor Muhammad Mas'ud Ahmed for showing me samples of postcards on which this had been done.

[105] It was a source of pride to Ahmad Riza that he never allowed a question to go unanswered. His followers were also proud of his ability to give an immediate response, including quotations (from memory) of Qur'an, hadis, and fiqh, on any question.

Burhan ul-Haqq Jabalpuri, a khalifa of Ahmad Riza, related that in 1921, shortly after a Khilafat Committee meeting held at Bareilly, Ahmad Riza was asked at his home in Bareilly whether India would ever gain its freedom from British domination, and if so how did he expect the appointment of a qazi-e shar' (judge of Islamic law) and a mufti-e shar' (jurisconsult) to take place on the basis of popular demand?[106] In response to the first part of the question, Ahmad Riza said that yes, India would surely become independent some day. But he needed time to think about the second half of the question. Some days later,

> [he] started making some special seating arrangements in the morning in the sitting area (*baithak*). The *takht* (elevated platform meant for sitting on) was set apart with three especially adorned chairs next to it. And, departing from usual practice, the Imam-e Ahl-e Sunnat [Ahmad Riza] himself sat down on a separate chair facing the takht. When the daily audience of people had assembled in the hall (darbar) the Sarkar-e A'la Hazrat [Ahmad Riza] said:
>
> 'The country will definitely become free of English domination. The government of this country will be established on a popular basis (*jamhuri bunyad*). But there will be great difficulty in appointing (*taqarrur*) a qazi-e shar' and a mufti-e shar' on the basis of Islamic shari'a law.
>
> Because in the country's fundamental laws [constitution] there will be no clear [course of] action on the basis of which the qazi-e shar' and the mufti-e shar' may be appointed in the correct manner, I am today laying the foundations for this [process] so that this . . . may continue and no difficulty be experienced after independence'. Then he said, 'Today, I am appointing . . . Maulana Amjad 'Ali A'zami the qazi-e shar' for the entire Indian nation' . . . . And, accompanied with supplications for [him], he seated him on the chair singled out for the qazi-e shar'.[107]

In this way, Ahmad Riza also appointed two mufti-e shar' to assist the qazi, seating each one on either side of him. One of these was his younger son, Mustafa Riza Khan, the other Burhan ul-Haqq, in whose biography this incident is related.

This passage is striking for several reasons. First, one sees an echo of the elective process of the first 'rightly guided' caliphs, one that was not institutionalized but nevertheless stamped by the consensual

[106] Muhammad Ramazan 'Abd ul-'Aziz Rizwi, *Tazkira-e Hazrat Burhan-e Millat* (Jabalpur: Astana 'Aliyya Rizwiyya Salamiyya Burhaniyya, 1985), pp. 20–1.

[107] Ibid., pp. 21–2.

approval (ijma') of the community. Elements of both direct appointment and election were therefore present. One imagines that Ahmad Riza's choice was approved by all those present. The qazi-e shar' and his two assistant muftis were also, it is important to note, being appointed for all of India: they were to adjudicate, thus, between Muslims of all schools of thought, not just the Ahl-e Sunnat. This was in keeping, one supposes, with the latters' claim to be representative of the Ahl-e Sunnat throughout the Muslim world, rather than a merely local school of thought. And finally, one must note the ad hoc nature of the solution (which too, of course, has precedents in early Islamic history). Did the solution ever carry practical weight, even within the Ahl-e Sunnat movement? Given that there is no further mention of this 'election' in the Ahl-e Sunnat literature, I doubt that it did.

What this incident tells us, I believe, is that Ahmad Riza did not look at the world in which he lived in political terms. This was a challenge that his followers had to face. Contrary to what later followers have chosen to read into his works, he himself seems to have offered no clear answer to the political dilemmas of early twentieth-century Muslims. His scholarly output, enormous as it was, concentrated largely on matters of belief and practice at the individual level.

The question of Ahmad Riza's attitude to the Hindus remains to be discussed. If the British were not important to him, the Hindus were for the most part not a significant concern either. He wrote about them only toward the end of his life, in the context of social conflicts generated by the Arya Samaj conversion of Muslims to Hinduism in the course of the so-called Shuddhi movement—the Muslims called it irtidad (apostacy)—and the cow slaughter issue. Additionally, Ahmad Riza opposed the political union of Hindus and Muslims in the various early twentieth-century movements already examined.

As with the British, he thought about the Hindus only when circumstances forced this upon him, often in a conflict situation. A passage from his *Malfuzat* gives us a glimpse of his deep-rooted sense of distance from the Hindus amidst whom he lived. They were kafirs, and were to be regarded with enmity for that reason.

Paradoxically, his characterization of the Hindu (a Brahman, no less) that he met on the occasion referred to as 'unclean', and his revulsion toward even the slightest physical contact with him, mirrors exactly Hindu concepts of ritual purity and impurity:

> Praise be to Allah, ever since I gained consciousness I have found only strong dislike for the enemies of Allah in my heart. Once I had gone to my village (*apne dehat ko*). Some rural courtcase arose and our servants (mulazim) from all four directions had to go to Badayun [to appear in court]. I was left all alone. This was a time when I suffered from severe colic pain. That day the pain started from the time of zuhr (mid-day) . . . I couldn't stand up for the namaz (prayer). [Ahmad Riza then relates that he supplicated Allah and the Prophet for help, this plea was heard, and he was able to offer the namaz. But the pain returned just as severely as before, and he decided to lie down. While he was lying there,] a Brahman from the village passed by in front of me. (The wretch himself professed something close to tauhid and deceitfully inclined toward the Muslims in order to please me.) The gate was open. Seeing me he came in. And putting his hand on my stomach he asked, 'Is this where it hurts?' Feeling his impure (*najis*) hand touching my body I felt such revulsion (*karahat, nafrat*) that I forgot my pain. And I began to experience a pain even greater than this, [knowing that] a kafir's hand was on my stomach. This is the kind of enmity (*'adawat*) that one should [cultivate toward kafirs].[108]

In answer to the question, 'Ahmad Riza: pro-British, anti-Hindu?' I would say that, while he did not oppose the British presence in India because Indian Muslims were free to live their lives in accordance with the shari'a without hindrance, he did not accept the jurisdiction of the British Indian government over himself as an Indian Muslim, or over the Muslim community in general either. His refusal to appear in a Badayun court in 1916 seems to me to be a clear demonstration of his belief that the Muslim community could—and should—be internally self-governing under the British Indian state. As for his stand on joint action with Hindus, he opposed this consistently through the course of the Khilafat and Non-Cooperation movements. For Ahmad Riza, direct political action against the British in co-operation with non-Muslims, and even with Muslims of whom he disapproved on shar'i grounds, was to sacrifice principle for tactical gain.

108 Ahmad Riza Khan, *Malfuzat*, vol. 2, pp. 78–9.

EPILOGUE

Ahl-e Sunnat Debates on Pakistan

In the previous chapter I considered the reasons why the Ahl-e Sunnat movement did not support the nationwide Khilafat movement in 1919–20, nor join with the Jam'iyyat-e 'Ulama'-e Hind in its endeavour to launch an anti-British struggle in a Hindu–Muslim partnership. I would like now to indicate some of the directions in which Ahmad Riza's followers led the movement after his death in 1921, particularly in relation to the Pakistan question. In order to do this as concisely and as clearly as possible, I have chosen to focus on the contributions of three men. All personally close to Ahmad Riza, each took a different stand in the 1940s on Pakistan and the Muslim League.

Na'im ud-Din Muradabadi

Born in 1882 in Muradabad, Na'im ud-Din was a precocious student. He had memorized the Qur'an by the age of eight, and then learned Persian, Arabic, tibb (Yunani medicine), and a good part of the dars-e nizami syllabus[1] under the personal direction of his father and other teachers. At the age of fourteen or thereabouts, he joined Muradabad's Madrasa Imdadiyya, where he was taught

[1] The sources (for which see note 2 below) say 'up to Mulla Hasan'. According to Sufi's *Al-Minhaj*, in which he gives the titles of all the books taught at Deoband's Dar al-'Ulum, this book was taught in the third of an eight-year course. I assume the curricula of most madrasas in the late nineteenth century were similar. Sufi, *Al-Minhaj*, p. 130.

logic, philosophy, and hadis by one Sayyid Shah Gul Muhammad, the school's muhtamim (manager).[2] Na'im ud-Din completed the dars-e nizami syllabus by the time he was nineteen, then stayed on at the madrasa another year to study the art of fatwa-writing. He graduated in 1902, aged twenty. Shortly thereafter, he sought and received discipleship (bai'a) from his erstwhile teacher, Sayyid Gul Muhammad.[3]

The Madrasa Imdadiyya where Na'im ud-Din studied is said to have been located near another madrasa, the Madrasa-e Shahi. This latter had been personally founded by Maulana Muhammad Qasim Nanautawi (d. 1877), and was organized on principles similar to those operative at the Dar al-'Ulum at Deoband.[4] During his lifetime Muhammad Qasim had occasionally taught there, though that was of course before Na'im ud-Din's time. What impact this proximity to a Deobandi school may have had on the young Na'im ud-Din is unknown.

Although the biography is uninterested in chronology, which would have helped us map Na'im ud-Din's intellectual development, however roughly, a few details mentioned therein suggest that his loyalty to the Ahl-Sunnat cause may have developed only gradually. His father Mu'in ud-Din had been a disciple (murid) of Muhammad Qasim Nanautawi. According to the biography, it was

[2] Mahmud Ahmad Qadiri, *Tazkira-e 'Ulama'-e Ahl-e Sunnat*, pp. 252–3; Ghulam Mu'in ud-Din Na'imi, 'Tazkira al-Ma'ruf Hayat-e Sadr al-Afazil. Tajdar-e Ahl-e Sunnat Sultan al-'Ulum Sadar al-Afazil Ustad al-'Ulama' Hazrat Maulana Sayyid Muhammad Na'im ud-Din Muradabadi ke Zindagi ke Halat Tayyiba ke Sath Musalmanon ki Dini o Siyasi Rahnuma'i', in *Sawad-e A'zam*, vol. 2 (Lahore: Na'imi Dawakhana, 12–19 Zu'l Hijja 1378/19-26 June 1959), pp. 5–6. Mu'in ud-Din's biography is hereafter cited as 'Hayat-e Sadr al-Afazil'. I should note that although it is ascribed to a single author, it consists in fact of articles by more than one person. The longest memoir is that of Ghulam Mu'in ud-Din 'Na'imi, who is named the author of the Tazkira.

[3] He had travelled to Pilibhit in search of a well-known pir there, Shah Ji Muhammad Sher Miyan of Pilibhit; but the latter advised him to go back to Muradabad and become Sayyid Gul Muhammad's murid. 'Hayat-e Sadr al-Afazil', p. 6.

[4] That is to say, financially dependent on personal contributions from supporters rather than on landownership or other forms of fixed income. See Metcalf, *Islamic Revival*, pp. 127–8. Some additional information on the Madrasa-e Shahi is also available in Ziyaud-Din A. Desai, *Centres of Islamic Learning in India*, pp. 35–6. Unfortunately I have no information on the Madrasa Imdadiyya which Na'im ud-Din attended.

not until the early twentieth century, long after Muhammad Qasim's death, that Mu'in ud-Din learned the 'truth' about his dead pir:

Maulana Mu'in ud-Din took bai'a at the hands of Muhammad Qasim Nanautawi. At this time, the Wahhabi used to hide his Wahhabism well. Thus, Maulawi Qasim permitted Maulana Mu'in ud-Din to attend milad sharif, do qiyam at the salat o salam [stand up when praying for benediction for the Prophet], and taught him ways full of baraka. When others told Maulana Mu'in ud-Din that Muhammad Qasim was a Wahhabi, he replied, 'How can I accept this? He himself told me about the baraka of milad sharif, . . . and gave me permission to do this'. But when he was shown the fatwa *Husam al-Haramain* [by Ahmad Riza Khan] and *Tahzir al-Nas* by Maulawi Qasim Nanautawi, in which [the latter] had denied the finality of [Muhammad's] prophethood, and the contents of *Husam al-Haramain* were compared with those of *Tahzir al-Nas*, he dissolved his tie of discipleship to Qasim Nanautawi, and became A'la Hazrat's [Ahmad Riza Khan's] disciple.[5]

This extraordinary event receives no further comment in the biography. Yet given the fact that a disciple's tie to his sufi master is believed to be for life, and indeed to persist even after the pir's death, and given the considerable animosity that characterized the Ahl-e Sunnat's relations with Deoband, this decision by Na'im ud-Din's father must surely have been provoked by some prior event, and accompanied by considerable debate and argument. At any rate, it seems clear that Na'im ud-Din's father had ties with the Deobandi 'ulama' and that Na'im ud-Din grew up in a household which was sympathetic to Deobandi perspectives on din. If so, he must have broken away as a young man at some indeterminate—but crucial—point from his father, and to have persuaded him to sever his Deobandi ties accordingly.[6]

Another indication that Na'im ud-Din was not as a young man committed to the Ahl-Sunnat vision of din lies in the report that he contributed 'resolute' (*mustaqill*) articles published in Abu'l Kalam

[5] 'Hayat-e Sadr al-Afazil', p. 5.

[6] All this is, of course, conjecture, and one wonders why Mu'in ud-Din did not send his son to the Deobandi Madrasa-e Shahi in the first place. The fact that Ahmad Riza's *Husam al-Haramain* is mentioned in the text causes me to place this 'conversion' by Mu'in ud-Din in the early twentieth century, for *Husam* was written in 1905–6. On the other hand, the biographer, writing after the event, may well have added these details himself.

Azad's Calcutta-based *Al-Hilal* and *Al-Balagh*[7] in order to establish his place in the literary field and preach din through the written word. This information (like Mu'in ud-Din's transfer of discipleship) is intriguing, for the Ahl-e Sunnat and Abu'l Kalam Azad had little in common concerning Islam or politics.[8] In fact the Ahl-e Sunnat were in sympathy with the point of view represented by Azad's father Khair ud-Din (1831–1908), who believed strongly in the doctrine of taqlid and had written extensively against the Indian 'Wahhabis'.[9] Abu'l Kalam disagreed with his father on all of the above.

We do not know what caused Na'im ud-Din to change his views (if indeed this occurred as conjectured). To confuse matters further, the biography reports that simultaneously with his writing for *Al-Balagh* and *Al-Hilal* Na'im ud-Din was engaged in writing a book in defence of the Prophet's knowledge of the unseen ('ilm-e ghaib).[10] According to one account, someone showed this book to Ahmad Riza who liked it and asked to meet the author. However, another story, also related in the biography, has it that Na'im ud-Din came to Ahmad Riza's attention because he had written a series of

[7] This detail is related in both the biographical sketches available to me: Mahmud Ahmad Qadiri, *Tazkira-e 'Ulama'-e Ahl-e Sunnat*, p. 253, where the word used is 'mustaqill'; and 'Hayat-e Sadr al-Afazil', p. 18.

Al-Hilal appeared from July 1912 to December 1914, and again from June to December 1927. *Al-Balagh* appeared between November 1915 and March 1916. See Douglas, *Abul Kalam Azad*, p. 98, n. 3.

[8] As Douglas writes of *Al-Hilal*, 'As a religious journal, *al-Hilal* challenged traditional taqlid and offered Azad's fresh interpretation of Islam related to contemporary life. Politically, it challenged the position of loyalty to the British represented by Aligarh'. Douglas, *Abul Kalam Azad*, p. 100. On both counts, as earlier chapters have shown, the Ahl-e Sunnat position was at odds with Azad's.

[9] Ibid., pp. 33–5, 42–3. Khair ud-Din was also an important pir in his time in Calcutta. Azad rejected the institution of *piri-muridi* (the honour and devotion of disciples for their masters) with the same vehemence as he did his father's views on taqlid and 'Wahhabis'. See ibid., pp. 49–51.

[10] 'Hayat-e Sadr al-Afazil', p. 18. The title of the book was *Al-Kalimat al-'Uliyya li-I'la' 'ala 'Ilm al-Mustafa* (The Sublime Speech Elevating the Prophet's Knowledge). Mahmud Ahmad Qadiri adds that it was written in rebuttal of Maulana Salamat Ullah Rampuri's *I'lam al-Azkiya'* (Notification of the Wise . . .). *Tazkira-e 'Ulama'-e Ahl-e Sunnat*, p. 253. Ahmad Riza also addressed himself to questions arising from this book by Salamat Ullah Rampuri (d. 1813–14) in his *Daulat al-Makkiyya*, Part II.

articles published in a paper called *Nizam ul-Mulk* attacking the views of a 'Wahhabi' from Jodhpur.[11]

The broad outlines of Na'im ud-Din's subsequent career seem quite clear. Based in Muradabad, he devoted himself to defence of the Ahl-e Sunnat cause through his writings,[12] as well as debates with Deobandis, Ahl-e Hadis, Shi'is, Christians, and Aryas. He is said, for instance, to have persuaded an Arya of the falsity of the Hindu doctrine of transmigration of souls, and to have worsted another in debate when a Deobandi failed to do so.[13] Ahmad Riza is reported to have had such high regard for Na'im ud-Din's skill at debate that on important occasions, when the opponent was well known, he frequently appointed him the Ahl-e Sunnat representative (wakil) and sent him across the country at short notice.[14] Ahmad Riza's trust in his abilities was again evident in 1920–21 when he sent Na'im ud-Din at the head of a team of emissaries to Lucknow to accept 'Abd ul-Bari's *tauba-nama* (statement of repentance) for public comments made by the latter in the course of the Khilafat movement.[15] Some years later, according to Na'im ud-Din's biography, Muhammad 'Ali, one of the principal leaders of the Khilafat movement, personally came to Muradabad and did tauba in Na'im ud-Din's presence.[16]

[11] 'Hayat-e Sadr al-Afazil', pp. 6–7, 18.

[12] These included works defending the Prophet's knowledge of the unseen, works about isal-e sawab (transfer of merit), rebuttal of Muhammad Isma'il's *Taqwiyyat al-Iman*, and others. Ibid., p. 20.

[13] 'Hayat-e Sadr al-Afazil', pp. 7–8.

[14] Ibid., pp. 10–11, and passim.

[15] Na'im ud-Din was one of a small number of intermediaries in the protracted correspondence that took place between Ahmad Riza and 'Abd ul-Bari on this occasion. Ahmad Riza had listed 101 statements made by 'Abd ul-Bari for which he wanted the latter to do tauba, on grounds that these were alternatively kufr (expressive of unbelief), *zalal* (dishonourable), or haram (unlawful, forbidden). After a lengthy correspondence 'Abd ul-Bari is said to have done tauba, though he later refused to sign a document to that effect drawn up by Ahmad Riza. Na'im ud-Din was a witness, together with eleven others representing Ahmad Riza, to the tauba-nama. See Mustafa Riza Khan (compiler), *Al-Tari al-Dari li-Hafawat 'Abd ul-Bari* (Unexpected Correspondence [?] Regarding 'Abd ul-Bari's Errors), (Bareilly: Sunni Press, 1339/1921), pp. 3–27, 55.

[16] No date is given for this event, though we are told that it occurred three months before his death. As Muhammad 'Ali died in London in January 1931 (where he had

Attendant on Na'im ud-Din's skills as a persuader and debater were his organizational abilities. Unlike Ahmad Riza, whose style was essentially scholarly and solitary, Na'im ud-Din excelled at creating and managing institutions. Among his many achievements were the founding, around 1920, of a madrasa which subsequently expanded to become the Jam'iyya Na'imiyya, and leadership of the anti-Shuddhi organization 'Jama'at-e Riza-e Mustafa' which sent members to Agra, Ajmer, and to villages in neighbouring districts to convert former Muslims (the Malkana Rajputs) back to Islam in the 1920s.[17] In 1924, he created and edited (with the assistance of his pupil, Muhammad 'Umar Na'imi) a monthly journal, *Al-Sawad al-A'zam* (literally 'the great [that is to say, Sunni] majority'). In 1925 he also created a new body of Ahl-e Sunnat 'ulama', called the All-India Sunni Conference. The very name of the new organization indicates that it was intended to reach the Ahl-e Sunnat nationwide. In fact it was the Ahl-e Sunnat answer to the Jam'iyyat al-'Ulama'-e Hind and the Khilafat Committee, then the main 'ulama' organizations at the national level.

According to Na'im ud-Din's biography, the All-India Sunni Conference grew out of Na'im ud-Din's awareness of an increasingly anti-Muslim attitude among Hindus, exemplified not only in the Arya Samaj-led Shuddhi movement referred to above but also in Hindu assertiveness over the cow slaughter issue:

> After [the Shuddhi movement] the Hindus . . . started the Guru Gokul movement, by which they hoped to establish *gaushalas* (shelters for cows), colleges, *bhavans* (schools) . . . where young people would be admitted and given training which would result in their becoming severely anti-Muslim. [Na'im ud-Din] said that outwardly, this movement seeks to spread learning but the result will be that twenty or twenty-five years down, such people will . . . play Holi (Hindu spring festival celebrated with water) with blood . . . . Consequently he roused every Sunni 'alim and made [the 'ulama'] aware of these new dangers. He told them, 'If you have not become conscious [of the situation] yet, . . . prepare yourselves for that which is to happen'. He invited all the 'ulama' and masha'ikh (pirs) of the Ahl-e Sunnat, from all parts of the

---

gone to attend the Round Table Conference), this places the event in September or October 1930. 'Hayat-e Sadr al-Afazil', p. 74.

17 For details, see Chapter III. For the Shuddhi movement, see Thursby, *Hindu-Muslim Relations in British India*, pp. 136–58, and passim.

country, to Muradabad. For four days they gathered together and deliberated. At the end, the All-India Sunni Conference was established.[18]

Records of the 1925 meeting bear the biography out on the expression of anti-Hindu sentiment at the All-India Sunni Conference.[19] In line with arguments made by Ahmad Riza against the Jam'iyyat al-'Ulama'-e Hind and Khilafat leadership a few years previously, the All-India Sunni Conference rejected the principle of Hindu-Muslim unity as a means of achieving freedom.[20] Indeed, in his welcome address Hamid Riza Khan (Ahmad Riza's eldest son) rejected the goal of freedom itself, saying that since Swaraj would amount to Hindu *raj* he prayed that the Hindus would not succeed in their goal.[21] Instead, he and others spoke of the need to work for the education and economic uplift of Muslims, and for social issues on a national scale.

New to the Ahl-e Sunnat movement thus far was the projected sweep of the All-India Sunni Conference's influence. From the very beginning the organizers spoke of the need to set up branch affiliates at the state, district, and tahsil levels. In his address Hamid Riza Khan outlined a range of activities which the Conference would undertake. Important among these was tabligh (preaching), both against the Shuddhi movement, and against the 'false' teachings of other Muslim schools of thought. Tabligh would be carried out from madrasas to be set up throughout the country. 'The purpose of every madrasa is tabligh', he said. Students were to be trained in the principles of tabligh, and a select number of students as well as all

[18] 'Hayat-e Sadr al-Afazil', pp. 23–4.

[19] Muhammad Jalal ud-Din Qadiri (ed.), *Khutbat-e All-India Sunni Conference 1925–1947* (Gujarat, Pakistan: Maktaba Rizwiyya, 1978), pp. 122–230. There are several references to the distress caused to Muslims by the Arya-led Shuddhi movement. See, e.g., pp. 143–5, 175–6 (on the related Sangathan movement), 205–9.

[20] This position was also taken in the context of heightened Hindu-Muslim conflict during the 1920s. Thursby points out that as in earlier periods when an upsurge of violent conflict had been noted, this one 'correlated with steps in the devolution of political power' along the lines of the Montagu Reform Bill of 1918, and with 'the coincidence of the major religious festivals' of the two groups. Thursby, *Hindu-Muslim Relations in British India*, p. 72.

[21] *Khutbat-e All-India Sunni Conference*, p. 177.

teachers would be required to spend two days a week actively preaching.[22]

Hamid Riza also outlined a detailed hierarchy of madrasas to be set up throughout the country, affiliated to a Jam'iyyat-e 'Aliyya at the national level and going all the way down to the village level.[23] The madrasas would teach Qur'an, diniyat (religious subjects, not specified) using Amjad 'Ali A'zami's *Bahar-e Shari'at*,[24] arithmetic, and perhaps Persian and Arabic. Girls' schools were also to be set up, teaching diniyat, needlework and housekeeping. There were to be separate madrasas for Muslim boys attending English-language schools, in which religious instruction would be given for an hour each day. All madrasas would have a Dar al-Ifta, though important fatawa would have to be approved by the Jam'iyyat-e 'Aliyya before being issued. *Muballighs* (preachers), teachers, and debaters would also be trained under the aegis of the Jam'iyyat-e 'Aliyya, among other things.[25]

Finally, Hamid Riza suggested ways in which Indian Muslims could promote their economic welfare: instead of working under Hindu employers as servants, they should start businesses, no matter how small.[26] They should put aside some of their earnings to buy land at the earliest opportunity. Even if a man had inherited land, he should earn enough to buy himself some more. He advised everyone to put money aside for their children from birth. A paisa

[22] Ibid., p. 150. This emphasis on tabligh should be seen in the context of the rise of the Tablighi Jama'at around this time in Delhi. Led by Maulana Muhammad Ilyas (1885–1944), who studied at Deoband under Maulana Mahmud Hasan, the Tablighi Jama'at was the first organization of Indian 'ulama' to attempt to educate the mass of poor Muslims in the countryside. It started work among the Mewatis in Delhi. See Nadwi, *Life and Mission of Maulana Mohammad Ilyas*; Anwarul-Haq, *The Faith Movement of Mawlana Muhammad Ilyas* (London: George Allen & Unwin, 1972).

[23] *Khutbat-e All-India Sunni Conference*, pp. 143–50.

[24] A collection of fatawa, written by one of Ahmad Riza's close followers (khalifas), the *Bahar-e Shari'at* (currently available in 18 volumes) is widely used among the Ahl-e Sunnat. Its language is much simpler than Ahmad Riza's *Fatawa-e Rizwiyya* but follows the latter in argument and thinking.

[25] *Khutbat-e All-India Sunni Conference*, pp. 146, 148–50.

[26] Ibid., pp. 179–80.

a day, he said, would add up to a lot in fifteen years.[27] And they should cut down on their expenses, avoiding lavish wedding feasts. Better still, a man should not marry his child into a family that wanted to have a feast that would involve borrowing money.[28]

The 1925 meeting of the All-India Sunni Conference was attended, it is reported, by over two hundred and fifty learned men from all over the country.[29] An important supporter of the organization was Pir Jama'at 'Ali Shah from Panjab.[30] In his khutba he expressed strong support for the anti-Hindu, anti-Jam'iyyat-e 'Ulama'-e Hind stand of the leaders of the Conference.[31] He said that unity should not be sought with Hindus, or with 'free-thinking' Muslims such as the Ahmadis or Ahl-e Hadis. Unity already existed among the Ahl-e Sunnat wa Jama'at, who represented the vast majority of Muslims in India. The task before them was to carry out internal reform: to strengthen iman (faith), root out social evils like smoking and drinking, build more madrasas, and continue the work of tabligh.

In 1935 the All-India Sunni Conference met again at Badayun; and for a third time in April 1946, at Banaras. I turn to this 1946 meeting directly for its discussion of the Pakistan issue. It is said to have been attended by five hundred sufi shaikhs, seven thousand 'ulama', as well as two hundred thousand other 'Sunnis'.[32] Among

[27] Ibid., p. 181.

[28] Hamid Riza went into great detail in this speech on the problem of indebtedness. Among other remedies, he suggested the creation of a *bait al-mal* or treasury. Ibid., pp. 183–90.

[29] *Al-Sawad al-A'zam*, 4, 12 (Muradabad: Rabi' al-Akhir 1347/September 1928), 2.

[30] Gilmartin writes of Pir Jama'at 'Ali Shah (1841?–1951) that he came from a line of Qadiri pirs in Sialkot district, but was active in the reformist Naqshbandi order. 'Pir Jamaat Ali Shah's most burning religious concern was work in tabligh . . . He made extensive tours of Punjab and much of India, stressing the importance of the performance of religious duties according to shari'at and establishing mosques in towns and villages. This work greatly expanded his influence and led to contacts with powerful Muslims whose wealth he tapped for religious causes. By the opening of the twentieth century, Pir Jamaat Ali Shah could claim an extensive following, both in rural northern Punjab and among powerful Muslims elsewhere, which made his political influence comparable to that of any Chishti revival pirs'. Gilmartin, *Empire and Islam*, p. 60.

[31] The khutba is reproduced in *Khutbat-e All-India Sunni Conference*, pp. 195–217, from Sayyid Munawwar Husain Shah, *Malfuzat-e Amir al-Millat* (Lahore: 1976), pp. 171–203.

[32] *Khutbat-e All-India Sunni Conference*, p. 252. Introductory comment by the compiler

the leadership were Maulanas Na'im ud-Din Muradabadi, Mustafa Riza Khan (Ahmad Riza's younger son), Zafar ud-Din Bihari, and Sayyid Muhammad Ashrafi Jilani of Kachhochha. The last-named delivered the welcome address.

Unfortunately, neither the khutba delivered by Sayyid Muhammad[33] nor the formal resolutions adopted by the 1946 All-India Sunni Conference meeting, give us any insight into the debate that must have taken place on this occasion, and in preceding years, about the creation of Pakistan. Indeed, the khutba does not mention Pakistan in a political context at all until the very end. It focuses, as such khutbas did on previous occasions, on the need for 'Sunni' Muslims to improve their situation through tabligh, madrasas, and personal attention to din. One may guess that the reason for this surprising lack of discussion of what undoubtedly was an issue of paramount importance in 1946 may have been the problem that some 'ulama' had in supporting the Muslim League.[34]

At any rate, Sayyid Muhammad's khutba concentrates on the All-India Sunni Conference's educational and tablighi aspirations for the Ahl-e Sunnat throughout India. Occasionally he couched this sentiment by playing on the word *pakistan* in its literal meaning of 'a pure place'. He indicated for instance that Pakistan would come about naturally to the extent that Muslims became 'pure':

Because every Muslim must, from morning to night, be a Muslim, because every minute a person is governed by essentials, by the grace of education every

---

of the book.

[33] Sayyid Muhammad (1311/1893–94 to 1383/1963) was born in Rae Bareilly district. He was brought up by his maternal grandfather, Sayyid 'Ali Husain Ashrafi (1849/50–1936/37), who had addressed the first All-India Sunni Conference in 1925. Sayyid Muhammad studied the dars-e nizami at the Madrasa Nizamiyya, Firangi Mahal, Lucknow where Maulana 'Abd ul-Bari was one of his teachers. After eight years there, he went to Aligarh and studied with Maulana Lutf Ullah Aligarhi, then to Pilibhit, where he studied hadis with Maulana 'Abd ul-Muqtadir Badayuni. His maternal uncle, Maulana Ahmad Ashraf, was his pir. Sayyid Muhammad's accomplishments included the founding of a madrasa, Madrasa al-Hadis, in Delhi, converting some five thousand non-Muslims to Islam, and writing books, both prose and poetry. See Mahmud Ahmad Qadiri, *Tazkira-e 'Ulama'-e Ahl-e Sunnat*, pp. 235–6.

[34] That support of the League was the subject of considerable controversy amongst Ahl-e Sunnat 'ulama' becomes clear further in this Epilogue, when we study 'Muhammad Miyan' Marahrawi's position.

breath can become an Islamic breath. Then that breath will have that glory which we call Pakistan . . . .

[If all Muslims] live and die for Allah, then you may be sure that in the parched land between the Bay of Bengal and the Indian Ocean [you] will see Pakistan. When a community (qaum) becomes pure (*pak*) in knowledge, in deed, [and] in disposition, it transforms whichever place it sets foot on into a pure abode (pakistan).[35]

Sayyid Muhammad spoke at length about the lack of communication between the Ahl-e Sunnat in different parts of India, and their attendant failure to make a concerted effort to ameliorate their situation.[36] During the course of the four-day proceedings, resolutions were adopted to act on suggestions made on this occasion as well as in past conferences.

Addressing the Pakistan issue in the context of this larger concern for self-improvement toward the end of his khutba, Sayyid Muhammad affirmed the All-India Sunni Conference's support of the Muslim League in the demand for Pakistan. Ideally, he said, they would like all of India to be 'Pakistan', but recognizing that things change slowly, they supported the idea of a part of the country being singled out as a place to start. But this support was conditional, he said, on the Pakistan-to-be being subject to the laws of Islam:

Those Sunnis who have accepted this message [demand for a separate state] advanced by the [Muslim] League, and who go about canvassing support for the League, do so only to the extent that, in one part of Hindustan, the free governance of the Qur'an, of Islam, will prevail. In this [part], the lives and property of non-Muslim *zimmis* will enjoy protection according to the shari'a. They will be allowed to freely engage in social relations and practise their din . . . . If the League has adopted a path other than the one assumed by the Sunnis to have been taken, no Sunni will accept it.[37]

And again,

In Pakistan that offender (*mujrim*) will not be favoured, who, professing the kalima (articles of faith), calling him or herself a Sunni, is [nevertheless] irritated by the thought of an Islamic authority.[38]

[35] *Khutbat-e All-India Sunni Conference*, pp. 270–1.

[36] Ibid., p. 270, and passim.

[37] Ibid., p. 276.

[38] Ibid., p. 277.

Insofar as the All-India Sunni Conference was concerned, Sayyid Muhammad said, the Muslim League was but an 'interpreter' (tarjuman) of the Ahl-e Sunnat's passionate desire (*jazbat*) to see the recreation of that pristine state of affairs that had prevailed at the time of the 'rightly-guided' caliphs of Islam.[39] The Muslim League's goals were but temporary. It was the All-India Sunni Conference which would be needed in the future:

> If Sunnis have the right, as other communities do—and they do have the right—to stay alive, to protect their din, to arrange their future, to save their community (qaum) from destruction, to adorn their mosques and khanqahs, to keep their centres on the right track, then [the Sunnis] need the All-India Sunni Conference more than they do any other organization [at the state level?].[40]

The formal resolution on Pakistan adopted by the All-India Sunni Conference, however, gave little hint of the nuanced support indicated by Sayyid Muhammad in his khutba. It said:

> This session of the All-India Sunni Conference fully supports the demand for Pakistan, and announces that the 'ulama' and shaikhs of the Ahl-e Sunnat are prepared for whatever sacrifice may be necessary in the movement for the creation of an Islamic state (islami hukumat). And they consider it their duty to establish a state [guided by] the Qur'an, hadis, and the principles of fiqh.[41]

There is no suggestion, in anything we have seen of the proceedings of the Conference's 1946 meetings, that a large-scale migration (hijra) was envisaged, involving the uprooting of thousands of families leaving for a new home in Pakistan. It seems, rather, to have been assumed that the 'ulama' of the Ahl-e Sunnat would proceed as they had done in the past, attempting to inculcate din among Muslims throughout India and thereby deepen their influence. Along with this they would help create, in one part of the country, a state which would be governed by shari'a and which would usher in, they hoped, a life-style as close to their ideal as possible.

As for Na'im ud-Din Muradabadi, he never migrated to Pakistan. He was about sixty at the time of Partition, and died a year later in

39 Ibid., pp. 276, 278.

40 Ibid., p. 278.

41 Ibid., p. 283.

1948. But before his death, he managed to visit Karachi, Lahore, and other places in Pakistan, where he met with Ahl-e Sunnat 'ulama' and directed them in the organization of tablighi and other work.[42]

Shah Aulad-e Rasul 'Muhammad Miyan' Marahrawi

Shah Aulad-e Rasul (1892–1952), generally known as 'Muhammad Miyan', was born in Sitapur district (north of Lucknow). He was a third-generation descendant, on his father's side, of Sayyid Aulad-e Rasul (d. 1851, elder brother of Shah Al-e Rasul, Ahmad Riza's pir), and, going further back, of Shah Barkat Ullah (1660–1730), considered the founder of the Barkatiyya family. The Barkatiyya were Zaidi Sayyids tracing their descent back to Fatima, the Prophet's daughter. Although Muhammad Miyan's ancestors had moved to Marahra from Bilgram (in Hardoi district) in the seventeenth century, a branch of the family continued to live there into the early twentieth. This 'eastern' branch was of Shi'i persuasion.[43]

Muhammad Miyan was educated by a host of family elders and other 'ulama', memorizing the Qur'an, and learning Persian, Arabic, and the dars-e nizami from them. He completed his studies at the Madrasa 'Aliyya Qadiriyya at Badayun. And although he was never personally instructed by Ahmad Riza, he looked upon the latter as one of his teachers.[44] He was a prolific writer, having published about thirty books, including a family history and several on the political issues of his day. He received bai'a from his father, Shah Muhammad Isma'il Hasan 'Shah Ji' (1855–1914?).

Muhammad Miyan, as a Sayyid and a member of the family of Ahmad Riza's pir Shah Al-e Rasul, was naturally included in the

[42] 'Hayat-e Sadr al-Afazil', pp. 28–9. At Lahore, he is said to have stayed with Maulana Abu l Barakat Ahmad Qadiri, the manager (nazim) of the Anjuman-e Hizb ul-Ahnaf, an influential Panjabi organization that was part of the Ahl-e Sunnat movement. For more on this body, see Gilmartin, *Empire and Islam*, pp. 104, 164; Metcalf, *Islamic Revival*, p. 312.

[43] See Muhammad Miyan's *Khandan-e Barakat* (c. 1927), pp. 52–5. (No publication details are available.) Also see Chapter IV of this study for an account of the Barkatiyya family in the nineteenth century.

[44] *Khandan-e Barakat*, p. 53.

inner circle of Ahmad Riza's close associates. Ahmad Riza was on particularly close terms with Nuri Miyan (Muhammad Miyan's uncle and maternal grandfather, d. 1906).[45] After Nuri Miyan's death, Ahmad Riza used to attend his annual 'urs at Marahra; in addition, Ahmad Riza observed the 'urs of Shah Al-e Rasul for three days at his own home in Bareilly each year.

Muhammad Miyan's close links with Ahmad Riza and his khalifas is indicated, among other things, by the fact that he delivered the *khutba-e sadarat*, or chief address, at the first meeting of the Ansar al-Islam in April 1921 (22–24 Sha'ban 1339). This organization was created by Ahmad Riza in order to raise money for the Turkish cause and related concerns (such as protection of the Hijaz from non-Muslim rule).[46] Furthermore, Muhammad Miyan's positions on the major early twentieth-century debates examined in the previous chapter appear to have been in complete agreement with those taken by Ahmad Riza. Like Ahmad Riza, he believed that British India in the 1920s was a dar al-islam, that Hindu-Muslim unity in the course of the Khilafat movement was to be condemned, and that the Khilafat movement itself was but a means to achieve independence from British rule.[47] He also agreed with Ahmad Riza on the impermissibility of Muslims doing hijrat from British India in 1920.[48]

In these respects Muhammad Miyan was in agreement also with Na'im ud-Din, who had likewise rejected Hindu-Muslim unity and

[45] See, e.g., Ghulam Shabar Qadiri Nuri Badayuni, *Tazkira-e Nuri*, p. 14.

[46] See Shah Aulad-e Rasul, *Khutba-e Sadarat* (Marahra: Khanqah-e Barkatiyya, n.d.), 60 pp.

[47] Ibid., pp. 18, 21, 25–6, and passim. Also see S. Jamaluddin, 'Religiopolitical Ideas of a Twentieth Century Muslim Theologian—An Introduction', in *Marxist Miscellany*, 7 (March 1977), pp. 13–19. Jamaluddin interprets Muhammad Miyan's attitudes on these issues as an expression of his 'fierce class consciousness'. Because Muhammad Miyar came from a sufi and zamindari (landowning) family, he says, 'he attempted to divert the Muslims from the national movement in order to safeguard the vested interests of the zamindar class. The same class consciousness made him keep distance from the Congress'. Ibid., p. 14. This would imply that no zamindars, Hindu or Muslim, participated in the nationalist movement, which is manifestly not the case. Nor does class consciousness seem to have any bearing on political partnership with the Congress.

[48] *Khutba-e Sadara*, p. 49. Also see Raja Rashid Mahmud, *Tahrik-e Hijrat (1920)*, p. 94.

the Khilafat movement. Na'im ud-Din had supported the goals of the Ansar al-Islam, and had addressed its meetings in 1921 as had Muhammad Miyan.[49] Furthermore, both men had worked together in the Jama'at-e Riza-e Mustafa in the early 1920s against the Shuddhi movement of the Arya Samaj.[50]

By 1935–40, however, Muhammad Miyan had begun to move away from Na'im ud-Din and his associates in the All-India Sunni Conference over the question of what the leadership's attitude should be toward the Muslim League. Perhaps it was his disagreement on this important matter that motivated Muhammad Miyan around 1935 to create the Jama'at-e Ahl-e Sunnat, based in Marahra. This new body, of which Muhammad Miyan was president (sadr),[51] represented the opinions of sufi shaikhs and 'ulama' calling themselves Ahl-e Sunnat. It met annually in the course of a three-day 'urs for Muhammad Miyan's father, Shah Muhammad Isma'il 'Shah Ji'.

In 1946, a small number of Barkatiyya pirs associated with Muhammad Miyan began a monthly journal, the *Ahl-e Sunnat ki Awaz*, 'The Voice of the Ahl-e Sunnat', in which the Jama'at-e Ahl-e Sunnat's activities were reported. It is from this journal that we learn why Muhammad Miyan and his supporters objected to the Muslim League and the All-India Sunni Conference. It becomes clear from this that the Jama'at-e Ahl-e Sunnat's objections to the Muslim League were the main reason for its opposition to the creation of Pakistan.

The very first issue of the *Ahl-e Sunnat ki Awaz* notes that the Jama'at-e Ahl-e Sunnat adopted certain resolutions at its 1946 meeting. These included, importantly, the declarations that

> . . . we, the leaders of the Jama'at-e Ahl-e Sunnat, are free of (*bari*) and displeased with (*be-zar*) the Congress of the kafirs and polytheists, and with the

[49] *Al-Sawad al-A'zam*, 2, 5 (Sha'ban 1339/April 1924), 4.

[50] *Rudad-e Jama'at-e Riza-e Mustafa* (1342/1924), p. 15. No publication details are available.

[51] Among other office-bearers (in 1946) were Maulana Shah 'Hasan Miyan', the Vice-President (na'ib-e sadr), and Maulana Shah Al-e Mustafa 'Sayyid Miyan', the Chief Administrator (nazim). Both were sajjada-nishins at the Barkatiyya khanqah, as was Muhammad Miyan. See *Ahl-e Sunnat ki Awaz*, 1, 5 (Marahra: Khanqah-e Barkatiyya, n.d.), 2, 7.

> . . . Muslim League of the apostates (murtaddin) and hypocrites (munafiqin) . . . . The All-India Sunni Conference has arisen after twenty-three years wrapped in the cloak of the clandestine League, and standing before the touchstone of the pure sunna, has not yet purified itself of the strangers admitted into it. [On the contrary, it] is openly supporting the dark (muzlim) [the letter *sin* in the Arabic replaced by *zo'e*] League. Therefore, it is our shar'i duty to stay away from it. The newspaper *Dabdaba-e Sikandari* has adopted a policy of clearcut opposition to the sunna in its [slavish support] of the so-called Sunni Conference . . . . This . . . meeting expresses its strong disapproval of it.[52]

In this same meeting, the Jama'at-e Ahl-e Sunnat also voiced its opposition to the 'fitna' (affliction) of the Ahrar and Khaksar parties.[53]

An article written in February or March 1947 (Rabi' al-Akhir 1365) set out with clarity the Barkatiyya pirs' objections to the Muslim League. Its author, Hasan Miyan, wrote that the League did not care in the least whether its supporters wee Muslims or kafirs, as long as they were pro-League. Thus it was uninterested in Muslims whose faith was true to the shari'a, but who were not members of the League and did not look upon Muhammad 'Ali Jinnah as the 'prophet of politics' (siyasat ka nabi) or the 'protector of the law' (*qanun ka parwar-o-gar*), and did not accept Jinnah's and the League's 'new shari'a'.[54] The League's Pakistan would be open to every kafir, polytheist, Hindu, Christian, or Jew. It would have no place for true Muslims. Furthermore, in his view the current 'war' of the League with the Congress was purely tactical in nature, as were its expressions of love for all Muslims. The assurances it was giving the Muslims were designed to elicit support for its own political agenda; there was no truth to them. He said he was surprised that the All-India Sunni Conference did not see this, and reminded

[52] *Ahl-e Sunnat ki Awaz*, 1, 20–1. There was a fourth declaration, not quoted above, in which the Jama'at expressed its support of the newspaper *Al-Faqih* to which the *Dabdaba-e Sikandari* was opposed.

[53] Two urban Muslim organizations that arose in Panjab in the late 1920s and early 1930s. For details, see Gilmartin, *Empire and Islam*, pp. 96–9, 105, and references therein.

[54] Hasan Miyan, 'Leaguion ki islam-dosti aur muslim-nawazi ki haqiqat—League ke Pakistan men musalmanon ke li'e koi jagah nahin' (The Truth about the League's Love of Islam and Cherishing of Muslims—There is No Place for Muslims in the League's Pakistan), *Ahl-e Sunnat ki Awaz*, 2, 6–7.

them of the Qur'an verse (3:118, Yusuf 'Ali tr.), 'O ye who believe! Take not into your intimacy those outside your ranks . . . ', for the purpose of outsiders is to mislead.[55] In the current situation, he said, there was nothing to be done but to stay away from 'lovers of falsehood' like the League, the Congress, and others, and remain firm in their adherence to the thirteen-hundred-year-old shari'a.[56]

These arguments, representing the Jama'at-e Ahl-e Sunnat's reasons for opposing the League's Pakistan movement, are very similar to Ahmad Riza's own arguments in the early 1920s against Hindu–Muslim unity and the Khilafat movement. Like Hasan Miyan, who said that the Muslim League's purposes in wanting to create Pakistan were unrelated to the religious (dini) welfare of Muslims, Ahmad Riza had seen the Khilafat leaders' support of the Turkish khalifa as politically motivated, and therefore 'impure' or tainted. Contributors to the *Ahl-e Sunnat ki Awaz* indicated explicitly that Ahmad Riza was the model they held up for emulation, and maintained that those of the Ahl-e Sunnat who disagreed with them on Pakistan were not his true followers:

> There are those who were respectfully bending their knees before the Mujaddid-e A'zam [Ahmad Riza] yesterday and whose very breath trembled in the presence of his awesome glory. Today, on the contrary, . . . they have set themselves up as a mujaddid-e din and millat. Entrapping innocent people in their . . . net, they move with the wind of the times like a reed.[57]

The July 1947 issue (Sha'ban 1365) of the *Ahl-e Sunnat ki Awaz* was devoted solely to publication of correspondence between Muhammad Miyan and Na'im ud-Din Muradabadi. The very fact that this extensive correspondence, detailing their disagreements from 1938–39 to 1947, was made public in this way points to the fact that relations between them had reached a point of no return. The depth of the rift and some sense of the personal hurt caused to the Barkatiyya pirs by their difference of opinion with Na'im ud-Din

[55] Ibid., p. 8.

[56] Ibid., p. 9.

[57] *Ahl-e Sunnat ki Awaz*, part 1, p. 9. Though the writer's name is not indicated, it may have been Shah Al-e Mustafa Sayyid Miyan, the paper's manager (murattib). Ahmad Riza's name and views on Muslim participation in Congress-led movements were similarly evoked by Hasan Miyan, in *Ahl-e Sunnat ki Awaz*, 5. 2–3.

Muradabadi is indicated by Hasan Miyan's comment, following the correspondence, that although the Barkatiyya *astana* ('palace') had been the 'qibla and Ka'ba' of the Astana-e 'Aliyya Rizwiyya (Ahmad Riza's residence/khanqah), and of numerous others revered by the Ahl-e Sunnat, yet Na'im ud-Din had been 'ashamed' ('*ar*) to personally visit Muhammad Miyan at Marahra.[58]

BURHAN UL-HAQQ JABALPURI

While Na'im ud-Din and his associates in the Ahl-e Sunnat movement supported the League and Pakistan from the outside, and Muhammad Miyan and like-minded pirs opposed the League and Pakistan altogether, Burhan ul-Haqq Jabalpuri adopted yet another position. His career offers a complete contrast to the first two in that he played a leadership role in the Muslim League from his hometown of Jabalpur in the Central Provinces. Insofar as the Pakistan issue was concerned, he presents the picture of an important local politician rather than that of an 'alim anxious to establish whether the League's party members' beliefs were 'correct' or not.

Burhan ul-Haqq Jabalpuri (1892–1984) was born to a family that traced its descent to the first caliph Abu Bakr (d. 13/634) and therefore styled itself 'Siddiqi' (from the epithet 'siddiq', 'true', attached by Sunni Muslims to Abu Bakr's name). The family had lived at Jabalpur since about 1865. This was the year that Burhan ul-Haqq's grandfather, 'Abd ul-Karim, a *mir munshi* (religious teacher) and *kotwal* (city magistrate) in British service, came to Jabalpur from somewhere near Haidarabad as part of the Madras army.[59] He gave up his job a few years later and devoted himself to religious teaching. He was initiated into the Qadiri order by his pir, a man from the

[58] Hasan Miyan, 'Sadr al-Afazil khud apni khat o kitabat ki roshni men' ([Na'im ud-Din Muradabadi] in Light of His Own Correspondence), *Ahl-e Sunnat ki Awaz*, 5, 22, 23. The reference was to a protracted discussion, which ended in stalemate, as to where the two men should meet. Several locations were suggested, among them Bareilly (by Na'im ud-Din) and Marahra (by Muhammad Miyan).

[59] Muhammad Hamid Siddiqi Rizwi Salami Burhani, *Tazkira-e Hazrat Burhan-e Millat* (Jabalpur: Astana 'Aliyya Rizwiyya Salamiyya Burhaniyya, 1985), pp. 9, 12.

south Indian town of Vellore, and had also been admitted into the Naqshbandi order by another sufi teacher.[60] 'Abd ul-Karim corresponded with, though never met, Ahmad Riza, whom he held in high esteem.[61]

Burhan ul-Haqq's early education took place under the direction of family elders, among them his grandfather and father 'Abd us-Salam. 'Abd us-Salam, an 'alim, devoted his time to teaching at the Madrasa 'Id al-Islam and issuing fatawa from its Dar al-Ifta. In the 1890s, he associated himself with the Nadwat al-'Ulama', attending its annual meetings at Lucknow and elsewhere in a leadership role. A personal dispute with Shibli Nu'mani, a leader of the Nadwa, over proposed changes in the dars-e nizami syllabus, and disagreement with the Nadwa on more general matters, however, caused him to leave.[62] Henceforward, 'Abd us-Salam became active in opposing the Nadwa in concert with other Ahl-e Sunnat 'ulama'. In this capacity he came into close contact with Ahmad Riza. In 1895–96 Ahmad Riza gave him a sanad-e ijazat, a certificate linking him as a teacher to Ahmad Riza and his teachers in turn.[63]

The relationship between Ahmad Riza and Burhan ul-Haqq's father deepened over the years. Burhan ul-Haqq recalled that Ahmad Riza wrote or sent a telegram whenever a bereavement occurred in the family.[64] It was he who named Burhan ul-Haqq's brother, born in 1904, and then mourned his death a few years later. In 1908, Burhan ul-Haqq's uncle died within a day of the death of Ahmad Riza's brother, Hasan Riza. Each side condoled with the other at its loss.[65]

Growing up in this atmosphere of reverence for Ahmad Riza, Burhan ul-Haqq soon developed a passionate desire to meet him in person. He recalled that when he was about nine, he dreamt that he

60 Ibid., p. 12.

61 Burhan ul-Haqq Jabalpuri, *Ikram-e Imam Ahmad Riza* (Lahore: Markazi Majlis-e Riza, 1981), pp. 30–1.

62 Ibid., pp. 42–5.

63 Whether the sanad was in hadis, fiqh or some other field is not specified. *Ikram-e Imam Ahmad Riza*, p. 52.

64 Ibid., p. 35.

65 Ibid., pp. 36–8.

had fallen sick and was only cured when Ahmad Riza gave him a ta'wiz (amulet). Soon after he actually fell seriously ill with the plague; only when a ta'wiz from Ahmad Riza was tied to his body did he recover.[66] Some years later, in 1905–6 when he was fourteen, he was finally able to fulfill his ambition of meeting Ahmad Riza. That year Burhan ul-Haqq accompanied his father to Bombay to welcome Ahmad Riza back from the Haramain. Ahmad Riza, now recognized by Ahl-e Sunnat 'ulama' as the mujaddid or 'renewer' of the fourteenth Hijri century, had just scored what the Ahl-e Sunnat regarded as a special victory against the Deobandis in the course of his recent sojourn at the Haramain. He naturally left a deep impression on the young Burhan ul-Haqq during his ten-day stay in Bombay en route to Bareilly.[67]

In 1913–14 Burhan ul-Haqq and his father went to Bareilly. Ahmad Riza had sent for 'Abd us-Salam in connection with his dispute with certain Badayuni 'ulama' over the second azan (call to prayer) on Fridays, which had led them to file a case of libel against him.[68] Burhan ul-Haqq spent the next three years at Bareilly, attending personally to Ahmad Riza's needs, helping in the Dar al-Ifta, and taking classes at the Madrasa Manzar al-Islam.[69] From Ahmad Riza he learned *'ilm-e tauqit*, the precise calculation of time by means of the sun. Returning to Jabalpur in 1917, he was able to persuade Ahmad Riza to come on a visit in 1919. While there, Ahmad Riza performed Burhan ul-Haqq's dastar-bandi (tying of a turban, symbol of the completion of one's studies) at a large public function.[70] Burhan ul-Haqq also received a sanad-e khilafat, a testimonial to his close relationship with Ahmad Riza over the years.

[66] Ibid., pp. 55–6. Several years later, a similar event occurred in which Ahmad Riza was believed to have saved Burhan ul-Haqq's wife from almost certain death from the plague. Again, the cure followed a vision in which Ahmad Riza appeared to her, soon after which a ta'wiz was received in the mail. Ibid., pp. 64–5.

[67] See *Tazkira-e Hazrat Burhan-e Millat*, pp. 15–16; *Ikram-e Imam Ahmad Riza*, pp. 54–5.

[68] For details on this dispute, see Chapter VI above. Burhan ul-Haqq does not specify what Ahmad Riza wanted his father to do in his connection.

[69] Mustafa Riza Khan and Amjad 'Ali A'zami were his constant companions during these years. See *Ikram-e Imam Ahmad Riza*, p. 57.

[70] Ibid., pp. 67–8. Also see Chapter III for details on Ahmad Riza's Jabalpur trip.

In the 1920s, Burhan ul-Haqq followed Ahmad Riza's lead on the major issues, opposing the Khilafat movement, the Non-Cooperation movement, Hindu-Muslim unity, and the Hijrat movement.[71] In March 1921, he joined a delegation from the Jama'at-e Riza-e Mustafa at a Khilafat committee meeting at Bareilly. Presenting the delegation's point of view to the Committee, Burhan ul-Haqq debated with Abu'l Kalam Azad on the issue of Khilafat and Hindu–Muslim unity.[72]

The biographical sources are silent on Burhan ul-Haqq's activities between this point and Partition in 1947, though some information is available about his interests in the 1950s and beyond.[73] Unfortunately, therefore, I cannot tell whether he ever discussed with other Ahl-e Sunnat 'ulama' the course to be followed regarding the Muslim League and its demand for Pakistan.[74] I do not know what led him to join the League, or whether he had earlier been involved in other organizations like Na'im ud-Din Muradabadi's All-India Sunni Conference. The fact that he never moved to Pakistan despite his avid support for the League in the early forties raises a whole different set of questions about his relationship to the League and his support of a Muslim state versus his commitment to stay on in Jabalpur and maintain his ancestral dargah. On this, too, the sources are silent.

We can infer that Burhan ul-Haqq joined the League in the late 1930s when it was reorganized and revamped under the leadership of Jinnah.[75] In January 1940, Burhan ul-Haqq addressed a meeting

[71] As to this last, I infer that he opposed the Hijrat movement from the fact that many years later he accused Gandhi of having encouraged the Muslims to do hijrat in 1920. See Burhan ul-Haqq Jabalpuri, *Khutba-e Sadarat*, Muslim League Conference, District Jabalpur, 1–3 January 1940 (Jabalpur: n.d.), p. 2.

[72] *Ikram-e Imam Ahmad Riza*, pp. 106–9; *Tazkira-e Hazrat Burhan-e Millat*, p. 20.

[73] Ibid., pp. 23–4, 26–7, 37.

[74] The complete omission of any reference to Burhan ul-Haqq's membership of the Muslim League in the available biographical literature is curious. Perhaps it is connected with the inherent contradiction suggested by the fact, referred to below, that despite his being a member of the League he chose to remain in India after Partition. Or perhaps the Ahl-e Sunnat did not approve of his joining the League.

[75] There are several sources on Muslim League history. For the 1930s period, see, e.g., Stanley Wolpert, *Jinnah of Pakistan* (New York: Oxford University Press, 1984), pp. 140–54.

of the Jabalpur District Muslim League Conference as the chairman (sadr) of the welcome session (*majlis-e istiqbaliyya*).[76] In his speech, he pointed out that Muslims constituted only four per cent of the population of the Central Provinces, and that because they were so outnumbered by Hindus (the other 96 per cent) they were economically weak, poor, and helpless. He then went on to detail the manner in which the Hindus had taken advantage of this weakness in recent years,[77] and enumerated at length the wrongs that Muslims had suffered in the Central Provinces during the Hindu-dominated Congress ministry that had governed from 1937 to 1939.[78] All this was, of course, an echo of League arguments made in support of its 'two-nation theory', which held that Hindus and Muslims had never shared a common cultural, linguistic, or religious tradition and therefore could not live together as fellow citizens of the same country. Burhan ul-Haqq likened India to Europe, which consisted of separate countries, each with its own language, religions and culture. If it was acceptable for Europe to be politically divided into several states, he said, why should the Indian subcontinent be held to a different standard?[79] Beyond this, he went on to criticize recent attempts at the national level to bring the League and Congress together within a new constitutional framework.

During the next few years, Burhan ul-Haqq was actively involved in Muslim League politics at Jabalpur. In a 1941 letter addressed to Jinnah, he reported that the Muslim League in Jabalpur had set up a Municipal Parliamentary Board which would be contesting elections that November in those district wards in which Muslims constituted a majority.[80] Wolpert points out that it was precisely by

[76] Muhammad Burhan ul-Haqq, *Khutba-e Sadarat,* 15 pp.

[77] He said that by trying to substitute Hindi for Urdu in high schools, for instance, they were trying to make Muslim children forget their linguistic, cultural, and religious roots, and to assimilate them with Hindus. Ibid., p. 3.

[78] Ibid., pp. 8–9.

[79] Ibid., pp. 6, 8. As a means of underscoring the absurdity of the idea that either Europe or the subcontinent could ever form single states, he added that if the European nations would agree to merge all their countries and become a single nation, the Muslim League would drop its demand for a separate state!

[80] C. P. & Berar I:67, 'Correspondence of Qaide Azam Mr. M. Jinnah and Other Papers', Shamsul Hasan Collection. This collection is owned by Mr Khalid S. Hasan,

establishing such parliamentary boards throughout the country that Jinnah was able to extend the League's influence to towns and villages throughout the country.[81]

Further correspondence dating to 1943–46 reveals Burhan ul-Haqq directing administrative and political affairs in his area as President of the Jabalpur Town and District Muslim League. His correspondence with Jinnah and other national Muslim League leaders deals with a range of issues. In a letter that shows his concern about internal administrative organization, he suggests to Jinnah that the number of delegates allotted to each district be changed to reflect the number of fee-paying members in their districts.[82] Other letters reveal Burhan ul-Haqq protesting to local authorities over matters that Muslims perceived as injurious to their interests. One of these related to a proposal by the municipality to prohibit meat vendors going from house to house to sell meat. Burhan ul-Haqq argued that as it was overwhelmingly Muslims who engaged in this trade, this law would affect them adversely and have no impact on other religious groups.[83] Similarly, he protested against the decision of the military to prohibit Muslim sepoys from wearing beards.[84]

Letters written in 1946 reflect the growing atmosphere of conflict between Hindus and Muslims, and the violence simmering beneath the surface, ready to erupt at a moment's notice. In one of these, Burhan ul-Haqq protested the Hindu Mahasabha's use of loudspeakers fitted on *tongas* (horse-drawn passenger carriages) as they carried people to and fro through town.[85] In others, he referred to the killing

---

son of Shamsul Hasan, of Karachi. I am grateful to him for permission to photocopy Burhan ul-Haqq's correspondence included in the collection.

Burhan ul-Haqq is unlikely to have spoken and written English. His letter must have been written for him by someone else, then signed by him (in English).

[81] Wolpert, *Jinnah of Pakistan*, p. 142.

[82] C. P. & Berar II:13, in 'Correspondence'. The letter was dated April 3, 1943, and was acknowledged by Jinnah in an unsigned letter dated April 9, 1943.

[83] Ibid., 17. The municipal resolution prohibiting the sale of meat by hawkers was dated June 10, 1943. A mass meeting of Muslims, including dealers in the meat trade, protested the decision on June 24, 1943.

[84] Ibid., 19. This was the subject of a resolution of the Working Committee of the Muslim League of Jubbalpur, dated October 12, 1943.

[85] Ibid., 64. Letter to the Deputy Commissioner, Jubbalpur, dated October 21, 1946.

of Muslims in railway trains, and the public meetings of the Arya Samaj that incited Hindus to anti-Muslim violence. He pleaded with local authorities to take steps to prevent bloodshed.

This correspondence gives us a vivid glimpse of the local atmosphere of Hindu-Muslim hatred in Jabalpur immediately preceding Partition, and of the efforts of one Muslim League politician to defend Muslim interests in his town and district. But what we do not see so clearly, for lack of knowledge of the internal dialogue and debate, is the connection between Burhan ul-Haqq the Muslim League leader, and Burhan ul-Haqq the devoted follower of Ahmad Riza Khan and the Ahl-e Sunnat movement.

As I noted earlier, despite his Muslim League career Burhan ul-Haqq never migrated to Pakistan. While some of his children married and settled in Karachi, he remained in India. After his father's death in 1952, he became his sajjada-nishin. He appears to have continued to be an important local political figure, for it is reported that on his death in December 1984 tributes were paid to him by contemporary politicians, among them Rajiv Gandhi who happened to be in Jabalpur in the course of a national election campaign.[86]

Conclusion

What common ground can we find in the biographies of the three men examined here? At first sight there appears little, particularly if we contrast Burhan ul-Haqq to Na'im ud-Din and Muhammad Miyan. While the last two disagreed with one another on the course to be adopted, they clearly debated the Pakistan issue as 'ulama', concerned primarily that they act as Muslims in this matter, as in all others they had confronted before. For Burhan ul-Haqq, on the contrary, the first priority appears to have been to safeguard the political interests of Muslims against those of their rivals, whether Hindus or others.

Nevertheless, all three men, it is quite clear, believed firmly that

---

The Hindu Mahasabha, led by M. M. Malaviya, had an anti-Muslim stance.

86 *Tazkira-e Hazrat Burhan-e Millat*, pp. 37, 41.

as Muslims they must repudiate any alliance with Hindus regardless of the end sought to be promoted. This is the single common thread that runs through their lives on all the issues they faced in the early twentieth century. We may recall that Ahmad Riza too had rejected a Hindu-Muslim alliance in the early years of this century and that this had accounted in part for his opposition to the Khilafat movement. Consequently, there was continuity in this respect between Ahmad Riza and his three close followers.

Another principle that Ahmad Riza had consistently upheld was his refusal to associate with Muslims whose beliefs he judged to be 'wrong', or 'false'. Here only Muhammad Miyan appears to have followed his lead. Na'im ud-Din and Burhan ul-Haqq, both supportive of the Muslim League in one way or another, seem to have looked at the issue 'politically' and not to have asked whether the Muslims in the League were 'good' Muslims or not.

Perhaps the times seemed to them to call for a different approach. Indeed, there is something to suggest that if they had taken an anti-Muslim League position they would have lost the support and respect of ordinary Muslims around them. Hasan Miyan, for instance, wrote in 1946 that pro-League sympathy was so strong in Bareilly that if Na'im ud-Din and Muhammad Miyan had chosen Bareilly as the venue for their discussions public anger against Muhammad Miyan would have been too great for even Mustafa Riza Khan to contain.[87] According to him, in Marahra on the other hand the Muslims were not attracted to the League. As for Jabalpur, Burhan ul-Haqq's correspondence provides an indication of the kind of local harrassment that must have gone on on both sides. That the Muslims were pro-League can be readily believed.

A question that does not surface in the biographies, though it was clearly part of the debate over Pakistan, was the fate of the shrines and khanqahs that would be left behind if their caretakers migrated to Pakistan.[88] It is significant that regardless of what their positions

[87] Hasan Miyan, *Ahl-e Sunnat ki Awaz*, part 5. The reason for mentioning Mustafa Riza in this context was that he was deeply revered as a pir, and his authority would not normally have been challenged.

[88] Obviously, the closing down of madrasas also posed some of the same dilemmas, particularly if they were old and had an honoured tradition. But I assume that difficult

were on the merits of the League and of Pakistan, none of the ‘ulama’ whose lives I have briefly examined here left India at Partition.[89] Logically only Muhammad Miyan’s position would have dictated this course of action. However, the need to maintain the continuity of the khanqah and dargah established by his ancestors, and to observe the necessary ritual practices associated with them, apparently overrode other considerations for Burhan ul-Haqq despite his support of the League. Mustafa Riza Khan, a member of the All-India Sunni Conference who must therefore be assumed to have supported the demand for Pakistan, did not migrate either. He too had a khanqah to look after, that of his father Ahmad Riza Khan.

This is not to suggest that none of the Ahl-e Sunnat ‘ulama’ migrated to Pakistan, for several obviously did. Many migrated a few years after Partition rather than immediately, and set in place new schools, khanqahs and other structures for the spread of their movement. Given the tragic dimensions of the conflict, and the insecurity, uncertainty, and sheer danger to life at the time, it is not surprising that personal exigencies often dictated the practical steps that individual Muslims took with regard to the decision to stay or to leave.

---

as it may have been to abandon a madrasa, this could not compare to the difficulties associated with leaving ancestral shrines containing the remains of family elders. Given the reverence with which the Ahl-e Sunnat in particular regarded shrines, this must have been a very important consideration in the decision to migrate. It is probable that migration was considered only after ensuring that some members of the family stayed behind in order to look after the shrine.

89 Na‘im ud-Din, as earlier mentioned, was ailing at the time. Despite this, he did make a trip to Pakistan to help get new Ahl-e Sunnat organizations goir g there.

CONCLUSION

I began this study of the Ahl-e Sunnat wa Jama'at by insisting on the importance of taking its own terms of reference seriously, rejecting the appellation 'Barelwi' because its own members reject the name. Likewise, given its claim to be engaged in tajdid or renewal of the faith, I have also described the movement as 'reformist'. In the light of the Ahl-e Sunnat's defence of the veneration of 'saints' and its vision of the Prophet Muhammad as intercessor (at all times, not only on the Day of Judgment), miracle-worker, and the like, these claims have been regarded with some scepticism by contemporaneous South Asian Muslim movements of reform. Is the historian of religion wrong, then, in approaching a religious movement in a spirit of empathetic understanding from within? I believe not. Indeed, the phenomenological approach appears to be the only way 'short of conversion, [of enabling] one to enter . . . fully into the religious experience of other men'.[1] Beyond this, however, there remains a need for 'structured understanding of social process', as Roff indicates.[2] I would like to conclude this study by making some general comments in this direction. In order to do so, I draw on recent theoretical approaches

[1] James E. Royster, 'The Study of Muhammad: A Survey of Approaches from the Perspective of the History and Phenomenology of Religion', *Muslim World*, 62 (1972), 64.

[2] Roff, 'Pilgrimage and the History of Religions', in Martin (ed.), *Approaches to Islam in Religious Studies*, p. 78.

to the relation between the colonial state and an emerging South Asian public in the late nineteenth and early twentieth centuries.

The Ahl-e Sunnat movement, like those other Sunni Muslim movements which it debated and against which it defined itself in the late nineteenth century, arose at the height of the British empire. Like its rivals, it sought to offer Muslims a meaningful personal identity structured around the practice of religion. As Freitag has shown, Indians of all religious persuasions engaged in 'public arena' activities defined as 'cultural' precisely because the British Indian state, deeming such activities to be apolitical, refrained from interfering in them.

Among north Indian Muslims, a wide array of movements and leaders claimed the mantle of reform, ranging from Sir Sayyid Ahmad Khan on the one hand to the Ahl-e Sunnat on the other. Despite the differences between them, they shared important characteristics. Gilmartin describes the 'ulama' understanding of community as 'one defined in its essence by the shariat and by controlled personal behaviour'.[3] To quote Gilmartin,

> With the colonial state providing no symbolic definition of Muslim community in India, the assertion of 'community' solidarity required that the individual Muslim himself bring his (or her) inner life and sense of identity under self-conscious personal and rational control . . . . To many of the reformist ulama, the internalized control of behaviour that increasingly defined the community was . . . fundamentally modelled on the triumph of individual rationality (aql) over emotion, a process that went hand in hand with the triumph of *shariat* over local custom, and localized kin and caste based identities.[4]

This view of community in no way challenged the 'colonial sociology' of the British Indian state. That sociology was based on the assumption that the colonial state, informed by superior 'universal principles', and 'scientific' and 'rational' knowledge, was the only authority 'which allowed . . . the communities [to be ordered] into a rationalized political whole'.[5] Indian communities, by nature

[3] David Gilmartin, 'Democracy, Nationalism and the Public: A Speculation on Colonial Muslim Politics', *South Asia*, New Series, 14, 1 (June 1991), 134 (Special number, 'Aspects of the Public in Colonial South Asia').

[4] Ibid., 128–9.

[5] Ibid., 124.

'particularistic', required the presence of an outside arbiter to order them into a rational whole. The 'ulama' definition of community accommodated itself to this understanding of a multitude of particularistic groups existing under the umbrella of British rule.

As some scholars have recently begun to explore, the British policy of non-interference in religion was also informed by a dimly articulated view of the religious and cultural realm as feminine. As Freitag writes,

> the state saw activities most important to [the] colonial Other as being those that took place around religion, kinship, and cultural production; these activities were labeled 'private' or 'domestic', not public; because women took much responsibility for domestic activities, the men involved in those activities must be effeminate.... We might even go so far as to say that cultural production, itself, came to some significant extent to be gendered as feminine.[6]

Faisal Devji has examined the implications of shifting definitions of private and public in colonial India with reference to changing attitudes among the 'ulama' regarding women's education[7] and sufism. Devji sees the reformist 'ulama' appropriating the sufi discourse of love between God and man, which was implicitly critical of the legal culture of the 'ulama'. The sufis' antagonistic relationship with the 'ulama' nevertheless rested on an acceptance of the legal culture they represented.

In an independent move, the Muslim élite or shurafa (including among them the 'ulama') responded to the British takeover of the 'public' state and what Devji calls the 'moral' city (the locus of state

[6] Sandria B. Freitag, 'Introduction', in Sandria B. Freitag (ed.), *Culture as Contested Site: Popular Culture and the State in the Indian Subcontinent* (forthcoming).

[7] '[J]ust as the British were proceeding to "reform" the character and actions of their exotic, irrational Indian subjects through education, these same Indians were engaged in an identical task with their own "Others".' The 'ulama' (and the Muslim élite, or *shurafa,* more generally) began to advocate women's physical separation (and protection) from the outside world, now seen as morally corrupting. Faisal Fatehali Devji, 'Gender and the Politics of Space: The Movement for Women's Reform in Muslim India, 1857–1900', *South Asia,* 14, 1 (1991), 150.

power) by incorporating sufism, hitherto seen as private and anti-establishment, into their discourse. They

> were able to build their own private polity or political sphere... [locating it in] areas such as the mosque and the school (the courts and market being surrendered to the 'amoral' public sphere of colonialism), areas which were now seen as private. [This] privacy [was] confirmed by the fact that the mosque and school as sharif fiefs were paired in orthodox discourse with the traditionally private areas of the Sufi hospice or shrine and of the domestic realm.[8]

In realigning the public and private spheres during the height of colonial rule, Devji believes—accepting Benedict Anderson's now well-known argument about the connection between print technology and the growth of nationalism—that the 'ulama' (as part of the shurafa) used 'print capitalism' to imagine themselves anew. Print, unlike verbal exchange, is by nature declamatory, Devji points out, allowing of no 'dialogue or interaction', stressing instead 'the imperative, the uniform, and the linear'.[9] Accompanying this emphasis on publication, Devji also sees a spatial relocation of the 'ulama' from the city to the qasba, or small rural town, centre of kinship networks, family property, and (although Devji does not explicitly mention this) sufi hospices.

The relationship of the colonial state to Indians engaged in religious and cultural activity was by no means static. By the early twentieth century, underlying processes of social change were working toward the politicization of religious practice, as several of the scholars mentioned here have shown. Gilmartin in particular demonstrates the political role played by the emerging commercial Urdu press in Punjab in the early twentieth century. Rooted in the

[8] Ibid., 148. While the assumption that mosque and shrine, or 'ulama' and sufis, had been opposed until this point is to my mind an over simplification of a complex relationship, I accept the argument that a realignment of boundaries between the two roles was in process.

[9] Ibid., 149. As we have seen in the course of this book, however, print capitalism gave scholarly debate and disputation greater reach and influence than ever before.

marketplace (unlike the 'ulama' whose activities were centred in schools, mosques, and sufi shrines), newspaper editors, journalists, and publicists created an 'autonomous realm' that did not accept the British view of Indians as divided into so many particularistic communities. Unlike the 'ulama' again, this Muslim leadership used a rhetoric of emotion rather than restraint and reason. Gilmartin illustrates his argument by discussing the politicization of poetry (most notably by Muhammad Iqbal) and the mobilization of a Muslim 'public opinion' around issues such as defence of the Prophet Muhammad against denigration by Hindus.

Let me recapitulate Gilmartin's argument by referring specifically to one of the cases he mentions, that of the *Rangila Rasul* ('the Merry Prophet') in 1924, as this ties in with the importance of the Prophet to the Ahl-e Sunnat movement. *Rangila Rasul* was the title of a pamphlet satirizing the Prophet's sexual life. Published in Lahore in 1924, it was inspired by the anti-Muslim polemics of the Arya Samaj. The British, anxious to preserve public order, banned the pamphlet, but in 1927 the order was overturned by the Lahore High Court.[10] While all Muslims were united in condemning the pamphlet and in protecting the Prophet's honour, the 'ulama' (represented here by the Jam'iyyat-e 'Ulama'-e Hind) expressed their disapproval of uncontrolled action:

> If Muslims acted on the basis of 'feelings' that had been 'involuntarily' excited by the failure of the Government effectively to prosecute the pamphlet, then for that, in spite of the appeal to shariat, the ulama could not be held responsible . . . . If Muslims lost self-control, they declared, then 'the entire responsibility of exciting religious feelings and making law subservient to 'feelings', would have to devolve not on the ulama, but 'on the Government'.[11]

Opposing the 'ulama' was the Urdu press, represented here by Sayyid Ataullah Shah Bokhari, a poet, leader of the Khilafat movement, and later a leader of the Ahrar Party. Bokhari maintained that

> If the Hindus abuse the Prophet in a meeting held in a private building, . . . Muslims should not attend it. But if any Hindu in any open meeting or

[10] Gilmartin, 'Democracy, Nationalism and the Public', 134. Although Gilmartin does not mention the author's name, one may assume it was a Hindu.

[11] Ibid., 134.

procession uses obscene language about the Prophet he should be killed there and then. Any Muslim who would not be prepared to do this is not a true Muslim.[12]

As Gilmartin comments, for Bokhari 'it was the *public* display of the heart in the active protection of the honour of the Prophet that defined the real existence of a Muslim community during the *Rangila Rasul* crisis . . . . To control one's emotions in such a circumstance was in Bokhari's eyes almost a crime. His appeal was based not on the letter of the *shariat,* but on *action* in the name of the heart, as the most telling validator of Muslim identity'.[13]

Gilmartin sees the long-term significance of this agitation, and of a more protracted struggle between Sikhs and Muslims in the mid-1930s over the disputed Shahidganj mosque, as paving the way for the demand for Pakistan in the 1940s. A new 'public' that transcended the particularistic Muslim community ordered by the colonial state gradually emerged from this process. Because the journalist leaders of the *Rangila Rasul* and other agitations rejected the 'colonial sociology' of the British Indian state, a new political sphere, autonomous of that state, grew to challenge it by the 1940s. Although initially employing the rhetoric of emotion, under Jinnah's leadership, Gilmartin argues, 'the rhetoric of emotional nationalism . . . merged with the rhetoric of control and discipline'.[14]

Turning once more to the Ahl-e Sunnat wa Jama'at in light of these analyses, I find helpful Gilmartin's observation that the reformist 'ulama' defined community around the concepts of shari'a and a rhetoric of restraint and self-control, in order to create a new type of person. In this perspective, the Ahl-e Sunnat movement's claims to being 'reformist', or engaged in tajdid, are self-evident. I am reminded of small details about Ahmad Riza Khan's life-style as described by Zafar ud-Din Bihari: he entered the mosque with his right foot first, he exited it with his left; when sitting, he never stretched his legs out in the direction of the Ka'ba; he urged upon his followers the importance of having the right intention (niyya),

[12] Ibid., 134-5.

[13] Ibid., 135.

[14] Ibid., 138.

for a deed would be rewarded accordingly, and so on. The personal adab (etiquette) of 'ulama' of competing movements, such as the Deobandi or Firangi Mahali, likewise emphasized an ethic of personal restraint.

Nor was the Ahl-e Sunnat's focus on the Prophet Muhammad as a role model and object of veneration unique among the late nineteenth-century north Indian 'ulama'. The Deobandis, as sufis, also sought to develop a deep inner bond between master and disciple, and looked to the Prophet Muhammad as ultimate exemplar of how a Muslim should behave. Indeed, having indicated throughout this book the differences between the Ahl-e Sunnat and Deobandi 'ulama', it seems important to make the opposite point here, and to speculate that part of the explanation for the urgency and volume of anti-Deobandi writing on the part of the Ahl-e Sunnat 'ulama' (matched on the Deobandi side with equally fierce verbal and written attacks on the 'Barelwis') was not that they were so different, but that they were so similar. It became important for both sides to play up their differences in order to grow organizationally, for if they seemed too similar their separate existence would make no sense. Differences of degree were thus highlighted until they appeared to be insurmountable differences of kind.

Taking this thought a step further, I would argue that the Ahl-e Sunnat's real 'other' among Sunni 'ulama' movements was not Deoband but the Ahl-e Hadis, against whom they wrote relatively little. Unlike Deobandi and Ahl-e Sunnat 'ulama', those of the Ahl-e Hadis accepted the authority of the Qur'an and hadis alone. They denied the legitimacy of the four Sunni law schools (mazhab) and of the centuries'-old tradition of fiqh commentary related to these, as unhelpful accretions which kept Muslims from studying the original sources. It was they who urged individual Muslims knowledgeable in Arabic to engage in their own interpretation (ijtihad) of Qur'an and hadis. And in contrast to the Deobandis and Ahl-e Sunnat, the Ahl-e Hadis had no tolerance for sufism, regarding it as a 'danger to true religion'.[15] In social terms, the Ahl-e Hadis belonged to an exclusive élite, writing for the most part in Arabic

[15] Metcalf, *Islamic Revival*, p. 274. My knowledge of the Ahl-e Hadis movement is based on her account.

and Persian rather than Urdu.[16] Of all the 'ulama' groups to whom the Ahl-e Sunnat referred pejoratively as 'Wahhabi', the Ahl-e Hadis, who admired Ibn Taimiyya and had active ties with the Arabian Muwahhidun movement, were perhaps the only ones deserving of the label.

Contrasting these two polar opposites as I have, I return to the fact that all the nineteenth-century 'ulama', regardless of affiliation to one or other movement, looked to the Prophet Muhammad as exemplar. The Ahl-e Hadis, defining themselves as such, were of course making this very point, as were the Ahl-e Sunnat in their choice of name. The difference lay in their understanding of what it meant, as a practical matter, to follow the Prophet's way or sunna.

The Ahl-e Sunnat, in embracing the concept of prophetic intermediacy and a hierarchy of spiritual authority that continues through an unbroken lineage of 'saints', were in social terms embedded in a hierarchical ordering of society composed of shurafa (the élite) and *ajlaf* (common people). This was equally true of those 'ulama' groups, even the Ahl-e Hadis (and the Deobandis), who promoted a more egalitarian vision of the perfect Muslim society. I would argue that Ahl-e Sunnat teachings, despite their respect for hierarchy, nevertheless promoted a concept of the person who in his or her self-restrained adherence to the shari'a was as thoroughly 'modern' as that envisioned by other Indian 'ulama' at the time. If there is ambiguity here in the relation between respect for hierarchy and the call for individual responsibility, perhaps this was one of the keys to the appeal of the Ahl-e Sunnat. Perhaps this dual message was just what was needed in late nineteenth-century British India. In his presentation of the Ahl-e Sunnat message, however, Ahmad Riza was forceful and unambiguous.

It is intruiging to speculate that the emerging concept of personhood subsumed by the emphasis on the importance attached to exemplary personal behaviour modelled on the Prophet—in a context of shifting boundaries between the private and the public, as Devji has shown—was accompanied by a feminization of language. Freitag's insights into the gendered nature of cultural production,

[16] Ibid., p. 278.

and Gilmartin's work on the growing importance of the rhetoric of emotion in Muslim discourse in the early twentieth century point in this direction as well. For the Ahl-e Sunnat movement in the period studied here, Ahmad Riza's corpus of na't poetry in praise of the Prophet, evoking the sufi concepts of divine love, comes to mind. As shown, he employed the imagery of the Prophet as Allah's beloved, sometimes explicitly using the metaphor of a bride and bridegroom. Devoted to the Prophet, Ahmad Riza in turn frequently described himself as a lover of the Prophet.

Under Ahmad Riza's pen the language of love between God, the Prophet, and the poet (himself) became a tool with which to condemn those 'others' (chiefly Deobandis) with whose views he disagreed. But it never became political in the way Gilmartin describes happening with the commercial Urdu press of early twentieth-century Panjab. I believe the reason for this was that Ahmad Riza was never comfortable with public 'action'—and would have eschewed it even if he had lived during the *Rangila Rasul* controversy— because such action was rooted in the 'amoral' marketplace (to use Devji's felicitous term). The politicization of the Ahl-e Sunnat movement occurred under new leadership, as most forcefully demonstrated by the events of the azan dispute in 1914–17. Ahmad Riza confined his message to the world of the mosque, shrine, school and home (the domestic and private realm), refusing to involve himself in court or marketplace (the public sphere of colonialism). Younger leaders like Maulana 'Abd ul-Muqtadir Badayuni, opposing him in court over a libel case, were in fact signalling that they could no longer accept the more limited apolitical definition of community for which he stood. In 'Abd ul-Muqtadir, later a Khilafatist leader, one may see the process toward politicization of the Ahl-e Sunnat movement at work.

I would like to return, finally, to the question of texts, the use of which characterized all the nineteenth-century reformist movements in north India, as indeed elsewhere in the Muslim world. Texts are given meaning in context, as we know. It is therefore crucially important to attend to who uses them and how, in what situation, how they relate to oral traditions, to competing texts, and so on. While I agree with Devji that printed texts may be declamatory by nature and that their authors seek to give them unambiguous single meanings, they do so in a context of dialogue and interpretation that may not always be explicit. Muslims could not 'be' Muslim (in a religious sense) if they did not engage in the interpretation of their scriptural texts. Given that the Islamic tradition is inherently discursive, dialogical, and dialectical, as Fischer and Abedi point out (and compellingly illustrate) in their work on Iran in the 1960s and 1970s,[17] differences of interpretation are surely at the heart of Muslim self-definitions as this or that kind of 'Muslim'.

As this study has shown, under Ahmad Riza Khan's leadership the Ahl-e Sunnat movement interpreted both Qur'an and hadis in ways that supported its view of the Prophet as uniquely endowed by God. In lengthy exegesis of relevant Qur'anic passages, Ahmad Riza argued that God had gifted the Prophet with unimaginable abilities, including knowledge of the Day of Judgment. Citing hadis, he argued that Deobandis had inaccurately reported a hadis in which the Prophet had allegedly denied that he knew what lay on the other side of a wall. Likewise, Ahmad Riza accepted the authority of hadis classified as weak, including one (from Abu Da'ud) which related that the bodies of prophets do not decay after death, for Allah has forbidden the earth from consuming them.

While movements such as the Ahl-e Sunnat seek to impart single meanings to the texts around which they construct themselves, the texts themselves are constantly open to rereadings and reinterpretations by other people in other historical situations. This is happening anew in our own time in the Muslim world, as in the Muslim diaspora in the Western world. Ahmad Riza's writings and interpretations are today being edited, commented upon, and glossed by the Ahl-e Sunnat in publications in India, Pakistan and the U.K. A new 'canon' is thus under process of creation, which we would have to locate in its own specific late twentieth-century context.

[17] Michael M. J. Fischer and Mehdi Abedi, *Debating Muslims: Cultural Dialogues in Postmodernity and Tradition* (Madison: University of Wisconsin Press, 1990).

Glossary

abjad, the Arabic alphabet as used for chronograms
adab, (pl., *ādāb*), etiquette, proper behaviour
'ālim (pl., *'ulamā'*), scholar of Islamic theology and jurisprudence, on whom rests the interpretation of *sharī 'a*
'amal, practice, here specifically denoting phrases, numerical charts, etc., used by Sufis
anjuman, association
'aqida (pl., *'aqā'id*), article of faith, creed
āyat, literally 'sign,' verse of the Qur'an
azān (Ar., *adān*), call to prayer, consisting of seven formulae among them the profession of faith (*shahāda, kalima*) and the *takbīr*

bāb, literally 'gate', 'door', here, chapter in a book
bad-maẕhab, person with 'wrong' beliefs; the word *maẕhab* (Ar., *maḏhab*), literally one of the four main Sunni law schools (Hanafi, Shafi'i, Maliki, and Hanbali), is used in the Ahl-e Sunnat context in the more general sense of 'faith' or 'belief'
bai'a, pledge of allegiance of a sufi disciple to his master by grasping his hand
baraka (also *barkat*), literally 'blessing', power inherent in saintly persons or sacred objects. Also see *tabarrukāt*
bāṭil, false, baseless
bāṭin, hidden, esoteric. Opp. of *ẓāhir*
bayān, exposition, sermon
be-shar', literally 'without the law,' sufis regarded as deviant because they do not observe the injunctions of the *sharī 'a*
bid'a (also, *bid'at*) (pl., *bida'*, *bida't*), reprehensible innovation, opp. of *sunna.*
bid'at-e ḥasana, a 'good' *bid'a*

chandā, donation
chihlam, the fortieth day of mourning, or the period of forty days' mourning after a bereavement
chillā, forty days' seclusion, in which the sufi novice is completely separated from the world, and engaged only in prayer and meditation

dajjāl, the Antichrist or evil spirit who will appear before the end of the world to stir up anarchy and will then be killed by Jesus or the Mahdi; a term used in Ahl-e Sunnat sources to refer to Mirza Ghulam Ahmad (d. 1908), founder of the Aḥmadiyya movement
dālān, hall, washing place attached to a mosque
dār al-ḥarb, enemy territory, an area where Muslims are not in power and where the *sharī'a* is not in force. Opp. of *dār al-islām*
dargāh, literally 'court', the seat of spiritual authority represented by sufi shrines or tombs
dars-e niẓāmi, a course of studies taught in South Asian *madrasas* since the eighteenth century
dastār-bandi, literally 'tying of the turban', a ceremony in which a sufi appoints a successor or *sajjāda-nish in* by presenting his turban to the latter; also used of ceremony marking a student's completion of the *dars-e niẓāmi* syllabus
dīn, the faith. Opp. of *dunya*, 'the world'
dīwān, collection of poems
du'ā, petition; nonritual, personal prayer

e'tikāf, seclusion for prayer and devotional exercises

fanā, literally 'annihilation', total absorption of the devotee in Allah. Three stages were distinguished: *fanā fi'l shaikh*, complete spiritual unity with one's spiritual preceptor; *fanā fi'l rasul*, annihilation in the Prophet Muhammad; and *fanā fi Allah*, annihilation in the Divine
faqīh (pl., *fuqahā'*), a jurisprudent, one who is knowledgeable in *fiqh*
faqīr, literally 'poor', general name for a sufi or religious mendicant; a self-deprecatory way of referring to oneself
farẓ (Ar., *farḍ*), religious duty
fatwā (pl., *fatāwā*), legal opinion given by a *mufti*
fiqh, Islamic jurisprudence, based on the Qur'an and prophetic traditions (*sunna*), as well as *qiyās* and *ijmā'*. Different elaborations on matters of detail distinguish the four main Sunni law schools
fitna, turmoil, chaos; a state of anarchy which foreshadows the end of the world

gaddī, literally 'throne', seat of authority at a *dargāh* (q.v.)
ghair-muqallid, one who does not follow one of the main Sunni law schools,

but only accepts the authority of the Qur'an and *ḥadīṣ* (as well as *qiyās*) in matters of *fiqh*. In Ahl-e Sunnat literature, a (pejorative) name for the Ahl-e Ḥadīṣ

ghaus (Ar., *ghauth*), literally 'help[er]', title of the highest member of the hierarchy of saints, particularly 'Abd al-Qādir Jilāni (d. 1166)

ghusl, ritual ablution; ceremonial washing of a saint's tomb during an *'urs*

gumrāh, one who has lost his way, gone astray

gunāh, sin, offence

gyārhawīn, literally 'eleventh', rituals performed in commemoration of the death of Shaikh 'Abd al-Qādir Jilāni on the eleventh of every month

ḥadīṣ (Ar., *ḥadīth*), tradition from the Prophet, report of his words in a given situation. An individual *ḥadīṣ* consists of a text (*matn*) and a chain of transmitters (*isnād*). The most reliable sources of *ḥadīṣ* are considered by Muslims to be those of al-Bukhari (d. 870) and Muslim (d. 875), together known as the *ṣaḥīḥain*, 'the two correct ones'

ḥadīṣ qudsī, 'Divine Saying', the word of Allah reported by the Prophet in his words

ḥajj, the annual pilgrimage to Mecca, required of every Muslim at least once in his or her lifetime if economically feasible

ḥaqīqa(t), literally 'reality', the last stage on the sufi path or ṭarīqa

ḥarām, forbidden; one among five legal classifications of human action

hijra, emigration of Muslims, particularly from a land considered *dār al-ḥarb* (q.v.)

ijāzat, permission; in the sufi context, permission to admit disciples of one's own into a particular order or number of specified orders

ijmā', the consensus of scholars which, with Qur'an, *sunna*, and *qiyās*, constitutes one of the four bases of the Law

ijtihād, literally 'striving', 'effort', independent inquiry to establish the ruling of the *sharī'a* on a particular matter. The person qualified for the task is known as *mujtahid*. Opp. of *taqlīd*

'ilm-e ghaib, literally 'knowledge of the unseen', a form of knowledge considered by many Muslims to be accessible to Allah alone, but claimed by the Ahl-e Sunnat to also have been gifted by Allah to the Prophet

imkān-e naẓīr, literally 'the possibility of an equal', subject of a nineteenth century debate among north Indian 'ulamā' on whether Allah could make another prophet similar in every respect to Muhammad

irāda, inner purpose or motive, similar to *nīyya*

īsāl-e ṣawāb, the transfer of merit for a pious act to someone else, often deceased. Associated with intercession at saints' tombs in particular

istiftā, the act of asking for a *fatwā*, request for a legal opinion

jāgīr, land grant from government entitling owner to revenue therefrom

jamā'at, group, majority
janāza, funeral
jihād, literally 'holy war' against unbelievers. Also one's own struggle with one's baser instincts
jinn, beings made of smokeless fire, some good and some evil, constantly trying to possess human souls, who in turn try to control them

kāfir (pl., *kuffār*), literally 'ungrateful', infidels. See also *takfīr*
kalima, the profession of faith in Allah's unity and the prophethood of Muhammad
karāmat (pl., *karāmāt*), miracles performed by a saint
khalīfa, viceregent; successor to a sufi master
khānqah, sufi hospice, usually a large compound where the *pīr* and his family as well as devotees live. Often a school, a public kitchen and other facilities were attached
khāndān, a family, an extended kin group
khātam al-nabiyyīn, the seal of the Prophets, an epithet of Muhammad
khatma, the reading of the Qur'an in a single night
khuda, God

lāzim, obligatory

madrasa, a school or academy of learning where the Islamic sciences are taught
mā'rifa(t), spiritual 'knowledge' of God
maṣlaḥa (also *maṣlaḥat*), that which is conducive to good; expedient
mazār, literally 'place for a visit (*ziyāra*)', the tomb of a saint
mīlād, literally 'birthday', but used particularly for celebration of the Prophet's birth anniversary, generally accepted as being on 12 Rabi' al-Awwal, the third lunar month of the Hijri calendar
millat, community of believers
mubāḥ, legally indifferent in terms of the *sharī'a*
mubāhala, a procedure in which two opponents in a debate invoke the curse of Allah on the person who is wrong. Also see *munāẓara*
mufti, a jurisconsult, one who issues *fatawa*
mujaddid, a renewer of the *sharī'a*, expected once every Hijri century
mujtahid, one who is qualified to engage in *ijtihād*
munāẓara, oral debate, usually between 'ulamā'
murīd, literally 'one who is desirous', disciple to a personal *pīr*
murshid, teacher
murtadd, an apostate from Islam

nabī (pl., *anbiyā'*), prophet
na't, poetry in praise of the Prophet

na't-khwāni, recitation of *na't* verse
naẓar, gift to a sufi pir
niyya, intention

pīr, sufi master
pīri-murīdi, relation between spiritual guide and disciple, which entails absolute obedience of the *murīd* to his *pīr*; the term is used in a pejorative sense by those who associate the bond and its associated practices with 'popular' (i.e., 'unreformed') religion

qabr, a grave
qasba, an agricultural town dominated by Muslim service gentry
qaṣida-khwāni, recitation of long poem in praise of a king, an important person, Allah, or the Prophet
qaum, community, nation
qawwāli, singing with musical accompaniment at sufi devotional exercises, often leading to a state of ecstasy
qāẓī (Ar., *qāḍī*), judge of *sharī'a* law
qiyāmat, resurrection at the end of time
quṭb, literally 'pole', 'axis', the highest member of the hierarchy of saints around whom the world revolves; equivalent in sufi theory to the Ghauṣ-e A'zam, or Shaikh 'Abd al-Qādir Jilani

ra'ıs (pl., *ru'asā*), person of means respected in his community
rasūl, literally 'messenger', the Prophet Muhammad as bearer of the Qur'an, basis for the *sharī'a*
rawāfiẓ (Ar., *rawāfiḍ*), literally 'dissenters', used in Ahl-e Sunnat literature in a pejorative sense in reference to Shī'is

sajjāda-nishīn, literally 'one who sits on the prayer mat', successor to a *pīr*
ṣalāt o salām, prayer calling upon Allah's blessings on the Prophet
samā', literally 'hearing', listening to music, a controversial issue among sufis
sanad, certificate or testimonial
sayyid, descendant of the Prophet through his daughter Fatima and her sons Ḥasan and Ḥusain, a group highly venerated by the Ahl-e Sunnat movement
shaikh (Ar., *shaykh*), 'elder' or 'leader', in South Asia often used interchangeably with 'pir'
shajara, spiritual and/or family genealogy
sharī'a, the sacred law of Islam, comprising the totality of Allah's commands that regulate the life of every Muslim in relation to Allah and to those around him or her
shirk, idolatry, associating partners with Allah

silsila, chain linking an individual through his or her sufi master ultimately to the Prophet; those with similar chains or *silsilas* belonged to the same sufi *ṭarīqa*

sunna, the 'way' or 'path' of the Prophet Muhammad, as known to Muslims through the *ḥadīṣ* literature. Everything the Prophet is reported to have said, done, or advised others to do, is thus part of his *sunna*. The Ahl-e Sunnat wa Jama'at defined themselves as followers of the prophetic *sunna*

sūra, a chapter of the Qur'an

tabarrukāt, objects filled with *baraka* or grace; sacred relics

tablīgh, preaching

tajdīd, renewal of the Law

takfīr, declaring someone an infidel or unbeliever (*kāfir*)

taqlīd, literally 'imitation', following one of the Sunni law schools in preference to *ijtihād*. As Hanafis, most Sunni Muslims in nineteenth century India were *muqallids*, adherers of the Hanafi school of law

ṭarīqa, path, sufi order. In South Asia, the Naqshbandi, Chishti, and Qadiri orders were the most important nineteenth century orders

tasawwuf, sufism

tauba, to repent; the first step on the sufi path

ta'ziya, replica of a tomb of Ḥasan and Ḥusain, carried in public processions during Muḥarram

ṭibb, Yunani medicine

umma, community of Muslims

'urs, literally 'wedding', celebration of a saint's death anniversary when his soul is believed to unite with Allah

wali, 'friend' (of God), sufi saint

wa'z, sermon

wasīla, means of access, intermediary

wuzu (Ar., *wudu*), ritual ablution before prayer

zakāt, mandatory alms-tax on accrued wealth

ziyāra, to visit, specifically the shrines of dead saints in veneration and supplication of them

Bibliography

Works in Urdu

Journals and Newspapers

Ahl-e Sunnat ki Awaz (Marahra: Khanqah-e Barkatiyya, n.d.), 1946.

Ashrafiyya (Mubarakpur, Azamgarh). Articles by Mahmud Ahmad Qadiri, 'Malik al-'Ulama' Maulana Muhammad Zafar ud-Din Bihari aur Khidmat-e Hadis', 1 (February 1977), 15–20; 2 (April 1977), 25–30; 3 (July 1977), 15–21.

Dabdaba-e Sikandari (Rampur), 1908–22.

Al-Sawad al-A'zam (Muradabad), 1920.

Tuhfa-e Hanafiyya (Patna), 1315/1898 to 1325/1908. Also known as *Makhzan-e Tahqiq*.

Books and Articles

WORKS BY AHMAD RIZA KHAN

Anwar al-Intibah fi Hill Nida Ya Rasul Allah (Karachi: Bazm-e Qasimi Barkati, 1986).

Al-'Ataya li-Nabawiyya fi'l Fatawa al-Rizwiyya, vol. 1 (Bombay: Rizwi Academy, 1405/1984–85).

———, vols. 2 and 3 (Sambhal, Muradabad: Maktaba Na'imiyya, n.d.).

———, vol. 4 (Ramnagar, Nainital: Madrasa Miftah al-'Ulum, 1406/1986).

———, vol. 5 (Lahore: Maktaba Nabawiyya, 1392/1972).

———, vols. 6 and 7 (Mubarakpur, Azamgarh: Sunni Dar al-Isha'at, 1981 and 1987).

———, vol. 10, part 1 (Besalpur, Pilibhit: Maktaba Riza Iwan 'Irfan, n.d.).

———, vol. 11 (Saudagaran, Bareilly: Idara-e Isha'at-e Tasnifat-e Riza, 1402/1981–82).

Al-Daulat al-Makkiyya bi'l Madat al-Ghaibiyya (Karachi: Maktaba Rizwiyya, n.d.).

Dawam al-'Aish fi'l Ummat min Quraish (Lahore: Maktaba Rizwiyya, 1400/1980).

E'tiqad wa'l Ahbab fi'l Jamil wa'l Mustafa wa'l Al wa'l Ashab (Lahore: Farid Book Stall, n.d.).

Fatawa al-Haramain bi-Rajf Nadwat al-Main (Bareilly: Matba' Ahl-e Sunnat wa Jama'at, 1317/1899–1900).

Fatawa al-Qudwa li-Kashf Dafin al-Nadwa (1313/1895–96). Publication information unavailable.

Fatawa al-Sunna li-Iljam al-Fitna (Bareilly: Matba' Ahl-e Sunnat wa Jama'at, 1314/1896–97).

Hada'iq-e Bakhshish (Karachi: Medina Publishing Co., 1976).

Husam al-Haramain 'ala Manhar al-Kufr wa'l Main (Lahore: Maktaba Nabawiyya, 1405/1985).

Ihlak al-Wahhabiyyin 'ala Tauhin Qubur al-Muslimin (Bareilly: Hasani Press, 1322/1904–5).

I'lam al-A'lam ba-an Hindustan Dar al-Islam (Bareilly: Hasani Press, 1306/1888–89). Reprinted in *Do Ahamm Fatwe* (Lahore: Maktaba Rizwiyya, 1977).

Iqamat al-Qiyamat 'ala Ta'in al-Qiyam li-Nabi Tihamat al-Jaza al-Muhya al-Ghalmat Kanhaiyya (Karachi: Barkati Publishers, 1986).

Al-Kaukab al-Shahabiyya fi Kufriyat Abi Wahhabiyya (Lahore: Nuri Book Depot, n.d.).

Kafl al-Faqih al-Fahim fi Ahkam Qirtas al-Darahim (Lahore: Shabir Brothers, n.d.).

Al-Mahajjat al-Mu'tamana fi Ayat al-Mumtahana (1339/1920), in *Rasa'il-e Rizwiyya*, vol. 2 (Lahore: Maktaba Hamidiyya, 1976).

Majma'-e Rasa'il: Mas'ala Nur aur Saya (Karachi: Idara-e Tahqiqat-e Imam Ahmad Riza, 1406/1985).

Majma'-e Rasa'il: Radd-e Mirza'iyyat (Karachi: Idara-e Tasnifat-e Imam Ahmad Riza, 1406/1985).

Majma'-e Rasa'il: Radd-e Rawafiz (Lahore: Markazi Majlis-e Riza, 1406/1986).

Maktubat-e Imam Ahmad Riza Khan Barelwi (Lahore: Maktaba Nabawiyya, 1986).

Malfuzat-e A'la Hazrat, 4 vols. (Gujarat, Pakistan: Fazl-e Nur Academy, n.d.).

Nahj al-Salama fi Hukm Taqbil al-Ibhamain fi'l Iqama (Bareilly: Matba' Ahl-e Sunnat wa Jama'at, 1333/1914–15).

Naqa' al-Salafa fi Ahkam al-Bai'a wa'l Khilafa (Sialkot, Pakistan: Maktaba Mihiriyya Rizwiyya, 1318/1900).

Rasa'il-e Rizwiyya (Bareilly: Idara-e Isha'at-e Tasnifat-e Raza, n.d.).

———, vol. 2 (Lahore: Maktaba Hamidiyya, 1396/1976).

———, vol. 5 (Faisalabad: Nuri Book Depot, 1982).

Shumul al-Islam li-Usul al-Rasul al-Karam (Bareilly: Hasani Press, 1315/1897–98).

Subhan al-Subuh 'an 'Aib Kizb Maqbuh (Bareilly: Matba' Ahl-e Sunnat wa Jama'at, 1307/1889–90).

Tadbir-e Falah wa Nijat wa Islah (Bareilly: Hasani Press, 1331/1913).

Tajalli al-Yaqin ba-an Nabiyana al-Sayyid al-Mursilin (Lahore: Hamid and Co., 1401/1980).

Tamhid al-Iman ba-Ayat al-Qur'an (Bombay: Raza Academy, n.d.). Also see English tr. by G. D. Qureshi cited under 'Works in English'.

OTHER AHL-E SUNNAT WORKS

(a) Primary Sources

Amjad 'Ali A'zami, *Bahar-e Shari'at*, 18 vols. (Bareilly: Qadiri Book Depot, n.d.).

Aulad-e Rasul 'Muhammad Miyan' Marahrawi, *Khandan-e Barakat* (Marahra: c. 1927).

———, *Khutba-e Sadarat*, Ansar al-Islam, 22-24 Sha'ban 1339/April 1921 (Marahra: Khanqah-e Barkatiyya, n.d.).

Burhan ul-Haqq Jabalpuri, *Ikram-e Imam Ahmad Riza* (Lahore: Markazi Majlis-e Riza, 1981).

———, *Khutba-e Sadarat*, Muslim League Conference, District Jabalpur, 1–3 January 1940 (Jabalpur: n.d.).

Hamid Riza Khan, *Murasalat-e Sunnat wa Nadwa* (Bareilly: 1313/1895–96).

Hasan Riza Khan, *Samsam-e Hasan bar Dabir-e Fitan* (Azimabad [Patna]: Matba' Hanafiyya, 1318/1900).

———, *Sawalat-e Haqa'iq-numa ba-Ru'asa Nadwat al-'Ulama'* (Badayun: Victoria Press, 1313/1895-96).

Hasnain Riza Khan, *Sirat-e A'la Hazrat* (Karachi: Maktaba Qasimiyya Barkatiyya, 1986).

Muhammad Jalal ud-Din Qadiri (ed.), *Khutbat-e All-India Sunni Conference 1925-1947* (Gujarat, Pakistan: Maktaba Rizwiyya, 1978).

Mustafa Riza Khan, *Al-Tari al-Dari li-Hafawat 'Abd ul-Bari* (Bareilly: Sunni Press, 1339/1912–13).

Rudad-e Jama'at-e Riza-e Mustafa (1342/1924).

Zafar ud-Din Bihari, *Hayat-e A'la Hazrat*, vol. 1 (Karachi: Maktaba Rizwiyya, 1938).

———, *Chaudhwin Sadi ke Mujaddid* (Lahore: Maktaba Rizwiyya, 1980).

(b) Secondary Sources

Ghulam Shabbar Qadiri Nuri Badayuni, *Tazkira-e Nuri: Mufassal Halat o Sawanih-e Abu'l Husain Nuri Miyan* (La'ilpur: 1968).

Mahmud Ahmad Qadiri, *Tazkira-e 'Ulama'-e Ahl-e Sunnat* (Muzaffarpur, Bihar: Khanqah-e Qadiriyya Ashrafiyya, 1391/1971).

Mas'ud Ahmed, Muhammad, *Fazil Barelwi aur Tark-e Mawalat* (Lahore: Riza Publications, 1978).

——, *Fazil Barelwi 'Ulama'-e Hijaz ki Nazar men* (Mubarakpur, Azamgarh: Al-Majma' al-Islami, 1981).

——, *Imam Ahmad Riza aur 'Alam-e Islam* (Karachi: Idara-e Tahqiqat-e Imam Ahmad Riza, 1983).

Muhammad Hamid Siddiqi Rizwi, *Tazkira-e Hazrat Burhan-e Millat* (Jabalpur: Astana 'Aliyya Rizwiyya Salamiyya Burhaniyya, 1985).

Muhammad Mahbub 'Ali Khan, *Buland Paya Hayat-e Hashmat 'Ali* (Kanpur: Arakin-e Bazm-e Qadiri Rizwi, 1380/1960–61).

Mu'in ud-Din Na'imi, 'Tazkira al-Ma'ruf Hayat-e Sadr al-Afazil', *Sawad-e A'zam* (Lahore: Na'imi Dawakhana, 1378/1959).

Razi Haidar, Khwaja, *Tazkira-e Muhaddis Surati* (Karachi: Surati Academy, n.d.).

Sayyid Mahmud Ahmad Rizwi, *Sayyidi Abu'l Barakat* (Lahore: Tabligh Department, Hizb al-Ahnaf, 1979).

OTHER URDU WORKS

[Anon.], *'Ilm o Agahi* (Karachi: Government National College, 1974–75).

Bedar, Abid Raza, *Raza Library* (Rampur: Institute of Oriental Studies, 1966).

Imdad Ullah Makki, Haji, *Faisla-e Haft Mas'ala*. Reprinted, with commentary by Muhammad Khalil Khan Qadiri Barkati Maraharwi (Lahore: Farid Book Stall, 1406/1986).

Muhammad al-Hasani, Sayyid, *Sirat-e Maulana Sayyid Muhammad 'Ali Mungeri, Bani-e Nadwat al-'Ulama'* (Lucknow: Shahi Press, 1962).

Mushir ul-Haqq, 'Unniswin Sadi ke Hindustan ki Hai'at Shar'i: Shah 'Abd ul-'Aziz ke Fatawa-e Dar ul-Harb ka ek 'Ilmi Tajziya', *Burhan*: 63, 4 (October 1969), 221–44.

Rahman 'Ali, Maulawi, *Tazkira-e 'Ulama'-e Hind*, tr. Muhammad Ayub Qadiri (Karachi: Pakistan Historical Society, no. 16, 1961).

Raja Rashid Mahmud, *Tahrik-e Hijrat 1920: Ek Tarikh, Ek Tajziya* (Lahore: Maktaba 'Aliyya, 1986).

Works in English

Unpublished Private Papers

Shams ul-Hasan Collection, Karachi.

Published Works

Ahmad, Aziz, *Studies in Islamic Culture in the Indian Environment* (Oxford: Clarendon Press, 1964).

———, 'Afghani's Indian Contacts', *Journal of the American Oriental Society*, 89:3 (1969), 476–504.

Ahmad Khan, Mu'in-ud-Din, *History of the Fara'izi Movement in Bengal (1818–1906)* (Karachi: Pakistan Historical Society, 1965).

Ahmed, Rafiuddin, *The Bengal Muslims 1871–1906: A Quest for Identity* (Delhi: Oxford University Press, 1981).

Alam, Muzaffar, *The Crisis of Empire in Mughal North India: Awadh and the Punjab, 1707–1748* (Delhi: Oxford University Press, 1986).

Alavi, Hamza, 'Pakistan and Islam: Ethnicity and Ideology', in F. Halliday and H. Alavi (eds.), *State and Ideology in the Middle East and Pakistan* (New York: Monthly Review Press, 1988), pp. 64–111.

Anderson, Benedict, *Imagined Communities: Reflections on the Origin and Spread of Nationalism* (London: Verso, 1983).

Arnold, T. W., *The Caliphate* (London: Routledge and Kegan Paul, 1965).

Awn, Peter, J., *Satan's Tragedy and Redemption: Iblis in Sufi Psychology* (Leiden: E. J. Brill, 1983).

Al-A'zami, M. Mustafa, *On Schacht's Origins of Jurisprudence* (New York: John Wiley and Sons, 1985).

Baghel, Amar Singh, *Gazetteer of India, Uttar Pradesh: Rampur District* (Lucknow: Government of India, 1974).

Baljon, J. M. S., *Religion and Thought of Shah Wali Allah Dihlawi 1703-1762* (Leiden: E. J. Brill, 1986).

Barnett, Richard B., *North India Between Empires: Awadh, the Mughals, and the British, 1720 – 1801* (Berkeley: University of California Press, 1980).

Bayly, C. A., 'The Small Town and Islamic Gentry in North India: The Case of Kara', in Kenneth Ballhatchet and John Harrison (eds.), *The City in South Asia: Pre-Modern and Modern* (London: School of Oriental and African Studies, University of London, 1980), pp. 20–48.

———, *Rulers, Townsmen and Bazaars: North Indian Society in the Age of British Expansion, 1770 –1870* (Cambridge: Cambridge University Press, 1983).

Brennan, Lance, 'Social Change in Rohilkhand 1801–1833', *Indian Economic and Social History Review*, vii:4 (December 1970), 443–66.

———, 'The Local Face of Nationalism: Congress Politics in Rohilkhand in the 1920s', *South Asia: Journal of South Asian Studies*, 5 (1976?) 9–19.

———, 'A Case of Attempted Segmental Modernization: Rampur State, 1930–1939', *Comparative Studies in Society and History*, 23 (1981), 350–81.

Briggs, F. S., 'The Indian Hijrat of 1920', *Muslim World*, 20: II (April 1930), 164–8.

Brinner, William M., 'Prophet and Saint: The Two Exemplars of Islam', in John S. Hawley (ed.), *Saints and Virtues* (Berkeley: University of California Press, 1987), pp. 36–51.

Brodkin, E. I., 'The Struggle for Succession: Rebels and Loyalists in the Indian Mutiny of 1857', *Modern Asian Studies*, 6:3 (1972), 277–90.

———, 'British India and the Abuses of Power: Rohilkhand Under Early Company Rule', *Indian Economic and Social History Review*, x:2 (June 1973), 129–56.

Brown, Judith, *Gandhi's Rise to Power: Indian Politics 1915–1922* (Cambridge: Cambridge University Press, 1972).

Brown, Peter, 'Relics and Social Status in the Age of Gregory of Tours', The Stenton Lecture 1976, University of Reading, 1977.

———, 'The Saint as Exemplar in Late Antiquity', in John S. Hawley (ed.), *Saints and Virtues* (Berkeley: University of California Press, 1987), pp. 3–14.

Cole, J. R. I., *Roots of North Indian Shi'ism in Iran and Iraq: Religion and State in Awadh, 1722–1859* (Delhi: Oxford University Press, 1989).

Coulson, N. J., *A History of Islamic Law* (Edinburgh: Edinburgh University Press, 1964).

Currie, P. M., *The Shrine and Cult of Mu'in al-din Chishti of Ajmer* (Delhi: Oxford University Press, 1989).

Das, Veena, 'For a Folk-Theology and Theological Anthropology of Islam', *Contributions to Indian Sociology*, 18:2 (July-December 1984), 293–300.

Denny, Frederick M., 'Islamic Ritual: Perspectives and Theories', in Richard C. Martin (ed.), *Approaches to Islam in Religious Studies* (Tucson: University of Arizona Press, 1985), pp. 63–77.

Desai, Ziyaud-Din A., *Centres of Islamic Learning in India* (Delhi: Ministry of Information and Broadcasting, Government of India, 1978).

Devji, Faisal Fatehali, 'Gender and the Politics of Space: The Movement for Women's Reform in Muslim India, 1857–1900', *South Asia*, 14:1 (1991), 141–53.

Digby, Simon, 'The Sufi Shaikh as a Source of Authority in Medieaval India', in Marc Gaborieau (ed.), *Islam and Society in South Asia* (Paris: Ecole des Hautes Etudes en Sciences Sociales, 1986), Collection 'Purusartha', vol. 9, pp. 57–77.

Douglas, Ian Henderson, *Abul Kalam Azad: An Intellectual and Religious Biography*, eds. Gail Minault and Christian W. Troll (Delhi: Oxford University Press, 1988).

Eaton, Richard M., *Sufis of Bijapur 1300 –1700: Social Roles of Sufis in Medieval India* (Princeton: Princeton University Press, 1978).

———, 'Court of Man, Court of God: Local Perceptions of the Shrine of Baba Farid, Pakpattan, Punjab', *Contributions to Asian Studies*, 17 (Leiden: E. J. Brill, 1982), 44–61.

Ehsan Elahi Zaheer, *Bareilavis: History and Beliefs* (Lahore: Idara Tarjuman al-Sunnah, 1986).

Eickelman, Dale F., 'The Art of Memory: Islamic Education and Its Social Reproduction', *Comparative Studies in Society and History*, 20 (1978), 485–516.

———, 'The Study of Islam in Local Contexts', *Contributions to Asian Studies*, 17 (Leiden: E. J. Brill, 1982), 1–16.

Encyclopaedia of Islam, 2nd ed. (Leiden, 1954-).

Ewing, Katherine P., 'Ambiguity and *Shari'at*—A Perspective on the Problem of Moral Principles in Tension', in Katherine P. Ewing (ed.), *Shari'at and Ambiguity in South Asian Islam* (Delhi: Oxford University Press, 1988), pp. 1–22.

Farooqi, Burhan Ahmad, *The Mujaddid's Conception of Tawhid* (Lahore: Sh. Muhammad Ashraf, 1940).

Freitag, Sandria B., 'Ambiguous Public Arenas and Coherent Personal Practice: Kanpur Muslims 1913–1931', in Katherine P. Ewing (ed.), *Shari'at and Ambiguity in South Asian Islam* (Delhi: Oxford University Press, 1988), pp. 143–163.

———, *Collective Action and Community: Public Arenas and the Emergence of Communalism in North India* (Berkeley: University of California Press, 1989).

———(ed.), *Culture as Contested Site: Popular Culture and the State in the Indian Subcontinent* (forthcoming).

Friedmann, Yohanan, *Shaykh Ahmad Sirhindi: An Outline of His Thought and a Study of His Image in the Eyes of Posterity* (Montreal and London: McGill-Queen's University Press, 1971).

———, 'The Attitude of the *Jam'iyyat-i 'Ulama-i Hind* to the Indian National Movement and the Establishment of Pakistan', *Asian and African Studies*, 7 (1971), 157–80.

———, 'The Jam'iyyat al-'Ulama-i Hind in the Wake of Partition', *Asian and African Studies*, 11:2 (1976), 181–211.

———, *Prophecy Continuous: Aspects of Ahmadi Religious Thought and Its Medieval Background* (Berkeley: University of California Press, 1989).

General Instructions for Pilgrims to the Hedjaz and a Manual for the Guidance of

Officers and Others Concerned in the Red Sea Pilgrim Traffic (Calcutta: Superintendent of Government Printing, 1922).

Gilmartin, David, *Empire and Islam: Punjab and the Making of Pakistan* (Berkeley: University of California Press, 1988).

———, 'Democracy, Nationalism and the Public: A Speculation on Colonial Muslim Politics', *South Asia*, 14:1 (1991), 123–40.

Goldziher, Ignaz, *Muslim Studies*, vol. 2, tr. and ed. S. M. Stern (Chicago: Aldine, 1971).

———, *Introduction to Islamic Theology and Law*, tr. Andras and Ruth Hamori (Princeton: Princeton University Press, 1981).

Graham, William A., *Divine Word and Prophetic Word in Early Islam: A Reconsideration of the Sources, with Special Reference to the Divine Saying or Hadith Qudsi* (The Hague, Paris: Mouton, 1977).

———, 'Islam in the Mirror of Ritual', in Richard G. Hovannisian and Speros Vryonis (eds.), *Islam's Understanding of Itself* (Malibu: Undena Publications, 1983) pp. 53–71.

———, 'Qur'an as Spoken Word: An Islamic Contribution to the Understanding of Scripture', in Richard C. Martin (ed.), *Approaches to Islam in Religious Studies* (Tucson: University of Arizona Press, 1985), pp. 23–40.

———, *Beyond the Written Word: Oral Aspects of Scripture in the History of Religion* (Cambridge: Cambridge University Press, 1987).

Guillaume, Alfred, *The Traditions of Islam: An Introduction to the Study of the Hadith Literature* (Oxford: Clarendon Press, 1924).

Hallaq, Wael B., 'Was the Gate of Ijtihad Closed?' *International Journal of Middle East Studies*, 16 (1984), 3–41.

Hansen, Katheryn, 'The Birth of Hindi Drama in Benaras, 1868–1885', in Sandria B. Freitag (ed.), *Culture and Power in Banaras: Community, Performance, and Environment, 1800–1980* (Berkeley: University of California Press, 1989), pp. 62–92.

Haq, M. Anwarul, *The Faith Movement of Mawlana Muhammad Ilyas* (London: George Allen & Unwin, 1972).

Hardy, Peter, *Partners in Freedom—and True Muslims: The Political Thought of Some Muslim Scholars in British India 1912–1947* (Lund: Studentlitteratur, 1971).

———, *The Muslims of British India* (Cambridge: Cambridge University Press, 1972).

Harington, J. H., 'Remarks Upon the Authorities of Mosulman Law', *Asiatic Researches*, 10 (1811).

Haroon, Mohammed, *Cataloguing of Indian Muslim Names* (Lahore: Islamic Book Centre, 1986).

Hourani, Albert, *Arabic Thought in the Liberal Age, 1798–1939* (Cambridge: Cambridge University Press, 1983).

Husain, Iqbal, *The Ruhela Chieftaincies: The Rise and Fall of Ruhela Power in India in the Eighteenth Century* (Delhi: Oxford University Press, 1994).

Imperial Gazetteer of India, VII, XVII, XXI (c. 1909).

Irvine, William, 'The Bangash Nawabs of Farrukhabad—A Chronicle (1713–1857), Part I', *Journal of the Asiatic Society of Bengal*, 4 (1878), 259–383.

———, 'The Bangash Nawabs of Farrukhabad—A Chronicle (1713–1857), Part II', *Journal of the Asiatic Society of Bengal*, 48:2 (1979), 49–170.

J. R. C., 'Notice of the Peculiar Tenets Held by the Followers of Syed Ahmed, Taken Chiefly from the "Sirat-ul-Mustaqim", a Principal Treatise of that Sect, Written by Moulavi Mahommed Ismail', *Journal of the Asiatic Society of Bengal*, 1 (1832), 479–98.

Jamaluddin, Syed, 'Religiopolitical Ideas of a Twentieth Century Muslim Theologian—An Introduction', *Marxist Miscellany*, 7 (1977), 13–19.

———, 'The Barelvis and the Khilafat Movement', in Mushirul Hasan (ed.), *Communal and Pan-Islamic Trends in Colonial India* (Delhi: Manohar, 1981), pp. 400–13.

Jilani, 'Abd al-Qadir, *Futuh al-Ghaib ('The Revelations of the Unseen')*, tr. Aftab ud-Din Ahmad (Lahore: Sh. Muhammad Ashraf, 1967).

Jones, Kenneth W., *Arya Dharm: Hindu Consciousness in 19th-Century Punjab* (Berkeley: University of California Press, 1976).

———, *Socio-Religious Reform Movements in British India*, The New Cambridge History of India, III: I (Cambridge: Cambridge University Press, 1989).

Joshi, Esha B., *Gazetteer of India, Uttar Pradesh: Bareilly District* (Lucknow: Government of Uttar Pradesh, 1968).

Keddie, Nikki R., *Sayyid Jamal ad-Din 'al-Afghani': A Political Biography* (Berkeley: University of California Press, 1972).

———, *An Islamic Response to Imperialism: Political and Religious Writings of Sayyid Jamal ad-Din 'al-Afghani'* (Berkeley: University of California Press, 1983).

Kerr, Malcolm H., *Islamic Reform: The Political and Legal Theories of Muhammad 'Abduh and Rashid Rida* (Berkeley: University of California Press, 1966).

Kozlowski, Gregory C., *Muslim Endowments and Society in British India* (Cambridge: Cambridge University Press, 1985).

Kramer, Martin, *Islam Assembled: The Advent of the Muslim Congresses* (New York: Columbia University Press, 1986).

Lal Baha, 'The Hijrat Movement and the North-West Frontier Province', *Islamic Studies*, XVIII:3 (Autumn 1979), 231–42.

Lelyveld, David, *Aligarh's First Generation: Muslim Solidarity in British India* (Princeton: Princeton University Press, 1978).

Liyaqat Hussain Moini, Syed, 'Rituals and Customary Practices at the Dargah of Ajmer', in Christian W. Troll (ed.), *Muslim Shrines in India* (Delhi: Oxford University Press, 1989), pp. 60–75.

Mas'ud Ahmed, Muhammad, *Neglected Genius of the East: An Introduction to the Life and Works of Mawlana Ahmad Rida Khan of Bareilly (India) 1272/1856–1340/1921* (Lahore: Rida Academy, 1987).

Meer Hassan Ali, Mrs., *Observations on the Mussulmauns of India: Descriptive of their Manners, Customs, Habits, and Religious Opinions. Made during a Twelve Years' Residence in Their Immediate Society* (London, 1832), Idarah-i Adabiyat-i Delli reprint, vol. 2, 1973.

Metcalf, Barbara D., *Islamic Revival in British India: Deoband 1860 –1900* (Princeton: Princeton University Press, 1982).

———(ed.), *Moral Conduct and Authority: The Place of Adab in South Asian Islam* (Berkeley: University of California Press, 1984).

———, 'Hakim Ajmal Khan: *Rais* of Delhi and Muslim "Leader",' in R. E. Frykenberg (ed.), *Delhi Through the Ages: Essays in Urban History, Culture and Society* (Delhi: Oxford University Press, 1986), pp. 299–315.

Minault, Gail, *The Khilafat Movement: Religious Symbolism and Political Mobilization in India* (New York: Columbia University Press, 1982).

———, 'Some Reflections on Islamic Revivalism vs. Assimilation among Muslims in India', *Contributions to Indian Sociology*, 18:2 (July-December 1984), 301–5.

Mir Shahamat 'Ali, tr., 'Translation of the *Takwiyat-ul-Iman* , Preceded by a Notice of the Author, Maulavi Isma'il Hajji', *Journal of the Royal Asiatic Society*, 13 (1852), 310–72.

Momen, Moojan, *An Introduction to Shi'i Islam: The History and Doctrines of Twelver Shi'ism* (Delhi: Oxford University Press, 1985).

Mujeeb, M., *The Indian Muslims* (Lahore: Mustafa Waheed, n.d.).

Nadwi, S. Abul Hasan 'Ali, *Life and Mission of Maulana Mohammad Ilyas*, tr. Mohammad Asif Kidwai (Lucknow: Academy of Islamic Research and Publications, 1979).

Neuman, Daniel M., *The Life of Music in North India: The Organization of an Artistic Tradition* (Detroit: Wayne State University Press, 1980).

Padwick, Constance E., *Muslim Devotions: A Study of Prayer-Manuals in Common Use* (London: S. P. C. K., 1961).

Peters, Rudolph, *Islam and Colonialism: The Doctrine of Jihad in Modern History* (The Hague: Mouton, 1979).

Pritchett, Frances W., *Marvelous Encounters: Folk Romance in Urdu and Hindi* (Delhi: Manohar, 1985).

Qadri, Anwar A., *Islamic Jurisprudence in the Modern World* (Lahore: Sh. Muhammad Ashraf, 1973).

Qureshi, I. H., *Ulema in Politics: A Study Relating to the Political Activities of the Ulema in the South-Asian Subcontinent from 1556 to 1947* (Karachi: Ma' aref, 1974).

———, *The Muslim Community of the Indo-Pakistan Subcontinent (610–1947): A Brief Historical Analysis* (Karachi: Ma'aref, 1977).

Qureshi, M. Naeem, 'The 'Ulama of British India and the Hijrat of 1920', *Modern Asian Studies*, 13:1 (1979), 41–59.

Rahbar, Daud, tr., *Urdu Letters of Mirza Asadullah Khan Ghalib* (Albany: State University of New York Press, 1987).

Reid, Anthony, 'Nineteenth-Century Pan-Islam in Indonesia and Malaysia', *Journal of Asian Studies*, XXVI:2, 1967, 267–83.

Rizvi, S. A. A., *Muslim Revivalist Movements in Northern India in the Sixteenth and Seventeenth Centuries* (Agra: Agra University, 1965).

———, *Shah Wali-Allah and His Times: A Study of Eighteenth Century Islam, Politics and Society in India* (Canberra: Ma'rifat Publishing House, 1980).

———, *A History of Sufism in India*, vol. 2 (Delhi: Munshi Manoharlal, 1983).

Robinson, Francis, *Atlas of the Islamic World since 1500* (New York: Facts on File, 1982).

———, 'Islam and Muslim Society in South Asia', *Contributions to Indian Sociology*, 17 (1983), 185–203.

———, 'The 'Ulama of Farangi Mahall and Their *Adab*', in Barbara D. Metcalf (ed.), *Moral Conduct and Authority: The Place of Adab in South Asian Islam* (Berkeley: University of California Press, 1984), pp. 152–83.

Roff, William R., 'Sanitation and Security: The Imperial Powers and the Nineteenth Century Hajj', *Arabian Studies*, VI (1982), 143–60.

———, 'Pilgrimage and the History of Religions: Theoretical Approaches to the *Hajj*', in Richard C. Martin (ed.), *Approaches to Islam in Religious Studies* (Tucson: University of Arizona Press, 1985), pp. 78–86.

———, 'Islam Obscured? Some Reflections on Studies of Islam and Society in Southeast Asia', *Archipel*, 29 (1985), 7–34.

———, 'Islamic Movements: One or Many?' in William R. Roff (ed.), *Islam and the Political Economy of Meaning* (Berkeley: University of California Press, 1987), pp. 31–52.

Royster, James E., 'The Study of Muhammad: A Survey of Approaches from the Perspective of the History and Phenomenology of Religion', *Muslim World*, 62 (1972), 49–70.

Rubin, U., 'Pre-existence and Light: Aspects of the Concept of Nur Muhammad', *Israel Oriental Studies*, V (1975), 62–119.

Russell, Ralph, and Khurshidul Islam, tr. and eds., *Ghalib 1797–1869, vol. 1: Life and Letters* (Cambridge: Harvard University Press, 1969).

Sadiq, Muhammad, *A History of Urdu Literature*, 2nd ed. (Delhi: Oxford University Press, 1984).

Schacht, Joseph, *The Origins of Muhammadan Jurisprudence* (Oxford: Clarendon Press, 1950).

——, *An Introduction to Islamic Law* (Oxford: Clarendon Press, 1964).

Schimmel, Annemarie, *Mystical Dimensions of Islam* (Chapel Hill: University of North Carolina Press, 1975).

——, 'The Golden Chain of "Sincere Muhammadans",' in Bruce B. Lawrence (ed.), *The Rose and the Rock: Mystical and Rational Elements in the Intellectual History of South Asian Islam* (Durham: Duke University Program in Comparative Studies on Southern Asia, 1979), pp. 104–34.

——, 'The Sufis and the Shahada', in Richard G. Hovannisian and Speros Vryonis (eds.), *Islam's Understanding of Itself* (Malibu: Undena Publications, 1983), pp. 103–25.

——, *And Muhammad Is His Messenger: The Veneration of the Prophet in Islamic Piety* (Lahore: Vanguard, 1987).

Sharar, Abdul Halim, *Lucknow: The Last Phase of an Oriental Culture*, tr. and ed. E. S. Harcourt and Fakhir Hussain (Delhi: Oxford University Press, 1989).

Siddiqi, M. Zameeruddin, 'The Resurgence of the Chishti Silsilah in the Punjab during the Eighteenth Century', *Proceedings of the Indian History Congress, 1970* (New Delhi: Indian History Congress, 1971), 1, 408–12.

Siddiqi, Muhammad Zubayr, *Hadith Literature: Its Origins, Development, Special Features and Criticism* (Calcutta: Calcutta University Press, 1961).

Snouck C. Hungronje, *Mekka in the Latter Part of the 19th Century: Daily Life, Customs and Learning—the Moslims of the East-Indian-Archipelago*, tr. J. H. Monahan (London: Luzac and Co., 1931). Reprint (Leiden: E.J. Brill, 1970).

Stokes, Eric, *The Peasant Armed: The Indian Revolt of 1857*, ed. C. A. Bayly (Oxford: Clarendon Press, 1986).

Strachey, Sir John, *Hastings and the Rohilla War* (Oxford: Clarendon Press, 1892). Indian reprint (Delhi: Prabha Publications, 1985).

Subhan, John A., *Sufism, Its Saints and Shrines* (New York: Samuel Weiser, 1970).

Sufi, G. M. D., *Al-Minhaj, Being the Evolution of Curriculum in the Muslim Educational Institutions of India* (Delhi: Idarah-i Adabiyat-i Delli, 1941).

Tabataba'i, Sayyid Muhammad Husayn, *Shi'ite Islam* (Albany: State University of New York Press, 1975).

Thursby, G. R., *Hindu–Muslim Relations in British India: A Study of*

Controversy, Conflict, and Communal Movements in Northern India 1923–1928 (Leiden: E. J. Brill, 1975).

Troll, Christian W., *Sayyid Ahmad Khan: A Reinterpretation of Muslim Theology* (Delhi: Vikas, 1978).

———(ed.), *Muslim Shrines* in India (Delhi: Oxford University Press, 1989).

Turner, Victor, *Dramas, Fields, and Metaphors: Symbolic Action in Human Society* (Ithaca and London: Cornell University Press, 1974).

van der Veer, Peter, *Religious Nationalism: Hindus and Muslims in India* (Berkeley: University of California Press, 1994).

Van Gennep, Arnold, *The Rites of Passage* (Chicago: University of Chicago Press, 1960).

Voll, John, 'Muhammad Hayya al-Sindi and Muhammad ibn 'Abd al-Wahhab: An Analysis of an Intellectual Group in Eighteenth-Century Madina', *Bulletin of the School of African and Oriental Studies*, 38 (1975), 32–9.

Waugh, Earle, 'Following the Beloved: Muhammad as Model in the Sufi Tradition', in Frank E. Reynolds and Donald Capps (eds.), *The Biographical Process: Studies in the History and Psychology of Religion* (The Hague, Paris: Mouton, 1976), pp. 63–85.

Wensinck, A. J., *A Handbook of Early Muhammadan Tradition* (Leiden: E. J. Brill, 1960).

Whitcombe, Elizabeth, *Agrarian Conditions in Northern India: The United Provinces under British Rule, 1860–1900* (Berkeley: University of California Press, 1972).

Wolpert, Stanley, *A New History of India*, 2nd ed. (New York: Oxford University Press, 1982).

——, *Jinnah of Pakistan* (New York: Oxford University Press, 1984).

Yaduvansh, Uma, 'The Decline of the Role of the *Qadis* in India, 1793–1876', *Studies in Islam*, 6 (1969), 155–71.

Unpublished Papers and Dissertations

Ewing, Katherine Pratt, 'The *Pir* or Sufi Saint in Pakistani Islam', Ph.D. dissertation, Department of Anthropology, University of Chicago, 1980.

Mas'ud, Muhammad Khalid, 'Trends in the Interpretation of Islamic Law as Reflected in the *Fatawa* Literature of Deoband School: A study of the Attitudes of the 'Ulama of Deoband to certain Social Problems and Inventions'. M. A. thesis, Institute of Islamic Studies, McGill University (Montreal, 1969).

Pearson, Harlan Otto, 'Islamic Reform and Revival in Nineteenth Century India: The Tariqah-i Muhammadiyah', Ph.D. dissertation, Department of History, Duke University, 1979.

Qureshi, G. D., 'Preface to the Islamic Faith', tr. of Ahmad Riza Khan's *Tamhid al-Iman ba-Ayat al-Qur'an* (Stockport: Majlis-e Raza, n.d.), cyclostyle.

Valensi, Lucette, 'Le jardin de l'académie, ou comment se forme une école de pensée'. Paper presented at Colloquium on Modes of Transmission of Religious Culture in Islam, Princeton University, jointly sponsored by the Department of Near Eastern Studies, Princeton University, and the Ecole des Hautes Etudes en Sciences Sociales, Paris, 28–30 April 1989.

Interviews

Ahmad, Maulana Khalil, grandson of Maulana Didar 'Ali, founder of the Dar al-'Ulum Hizb al-Ahnaf. Teaches at the Dar al-'Ulum. 29 November 1986, at Lahore.

Amritsari, Hakim Muhammad Musa, President, Markazi Majlis-e Riza, Nuri Masjid, Lahore; an authority on the Ahl-e Sunnat in current-day Pakistan. 19 November 1986, at Lahore.

Faiz, Maulana Faiz Ahmad, Imam at mosque in Golra Sharif, site of Pir Mehr 'Ali Shah's shrine. 14 November 1986, at Golra Sharif.

Faruqi, Maulana Abu'l Hasan Zaid, of Chitli Qabr, Old Delhi. Author of several books in rebuttal of 'Wahhabis'. 24 June 1987, at Old Delhi.

Husain, Professor Abrar, Professor of Statistics at a Rawalpindi college, has studied Ahmad Riza's works related to mathematics specifically those in which Ahmad Riza rebutted aspects of Newton's and Einstein's theories. 14 November 1986, at Rawalpindi.

Husain, Sayyid E'jaz, a disciple of Ahmad Riza Khan and resident of Bareilly. 17 April 1987, at Bareilly.

Ja'far, Shaikh Muhammad, Secretary-General of the World Federation of Islamic Missions, Karachi. A disciple (murid) of Maulana 'Abd ul-Alim Siddiqi Meruthi (who was a follower of Ahmad Riza). 25 October 1986, at Karachi.

Khan, Maulana Akhtar Riza ('Azhari Miyan'), great-grandson of Ahmad Riza (through descent from Hamid Riza Khan; younger brother of Subhan Riza below), Sadr of the Markazi Dar al-Ifta, Bareilly, and of the All-India Sunni Jam'iyyat al-'Ulama'. 5 May 1987, at New Delhi; 16 October, at Bareilly.

Khan, Maulana Khalid 'Ali, grandson of Mustafa Riza Khan (Ahmad Riza's younger son, d. 1981). 16 October 1987, at Bareilly.

Khan, Maulana Subhan Riza ('Subhani Miyan'), great-grandson of Ahmad Riza (through descent from Hamid Riza Khan [d. 1943], Ahmad Riza's eldest son). Current Sadr (head) of the Madrasa Manzar al-Islam, Bareilly. 17 April and 16 October 1987, at Bareilly.

Khan, Maulana Tahsin Riza, grandson of Maulana Hasan Riza Khan (d.

1908), presently Sadr-e Mudarris at the Jam'iyya Nuriyya, Bareilly. Founded the Jama'at Islah al-'Ulum in February 1982, the purpose of which is to eradicate practices contrary to the shari'a (*bid'a*). 17 and 18 April 1987, at Bareilly.

Khan, Muhammad Zuhur ud-Din, publisher of books on the Ahl-e Sunnat movement. Owner of Maktaba Rizwiyya, Gujarat (Pakistan), and authority on political dimensions of the movement. 21 and 23 November 1986, at Lahore.

Mahmud, Raja Rashid, of the Panjab Textbook Society, and author of a history of the Hijrat movement in 1920. 29 November 1986, at Lahore.

Na'imi, Maulana Muhammad Athar, grandson of Muhammad 'Umar Na'imi (a disciple of Na'im ud-Din Muradabadi and assistant editor of the journal *Al-Sawad al-A'zam* published by Na'im ud-Din). Member, Central Roiyat-e Hilal Committee, Sind, and Honorary Khatib at Jame' Masjid Arambagh, Karachi. 10 and 11 November 1987, at Karachi.

Na'imi, Maulana Rizwan ud-Din, grandson of Na'im ud-Din Muradabadi. 19 October 1987, at Muradabad.

Niyazi, Dr. Mustafa Husain Nizami, son of Maulana Niyaz Ahmad who founded the Khanqah-e Niyaziyya at Bareilly and whose 'urs Ahmad Riza is reported to have attended each year. 19 April 1987, at Bareilly.

Okarwi, Kaukab Noorani, Chairman of the Okarwi Academy, Karachi. 19 October 1986, at Karachi.

Qadiri, Maulana 'Abd ul-Hakim Sharf, teacher at Jam'iyya Nizamiyya Rizwiyya, Lahore, and author of several books on aspects of Ahl-e Sunnat belief and practice. 18–20, 23 November 1986, at Lahore.

Qadiri, Maulana Ghulam 'Ali Okarwi, a student of Sayyid Abu'l Barakat (son of Didar 'Ali, founder of the Dar al-'Ulum Hizb al-Ahnaf, Lahore), and teacher of *fiqh* and *hadis*. 29 October 1986, at Karachi.

Rana, Professor Ghulam Sarwar, Assistant Professor, Political Science Department, Government College, Lahore. Interested in the role of sufis in the creation of Pakistan. 22 November 1986, at Lahore.

Sarwar, Mufti Ghulam, of Jam'iyya Ghausiyya, Lahore, author of a work on the economic aspects of the Nizam-e Mustafa. Became a disciple of Mustafa Riza Khan (Ahmad Riza's younger son) in 1980. 21 and 22 November 1986, at Lahore.

Siddiqui, Professor Bashir Ahmad, Department of Islamic Studies, Panjab University, Lahore. 27 November 1986, at Lahore.

Waqar ud-Din, Maulana, teacher of *hadis* and *mufti* at Madrasa Amjadiyya, Karachi. 12 August 1986, at East Meadow, New York.

Index